Carving Up the Globe
AN ATLAS OF DIPLOMACY

Library of Congress Cataloging-in-Publication Data

Names: Ruthven, Malise, editor.
Title: Carving up the globe : an atlas of diplomacy / Malise Ruthven, general editor.
Description: Cambridge, Massachusetts : Harvard University Press, 2018. | Includes bibli-
ographical references.
Identifiers: LCCN 2017045515| ISBN 9780674976245 (alk. paper)
Subjects: Political geography—Maps. | Treaties—History—Maps. | World politics—Maps.
Classification: LCC G1046.F1 C3 2018 | DDC 327.73—dc23
LC record available at https://lccn.loc.gov/2017045515

Carving Up the Globe
AN ATLAS OF DIPLOMACY

INTRODUCTION & CONTRIBUTING EDITOR
Malise Ruthven

CONTRIBUTORS
Andrew Avenell
Henry Bewicke
Caroline Chapman
Elizabeth Wyse

THE BELKNAP PRESS of HARVARD UNIVERSITY PRESS
Cambridge, Massachussets, and London, England
2018

Contents

Introduction

A French political cartoon of 1898 shows the imperial powers carving up China, overlooked by a helpless Qing official, a reflection of the "unequal treaties" of the 19th and early 20th centuries, which had forced China to concede territory and sovereignty.

Diplomacy may have existed from the earliest recorded time. Documents from Late Sumeria (mid-18th–century BCE Mesopotamia) and Akhenatan's Egypt (14th century BCE) indicate that envoys traveled between royal courts to communicate matters of war and peace, while the ancient Greeks, living as they did in a region where city states competed against each other for power and territory, developed an elaborate apparatus of international intercourse. At the other end of the ancient world the Chinese military strategist Sun Tzu (d. 496 BCE), who also lived during an era of warring states, wrote of the need for aspiring leaders to establish allies, barter land, and sign treaties with rivals, with emphasis on the role of an idealized "persuader/diplomat."

As Harold Nicolson, the British diplomat-turned-writer, wrote in *The Evolution of Diplomatic Method* (1954) the ancient Greeks evolved a number of principles that would come to be accepted as part of the diplomatic canon, covering issues including "the declaration of war, the conclusion of peace, the ratification of treaties, arbitration, neutrality, the exchange of ambassadors, the functions of a consul and certain rules of war," according to which it was regarded as impious to make a surprise attack upon a neighbor or to start what they called an "unheralded and truceless war." The Romans regarded treaties as a type of legal contract, and would often exercise legal ingenuity to evade terms that had been agreed and ratified, using offensive diplomacy, with the threat of their powerful armies, to get what they wanted without fighting. But they recognized a type of diplomatic immunity under the *ius gentium* ("law of nations") covering visiting ambassadors and their staffs. Visiting envoys were accommodated at a reception center called the "Graecostasis," paid for by the state, where they waited before being invited to address the Senate and to answer questions put to them by senators.

While the Western Roman Empire descended into disorder, some Roman practices were taken over by its successor in the east, the Byzantine Empire, and its emperors are said to have been the first to organize a special department of government for dealing with external affairs, and to train professional negotiators to serve as ambassadors for foreign courts. The arrival of Islam, which conquered much of western Asia and North Africa after the death of the Prophet Muhammad in 632 CE, introduced a new dynamic into the historical canvas. Inspired by Muhammad's engagements – both military and diplomatic – with his original pagan enemies, as well as by his religious preaching, Muslim armies waged a series of brilliant campaigns, creating an empire that stretched from Spain to the Indus valley. After failing to take Constantinople the Umayyad caliphs who ruled from Damascus negotiated peace treaties with their Byzantine enemies, paid tribute to the emperors to prevent attacks during periods of civil strife within their domains, and arranged for exchanges of prisoners. Diplomatic contacts continued under the Abbasids who replaced the Umayyads in 750, with Byzantine emissaries lavishly entertained in Baghdad and provided with gifts and robes of honor before their departure. The Frankish ruler Pepin, whose father Charles Martel had defeated the Spanish Umayyads at the Battle of Tours in 732, is reported to have sent envoys to the Abbasid court in Baghdad, with regular exchanges taking place between his successor Charlemagne and the Abbasid ruler Harun al-Rashid.

While diplomatic contacts between between rulers – both Christian and Muslim – existed on an ad hoc basis, the Venetians were the first true professionals in the field. The Venetian Republic was the first state to preserve its diplomatic archives in systematic form. Documents covering a formidable nine centuries, from 883 to 1797, contain the instructions to, and official despatches from, ambassadors it sent abroad. More than 12,000 of these documents have survived, giving unparalleled insight into the diplomacy of the medieval and early modern periods.

At its most basic, the primary concern of diplomacy is the "transition from a state of peace to a state of war, and vice versa; in other words, dealing with the interface of conflict and peace-making."[1] Any such formulation, however, must entail a vast array of discourses and human interactions. International diplomacy, whether medieval or modern, has been aptly described as a "skilled and difficult art."[2] Its moral and political complexities may be captured in two quotations of equal resonance. The first is from Sir Henry Wotton. In 1604 Wotton was on his way to Venice as envoy of James I, the first king of Great Britain (combining the thrones of England and Scotland), when Wotton famously stated that "an ambassador is an honest man sent to lie abroad for the good of his country."[3] The remark not only annoyed his boss but evoked the famed duplicity of the Venetian Republic to which he was being sent. The second is from a famous diplomatist, François de Callières, who had served as a spy and then as an official envoy for Louis XIV in Germany, the Netherlands and Poland. "A diplomatist," he wrote in his celebrated tract *De la manière de négiciér avec les Souverains,* "should remember that open dealing is the basis of confidence; he should share freely with others everything except what it is his duty to conceal…. It is a fundamental error, and one widely held, that a clever negotiator must be a master of deceit. Deceit is indeed the measure of the smallness of mind of him who uses it; it proves that he does not possess sufficient intelligence to achieve results by just and reasonable means."[4]

Broadly speaking, international diplomacy may be grouped very roughly into two main historical eras – before and after the Peace of Westphalia (1648). In the long passage of time before the Reformation challenged papal authority the Vatican played an important part in maintaining peace in Europe. While the word "diplomacy," derived from the *diploma* – folded letter – of the Greeks, is of fairly recent provenance (dating from 1796), the conduct of professional diplomacy can be traced to the later middle ages, when dynastic relations between different kings and lords gave ground to more systemic relations between emerging European powers. In western Europe, where Latin was the lingua franca and the pope's authority was regarded as absolute, the Holy See, with its cadre of religious professionals, played a vital if not always uncontested role. The pope could authorize ecclesiastical "reforms" – as when Adrian IV, the only Englishman to have sat on the papal throne, may have issued a bull in 1155 granting the right of the English King Henry II to invade and govern Ireland and to enforce the Gregorian Reforms on its semi-autonomous Christian Church (although some scholars consider this bull to have been a forgery). Popes could grant titles to what were seen as virgin territories, as in 1494 when Alexander VI established the Treaty of Tordesillas dividing the western hemisphere between Spain and Portugal. They could act as mediators in territorial disputes between different Christian princes – for example, they encouraged alliances between Italian city states and made peace between them as with the Peace of Lodi (1454), which ended the War of the Milanese Succession when Milan was pitted against Venice and Florence.

Until early modern times it was the pope who alone had representatives in all Christian courts. Rome itself was a kind of League of Nations and, arguably, just as ineffective. But with every ruler in western Christendom having his agents in the Holy See, it is not difficult to imagine the amount of undocumented diplomatic groundwork that took place in Rome or in the papal palace in Avignon. At a time when nearly all diplomacy was dynastic, governed by marriages between ruling houses, the pope could influence politics across different swathes of territory by granting exemption in cases where marriage was forbidden because of consanguinity. This was an important diplomatic lever, because prior to 1215 marriage under western canon law was prohibited up to the seventh degree, which meant that sixth cousins were forbidden to marry. The pope could also annul marriages: indeed it was the refusal of Clement VII to do so in the case of Henry VIII and Catherine of Aragon that caused the break between England and Rome in 1533.

The parchment scrolls contained in medieval chancelleries, treasuries and "wardrobes" (which were not just items of furniture, but offices of state with clerks and cash that could be used for diplomatic purposes) tell us much about medieval diplomatic practice, even if individual practitioners are unknown or forgotten. For example, a Latin text dating from the reign of Edward II (1307–27), when the English king held territories in Gascony as a vassal of his father-in-law Philip IV and later his brother-in-law Charles IV, instructs the archivist or *custos processum* to keep all his documents safe, "to be shown by him when required to the commissioners, envoys and proctors of the king for counsels and treaties, and to make them available when wanted." Armed with these documents, the English diplomats should observe the following procedures when dealing with their French counterparts: "Call attention to the care with which the king has observed the papal arbitration; Be careful not to conceded the slightest legal acknowledgement to the occupation of any part of Gascony by the French; Devise means to postpone cases regarded the demesnes of the king in the duchy until he has been informed about its ancient right, liberties and customs; Cite reasons by which the king can escape from continuing in his vassalage to the French throne; Try to obtain a change of precedence in English cases before the Parlement in Paris." Such efforts may not have prevented the outbreak of the Hundred Years' War (1337–1453) between the English Plantagenets and the French House of Valois, which resulted from English claims to the throne of France. But the documents reveal what might be called the beginnings of a *foreign* policy, with dynastic relationships giving ground to what we have come to regard retrospectively as the *national* interest.

The breakdown of papal authority following the Reformation and wars of religion led to the post-Westphalian era when a new culture of international diplomacy based on the idea of national sovereignty came to the fore. The Peace of Westphalia (1648) is generally regarded as a watershed in the development of modern political thought and norms of international relations, where notions of human sovereignty rooted in this-worldly secular reality triumphed over the absolutism of rulers claiming their mandate from God. In so doing it established the basis for the present-day international system whereby states – territorial units controlled by sovereign governments – became the primary actors in international affairs. Given the formal recognition it accorded to religious diversity in Europe, it is hardly surprising that the Holy See saw the Peace of Westphalia as a threat to its hegemony, with Pope Innocent X condemning it as "null, void, invalid, iniquitous, unjust, damnable, reprobate, inane, empty of meaning and effect for all time."

A process of peace-making lasting more than five years, as well as creating hundreds of pages of text, the Congress of Westphalia resulted in the two landmark treaties of Munster and Osnabruck (known collectively as the Peace of Westphalia) that ended the Thirty Years' War between Protestant and Catholic states that had devastated Germany after the Reformation. Altogether the Congress involved some 190 delegations representing 140 imperial "estates" – the Holy Roman Empire's constituent elements including territorial lords and imperial cities – along with 38 other "interested parties." A key turning point in what has been described as "a complex story of formal diplomacy and backdoor intrigue amid changing battlefield conditions"[5] came when Catholic troops of the Habsburg Emperor Ferdinand III suffered a catastrophic defeat by a Swedish army at the Battle of Junkau near Prague in 1645. The setback weakened the emperor's hand, obliging him to allow the estates of the empire to participate as independent parties in the peace process.

The arrangements finally agreed upon at Westphalia are widely seen as having laid the foundations for the modern national state. As well as fixing territorial boundaries (many of which would be challenged and contested in subsequent wars) Westphalia represented a paradigm shift in the relations between rulers and subjects. Whereas previously individuals might have overlapping or contested allegiances between, say, a Protestant monarch and the pope, or a Catholic monarch and his Protestant subjects, from now on inhabitants of a given state were deemed to be subjects to the laws and edicts of the state in which they resided. The formula *cuius regio, eius religio* – "religion belongs to the ruler" – first articulated at the Peace of Augsburg in 1555, and ratified by Westphalia, greatly increased the power of state machinery. Far from being an edict of tolerance, monarchs initially felt free to persecute or discriminate against religious dissenters within their domains. In 1685, for example, France's Louis XIV enforced Catholic conformity by revoking the Edict of Nantes allowing freedom of worship to the Protestant Huguenots, passed by his grandfather Henry IV in 1498. Even in England, which Enlightenment writers such as Voltaire admired for its liberties, Catholics only won the right to sit as members of parliament in 1829. Nevertheless Westphalia established a template that would guide diplomatic relations for more than a century and a half, and still remains highly relevant in a world of nation states. As the historian Wayne Te Brake has written, "the Peace of Westphalia stands even today as one of the greatest achievements in European diplomatic history."[6]

Another great milestone in the development of diplomatic practice is the 1815 Congress of Vienna that followed the Napoleonic wars in Europe. The Congress, attended by the Emperors of Russia and Austria, the King of Prussia, the Austrian statesman Metternich, the French diplomat Talleyrand (who had abandoned Napoleon's service) and the British Foreign Secretary Castlereagh (three men who were arguably the greatest diplomatists of their time), laid down the general foundations for a peace in Europe after a quarter of a century of war, a peace that lasted some four decades, and prevented wider conflicts from erupting in mainland Europe for almost a century. As well as serving peace, the Congress laid down certain rules of procedure that have regulated diplomatic practice up to the present. The diplomatic hierarchy established at Vienna and at Aix-la-Chapelle in 1818 determined the ranking or classes of representatives with ambassadors, papal legates, and papal nuncios, at the top, followed by envoys extraordinary and ministers plenipotentiary, ministers resident and finally chargés d'affaires. The systematizing of ranking in a status-conscious era helped to oil the wheels of diplomatic intercourse, avoiding conflicts over precedence. This highly contentious issue was resolved by agreeing that the order of priority within each rank should be based on the length of service in that country, rather than relying on the more subjective, and probably more contentious, basis of the relative importance of the sovereign or state the diplomat represented. The ambassador who was senior in terms of length of service in a country should be doyen or dean of the diplomatic corps in that country, a role that often fell – by default, as it were – to the long serving papal nuncios.

A global order based on the idea of national sovereignty, founded in Westphalia and refined in Vienna, has now spread across the globe, as virtually the whole of humanity (barring small remote communities of indigenous peoples) is locked into the international system with its international borders and frontier controls. As a type of international engineering the system is very far from flawless: witness the catastrophe of 1914 when the diplomatic alliances forged at the Congress of Vienna in the wake of the Napoleonic wars broke down catastrophically, leading to millions of deaths in battle, along with massive destruction and famine. The first attempt at creating a transnational organization based on Westphalian principles – the League of Nations – collapsed, not least because its architect, US President Woodrow Wilson, failed to sell his plan to the American people, so it was never ratified by the US Congress. With 21st-century hindsight, the peace from 1918 to 1939 was no more than an uneasy truce. Versailles, with its punitive repercussions, was a *diktat*, not a peace. As the economist John Maynard Keynes recognized, prophetically, in *The Economic Consequence of the Peace* (1919), the fate of Europe was intertwined with that of Germany – with Germany crippled, the entire European economy would suffer: "An inefficient, unemployed, disorganized Europe faces us, torn by internal strife, and international hate, fighting, starving pillaging and lying."[7] But the system survived nonetheless.

After what might be described as two more rounds of conflict, the six-year "hot war" from 1939–45 and the Cold War between 1945 and 1991, the Westphalian system reasserted itself: powerful forces – economic, political and military – are ranged to protect the *idea* of national sovereignty in the face of its numerous challenges. Indeed it may be argued that some of the challenges to local and regional claims of sovereignty, for example by Palestinians facing Jewish extremists in Palestine, or by Buddhist monks in Chinese-occupied Tibet, are really compliments to this idea: they want their sovereignty recognized over territories claimed by others who reject their claims – the challenge is not to the idea of national sovereignty as such. More universalist claims, such as those posed by Marxist-Leninist ideology, foundered with the collapse of the Soviet Union in 1991 and its replacement by the Commonwealth of Independent States. In the wars that followed de-colonization there were conflicts over frontiers and over which groups or factions should inherit the colonial mantle. But the principle of state sovereignty – of the Wilsonian idea that a "people," however understood or configured, has the right to assert its independence, still had the force of planetary consensus. The rise of national populism in eastern Europe, and even the small British majority in favor of "Brexit" in the 2016 referendum, attest to the importance people attach to their national identities. At the time of writing the one great exception – a vision of Islamic universalism that harks back to a transnational caliphate embracing different peoples and tribes under the rule of God and his deputies – appears to be on the retreat in those regions – Syria and Iraq – where it first appeared at the end of the period known as Late Antiquity.

The Westphalian system, like all human constructs, may be flawed, but it has delivered to a significant degree. Landmarks include the abolition of slavery in the 19th and early 20th centuries, with admission of countries such as Ethiopia (1923) and Saudi Arabia (1956) to international bodies conditional on its formal abolition. While this has not prevented the re-emergence of slavery under modern conditions of human trafficking, the fact that formal prohibitions exist in the international system gives diplomats the legal and moral authority to work against its spread. Similar arguments apply to the abolition of genocide and torture under various conventions, with the admittedly rare possibility that perpetrators may be held to account. Another landmark is the Limited Test Ban Treaty between the US, the UK, and the Soviet Union in 1963, which banned signatories from conducting atmospheric and above-ground nuclear explosions, a turning point in the Cold War that was followed by the 1968 Nuclear Non-Proliferation Treaty (NPT), now signed by 190 nations with some notable exceptions (including Israel, India, Pakistan and North Korea which signed originally but withdrew from the treaty in 2003). While doubtless flawed, partly on account of these exceptions, the NPT nevertheless represents an international standard against the spread of nuclear weapons, and establishes an inspection regime with the scientific expertise and moral authority to check the spread of weapons of mass destruction. It was the moral authority of the NPT, to which Iran is signatory, and months of skillful diplomacy conducted in the heat of hostility from Israel and powerful lobbying within the United States, that enabled the Obama administration to secure its most signal foreign policy achievement: the landmark nuclear deal with Iran and the P5+1 groups of world powers comprising the United States, the United Kingdom, France, China, Russia, and Germany, which allowed Iran to develop nuclear energy without nuclear weapons. When facing current global challenges such as international terrorism (military or other forms of destructive activity by groups or individuals who have not been formally authorized or sanctioned by internationally recognized governments) along with the growing dangers to human safety posed by industrially-driven climate change, the international system, based on Westphalian principles, is still the primary field of action.

However, while traditional or "first generation" diplomacy based on state sovereignty and territoriality may deal with such issues as war and peace between states, trade disputes, regulations for communications and transport, the newer "second generation" diplomacy deals with a whole raft of supranational issues, including human rights, gender issues, humanitarian interventions, and fair trade questions, which are brought to public attention by an increasingly globalized media. "Second generation" diplomacy is far from new. After World War I and the Communist revolution in Russia the US President Woodrow Wilson used modern propaganda techniques, including film and music, celebrity speakers, and photographic shows, to win Europeans over from communism, a tactic repeated after World War II when the CIA secretly sponsored abstract expressionism and other avant-garde genres to undermine the "progressive" image held by the Soviet Union among left-leaning circles in the West.

In recent times, globalization has greatly accelerated such exercises in the use of "soft-power," eroding the leverage of state-appointed officials as the dominant agents in the conduct of diplomacy. International NGOs, for example, are now increasingly visible actors on the world stage. In the field of human rights, organizations such as Amnesty International and Human Rights Watch draw attention to abuses to which governments must respond; while in the military domain, a figure such as Diana Princess of Wales – a global celebrity outside of governmental control – has been widely credited with the success of the Ottawa Mine Ban Treaty, signed by 122 governments in the weeks following her death in 1997. Given the power that social media now have in reflecting or generating responses to events, whether these actually happen, or are invented as "fake news," the long-term sustainability of a world order based on the principles of Westphalian sovereignty is open to question.

At the same time, the long-upheld rights and privileges of the diplomatic corps, the guardians of the Westphalian system, are also being challenged. The Vienna Convention on Diplomatic Relations (1961), a milestone in international law, has been ratified by 191 states or state parties, including Nationalist China (Taiwan), the UN observer states of the Holy See, and Palestine. The product of a long evolution going back to the 1815 Congress of Vienna, which first tried to codify the ad hoc practice of diplomatic immunity into law, the Convention establishes the conditions under which accredited diplomats have immunity from arrest or detention (articles 32 and 29), their exemption from most taxes and customs duties (articles 34 and 36), the obligation of host countries towards diplomatic missions and their premises, such as embassies and private residences of diplomats (articles 22 and 30), the rights of free communication between diplomats and their host countries via the "diplomatic bag" (which must not be opened even when abuse is suspected), and the inviolability of diplomatic couriers from arrest or detention (article 27). With family members enjoying most of the immunities and protections of diplomats themselves (article 37), the Convention can be seen as an enabling rubric for the "champagne and canapé" lifestyles enjoyed by diplomats, a condition that makes diplomacy a sought-after profession for élites the world over, but which may fall hard on the budgets of poorer countries whose peoples are subjected to much lower living standards.

Although the immunities enjoyed by diplomats and their staffs and the inviolability of embassies are considered essential to the working of international relations, they have been challenged by human rights organizations for harboring abuses such as slavery and human trafficking. While the Convention protects diplomats from criminal, civil, and administrative jurisdiction in pursuance of their duties, there is virtually no agreement regarding their private and unofficial activities, to the point where it is widely accepted that diplomatic agents enjoy constant immunity. At the lower end of the scale this prevents anyone with a cherished CD plate on their vehicle paying for a traffic violation. According to the British Foreign Office in 2013 the United Kingdom was owed more than £95m ($125m) in unpaid congestion charges and parking fines incurred by foreign diplomats since February 2003. In 2011, New York was said to be owed more than $17m in unpaid parking tickets racked up by foreign diplomats. At the upper end of the scale there have been much more serious charges, including rape and physical abuse. Between 1999 and 2004, 122 serious offenses were committed in the UK alone, including murder by a Colombian diplomat and accusation of rape and child abuse by a Moroccan official. Other cases included an arranged sham marriage by a Nigerian diplomat; robbery and assault by Angolan diplomats; and human trafficking and sexual assault by a Saudi diplomat. Diplomatic bags, of course, have been widely used for smuggling drugs and other forms of contraband. Perhaps the most bizarre example of diplomatic bag misuse occurred in 1984 when Umaru Dikko, an exiled Nigerian politician, was kidnapped in London, sedated and placed in a "diplomatic branded package" to be flown to face charges of corruption in Nigeria. Suspecting terrorism, however, customs officials insisted on opening the package and the plot was exposed. Seventeen men were arrested, leading to the arrest of one Nigerian agent and three Israeli operatives who had been hired to help with the plot. As both Nigerian and Israeli governments denied any involvement, the plotters could not claim diplomatic immunity, and received sentences of four to six years imprisonment before being deported to their homelands. A more positive – or at least ambiguous – example of diplomatic immunity is the role of embassies in providing political asylum. A famous example is that of Cardinal József Mindszenty, leader of the Catholic Church in Poland, who took refuge in the US embassy in Budapest when the Soviet Union suppressed the Hungarian uprising in November 1956. He remained there for 15 years, before being allowed to leave for Austria where he died in 1975.

At the time of writing, Julian Assange, the Australian computer programmer and information campaigner who founded the Wikileaks organization, has been living in asylum at the Ecuadorian embassy in London. Wanted by the United States on various charges for exposing classified documents, as well as charges in Sweden arising from a disputed sexual encounter, his home is now an office converted into a studio, equipped with a bed, telephone, sunlamp, shower, treadmill, and kitchenette. In a statement the Ecuador government said it was granting Assange asylum because of the threat represented by the US secret investigation into his activities, as well as calls for his assassination by American politicians. In an era of information transparency exemplified by Wikileaks, it is difficult to see how the Vienna Convention's barriers, aimed at maintaining diplomatic confidentiality, are likely to endure.

MALISE RUTHVEN
London 2017

References:
[1] Joseph M Siracusa *Diplomacy: A Very Short Introduction* (Oxford OUP 2010) p 1
[2] Jeremy Black *A History of Diplomacy* (London Reaktion Books 2010) p 40
[3] ibid p 59
[4] Harold Nicolson *The Evolution of Diplomatic Method* (London Constable 1954) p 63
[5] Wayne Te Brake *Religious War and Religious Peace in Early Modern Europe* (Cambridge CUP 2017), p 253
[6] ibid p 246
[7] Siracusa p 53

2550–334 BCE

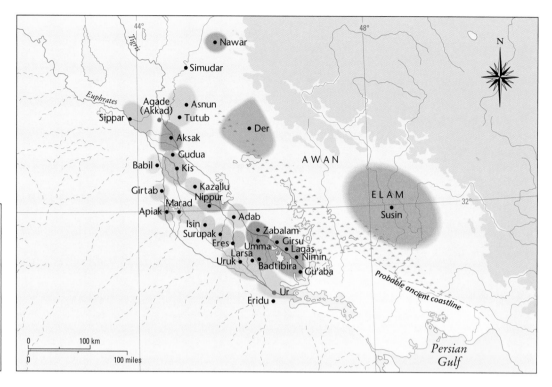

Treaty of Mesilim
2550 BCE

- Leading city or Regional power
- City with surrounding lands
- ELAM Peoples/Tribes
- Marshland
- Contour over 1000 metres

TREATY OF MESILIM 2550 BCE

The world's first recorded treaty was a peace agreement between two of the warring kingdoms of Mesopotamia, Lagash and Umma. Following a dispute about the use of an irrigation canal, these two kingdoms agreed to set a border between their territories, to be marked by an inscribed stele. A transcribed version of the cuneiform inscription is held by the Louvre Museum. It opens with these words: "By the immutable word of Enlil, king of the lands, father of the gods, Ningirsu and Shara set a boundary to their lands." Mesilim, a king of Kish, was the arbiter of the agreement.

THE "ETERNAL" TREATY 1259 BCE

This treaty was concluded 15 years after the Battle of Qadesh, which took place between the Egyptians under Rameses II and the Hittites under Muwatallis, in Syria, southwest of Homs, on the River Orontes, and ended in a stalemate. The treaty was intended to establish "peace and brotherhood" for all time and protestations were made by both rulers of love and esteem, despite mutual hostility. Separate versions were composed in each capital, one in Akkadian, one in Egyptian, and then were sent to the other capital to be translated. There were very few discrepancies between the two versions, indicating that the terms of the agreement had been discussed beforehand. The treaty recognized the territorial status quo, ensuring that each side maintained the peace and integrity of their homeland.

FOUNDATION OF PELOPONNESIAN LEAGUE c. 600 BCE

By the end of the 7th century BCE Sparta had become the most powerful city in the Peloponnese, exploiting military intervention to gain powerful allies, eventually forming a defensive League, with Sparta as the hegemon. A Council of Allies controlled the League, consisting of the Assembly of Spartiates and the Congress of Allies. Each allied state had one vote in Congress, however League resolutions did not bind Sparta.

FOEDUS CASSIANUM 493 BCE

This agreement between the nascent Roman Republic and the Latin League followed a Roman victory at the Battle of Lake Regillius. It ended hostilities between the Latin League and Rome, recognizing Rome as equal in power to all the combined members of the League. It was also agreed that the Roman and Latin armies would join to provide mutual defense against the Italic tribes.

FIRST TREATY BETWEEN ROME AND CARTHAGE 509 BCE

Carthage was the dominant power in the west Mediterranean, and the treaty regulated relations with the fledgling Roman republic, recognizing its emergence onto the international stage. Roman shipping was forbidden to enter the Gulf of Carthage, while the Carthaginians agreed not to attack certain towns that were "subject to Rome."

FOUNDATION OF DELIAN LEAGUE 478 BCE
In 478 BCE several Ionian city-states joined together, forming the Delian League, which would provide protection against the Persians. Athens was the hegemon (head) because of her naval supremacy. This was a free confederation of autonomous cities, with representatives, an admiral, and treasurers. The treasury itself was located on the island of Delos.

TREATY BETWEEN SEGESTA AND ATHENS 458 BCE
This was a treaty of cooperation between Athens and the city-state of Segesta, an important trading centre on the north-west coast of Sicily.

THE PEACE OF CALLIAS, c. 448 BCE
Negotiated by the Athenian diplomat Callias, this was said to be a peace treaty between Persia and an Athenian-led Greek alliance, ending half a century of conflict between the two powers in the eastern Mediterranean. Spheres of influence were agreed, with Persia accepting the autonomy of the Greek city-states in Asia Minor.

PEACE OF NICIAS 421 BCE
This treaty marked the end of the Archidamian War (431–21 BCE), the first part of the Peloponnese War (431–04 BCE) named after the Spartan king Archidamus II. Although the Athenians had won the war, they had not destroyed Sparta. The Spartans betrayed their allies, Corinth and Megara, accepting Athenian occupation of territories belonging to these cities. They also failed to enlist the support of some of their main allies, including Thebes, which refused to sign the treaty. Almost as soon as it was signed the treaty collapsed.

TREATIES BETWEEN PERSIA AND SPARTA 412 BCE
When Athens backed the Persian rebel Amorges, they broke the agreement between the Achaemenid king and the Delian League, in which both sides promised not to interfere in each other's political affairs. Persia therefore shared its distrust of Athens with Sparta, Athens' enemy, and they concluded an agreement of mutual aid in 412 BCE, effectively handing western Asia Minor to the Persians in exchange for financial support of their fleet.

THIRD TREATY BETWEEN PERSIA AND SPARTA 411 BCE
In this treaty the Spartans relinquished their role as the liberators of Greece. They needed Persian support, but the Persians – who had eliminated the Persian rebel Amorges – were in a powerful position and could demand whatever they wanted.

TREATY BETWEEN MACEDONIA AND THE CHALCIDIAN LEAGUE 393 BCE
Following the Illyrian invasion of Macedonia in 393 BCE, Amyntas was driven out and Argaeus II was installed on the throne. He went on to form an alliance with the Chalcidians in order to protect his country from further threats from Illyria.

PEACE OF ANTALCIDAS 386 BCE
This treaty ended the Corinthian War (395–386 BCE), temporarily securing Spartan domination in mainland Greece, while recognizing Persian control of the Greek cities of Asia Minor.

SECOND TREATY BETWEEN ROME AND CARTHAGE 348 BCE
After the Second Sicilian War, Rome and Carthage signed a reciprocal treaty allowing Romans to trade in the Carthaginian colony of Sicily, while Carthaginians were allowed to trade in Rome. The Romans agreed not to settle in Sicily and to hand over any settlements to Carthage. In return, Carthage returned captured cities in Latium.

PEACE OF PHILOCRATES 346 BCE
Named after an Athenian diplomat, this peace was negotiated between Athens and Macedonia under King Philip II, ending a war that had started in 356 BCE. All of central and southern Greece was under Philip's control; the Phocian defense of Thermopylae had failed. Philip II's reform of the Macedonian army and his establishment of the effective Macedonian phalanx had contributed to his military success and domination.

FOUNDATION OF HELLENIC LEAGUE 338 BCE
Sometimes called the League of Corinth, this federation of Greek city-states was formed by Philip of Macedon 338/337 BCE. Facing a common enemy, Persia, this was the first time in history that the majority of Greek states, with the exception of Sparta, formed a unified political entity.

ISPOLITEIA c. 330 BCE
This was treaty of equal citizenship rights between the city-states of Greece. It was enacted as a result of mutual agreements between individual states or through an exchange of individual decrees, and consolidated good diplomatic relations.

PEACE TREATY BETWEEN THE SENONES GAULS AND ROME 334 BCE
The Senones Gauls were one of the several Gallic tribes that invaded Italy in the 4th century, culminating in the sack of Rome in 386 BCE. When

Thirty Years' Peace 445 BCE

Sparta and Athens were initiallly allied against the existential threat of Persian invasion, and at their respective military strengths dovetailed perfectly; the Athenian navy destroyed the Persian fleet at Salamis (480 BCE), the Spartan-led land army were victorious at Plataea (479 BCE). Thereafter, their paths, and interests, increasingly diverged. Sparta, accustomed to pole position in the shifting confederacies of Greek city-states, became an increasingly sullen spectator as Athens wrested leadership, first of the counterattack against Persia, then of a league of city-states formed at Delos (477 BCE) which soon evolved into an Athenian empire. The series of conflicts that ensued came close to establishing Athenian supremacy on the Greek mainland, but a calamitous diversion against Persian Egypt and a Boeotian revolt persuaded the Athenians to seek peace with Sparta.

The Thirty Years' Peace was the outcome of these negotiations, concluded between the Delian League led by Athens, and Sparta's Peloponnesian Alliance. Its provisions attempted to crystallize a rare moment of parity. After Athens agreed to relinquish cities seized from its adversary during the conflict, their respective leagues were then deemed sacrosanct, and free from interference. However, states neutral at the time of the agreement were free to join either alliance. Any disagreements were to be submitted to third party arbitration. Athens also pledged not to exploit its naval and commercial supremacy to obstruct inter-state trade. The actual agreement has not survived, although Pausanias describes a copy inscribed in bronze at Olympia.

For a time, the Peace held: when Samos rebelled against Athenian hegemony (440 BCE), the Spartans refrained from becoming involved. But after a decade, diplomacy began to fray. Each alliance was tiered, with the main protagonists having senior allies, each of which had their own portfolio of minion states, all vying to improve their place in the pecking order. The Peace's collapse was triggered by two putative vassals of Corinth, Sparta's main ally, Corcyra and Potidaea. Athenian interventions in these disputes were deemed violations of the Peace, although the position was complex: Corcyra claimed it was a "neutral" by the Peace's definition, while Potidaea was a tributary of Athens as well as a colony of Corinth. Finally, an exasperated Athens slapped a trade embargo on its neighbor, Megara. Corinth protested to its protector Sparta. An assembly was held in Sparta to determine action, at which an (uninvited) Athenian delegation spoke in defense of their actions, but to no effect. Sparta declared war, although its ultimate triumph would prove pyrrhic. Its brief hegemony would be swept aside, first by Thebes, then by the invasion of Macedonia.

The Thirty Years' Peace 445 BCE
between Athens and Sparta

- Athenian state territory
- Athenian Empire
- Spartan state territory
- The Peolpennesian League

Black Sea

THRACE

P E

Byzantium ●
Perinthus ●   ● Chalcedon

Thasos

Samothrace   Aegospotami
● Acanthus   ● Lampsacus

PHRYGIA

Lemnos   ● Ilium
               (Troy)

Tenedos

P E R S I A N

Nisoi

A e g e a n   Lesbos
               Mytilene ●   LYDIA

Skopelos

Sea   A S I A   M I N O R

                    Chios   ● Phocaea   ● Sardis
EUBOEA   ● Smyrna
es   ● Eretria
TIA ● Deceleia
Plataea   Teos
gara ● Carystus   E M P I R E
● Athens   Andros   ● Ephesus ● Magnesia
Piraeus   ● Priene   CARIA
               Tenos   Ikaria   Samos
● Troizen   ● Miletus

C y c l a d e s

               Naxos   ● Halicarnassus

                    Kos

               Rhodes

Sea of Crete

                    0   100 km
                    0   100 miles

Crete

M e d i t e r r a n e a n   S e a

The World in 1 CE

The world in 1 CE was dominated by the expansionist momentum of the Roman Empire, whose influence, and in some cases dominion, extended into the Middle East and Africa. Beyond the imperial borders the Parthians were increasingly powerful, whilst the incursions of the Germanic tribes were proving troublesome and difficult to subdue. Diplomacy played an important part in the Roman world, and the Romans were known to recognize certain diplomatic procedures: protocol, formal meetings, respect for treaties. They were also masters of offensive diplomacy, where the threat of their powerful army secured compliance from subject peoples. Further east in China the Han were also experiencing an expansionist era, opening up to their Asian neighbors, and establishing diplomatic relations as well as the Silk Road, the overland trading route with the Roman Empire.

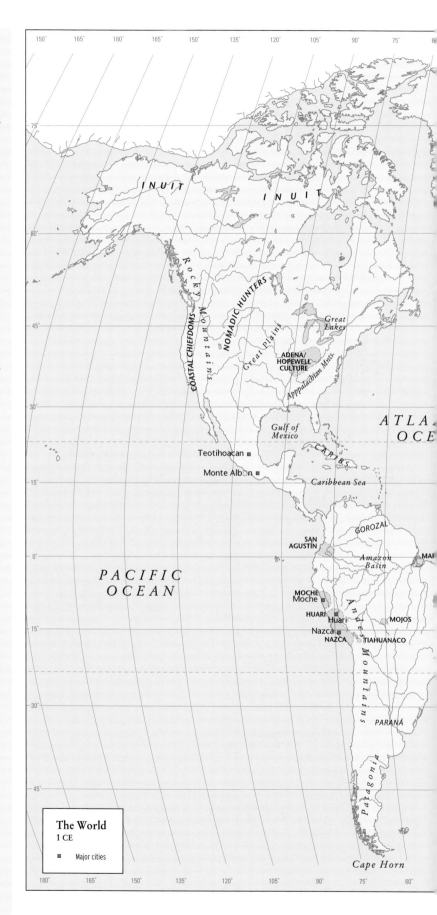

The World
1 CE

■ Major cities

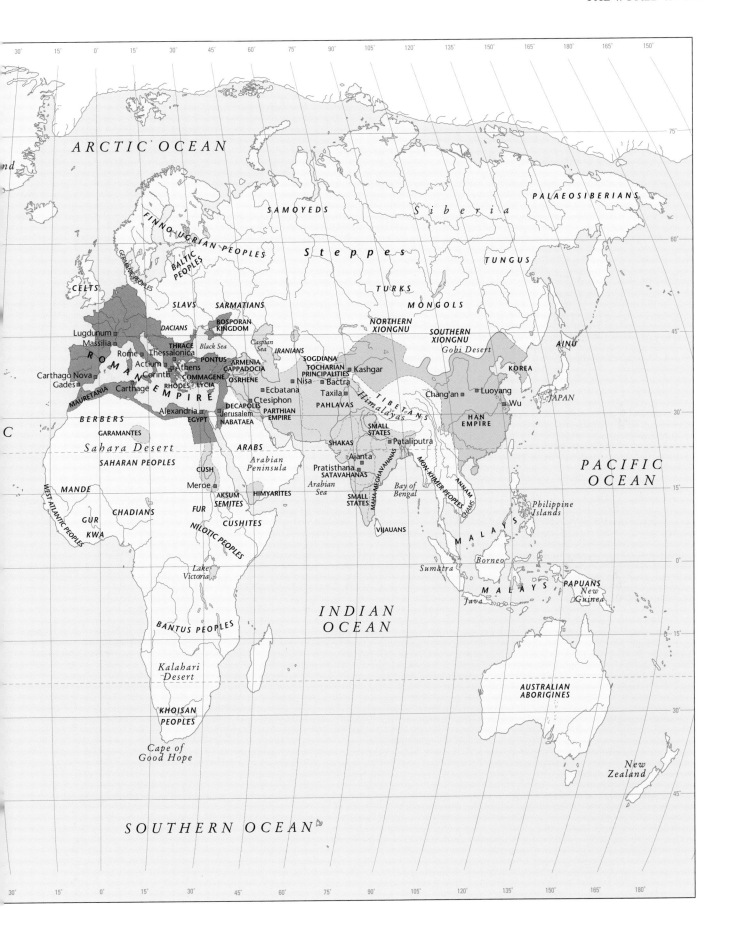

ARCTIC OCEAN

PALAEOSIBERIANS

Siberia

SAMOYEDS

Steppes

TUNGUS

FINNO-UGRIAN PEOPLES

BALTIC
PEOPLES

TURKS

MONGOLS

AINU

CELTS

SLAVS

SARMATIANS

NORTHERN
XIONGNU

Gobi Desert

SOUTHERN
XIONGNU

DACIANS

BOSPORAN
KINGDOM

KOREA

Lugdunum

Massilia

Black Sea

*Caspian
Sea*

IRANIANS

SOGDIANA
TOCHARIAN
PRINCIPALITIES

Kashgar

THRACE

Rome

Thessalonica

PONTUS

ARMENIA
CAPPADOCIA

Chang'an

Luoyang

Actium

COMMAGENE

OSRHENE

Nisa

Bactra

R O M A N

Athens

Corinth

RHODES

LYCIA

Ecbatana

Taxila

Japan

Carthago Nova

Himalayas

Wu

Gades

Carthage

Ctesiphon

PAHLAVAS

TIBETANS

MAURETANIA

E M P I R E

DECAPOLIS

Jerusalem

PARTHIAN
EMPIRE

HAN
EMPIRE

Alexandria

NABATAEA

BERBERS

EGYPT

GARAMANTES

ARABS

SHAKAS

SMALL
STATES

Pataliputra

Sahara Desert

SAHARAN PEOPLES

*Arabian
Peninsula*

Ajanta

MAHA-MEGHAVAHANAS

CUSH

Pratisthana

SATAVAHANAS

MANDE

Meroe

*Arabian
Sea*

*Bay of
Bengal*

MON-KHMER-PEOPLES

PACIFIC
OCEAN

WEST-ATLANTIC PEOPLES

AKSUM
SEMITES

HIMYARITES

SMALL
STATES

ANNAM

*Philippine
Islands*

GUR

FUR

CHADIANS

CUSHITES

CHAMS

KWA

NILOTIC PEOPLES

VIJAUANS

M A L A Y S

Borneo

Sumatra

INDIAN
OCEAN

M A L A Y S

PAPUANS
*New
Guinea*

Java

*Lake
Victoria*

BANTUS PEOPLES

*Kalahari
Desert*

AUSTRALIAN
ABORIGINES

*New
Zealand*

KHOISAN
PEOPLES

*Cape of
Good Hope*

SOUTHERN OCEAN

320 BCE–313 CE

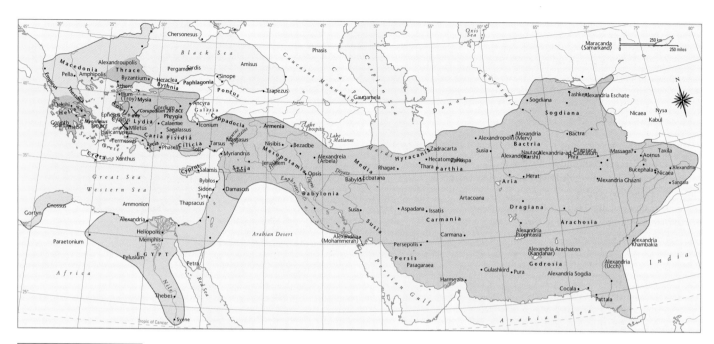

The Treaty of the Triparadisus
320 BCE

- Seleucid Kingdom
- Antigonid Kingdom
- Ptolemaic Kingdom
- Hellenistic Province
- Territorial boundaries
- Major battles with date

Ebro Treaty
226 BCE

the Senones sued for peace some 50 years later they were recognizing Rome's growing ascendancy in central Italy.

FIRST TREATY OF THE TRIPARADISUS 320 BCE

The death of Alexander the Great, son of Philip II of Macdeonia, in 323 BCE was followed by a series of conflicts as various contenders, the Diadochi, disputed the succession to his Empire. Perdiccas, Alexander's leading cavalry commander, assumed overall command of the Empire, rewarding his supporters with satrapies (administrative divisions) of the former Empire. Disputes soon broke out and Perdiccas was murdered by his own generals. The subsequent treaty divided dominance over the Empire between Ptolemy (Egypt), Antipater (Europe) and Antigonus (Asia).

THIRD TREATY BETWEEN ROME AND CARTHAGE 306 BCE

Amidst unrest in southern Italy, notably the Roman wars against the Samnites, and attempts by Agathocles of Sicily to eject the Carthaginians, a treaty was concluded that stipulated that Rome would not enter Sicily, while the Carthaginians would not enter the Italian peninsula.

FOURTH TREATY BETWEEN ROME AND CARTHAGE 279 BCE

Syracuse, allied with Pyrrhus, the Greek commander and king of Epirus and Macedon, joined with the Sicilians to eject the Carthaginians. The treaty between Rome and Carthage agreed on mutual

assistance against this threat, and stipulated that Carthage would supply warships and would provide aid to Rome by sea, while each side was responsible for supplying armed men.

TREATY OF LUTATIUS 241 BCE

This treaty ended the first Punic War (264–241 BCE), a battle for dominance in the Mediterranean between Romans and Carthaginians, which centered on the island of Sicily. The treaty demanded that the Carthaginians evacuate the island of Sicily and the islands between Sicily and Italy, and pay a ransom of 3,200 talents, while freeing all Roman prisoners – Carthaginian prisoners would only be released on payment of a ransom. Both sides agreed not to make war on the opposing side's allies.

EBRO TREATY 226 BCE

Following Carthaginian expansion northwest of the Ebro River in Spain, the Ebro Treaty – signed by the Roman reppublic and the Carthaginian Hasdrubal the Fair – prohibited the Carthaginians from crossing the Ebro River with warlike intent, but allowed them a free hand to the south, accounting for much of the Iberian peninsula. This allowed the Romans to concentrate on the threat from the Gauls of the Po Valley.

MACEDONIAN-CARTHAGINIAN TREATY 215 BCE

Philip V of Macedonia feared Roman expansion, and allied himself with Rome's main enemy, the Carthaginian Hannibal, following Hannibal's victories in the Second Punic War.

TREATY OF PHOENICE 205 BCE

Following Philip V's alliance with Carthage, the Romans allied with the Aetolian League, and the First Macedonian War (215–205 BCE) ensued. This treaty recognized Macedonia's position, including the capture of Illyria. However, Philip was required to forego his alliance with Carthage.

TREATY OF TEMPE 196 BCE

This was the treaty that ended the Second Macedonian War (200–198 BCE) between Rome and Philip V of Macedonia. Following the Roman victory at Cynoscephalae the Macedonians were forced to give up possessions in Greece and Asia and pay an indemnity to Rome.

TREATY OF APAMEA 188 BCE

The expansion of Seleucid King Antiochus III into Europe was halted by the Romans at the Battles of Thermopylae (191 BCE) and Magnesia (190 BCE). The Treaty of Apamea forced Antiochus to abandon Europe and all Asia west of the Taurus Mountains. He also gave up his war elephants and curtailed his navy. He had to agree not to harbor Roman fugitives on his territory and was forced to pay the costs of the war. This treaty allowed Rome to extend its hegemony in the eastern Mediterranean.

TREATY OF DARDANUS 85 BCE

The First Mithridatic War (89–85 BCE) was a challenge to Rome's expanding power in the east Mediterranean. King Mithridates of Pontus led the revolt of several Greek city-states, but Roman victory forced him to surrender his conquests in Asia to the Romans. He also gave up 70 ships and paid an indemnity. He was recognized as King of Pontus, and allowed to retain his Black Sea possessions.

PACT OF MISENUM 39 BCE

The Sicilian revolt against the Second Triumvirate of the Roman Republic (44–36 BCE) was led by Sextus Pompey, who became an important force in the civil war that engulfed Rome following Julius Caesar's assassination in 44 BCE. Sextus captured several Sicilian cities and prevented shipments of grain from reaching Rome. The Pact of Misenum recognized Sextus as ruler of Sardinia, Corsica and Sicily as long as he agreed to end the blockade.

TREATY OF RHANDEIA 63 CE

The Roman-Parthian War (58–64 CE) was fought over the buffer state of Armenia. When the Parthians installed their own candidate on the Armenian throne, Rome intervened and installed their own candidate. After inconclusive hostilities, the Parthians won a resounding victory at Rhandeia.

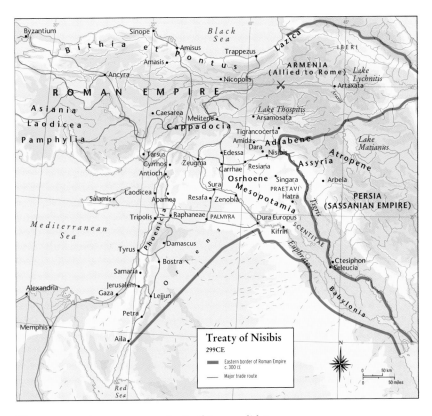

Treaty of Nisibis
299CE

— Eastern border of Roman Empire c. 300 CE

— Major trade route

The compromise treaty agreed a Parthian candidate would sit on the Armenian throne, but only with the formal approval of the Roman Emperor.

PEACE OF NISIBIS 299

This was the first treaty signed between the Romans and Sassanians, ending their war of 296–99. It followed a successful campaign by the Roman Caesar Galerius, who had defeated Shah Narseh in two successive battles, capturing his treasury, harem and wife. Galerius went on to capture the Sassanian capital, Ctesiphon. When Narseh sued for peace, Galerius demanded the total submission and subjugation of the Sassanian Empire. Emperor Diocletian was more moderate, recognizing the Tigris as the boundary between the two empires, but demanding the cession of five Persian satrapies to Rome. Diocletian strengthened his defensive lines along the border of the Eastern Roman Empire and peace ensued for the next 40 years.

EDICT OF MILAN 313

At a meeting in Milan between the Western and Eastern Roman Emperors, Constantine and Licinius respectively, the focus of attention was the general welfare of the Empire. Rome abandoned its persecution of Christians, guaranteeing them full religious freedom, and setting them on an equal footing with other religions.

363–716

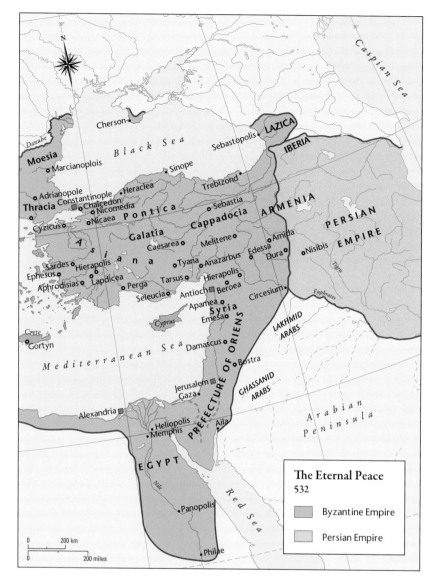

The Eternal Peace
532

Byzantine Empire

Persian Empire

PEACE OF ACILISENE 387

This treaty divided Armenia between the East Roman Empire and the Sassanid Empire. Persia received the greater share. Rome was finally forced to concede the loss of Kartli-Iberia (the area of present-day eastern Georgia) to the Sassanians, and from this point Zoroastrianism grew in importance in the region.

TREATY OF MARGUS 435

Attila, the leader of the Huns, forced the Eastern Roman Empire to award the Huns many concessions, including conceding merchants' rights, the return of Hunnish fugitives, and an increase in tribute paid by the Eastern Empire to the Huns to 700 pounds of gold annually. The treaty was signed in Margus, in modern-day Serbia.

THE ETERNAL PEACE 532

Justinian, who became Byzantine Emperor in 527, was eager to disengage himself from ongoing conflict with his Persian neighbors. After a period of uneasy peace between the Byzantines and Persians between 506 and 525, Shah Karvad had once again declared war on the Byzantines. Justinian sent envoys to Karvad, hoping to end the war, but Karvad refused to negotiate. Following Karvad's death in 531, his son Khusrau was eager for peace. The result was the treaty of "Eternal Peace." The empires agreed to regain their former territories, restoring the status quo. The Byzantines had to pay 11,000 pounds of gold as a tribute. Kartli-Iberia (eastern Georgia) remained in Persian hands, but the Iberians could choose to remain in the Byzantine Empire or return to their homeland. Justinian paid a heavy price for peace in the east, but the Eternal Peace left him free to focus on the West, where he saw the opportunity to retake imperial lands that had been occupied by barbarians following the fall of the Western Roman Empire in 476.

THE FIFTY-YEAR PEACE 562

Sometimes called the Treaty of Dara (after the town in southern Turkey where negotiations took place), this treaty between the Byzantine Emperor Justinian I and the Sassanid king, Khosrau I, ended the 20-year long war over the Caucasian kingdom of Lazica (formerly Colchis) on the shores of the Black Sea. The Sassanians agreed to evacuate Lazica in exchange for an annual subsidy. Christians in Persia were promised freedom of religion. The treaty, intended to last 50 years, actually lasted just ten.

TREATY OF ANDELOT 587

Gontran, the Merovingian King of Burgundy (561–92) signed a treaty with Queen Brunhilda

TREATY BETWEEN ROME AND THE SASSANIAN EMPIRE 363

Following Sassanian incursions into Rome's eastern territories, the Emperor Julian led an expedition against the Sassanian Empire. The two sides clashed outside the walls of the Persian capital, Ctesiphon, where Rome won a tactical victory. However, Emperor Julian was killed following the Battle of Samarra, and the Romans were forced to withdraw westwards, because their supply lines were becoming increasingly over-extended. Rome was forced to sign a humiliating peace treaty, losing much of northeastern Mesopotamia, including the cities of Nisibis and Singara, whose inhabitants were expelled following the Persian takeover. However, the terms of the treaty at least stipulateded that the emperor was able to ensure the safe withdrawal of his army.

of Austrasia. Brunhilda agreed that Guntram would adopt her child, his nephew Childebert II, making him his son and heir. With his uncle's help Childebert supressed the revolt of the nobles, seizing the castle of Woëwre. On Guntram's death Childebert annexed the kingdom of Burgundy.

TREATY OF HUDAYBIYYA 628

In 628 Muhammad and his followers made a peaceful pilgrimage to Mecca, but were halted by the Quraysh tribe at a place called Hudaibiya, just outside the city, where they made a diplomatic agreement. Both sides agreed to peace for a period of ten years; Muhammad and his followers were permitted to make a pilgrimage (*Umrah*) in the following year to Mecca, providing they remained unarmed. While many felt that Muhammad had made too many concessions, he insisted that his followers adhered to the terms of the treaty.

ILI RIVER TREATY 638

The Western Turkic Khaganate in present-day Turkestan was divided between warring tribes. Five tribes to the northeast and five to the southwest formed rival factions, with the Ili River forming a border. After a protracted civil war between the two factions the Ili River Treaty split the Khaganate into independent states.

THE BAQT 641

The Baqt (or Bakt) is believed to be the longest-lasting treaty in history, ushering in an understanding between the Christians of Makuria (Nubia) and the Muslim rulers of Egypt, which lasted some 700 years. There is no written record the treaty, but oral tradition reports that the Muslim conquerors of Egypt agreed that they would not attack the Nubians, and the Nubians agreed not to attack Egypt. Free trade and travel was allowed between the territories, fugitives and escaped slaves were to be extradited. The Nubians were obliged to build a mosque for Muslim visitors and residents. The Egyptians were under no obligation to protect Nubia from attacks by third parties. Finally, 360 slaves were to be sent annually from Makuria to Egypt – it is possible wheat and lentils were sent south in exchange.

TREATY OF ORIHUELA 713

This was the agreement of capitulation between conquering Arabs and Theodomir, the Visigothic king of Murcia, who surrendered the city of Orihuela in 713, just two years after the Muslims first entered Spain. The Spanish inhabitants were impressed by the tolerance, especially in religious matters, displayed by Muslim conquerors to subject

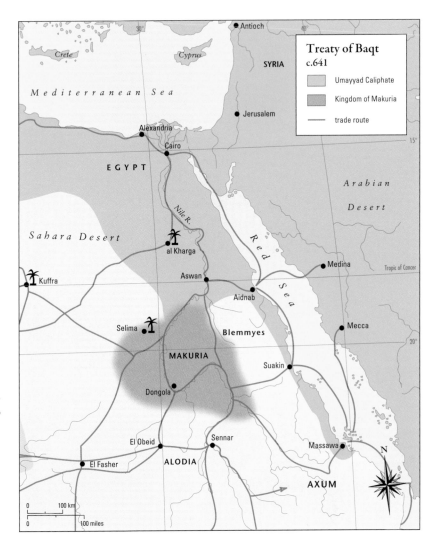

peoples. The Christians were allowed to practice their own religion, as long as they paid taxes and did not challenge their Muslim conquerors.

BYZANTINE-BULGARIAN TREATY 716

This peace treaty was agreed under Emperor Theodosius III, following the Bulgarians' support of the deposed Emperor Justinian II, when they sent a 15,000-strong army to Constantinople. The treaty agreed the border between Byzantium and Bulgaria at "Melones in Thrace," which was defined by a trench, extending for some 81 miles (130 km). The Byzantine Empire continued to pay tribute to Bulgaria, and both sides agreed to exchange political refugees who were charged with conspiracy against the legal ruler. The treaty also attempted to regulate the trade between the two countries, only allowing trade in goods that were stamped with a state seal. Bulgarian merchants were effectively given official access to Europe's largest market in Constantinople.

783–843

PEACE TREATY BETWEEN CHINA AND TIBET 783

Following Tibetan troops' incursion into Tang China and the capture of the Tang capital Chang'an, hostilities between Tang China and Tibet were ongoing. The Dunhuang oasis fell to the Tibetans and Tibetan was fast becoming the lingua franca of the region. Several attempts were made to negotiate peace treaties. In 783 a peace treaty was agreed, giving Tibet all the lands in Qinghai. This marked the beginning of the Tang dynasty's decline.

PAX NICEPHORI 803–814

Starting in 803, a series of negotiations between Emperor Nikephoros I of Byzantium and the Frankish ruler Charlemagne attempted to settle border disputes between Byzantium and the Franks. Nikephoros refused to recognize Charlemagne's title (he was crowned Emperor of the Romans in 800), although some steps were made towards agreements over disputed Italian territories. A shift in Venetian loyalties towards the Franks led to a period of naval conflict with Byzantium in the Adriatic, and Italy suffered from political and military instability. After the death of Charlemagne's son, King Pepin, the ruler of Lombardy, in 810, ongoing negotiations were successfully concluded, recognizing the borders between the Frankish and Byzantine domains.

PEACE OF AACHEN 812

During the protracted series of negotiations between Charlemagne and the Byzantine Empire the Peace of Aachen confirmed Dalmatian Croatia, with the exception of some Byzantine cities and islands, as under Frankish domain. Some of the borders remained unclear and Pople Leo V sent an embassy to Aachen in 817 to clarify them.

TREATY OF HEILIGEN 811

Following a meeting between Charlemagne and the Danish King Hemming at the River Eider, twelve Franks and twelve Danes agreed the border between Franks and Danes. The River Eider had long been the border between the settlements of the Angles and Saxons, although Hemming's predecessor Gudfred had made incursions into the lands south of the Eider. When he was killed on campaign, Hemming determined to make his peace with the Franks and agree spheres of influence. The Eider border held fast for many centuries, marking the division between Danish Schleswig and German Holstein. This division was disputed in the 19th century and only resolved after World War I.

BYZANTINE-BULGARIAN TREATY 815

In 815, the Bulgarians, under the rule of Khan Omurtag, decided that they needed to consolidate their territory and authority, especially when there was a risk of a Frankish-Byzantine alliance. So Omurtag concluded a 30-year peace treaty with the Byzantines, which confirmed a border in Thrace, and exchanged captured Slavs who remained in Byzantium with prisoners of war held in Bulgaria. The Byzantines also agreed to offer two head sof cattle for each released prisoner. The treaty held fast, and when, in 821, Thomas the Slav rebelled against the Byzantine Emperor and laid siege to Constantinople, Khan Omurtag sent an army to help Emperor Michael II put down the rebellion.

PEACE TREATY BETWEEN CHINA AND TIBET 822

The Tibetan Empire had reached its largest extent at the end of the 8th century. In 822 a treaty was agreed between Tang China and Tibet and its terms were inscribed on a *Doring* (pillar) that stands outside the Jokhang Temple in Lhasa. The treaty clearly demarcated the border between Tibet and China, with the words "Tibetans shall be happy in the land of Tibet, and Chinese shall be happy in the land of China." The treaty was observed by both sides and peace prevailed between China and Tibet for a quarter of a century.

PACTUM SICARDI 836

This treaty was signed between the warring duchy of Naples, including Sorrento and Amalfi, and the Lombard prince of Benevento, Sicard. The treaty

Peace Treaty Between China and Tibet
822

	Tibetan Empire, c. 800
	Chinese Empire under the T'ang Dynasty
——	Road or trade route
---	Sea trade route

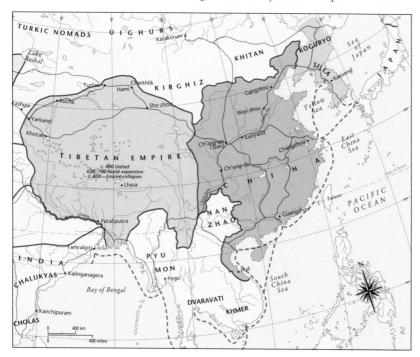

agreed the rights of merchants from all three cities (Naples, Sorrento and Amalfi) to travel through Sicard's domains. However, he did not abjure his rights of enforcement over the illegal slave trade in Lombards and trade in stolen merchandise. One clause in the treaty gave shipping companies the rights over property lost during shipwrecks (*lex naufragii*). However, peace lasted no more than a year. The Duke of Naples called in the aid of Saracens against Benevento, and in 838 Sicard captured Amalfi.

TREATY OF VERDUN 843

Frankish empire-building tended to be bedevilled by laws of inheritance. Roman Gaul's descent into anarchy in the 5th century was relatively short-lived, and the territory was reunited by the conquests of the Merovingian Clovis I. His death in 511 saw partition of his hard-won dominion between four sons. The Merovingian dynasty was wracked with internecine strife, but resolute against outside aggressors: most notably ending Islamic expansion decisively at Tours (732). The son of Charles Martel, the victorious general at Tours, Pepin the Short, would bundle the last Merovingian into a monastery and found the Carolingian dynasty, leaving his son, Charlemagne (r. 768–814), an approximation of modern France.

After a co-ruling brother died early, Charlemagne amassed an empire extending from northern Spain to Saxony and Lombardy, and coronation as Holy Roman Emperor by a grateful pope (800). His centralizing reforms - and sole surviving son – maintained the empire's territorial integrity. But when that son, Louis the Pious, died in 840, there were three sons and fresh partition and civil war ensued. That war was concluded by the Treaty of Verdun. The treaty was clearly provisional, crudely parcelling the empire between the three brothers. The middle kingdom allotted to the eldest brother, Lothair, stretched from the Low Countries of Friesia on the North Sea to Lombardy, lacking either cultural unity or military defensibility, and would rapidly dissolve.

However, in quite different ways, his younger siblings' kingdoms of East and West Francia proved oddly enduring. The Carolingian dynasty would disintegrate, as its disparate constituents "spewed forth kinglets," according to contemporary Benedictine chronicler, Regino of Prüm. In the east, the nobility sought to quell the turmoil through the novel device of electing a ruler in 911. Subsequently, the Ottonian dynasty restored dynastic rule and briefly restored Charlemagne's empire under Otto the Great (962–73). Eventually, renewed discord would see the reassertion of the electoral system,

and the remarkable longevity of the Holy Roman Empire, whose heartland would give rise to the German state. A variant on the imperial electorate would develop in the Swiss cantons. In West Francia, the Roman imprint of centralized rule vied with the centrifugal drive for autonomy of regional Frankish warlords. The kingdom of France came about through the remarkable resilience of the Capetian Dynasty (987–1328). Thereafter, the House of Valois (1328–1589), survived near extinction at English hands in the Hundred Years' War (1337–1453) to establish France as a major European power. Lothair's original middle kingdom was destined to fragmentation, and to become the battleground of choice of the developing powers on its flanks. The inhabitants of its shifting constituent states learned to live by their wits, developing a flair for trade, and nimble alliances, giving rise to the commercial powerhouses of Renaissance Italy and the provinces of Holland and Flanders.

855–1018

TREATY OF PRÜM 855

This was the second of three treaties that divided the Carolingian Empire (*see Treaty of Verdun, p 27*). The Holy Roman Emperor Lothair I had already seen the domain of his father, Louis the Pious, divided between himself and his two younger brothers, Louis the German and Charles the Bald. His domain now consisted of the realm of Middle Francia, which included the cities of Aachen and Rome. The dying Emperor further divided his realm between his three sons: he granted his eldest son Louis II the imperial crown and the kingdom of Italy; Lothair II was granted Frisia and parts of Austrasia, including the capital of Aachen, later to be known as Lotharingia; Charles became king of Provence, and much of Burgundy.

TREATY OF MERSEN 870

Concluded at Mersen (Meerssen) in Holland in August 870, this was a treaty between Charles the Bald and his half-brother Louis the German, which divided the kingdom of their nepew Lothair II, who had died the previous year, between them. Charles's portion was afterwards called Lorraine, while Louis received the greater part of the diocese of Besancon. The two realms were divided by the valleys of the Meuse and Moselle and the Jura Mountains. While the treaty appeared to create a clear division between the Teutonic and Romance races, it came to an end just nine years later in 879.

TREATY OF RIBEMONT 880

The last of the treaties that partitioned the Frankish Empire, the Treaty of Ribemont was concluded between the German King Louis the Younger and the kings of western Francia, his nephews Louis III and Carloman. In 879 Louis the Younger had invaded West Francia, reaching as far as Verdun, but retreating after his nephews had given their share of Lotharingia (Lorraine) to him. The Treaty of Ribemont confirmed this agreement, leaving Louis the Younger to confront the threat of Boso of Provence, a noble of Carolingian descent, who had declared himself King of Provence.

TREATY OF ALFRED AND GUTHRUM 878–90

The agreement, in Old English, between King Alfred of Wessex and Guthrum, the Viking king of East Anglia, established the border between their kingdoms and regulated relations between English and Danish subjects: "And we all agreed on the day when the oaths were sworn, that no slaves nor freemen might go without permission into the army of the Danes, any more than any of theirs to us." The Viking raids of the mid-9th century had steadily turned into colonizing ventures. The arrival of a large Viking warband in East Anglia in 865 signalled a decade of intense Viking activity, including the conquest of Mercia and Northumbria. Alfred, fending off Viking incursions into his own kingdom of Wessex in 878, barely escaped with his own life, but the decisive Battle of Edington saved the throne for Alfred and the Treaty of Wedmore bought him some breathing space. Under the terms of the treaty, Guthrum agreed to convert to Christianity and accepted Alfred as his adopted father. However, there is no document in existence that records this treaty, and it seems likely that territorial agreements were consolidated in this later treaty, which still survives in Corpus Christi College, Cambridge.

RUS-BYZANTINE TREATY 907

This treaty was concluded following Oleg of Novgorod's raid against Constantinople – he was said to have evaded capture and fixed his shield to the gates of the imperial capital. The agreement regulates the life of the Varangian (the Vikings who ruled Kievan Rus from the 9th–11th centuries) merchants in Constantinople, with stipulations about entry into the city, the quarter of the city in which they were permitted to live.

RUS-BYZANTINE TREATY 911

The wealth of Kievan Rus was dependent on its trading relationship with Byzantium: in 911 Byzantium signed a treaty with Kievan Rus, the earliest written source of Old Russian law. The treaty opens with a list of the envoys from Rus, followed with this statement: "In the first place we make an agreement with you Greeks to love each other with our souls and as much as is in our power." The treaty deals with the life of the Varangian

---

Treaty of Saint-Clair-sur-Epte 911

- Granted to Rollo (Count of Normandy), 911
- Acquired 924
- Aquired 933
- Added 1051
- ● Place name of Scandinavian origin

merchant colony in Constantinople, codifying criminal, inheritance, and maritime law, as well as dealing with the ransom of captives, exchange of criminals and status of mercenaries in the service of Byzantium.

TREATY OF SAINT-CLAIR-SUR-EPTE 911
This treaty was concluded between the French king, Charles the Simple, and the Viking chieftain Rollo, in the autumn of 911, and permitted the Vikings to settle in Neustria (the western part of the Frankish kingdom, corresponding to the north of modern France), in exchange for protection against raids by other "Northmen." Earlier that year the Vikings, led by Rollo, had attacked Paris and lay siege to Chartres. The combined forces of Neustria, Burgundy and Dijon defeated Rollo at the Battle of Chartres and Charles the Simple decided to negotiate. The land that was granted Rollo for settlement corresponded to upper Normandy. Eventually, Vikings would settle a region that extended west beyond the Seine, which became the duchy of Normandy, named after the Norsemen.

TREATY OF BONN 921
This treaty of friendship and mutual recognition between Charles the Simple of France and Henry the Fowler of Germany was signed on a ship in the middle of the Rhine, the border between the two kingdoms. The treaty recognized that border and the legitimacy of the two monarchs, hence the division of the Frankish Empire. The treaty was ineffective; by June 923 Charles had been captured at the Battle of Soissons and in 925 Henry annexed Lotharingia.

RUS-BYZANTINE TREATY 945
In the early 940s Kievan Rus undertook a naval expedition against Byzantium. The Rus fleet was dispelled at Constantinople, but the attackers ravaged the surrounding countryside. A surprise attack on the Rus fleet off the coast of Thrace, who were on their way home laden with booty, was successful, and most of their ships were destroyed. The treaty of 945 was therefore more advantageous to the Byzantines than the treaty of 911, allowing them to administer the mouth of the Dnieper River jointly with Rus, and apprehend any Rus shipping that did not bear the charter of a Kievan prince.

PEACE OF MERSEBURG 1002
A struggle for succession after the death of Emepror Otto III between the Bavarian duke Henry IV and Meissen margrave Eckard I, ended with the murder in 1002 of Eckhard. The Polish Duke Boleslaw I, a supporter of Eckhard, took over the Margraviate of Meissen and March of Lusatia, including the cities of Meissen and Bautzen, recently conquered by Germans, who the inhabitants had ejected. Meanwhile Henry IV had been crowned Emperor in June 1002. The dispute was resolved at a Hoftag (imperial meeting) held at Merseburg, which granted the Lusatian march and the eastern part of Meissen to Bolselaw as a fief; in return Boleslaw pledged allegiance to Henry II.

TREATY OF CHANYUAN 1004
This treaty was a major turning point in relations between the Northern Song (960–1127) and Liao dynasties (916–1125). The Chanyuan Treaty forced the Northern Song, who regarded themselves as the legitimate rulers of the Central Kingdom, to recognize the legitimacy of the Liao, a people of nomadic origin (Khitan) who rose in northeastern China. The Treaty was the peaceful end to many years of conflict, culminating in a major Liao invasion of Song territory, reaching as far as Pien-ching (present-day Kaifeng). Under the terms of the treaty the Song agreed to pay a large sum in annual tribute, and the two emperors recognized each other as equals. This relationship lasted until 1125.

PEACE OF POZNAN 1005
In 1003 Bolselaw I conquered the duchy of Bohemia and refused to give Henry II his oath of allegiance. His court became a focus of opposition to Henry II. In 1004 Henry attacked, evicting Boleslaw from Bohemia, then besieging the Lusatian fortress of Bautzen and incorporating it into the duchy of Saxony. A further invasion of Poland in 1005 was disrupted by the guerrilla tactics of Boleslaw's troops. In the resulting peace treaty, negotiated at Poznan, Poland gave up Lusatia and Meissen but retained Slovakia and Moravia.

PEACE OF MERSEBURG 1013
Warfare between Boleslaw I and Emperor Henry II continued intermittently from 1007–13, and in 1008 Boleslaw I once again took control of Lusatia. Henry II was eager to resolve these problems before his coronation in Rome, scheduled to take place in 1013. The Peace of Merseburg granted Boleslaw the Lusatian march and Upper Lusatia as a fief. In turn, Boleslaw pledged allegiance to Henry II and agreed to support his campaign to Rome. Boleslaw reneged on these promises, intriguing with the antipope Gregory VI against Henry II, who was nevertheless crowned Emperor in February 1014.

PEACE OF BAUTZEN 1018
Following Boleslaw's betrayal of his promise to support Henry II in Rome, the newly crowned Emperor resumed hostilities. His campaign of

The World in 1000 CE

The second millennium dawned with few dominant imperial powers; the last pan-Muslim caliphate, the Abbasids, had long since fragmented into multiple dynasties, from the Zirids of Northwest Africa to the Qarakhanids of Central Asia. In the expanding Islamic world diplomacy was seen as an auxiliary to, or a substitute, for war. Emissaries might be sent to foreign rulers advising them to accept Islam before war broke out. In the Mediterranean, Byzantium produced the first professional diplomats, whose first priority was to establish trading relationships and, inevitably, to gather information about neighboring states. Byzantium's neighbors were drawn into a complex network of international relations, ultimately controlled by the Empire, which greatly preferred diplomacy to war. Further west, the Carolingians attempted to define their status and legitimacy with relation to Byzantine emperors and Roman popes, and friendships and alliances were made and broken with great frequency.

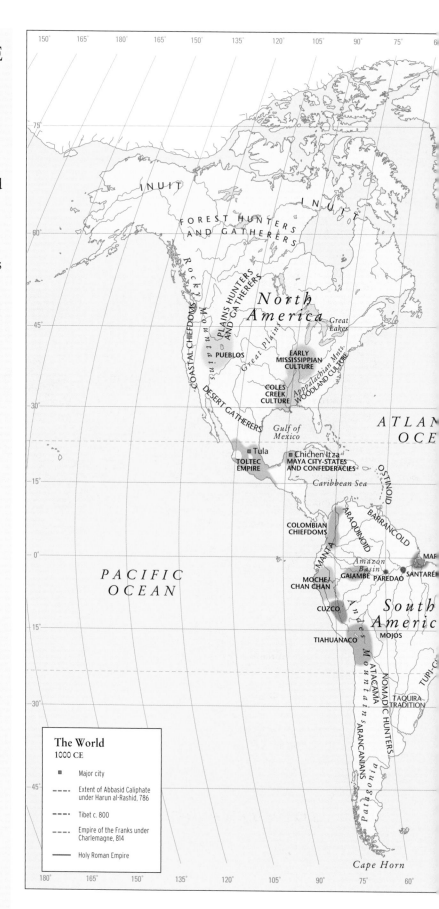

The World
1000 CE

- ■ Major city
- ----- Extent of Abbasid Caliphate under Harun al-Rashid, 786
- ---- Tibet c. 800
- ---- Empire of the Franks under Charlemagne, 814
- ——— Holy Roman Empire

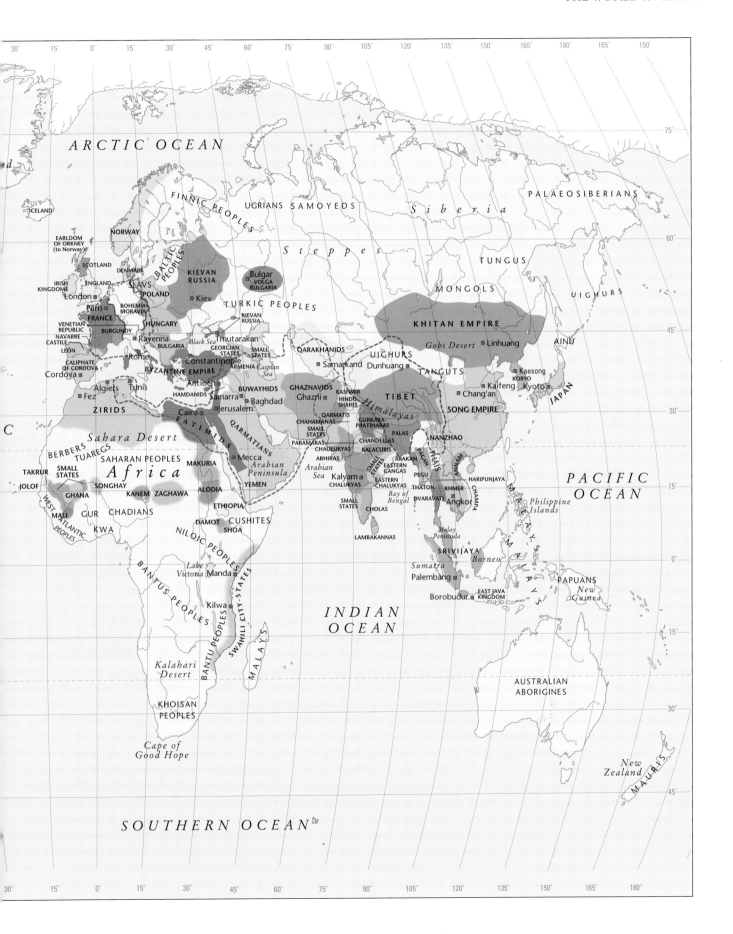

ARCTIC OCEAN

ICELAND

EARLDOM
OF ORKNEY
(to Norway)

NORWAY

FINNIC PEOPLES

UGRIANS SAMOYEDS

Siberia

PALAEOSIBERIANS

SCOTLAND

DENMARK

BALTIC
PEOPLES

Steppes

TUNGUS

IRISH
KINGDOMS

ENGLAND

SLAVS

London

POLAND

KIEVAN
RUSSIA

Kiev

Bulgar
VOLGA
BULGARIA

MONGOLS

UIGHURS

Paris

FRANCE

BOHEMIA
MORAVIA

HUNGARY

TURKIC PEOPLES

KHITAN EMPIRE

KIEVAN
RUSSIA

Gobi Desert

Linhuang

AINU

VENETIAN
REPUBLIC

BURGUNDY

Ravenna

BULGARIA

Black Sea

Tmutarakan

GEORGIAN
STATES

SMALL
STATES

QARAKHANIDS

UIGHURS

TANGUTS

Kaesong
KORYO

NAVARRE
CASTILE

LEÓN

Rome

Samarkand

Dunhuang

Kaifeng Kyoto

Chang'an

JAPAN

CALIPHATE
OF CORDOVA

Cordova

BYZANTINE EMPIRE

Constantinople

ARMENIA

*Caspian
Sea*

GHAZNAVIDS

KASHMIR
HINDU
SHAHIS

TIBET

Himalayas

SONG EMPIRE

Antioch

Ghazni

Algiers Tunis

HAMDANIDS

Samarra

BUWAYHIDS

Fez

ZIRIDS

Cairo

Baghdad

QARMATIS

CHAHAMANAS
SMALL
STATES

GURKARA-
PRATIHARAS

PALAS

NANZHAO

Sahara Desert

FATIMIDS

Jerusalem

QARMATIANS

PARAMARAS

ABHIRAS

CHANDELLAS

KALACURIS

ARAKAN

PAGAN

ANNAM

BERBERS

TUAREGS

SAHARAN PEOPLES

Africa

Mecca

*Arabian
Peninsula*

*Arabian
Sea*

CHAULUKYAS

SMALL
STATES

EASTERN
GANGAS

THAIS

CHAMPA

PACIFIC
OCEAN

TAKRUR

SMALL
STATES

MAKURIA

YEMEN

Kalyam

EASTERN
CHALUKYAS

PEGU

HARIPUNJAYA

JOLOF

SONGHAY

ALODIA

CHAULUKYAS

THATON

KHMER

DVARAVATI

GHANA

KANEM ZAGHAWA

SMALL
STATES

Angkor

*Philippine
Islands*

MALI

GUR

CHADIANS

ETHIOPIA

CHOLAS

Bay of
Bengal

*WEST
ATLANTIC
PEOPLES*

KWA

DAMOT

CUSHITES

SHOA

LAMBAKANNAS

SMALL
STATES

NILOIC PEOPLES

*Malay
Peninsula*

SRIVIJAYA

Borneo

Sumatra

PAPUANS
*New
Guinea*

*Lake
Victoria*

Manda

Palembang

EAST JAVA
KINGDOM

BANTUS PEOPLES

Borobudur

INDIAN
OCEAN

Kilwa

SWAHILI CITY-STATES

MALAYS

*Kalahari
Desert*

AUSTRALIAN
ABORIGINES

KHOISAN
PEOPLES

*Cape of
Good Hope*

*New
Zealand*

MAURIS

SOUTHERN OCEAN

1033–1143

1015, which passed through Lusatia, failed and the Emperor withdrew. In 1017 Henry's attempt to besiege Niemcza was turned back by a brave Polish defense. Henry withdrew and later that year Boleslaw again invaded German territory, between the Mulde and Elbe Rivers. Under the terms of the Peace of Bautzen Boleslaw I retained the Lusatian march and Upper Lusatia, and both sides exchanged hostages. Boleslaw's marriage with the first daughter of Margrave Eckard strengthened dynastic ties. Henry did not renew his campaigns against his Polish enemy, and also agreed to send him 300 knights to support his expedition to Kiev in 1018.

PEACE OF MERSEBURG 1033
The question of Polish succession had been disputed by King Mieszko II and his half-brothers, Bezprym, Otto and Dietric, ever since the death of King Boleslaw I (crowned 1025). In 1028 and 1030 Mieszko had attacked the eastern marches of Saxony, but was repulsed by Conrad II and forced to make peace, renouncing his claims to the Lusatian march and Upper Lusatia. In 1032 Mieszko's half-brother Bezprym, supported by Yaroslav I of Kiev, ousted Mieszko and assumed power. He was notoriously savage and cruel, and was murdered soon after, and Mieszko resumed power. In 1033 Conrad received Mieszko's submission at Merseburg, and it was agreed that Mieszko would renounce his territorial claims and his title of king. Poland was divided into three parts, between Mieszko and his two half-brothers Otto and Dietric, although Mieszko was recognized as the superior. When Otto died from natural causes later that year Mieszko repudiated the treaty; he prevented Dietric from assuming power in Pomerania, reunited the Polish lands, and continued to use the title of king.

TREATY OF MELFI 1059
This treaty, signed between Pope Nicholas II and the Norman princes Robert Guiscard and Richard I of Capua was a decisive turning point for Normans in Italy, securing their legitimacy. The Norman conquest of southern Italy had started in 999 when Norman knights, in the service of the Byzantines and Lombards, had arrived in Italy and seen the rich opportunities for wealth and trade available in the Mediterranean, and gone on to establish a patchwork of fiefdoms and independent states there. Pope Nicholas II confirmed the investiture of Robert Guiscard with the title of duke, as well as his right to possessions in Apulia and Calabria. Richard Drengot was confirmed as Count of Aversa and Prince of Capua. Sicily – then under Muslim control – was promised to the Normans, who were commissioned to seize it under the authority of the Holy See.

TREATY OF CEPRANO 1080
Signed in June, 1080, Pope Gregory VII established an alliance with Duke Robert Guiscard and recognized his conquests. The treaty followed a turbulent period of uprisings in Apulia, which had led to papal misgivings about Norman rule in southern Italy – in fact Guiscard had been excommunicated in 1074. Pope Gregory needed a protector against Henry IV; Guiscard renewed his vassalage, but also sought Gregory's sanction for the conquest of the Eastern Empire.

BYZANTINE-VENETIAN TREATY 1082
This trade and defense pact provided the Venetians with generous trading concessions, in return for their military support in the Byzantine Empire's war against the Normans. The Venetians were allowed to engage in tax-free trade throughout the Empire, and were also given control of the main harbor facilities in Constantinople. They were also granted their own district within Constantinople. These substantial concessions granted by the Emperor led to a massive shift in the political and economic power balance between Venice and Byzantium.

TREATY OF CAEN 1091
On his death-bed William the Conqueror gave England to his second son William Rufus and the duchy of Normandy to his first son Robert. In 1091 William Rufus led an expedition to Normandy, and a treaty was signed at Caen before any military engagement had begun. The two brothers agreed to end their rivalry, and England was left with several territories in Normandy.

TREATY OF ALTON 1101
When William Rufus, the son of William the Conqueror and successor to the English crown, died in 1100, his brother Henry seized the English throne, becoming King Henry I. This brought him into conflict with his elder brother, Duke Robert of Normandy, who was the rightful heir of William Rufus. Robert invaded England to claim the English crown and met Henry at Alton. Henry had the backing of the nobles and the Church, and was able to offer a diplomatic solution: Robert renounced his claim to the throne in exchange for an annual stipend and all but one of Henry's possessions in Normandy.

TREATY OF DEVOL 1108
Bohemond I, a crusader knight who had claimed the principality of Antioch, refused to honor an agreement to return conquered land to Byzantium and attacked the Empire. He was forced to surrender by Emperor Alexios I Komnenos and a treaty was

signed at Devol in western Macedonia. Bohemund became the liegeman of the emperor and promised to provide him with military support. He was allowed to retain the principality of Antioch and was granted Edessa, but was expected to give up previously held Byzantine territory. He was to restore the Greek bishop of Antioch, in exchange for as yet unconquered territory in Aleppo, Cappadocia, and Mesopotamia and an annual payment of 200 pounds of gold. His nephew Tancred, who remained in control in Antioch, refused to accept the terms of the treaty.

PACTUM CALIXTINUM 1122
Also called the Concordat of Worms, this was an agreement between Pope Calixtus II and the Holy Roman Emperor Henry V, which temporarily resolved the conflict between Church and state over the appointment of monks and bishops. Hitherto, the power of the secular ruler to invest bishops was seen as an important means of exercising political control. The Concordat agreed that the secular ruler would continue to invest bishops with secular power but no longer with sacred authority. This was an important step in a reform process, which aimed at granting the pope greater independence in his relations with the Holy Roman Emperor.

PACTUM WARMUNDI 1123
This agreement was between the Republic of Venice and Gormond (Latin *Warmundus*) of Picquigny, patriarch of Jersualem, who was acting on behalf of King Baldwin II of Jerusalem. The pact guaranteed Venetian naval support for the conquest of Muslim Tyre in the following year. In return the Venetians would be exempt from trade taxes, would extend their quarter in Acre and would be granted possession of one-third of the city and lordship of Tyre. This treaty was superseded some two years later by Baldwin II, who repudiated some of the earlier terms but upheld Venice's territorial rights and jurisdiction.

TREATY OF MIGNANO 1139
After the union of the Apulia and Calabria with the County of Sicily in 1127 there had been a decade of conflict in southern Italy. Moreover, in 1130 the antipope Anacletus II had crowned Roger of Sicily king. The legitimate pope Innocent II did not recognize this title, and many mainland vassals resented Roger's assertion of his authority. Throughout the 1130s Roger set about defeating these vassals; in 1137, the Emperor Lothair II and the pope conquered most of the south, although Roger quickly reclaimed his territories. Pope Innocent, accompanied by Prince Robert of Capua, marched

south to assert his authority but was captured by Roger's troops. Three days later, Innocent confirmed Roger as the king of Sicily at Mignano.

TREATY OF SHAOXING 1141
This treaty ended the military conflict between the Jin dynasty and the Southern Song. The Jin had rebelled against their erstwhile overlords, the Liao, in 1115, and although they had formed a temporary alliance with the Song against the Liao, within ten years they were invading Song territory, driving them south. After a period of protracted warfare, the treaty recognized the reality of foreign rule over all of China north of the River Huai; the Song's new domain was only half of the area previously claimed and they were forced to relinquish their old capital Kaifeng. The Song paid tribute to the Jin every year until 1164, reducing the Song to a tributary state.

TREATY OF ZAMORA 1143
The Battle of Valdevez took place in the summer of 1140 or 1141 between King Alfonso VII of León and Castile and his cousin Alfonso I of Portugal, who had decided to invade Galicia. The battle was a victory for the Portuguese who, according to the laws of chivalry, signed an armistice and exchanged prisoners. The Treaty of Zamora recognized Portuguese independence from the kingdom of León and both kings promised a lasting peace between their kingdoms.

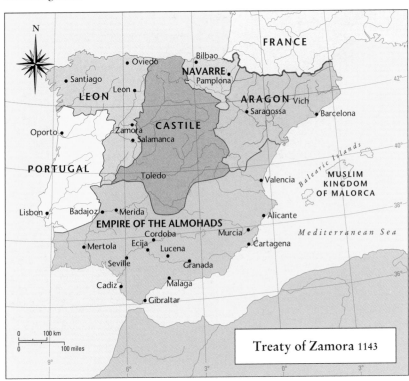

Treaty of Zamora 1143

1151–1204

TREATY OF TUDILEN 1151

In 1137 the kingdom of Aragon unified with the emerging county of Barcelona, under the rule of Count Ramón Berenguer IV. He led a series of major campaigns of reconquest against the Muslims, forming a coherent territory that included the Ebro valley as well as neighbouring Lower Aragon. In 1151 Alfonso VII of Castile concluded the Treaty of Tudilén with Count Berenguer, which set fixed limits to their respective zones in the future reconquest of the Iberian peninsula.

TREATY OF WALLINGFORD 1153

The civil war that had raged over the English crown (1135–53) between Empress Matilda, daughter of King Henry I of England, and her cousin King Stephen is known as "the anarchy." There was a breakdown of law and order, enabling rebel barons to gain power, especially in the north and East Anglia. It was brought to an end at Wallingford, on the banks of the Thames, later formally recorded at Winchester and signed at Westminster. Stephen was allowed to keep the throne until his death, when it would be passed on to Matilda's son Henry of Anjou, who later became Henry II.

TREATY OF CONSTANCE 1153

Elected German king in 1152, Frederick I Barbarossa was determined to assert the dominance of the Holy Roman Empire over the European monarchies. He signed the Treaty of Constance with Pope Eugenius III, promising not to concede any Italian land to the Byzantine emperor and to maintain the position of the papacy, supporting the pope against his enemies in Rome. Eugenius III promised that Frederick would receive his imperial crown. When Manuel of Byzantium offered Barbarossa the hand of a Byzantine princess in marriage in exchange for his support in the battle against Roger of Sicily, Barbarossa refused. He was crowned Holy Roman Emperor in 1155.

TREATY OF BENEVENTO 1156

After years of conflict with the Norman kings of Sicily, Pope Adrian IV found himself exposed in 1156 – the Byzantine army had been annihilated and Frederick Barbarossa had returned to Germany. The people had risen up against him in Rome and he was staying in Benevento. When the Sicilian army approached, the pope was forced to make terms. The kingship of William I was recognized over Sicily, as well as Calabria, Apulia, Campania, Capua, and newly conquered territories in central Italy. The pope had to forego much of his authority over the island; in exchange tribute was paid to the pope.

TREATY OF SAHAGUN 1158

When King Alfonso VII died in 1158 his realms were divided between his two sons: Sancho III became king of Castile and Fernado II became king of León. The treaty signed at Sahagun pledged to maintain peace and friendship, it also laid out plans for the future. They agreed to provide aid to each other against all other princes, with the exception of their uncle Ramon Berenguer IV, prince of Aragon. They agreed to partition Portugal and marked out the region of al-Andalus, at that time under the dominion of the Almohads, for future conquests.

TREATY OF WINDSOR 1175

This treaty was agreed between the representatives of King Henry II of England and Rory O'Connor,

The Anglo-Norman Invasion 1169-89

and The Treaty of Windsor 1175

UA NÉILL — Principal dynastic surnames

Ua Bric — Lesser dynastic surnames

→ English advance

Mac Óengussa

UA CERBAILL

54°

Ua Ragallaig

Ua Caíndelbáin

Ua Cellaig

Ua Congalaig

Bertram de Verdon 1189

Gilbert Pipard 1189

Hugh de Lacy 1172

UA MÁELSÉCHNAILL

MacCochláin

Ua Conchobair Failge

Dublin
Sept. 1170 taken

MacGilla Mocholmóc

MacFáeláin

CONNACHT

Ua hÉidin

Ua Matudáin

Ua Duinn

L E I N S T E R

TUADMUMU

Ua Dímmussaig

53°

Ua Cennétig

Ua Mórda

Ua Tuathail

UA BRIAIN

MacGilla Pátraic

Limerick

Ua Gormáin

Ua Cerbaill

Ua Máel Riaín

MACMURCHADA

Ua Duibir

Ua Nualláin

Wexford *May 1169 taken*

DESMUMU

Ua Bric

Ua Fáeláin

MACCARTHAIG

1 May 1169
Bannow landing
(Robert FitzStephen)

52°

Ua Caím

Cork

Waterford
Aug. 1170
taken

May 1170
Baginbun landing
(Raymond le Gros)

onnchada

17 Oct. 1171
Crook landing
(Henry II)

23 Aug.1170
Passage landing
(Strongbow)

7°

the High King of Ireland. It brought Ireland under English domination, forcing O'Connor to pay tribute to King Henry and owe fealty to him. Henry had presided over a series of Anglo-Norman invasions of Ireland from 1169 onwards, and the treaty acknowledged him as overlord of the conquered land, while O'Connor remained as overlord of the rest of Ireland.

TREATY OF VENICE 1177
By ivading Italy, Barbarossa had attempted to strike a decisive blow against Sicily and Pope Alexander III, who wanted to found a papacy that would be independent of the Emperor. The Lombard League was formed to defend against the Emperor. A series of Italian campaigns ensued, culminating in Barbarossa's defeat at the Battle of Legnano (1176); the Emperor was ready to sue for peace and end the schism within the Church. In the Treaty of Venice Emperor Frederick Barbarossa acknowledged Alexander III as the true pope, abandoning his support of the antipope Callixtus III. The Emperor recognized the temporal rights of the popes over the city of Rome, and a 15-year peace was concluded with William II of Sicily. A six-year truce was agreed with the Lombard League.

TREATY OF CAZORLA 1179
This was an agreement between Alfonso VIII, king of Castile and Alfonso II, king of Aragon, over the division of Muslim territories between their two kingdoms. While Aragon would expand in the territories to the south, Castile would consolidate all the territories beyond. This treaty was a foreshadowing of the two kingdoms that would emerge to dominate Spain in the following century: Castile-León and Aragon-Catalonia.

PEACE OF CONSTANCE 1183
This treaty was signed by Emperor Frederick Barbarossa and representatives of the Lombard League and confirmed the Treaty of Venice (1177). While the Italian cities were permitted to retain their own legislation and jurisdiction over their territories, they had to take an oath of fealty to the Holy Roman Emperor, and in the case of legal appeals submit to Imperial judges. Some Italian cities were administered directly by the Empire.

TREATY OF JAFFA 1192
The Third Crusade was a struggle that had started with the Muslim capture of Jerusalem in 1187 and had seen Richard I the Lionheart pitted against the Egyptian ruler Saladin. In 1191 Richard had helped to return the city of Acre to Crusader control and defeated Saladin at the battle of Arsuf. Richard lacked the troops necessary to march on Jerusalem and besiege the city, which was well-defended, and was unwilling to lead his army to certain destruction. Gravely ill, and faced with problems back in England – his brother John was intent on usurping his throne – Richard resolved to leave the Holy Land. The Treaty of Jaffa was Richard's attempt to capitalize on Saladin's weakness. It agreed a three-year cessation of hostilities, and that Saladin would allow Christian pilgrims to visit Holy Land sites within his territory, including Jerusalem. Richard surrendered the city of Ascalon to Saladin, but not before he had destroyed its defenses.

TREATY OF LE GOULET 1200
Signed by King John of England and King Philip II of France, this treaty was intended to finally settle the claims of the Angevin kings of England over French lands and to end the war over the duchy of Normandy. Philip recognized John as king of England, the legal heir of his brother Richard I, relinquishing his support of any other claimants. John recognized Philip as the suzerain of the continental lands in the Angevin Empire, and accepted the new borders of Normandy, promising not to support any rebellions fulminated by the counts of Flanders and Boulogne. Philip was to be paid 20,000 marks in acknowledgment of his recognition of John's sovereignty of Brittany.

PARTITIO TERRARIUM IMPERII ROMANIAE 1204
The Fourth Crusade (1202–04) was originally intended to conquer Muslim-controlled Jerusalem, but the majority of the crusaders became embroiled in a dispute over the Byzantine leadership, diverting to Constantinople and eventually capturing and sacking the city in 1204. A new feudal Crusader state was established by leaders of the Fourth Crusade on land taken from the Byzantine Empire. Known as the Latin Empire (or Empire of Romania) it lasted until 1261. According to the treaty, which agreed the distribution of the territories of the Byzantine Empire, Baldwin IX, count of Flanders, was crowned in Constantinople as the first Latin Emperor, while remaining Byzantine territories were shared amongst Crusaders and Venetians. The Latin Empire was weakened by constant warfare, in particular against the Bulgarians, and eventually fell when the Byzantines recaptured Constantinople.

TREATY OF SPEYER 1209
In this treaty Emperor Otto IV renounced the Concordat of Worms, ending the power struggle between pope and emperor, to claim authority over territories controlled by the pope, including Sicily.

1212–1234

GOLDEN BULL OF SICILY 1212

The Holy Roman Emperor Frederick II issued the Golden Bull in 1212 to confirm Ottokar I, a member of the Premyslid dynasty, as hereditary king of Bohemia. Ottokar's ancestor Vratislaus II had been elevated to king of Bohemia in 1085 by Emperor Henry IV, but his title was not hereditary and power struggles amongst the kings and nobles ensued. Ottokar had supported the election of Frederick II, then king of Sicily, in 1211, and the Golden Bull was issued when Frederick reached Basel for his coronation. It declared that the estates of Bohemia and Moravia were an autonomous and indivisible component of the Holy Roman Empire; the king of Bohemia was no longer subject to appointment by the Emperor, and he became the premier prince-elector of the Empire.

TREATY OF NYMPHAEUM 1214

Following the sack of Constantinople and creation of the Latin Empire in 1204, the Crusaders set about conquering new lands in Asia Minor. After a series of conquests in Bithynia (1204/05) and Nicaea (1207), there was a two-year truce, broken by the Latin victory against the Nicaean troops at the Ryndakos River in Bithynia in 1211. In 1214 The Treaty of Nymphaeum secured the extreme northwest of Asia Minor, which comprised the coasts of Bythinia and Mysia, for the Latins.

MAGNA CARTA 1215

One of the most famous legal documents in the world, Magna Carta was issued by King John (r. 1199–1216) in 1215 and became a cornerstone of British government. Much of the document addresses grievances related to his rule, but some of the fundamental values it upholds, which challenge the autocracy of the king and uphold the rights of the individual to justice and a fair trial, have appeared in much later constitutional documents, such as the US Bill of Rights (1791) and the European Convention on Human Rights (1950). King John's reign had been marked by strained relationships with the barons and the Church. He had raised an army to fight the French, which had been paid for by a tax called "scutage," which was much resented by the barons. He had rejected the appointment of Archbishop Stephen Langdon and been excommunicated by the pope, forcing him to put his kingdom under papal overlordship in 1213. When the rebel barons demanded that John cease his oppression of the English people, he refused to meet them; they renounced their oaths of allegiance to him and captured the city of London in May 1215. King John now had no choice but to negotiate, and Magna Carta (the Great Charter) was signed just a month later at Runnymede on the banks of the River Thames.

TREATY OF KINGSTON (alt. LAMBETH) 1217

As a result of King John's dispute with the papacy, in 1213 Pope Innocent III authorized King Philip II of France to invade England and remove John from the throne. It was decided that Philip's son Prince Louis would lead this expedition, but John's surrender to the overlordship of the pope in 1213 put paid to these plans. In 1216 Louis responded to pleas by English barons to help them oust the king. He landed at the island of Thanet, made his way to London, and claimed his hereditary right to the English crown through his wife Blanche of Castile. King John died in October that year and his young son Prince Henry was duly crowned Henry III, with William Marshall as regent. Louis continued to wage war and assert his right to the crown. A conference was arranged in 1217 near Kingston and a treaty was subsequently ratified at Lambeth, which brought a definitive end to Louis' ambitions: he surrendered his castles, released his supporters and persuaded his allies to lay down their arms.

GOLDEN CHARTER OF BERN 1218

Regarded as Bern's founding document, the charter establishes the town privileges of Bern, making it an Imperial Free city, and effectively independent. The charter's 54 articles contain extensive privileges, including the right to legislate independently. It is now believed that the Charter is a mid-13th-century forgery, made to formalize rights that the city had already held for some decades. These rights were formally confirmed by King Rudolf I in 1274.

NICAEAN-VENETIAN TREATY 1219

The Empire of Nicaea was a Byzantine successor state, founded by the Byzantine aristocracy after the sack of Constantinople in 1204. The Emperor of Nicaea, Theodore Laskaris, re-captured much of his territory from the Latins after defeating Emeperor Baldwin I at the Battle of Adrianople (1205), although the war against the Latins continued, with intermittent victories and defeats. In 1219 he issued a chrysobull giving Venetians the right to trade freely and without payment of dues throughout his territories. The trade arrangement was not reciprocal, but the Venetians agreed not to support the Latin Empire. The treaty was significant because it formally recognized the status of Laskaris.

TREATY WITH THE PRINCES OF THE CHURCH 1220

In 1220 Emperor Frederick II, who was grateful to the German bishops for their assistance in the election of his son Henry as king, made a treaty that became a major constitutional document of the Holy Roman Empire. Frederick relinquished a number of rights to the princes, including: the right to mint coinage; the right to levy tolls; the right to hold courts in their own territories. Frederick had given the spiritual princes a great deal of power within the Empire, mainly because he wanted to leave the northern part of the Empire secure while he dealt with problems in the south.

GOLDEN BULL 1222

The Golden Bull of 1222 was ratified by the Hungarian King Andrew II; it was the first written Hungarian constitution, and was considered to be a foundation document for the Hungarian nation, which curtailed the powers of the monarch. The Bull determined the principle of equality between nobles, and contained the "clause of resistance," which stated that if the king failed to keep his word, the nobles had to right to resist and oppose him. The nobility were also not obliged to go to war outside Hungary in support of the king, or to finance foreign wars.

TREATY OF MELUN 1226

Joan, countess of Flanders was married to Ferdinand of Portugal, who started a war against the king of France, which led to his capture. She was confronted, in 1224, by the so-called "false Baldwin," a hermit named Bertrand de Rains, who claimed to be her father, escaped from captivity. His initial popularity was probably stimulated by popular discontent with a weak government and a famine. Despite the fact that the man was obviously not Baldwin IX, many of the populace thought otherwise and a civil war ensued. False Baldwin made a triumphal process through Flanders, issuing decrees and proclamations, but was halted by a meeting with King Louis VIII of France in May 1225. He was unable to answer Louis' obvious questions and was captured and executed. Joan agreed, by the Treaty of Melun, to pay Louis VIII's expenses of 20,000 livres. She levied heavy indemnities on the towns that had supported Baldwin, and raised enough money to pay a ransom for Ferdinand and take him back. All the Flemish knights and burghers had to swear fidelity to the French king, and all Flemings had to renounce their loyalty to any count who opposed him.

GOLDEN BULL OF RIMINI 1226

Issued by Emperor Frederick II, the bull confirmed the Teutonic Knights' possessions in Prussia. Duke Konrad I of Masovia, who was waging crusades amongst the pagans of Prussia, enlisted the help of the Teutonic Knights, a Catholic military order founded in Acre at the end of the 12th century. The Bull decreed that Duke Konrad would equip the Knights in exchange for their support in Prussia.

TREATY OF PARIS 1229

Signed by Raymond VII of Toulouse and Louis IX of France (still a minor, so under the authority of his mother Blanche of Castile), this was the agreement that ended the Albigensian Crusade. This brutal 20-year military campaign was intended to eliminate the Cathar heresy in Languedoc, in the south of France. Under the terms of the treaty, Raymond's daughter Joan was to be married to Louis' brother Alfonso; they would become rulers of Toulouse after Raymond's death. Raymond also ceded more than half of his lands to Louis, and had to swear allegiance to Louis IX. The Cathars no longer had any political protection and Raymond and his vassals were ordered to hunt them down.

TREATY OF SAN GERMANO 1230

In 1227 Emperor Frederick II was excommunicated because of his delays in going on crusade to the Holy Land. The crisis was resolved three years later at San Germano. Frederick agreed that supporters of the papacy would be taken back into his favour and that he would not enter the duchy of Spoleto or other papal lands. He also agreed that the Church in Sicily would be free of taxation, that episocopal elections would follow rules laid down in the Fourth Lateran Council (1215) and that lands seized from the military orders would be returned to them.

TREATY OF CEPRANO 1230

Further negotiations took place to resolve some of the issues raised by the Treaty of San Germano, and some of the more stringent clauses were re-drafted in Frederick's favor. The borders between the kingdom of Sicily and the papal states were agreed, followed by a ceremony that symbolically ended Frederick's excommunication.

TREATY OF KRUSZIWCA 1230

This was a further treaty concluded between Konrad I of Masovia and the Teutonic Knights, which transferred the lands of Chelmno to the Knights, recognizing the independence of the Order and its rule over all the territories that had been conquered in Prussia and beyond the borders of Poland.

GOLDEN BULL OF RIETI 1234

A Bull of Pope Gregory IX, which confirmed the arrangements agreed at Krusziwca, but also, somewhat paradoxically, subjected the Teutonic Order exclusively to papal authority. With this

1236–1266

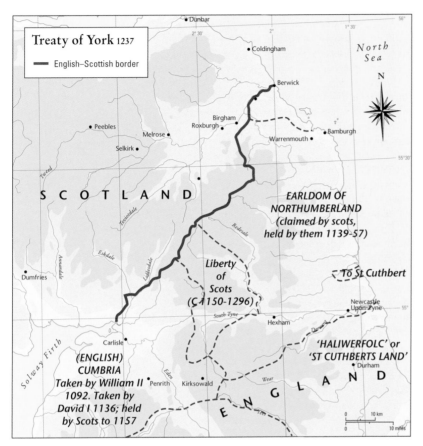

Treaty of York 1237

— English–Scottish border

North Sea

N

• Dunbar

• Coldingham

• Berwick

• Peebles

• Birgham
Roxburgh •

Melrose •

• Warrenmouth

• Bamburgh

Selkirk •

S C O T L A N D

EARLDOM OF NORTHUMBERLAND
(claimed by scots, held by them 1139-57)

Liberty of Scots
(c 1150-1296)

To St Cuthbert

Dumfries •

Newcastle Upon-Tyne

South Tyne

Hexham •

'HALIWERFOLC' or
'ST CUTHBERTS LAND'

• Durham

Carlisle •

(ENGLISH) CUMBRIA
Taken by William II 1092. Taken by David I 1136; held by Scots to 1157

Penrith •
Kirksowald •

Eden

Wear

E N G L A N D

0   10 km
0   10 miles

Solway Firth

decades of conflict followed and by 1237 Alexander II was monarch of a strong, independent Scotland. The treaty marked the end of Scotland's southward ambitions. Alexander gave up any claims to the northern counties of Cumberland, Westmoreland and Northumberland in exchange for estates within them, and swore fealty to the English king. Berwick on Tweed remained a matter of dispute for two centuries after the treaty was signed.

TREATY OF ALMIZRA 1244

Negotiated between Jaime I of Aragon and Infante Alfonso X of Castile, this treaty confirmed the essential points negotiated between Alfonso VIII of Castile and Alfonso II of Aragon in 1179. It confirmed the borders of Valencia, and agreed a frontier between Aragon and Castile. The treaty, which agreed that no Aragonese territory was adjacent to Moorish territory, effectively ended further Aragonese expansion in the peninsula.

TREATY OF JÁTIVA 1244

This treaty was signed between the Christian king Jaime I of Aragon and the Muslim commander Abu Bakr at Játiva in Spain, and marks the surrender of the Moorish city. The treaty offered generous terms to the conquered Moors, allowing them to retain the Castle of Játiva for two years before handing it over to the Christians.

Al AZRAQ TREATY 1245

When the Muslim commander Al-Azraq surrendered to King Jaime I of Aragon, following the capture of Cartagena, Al-Azraq became a Christian vassal and two castles, Alcala and Perpunchent, were granted to him. The treaty agreed that Cartagena would remain in Christian hands.

TREATY OF CHRISTBURG 1249

This treaty marked the end of the Prussian insurrection against their rulers, the Teutonic Knights. The treaty recognized that the overlordship of the Teutonic Knights was severe and granted the Prussians personal liberty: their rights of property, inheritance, trade, marriage, and legal representation were asserted. It was also agreed that Prussians could become clerics, enter religious orders, and receive the belt of knighthood if they were of noble birth. However, all these liberties would be removed if the Prussians apostasized or rebelled against the Knights, and all pagan customs were to be abandoned.

TREATY OF LÖDÖSE 1249

Norway had been enduring a protracted civil war, and supporters of the pretender to King Haakon's throne, Sigurd Ribbung, had been given help

agreement in place, the Knights felt they had legal immunity – they could ignore protests from the Duke of Masovia and the pope was in any case far away from the fringes of eastern Europe.

TREATY OF KREMMEN 1236

Signed between Duke Wartislaw III of Pomerania and Margrave John I and Otto III of Brandenburg, this treaty recognized the suzerainty of the Brandenburg margraves over his duchy of Pomerania-Demmin, and additional Pomeranian lands were ceded, in Wartislaw's lifetime, in accordance with the agreed terms. The dukes of Pomerania had become isolated following the defeat, in 1227, of their Danish protectors, and had no allies against the increasingly powerful Brandenburg dukes to the south.

TREATY OF YORK 1237

This treaty between Henry III of England and Alexander II of Scotland established a boundary between England and Scotland, much of which is still in place today, making it one of the oldest political borders in the world. Some fifty years earlier, King William I of Scotland had accepted Henry II of England as his feudal overlord. But

and sanctuary in Sweden. The resulting incursion into Swedish territory by King Haakon and his troops, with the intention of quelling the revolt, had only served to anger the Swedes. The Treaty of Lödöse between King Eric XI of Sweden and King Haakon IV of Norway negotiated mutual peace and friendship between the two kingdoms, and it was agreed that from now on neither kingdom would provide a haven for enemies of the other ruler.

TREATY OF LANDIN 1250
This treaty, signed between the margraves of Brandenburg, scions of the mighty German dynasty of Ascania, and Duke Barnim I of Pomerania-Stettin, brought a long-standing conflict to an end. Barnim was accepted as co-ruler, with his cousin Wartislaw II, of Pomerania-Stettin. In exchange he agreed to be a Brandenburg vassal.

TREATY OF CORBEIL 1258
Under the term of this treaty Louis IX renounced French claims to Rousillon and Barcelona in exchange for the yielding of Spanish claims to Provence and Languedoc. The treaty definitively separated the House of Barcelona from southern France, loosening the ties that existed between Catalonia and Languedoc.

PROVISIONS OF OXFORD 1258
The Provisions of Oxford were created in 1258 by a group of barons led by Simon de Montfort. The provisions forced Henry III of England to accept a new form of government, which put him under the authority of the elected "Council of Fifteen." This radical reform was a response to growing popular discontent, particularly aimed at the abuses of local officials. Written confirmations of the Provisions were sent to sheriffs in all of the counties of England.

TREATY OF PARIS 1259
This was an agreement between Louis IX of France and Henry III of England over lands lost by King John in the war of 1204. In return for keeping parts of Aquitaine and Gascony as a vassal of Louis, along with the cities of Limoges, Cahors and Périgueux, Henry agreed to renounce his claims on Normandy, Maine, Anjou, and Poitou. He retained the Channel Islands as peer of France and duke of Aquitaine.

TREATY OF NYMPHAEUM 1261
Nicaea had expanded in western Asia Minor throughout the 13th century, and had taken over much of the territory governed by the Byzantine Empire before the siege of Constantinople in 1204. The Nicaean fleet presented a major threat to Latin-controlled Byzantium, which was defended by a Venetian patrol. The Nicaean emperor Michael VIII Palaiologos sought an alliance with Venice's arch-rival, the republic of Genoa. Under the terms of this trade and defense pact, signed between the Empire of Nicaea and the republic of Genoa, the Genoans agreed to ally with the Nicaeans in case of war and to assist with their planned siege of Constantinople. In exchange the Genoans would receive tax and custom concessions.

OLD COVENANT 1262
Iceland, which had been settled by Norsemen in the late 19th century, was independent until it came under the control of Norway in 1262. Signed by Iceland's chieftains, the agreement accepted King Haakon IV of Norway as sovereign and Iceland became part of the Norwegian realm, although it retained its own parliament, laws and self-government. The union probably came about because of strife amongst the chieftains, as well as the growing influence of King Haakon, which he exerted through alliances with certain clan chiefs.

TREATY OF PIPTON 1265
The representatives of Prince Llywelyn ap Gruffydd met those of the Earl of Leicester, Simon de Montfort, at the castle of Pipton on the northern bank of the River Wye in June 1265 and drafted the Treaty of Pipton, subsequently signed by the captive King Henry III. De Montfort had defeated the unpopular King Henry at the Battle of Lewes (1264), and was effectively in a position of ultimate power. By the terms of the treaty, which Henry signed under duress, Llywelyn agreed to pay the king of England £20,000 over the next ten years. His price was recognition as prince of Wales and lordship over the lands he had recently conquered in Wales and the Marches.

DICTUM OF KENILWORTH 1266
In 1266, following the Second Barons' War, in which supporters of Simon de Montfort, Earl of Leicester, had rebelled against the much-resented King Henry III, terms were issued to the rebels. In the previous year de Montfort had been defeated and killed at the Battle of Evesham, when he confronted the troops of Henry's son Prince Edward, and Henry had regained his lost authority. Remnants of de Montfort's supporters had fled to Kenilworth Castle, where they were besieged by Prince Edward. Peace was concluded, with King Henry reaffirming Magna Carta, but repudiating the Provisions of Oxford (1258). A pardon was extended to the rebels, restoring confiscated land to previous owners, on condition that they paid penalties to the crown for their involvement in the revolt.

1266–1305

TREATY OF PERTH 1266

This peace treaty between Scotland and Norway settled their respective territorial claims. While Scotland gained the Hebrides and the Isle of Man, Norway's sovereignty over Orkney and Shetland was reaffirmed. Scotland also agreed to pay Norway a sum of 4,000 marks, and an annuity of 100 marks in perpetuity. The treaty was concluded between the nobles of King Magnus VI of Norway and King Alexander III of Scotland. There had been territorial disputes between the two kingdoms for many years, but the defeat of Magnus's father Haakon IV at the battle of Largs in 1263 put the Scots in a strong bargaining position.

TREATY OF BADAJOZ 1267

This treaty set out to resolve territorial disputes between Castile and Portugal. Alfonso X of Castile renounced his rights to the kingdom of the Algarve (dropping his title of "King of the Algarve"), while Alfonso III gave up Portuguese claims to the territories between the Guadiana and Gudalquivir Rivers. With a few minor exceptions, the Treaty of Badajoz defines the Portuguese frontiers to the present day.

TREATY OF MONTGOMERY 1267

This treaty, for the most part, confirmed the Treaty of Pipton, signed in 1265. Llywelyn ap Gruffydd was acknowledged as prince of all Wales, and his right to the homage and fealty of the Welsh lords was recognized. In return, he promised to pay the crown £126,666, paid homage to the king, and returned some of the lands he had taken in Cheshire and Shropshire.

TREATY OF VITERBO 1267

Baldwin II, the impoverished Latin Emperor, had come to western Europe seeking a crusade to regain his throne, following the capture of Constantinople by Greeks in 1261. William II Villehardouin, prince of Achaea, the principal vassal of the fading Latin Empire, was keen to gain a more powerful overlord. Under the terms of the treaty, made between Baldwin, William II, and Charles I of Sicily in the palace of Pope Clement IV at Viterbo, Baldwin made concessions in the Aegean to Charles, surrendering his rights to Achaea; Charles raised an army of 2,000 knights to reconquer Constantinople. In effect, the rights of the defunct Latin Empire were transferred from Baldwin to Charles.

PEACE OF PRESSBURG 1271

Signed in Pressburg (modern-day Bratislava) this treaty settled territorial disputes between Bohemia and Hungary. Under the agreement King Stephen V of Hungary renounced claims to parts of present-day Austria and Slovakia and King Ottaker II renounced claims on conquered territory in Hungary.

TREATY OF ABERCONWY 1277

In 1276 King Edward I declared Llywelyn ap Gruffydd, prince of Wales, a rebel. He gathered a huge army, attacking the heart of Gwynnedd. Llywelyn was forced to submit and sign the treaty of Aberconwy. Under the terms of this humiliating treaty, he lost most of his land east of the River Conwy and much of this land was handed to his turncoat brother, Dafydd. In addition, he had to pay the crown a fine of £50,000, although he did not lose his title of prince of Wales.

TREATY OF ORVIETO 1281

This treaty formalized the alliance between Charles I of Sicily, the Doge of Venice and Philip of Courtenay, the titular Latin Emperor. Its stated purpose was the dethronement of Michael VIII, ruler of the Byzantine Empire, in favor of Philip of Courtenay, and the forcible establishment of the Union of the Churches, which would bring the Greek Orthodox Church under the authority of the pope. The actual intention was to re-establish the Latin Empire, under the authority of Charles, and to restore Venetian trading privileges in Byzantium. Philip and Charles were to supply troops and cavalry, and the Venetians a fleet, for the planned invasion.

TREATY OF RHEINFELDEN 1283

Rudolf II was the youngest son of Count Rudolf of Habsburg, who – in 1273 – was elected king of the Romans, and captured the duchies of Austria, Styria and Carinthia from Ottokar II, king of Bohemia. In 1278, following the death of Ottokar, Count Rudolf had granted the Austrian and Styrian duchies to his sons Albert and Rudolf II. By the terms of the Treaty of Rheinfelden, primogeniture was enforced, and Rudolph II – then just eleven years old – had to give his duchy of Styria to his elder brother, Albert. To compensate, he was designated future king of the Romans, and appointed duke of Swabia.

ROSTOCK PEACE TREATY 1283

This treaty, signed by a number of Hanseatic towns as well as the dukes of Saxony and Pomerania, agreed to secure peace on land and sea as well as protection of taxes and other freedoms. All signatories agreed that for ten years they would avoid the use of force in exercising their rights.

TREATY OF BIRGHAM 1290

In 1286 Alexander III of Scotland died in a riding accident, without a male heir. His only surviving heir was his three-year-old granddaughter, Margaret, known as the Maid of Norway, who was the daughter of the king of Norway. At a parliament called soon after his death, the Scots nobles agreed to respect her succession, appointing six regents, known as the "Guardians of Scotland" to rule the kingdom while she was a minor. They decreed that Margaret should marry Prince Edward, the son of King Edward I of England, and he demanded that Margaret should be handed over to him, to be raised in the English court. By the terms of the Treaty of Birgham the Scottish Guardians and Edward I agreed the marriage contract, at the same time putting safeguards in place to protect Scotland's independence: Anglo-Scottish borders would be respected; Scottish laws, rights and freedoms would be preserved; the Scottish Church would be free from interference from the English Church.

TREATY OF TARASCON 1291

Jaime II, the younger brother of King Pedro III of Aragon and Catalonia, was crowned king of the Balearic Islands in 1276. The two brothers had several disputes about the distribution of their father's lands. In 1284 Pedro's troops captured the island of Sicily, bringing him into conflict with the pope, who allowed the French king, Philip III ("the Bold") to retaliate. Jaime sided with King Philip in the "Aragonese crusade," and was defeated. His nephew, Alfonso III of Aragon, annexed the Balearic Islands. The Treaty of Tarascon was the first attempt to settle these disputes, but Alfonso's sudden death voided the agreement.

AULD ALLIANCE 1295

Scotland and France pledged to support each other against the threat of attack from England. Their treaty of friendship was cemented by a marriage agreement between Jeanne de Valois, niece of King Philip the Fair of France, and Edward Balliol, son of John Balliol, the heir to the Scottish throne (the marriage did not actually take place). The Alliance enraged King Edward I of England, who raised his army in preparation for a war on Scotland.

TREATY OF ANAGNI 1295

During the reign of King Alfonso III the crown of Aragon reached a new peak of power. Following his death in 1291, the crown of Aragon passed to his brother Jaime II (known as "the Just"), who had already succeeded his father to the throne of Sicily in 1285. By the Treaty of Anagni, the Balearic Islands were restituted to King Jaime II of Majorca; King Jaime II of Aragon was recognized as king of Corsica and Sardinia by Pope Boniface VIII; he in turn agreed to return Sicily to the rule of the Angevin

dynasty. The Sicilians rejected this agreement, installing Jaime II's brother Frederick on the throne.

PEACE OF CALTABELLOTA 1302

According to this treaty, King Charles II of Naples agreed to give up his claim to the throne of Sicily during the lifetime of Frederick III of Sicily (r. 1295–1337), thus ending the conflict between the houses of Anjou and Aragon in the Mediterranean. The treaty reaffirmed Charles II's authority over the kingdom of Naples. The treaty terminated the War of the Sicilian Vespers (1282–1302), which started with an uprising of the native Sicilians, resentful of their French rulers' mistreatment, against Charles of Anjou. The war was fought in Sicily, Catalonia and the western Mediterranean between Charles I, and subsequently II of Anjou and the king of France on one side and, on the other, the kings of Aragon.

TREATY OF PARIS 1303

Signed between Philip IV of France and Edward I of England, this was the treaty that set the stage for the Hundred Years' War (1337–1453). Under the terms of the treaty, the French restored Gascony to England and agreed a marriage alliance between Philip's daughter and Edward's son. The treaty followed several inconclusive campaigns for control of the region in southwest France.

TREATY OF TORRELLAS 1304

In 1296 control over Murcia and the surrounding region, hitherto in the hands of Castile, was transferred to the kingdom of Aragon, following a series of conquests by King Jaime II of Aragon. In 1304, Jaime II and Fernando IV of Castile decided to fix new borders between their states in Andalusia. Under the Treaty of Torrellas the major part of Murcia was assigned to Castile.

TREATY OF ATHIS-SUR-ORGE 1305

By the terms of this treaty, the French recognized the independence of Flanders. It was signed between Philip IV of France and Robert III of Flanders at the conclusion of the Franco-Flemish War (1297–1305), during which Philip had attempted to tighten his control over the county of Flanders, which had enjoyed a large measure of independence within the French kingdom. The Flemish allied with King Edward I of England, although the first Scottish War of Independence meant his support was limited. After bitter sieges, conquest, armistice, and insurrection the war culminated in Flemish victory at the Battle of the Golden Spurs (1302). Independence came at a price; the Flemish agreed to relinquish the cities of Lille, Douai, and Orchies and paid exorbitant fines to Philip IV.

1305–1355

TREATY OF ELCHE 1305
Following the Treaty of Torrellas, signed the previous year, the crowns of Castile and Aragon met again to resolve some ongoing border disputes concerning the region of Murcia. Under the terms of the treaty the port city of Cartagena was returned to Castile.

TREATY OF SOLDIN 1309
Following the Brandenburg occupation of Pomerelia the Teutonic Knights were hired by the Poles to expel the Brandenburgers – they were evicted from Danzig in 1308. When there was a dispute about payment for this service between the Order and the Polish Duke Wladyslaw I, the Knights occupied Danzig, suppressing a revolt with great ferocity. By the terms of Soldin the Knights purchased Brandenburg's claims to the castles of Danzig, Shwetz and Dirschau and their hinterlands, giving the Teutonic Knights effective control of Pomeralia.

TREATY OF TEMPLIN 1317
This treaty concluded the war between the Margraviate of Brandenburg and Denmark leading a north German alliance, which was resisting Brandenburg expansionism. The decisive defeat of

the Brandenburgian margrave, Waldemar, at Gansee in 1316 forced a negotiation. Under the terms of the treaty Brandenburg transferred territory that she had won from Pomerania in 1236 to Mecklenburg and surrendered other territories to Pomerania-Wolgast.

TREATY OF NÖTEBORG 1323
Following a series of attacks on Novgorod from Swedish Finland, sometimes known as the Third Swedish Crusade, this peace treaty was concluded between the kingdom of Sweden and the republic of Novgorod. While the forces of Novgorod had been able to stop the Swedish advance, they had not been able to capture the fortress at Viborg, and this stalemate forced an agreement. The border between Novgorodian and Swedish territory on the Karelian Isthmus was agreed, with the western part of Karelia being integrated into Sweden, while the eastern part, and the county of Kexholm, remained under the rule of Novgorod.

TREATY OF PARIS 1323
By the terms of this treaty, Count Louis I of Flanders relinquished Flemish claims over the county of Zeeland and acknowledged the count of Holland as count of Zeeland. Count Floris IV of Holland had re-conquered Zeeland from Flanders (1222–34) and since then Zeeland had been ruled in personal union by Holland.

TREATY OF CORBEIL 1326
Renewing the Auld Alliance between France and Scotland, Robert I the Bruce and Charles IV of France once again agreed a treaty of mutual aid against England. From 1323 peace negotiations between Scotland and England had repeatedly collapsed because of England's refusal to recognize Robert I as king of Scotland. Diplomatic missions were sent across Europe to strengthen Scotland's position and in 1324 Pope John XXII recognized Robert as king.

TREATY OF NOVGOROD 1326
This was the treaty that marked the end of decades of border skirmishes between Norway and Novgorod in the northern region known as Finnmark. The treaty agreed a 40-year armistice, and rather than delineating a border it agreed which part of the native Sami people would pay tribute to Norway and which to Novgorod, creating a kind of buffer zone between the two countries.

TREATY OF EDINBURGH-NORTHAMPTON 1328
So-called because it was agreed by Robert the Bruce in Edinburgh Castle and by the teenage English

Treaty of Noteborg
1323

king, Edward III, in Northumberland, this was the treaty that Robert had long been striving for. England recognized Scotland's independence and in return Scotland paid England a sum of £20,000 and gave up any claims to Northumberland. A marriage was agreed between the two royal families. The treaty was the formal ending of the First War of Scottish Independence (1296–1328) a series of warring periods that had culminated in the English defeat at the Battle of Bannockburn (1314), which had effectively given Scotland de facto independence.

TREATY OF PAVIA 1329

This was the agreement that divided the House of Wittelsbach into two branches. Under the accord Emperor Louis IV granted the Electoral Palatinate, a fragmented historical territory of the Holy Roman Empire whose rulers served as prince-electors, to his brother Duke Rudolph's descendants – Rudolph II, Rupert I, and Rupert II. The Electoral Palatinate consisted of two parts: the Lower Palatinate of the Upper Rhine and the Upper Palatinate along the Bohemian border. Louis retained Upper Bavaria and inherited Lower Bavaria in 1234.

DECLARATION OF RHENSE 1338

Emperor Louis of Wittlesbach, who had been elected in 1314 and crowned by the archbishop of Mainz, argued that election by a majority of electors did not require papal confirmation. His election was disputed and his rival Frederick of Habsburg was consecrated by the archbishop of Cologne. This constitutional argument was settled in favor of Louis at the Battle of Mühldorf (1322). Pope John XII refused to accept Louis's legitimacy as emperor and excommunicated him. Louis warned the electors that their rights were being endangered and six electors responded with the Declaration of Rhense, which proclaimed that election by majority was valid and that any king-elect could assume his authority on election, without waiting for papal approbation. His legitimate power was therefore not dependent on the pope's will.

TRUCE OF ESPLECHIN 1340

The Hundred Years' War (1337–1453) was a series of episodic conflicts between France and England, stemming from Edward III of England's desire to maintain his sovereignty in Aquitaine and assert his claim as the legitimate ruler of France. The Truce of Espléchin marked the end of the first phase of the war, following the protracted English siege of Tournai. Philip VI arrived with the main French army but refused to meet the English in battle. Both sides needed to replenish their funds and Tournai

itself was running out of food, so a temporary truce was agreed, suspending hostilities on all fronts for nine months.

TREATY OF KALISZ 1343

The Teutonic Knights, and their ally Bohemia, had waged successful war in Poland from 1328–31, and Polish territory had been lost. When Casmir the Great (1333–70) ascended to the Polish throne he accepted the Knights' rule in Pomerania, agreed in the Treaty of Kalisz. In return he regained Kuyavia and the lands of Dobrzyn in the east. He nevertheless retained the title duke of Pomerania. He also became a patron of the Teutonic Order, which made symbolic feudal payments to the Polish king and provided military aid.

TREATY OF STRASLUND 1354

This treaty settled border disputes that were the result of the war for Rugian succession between the duchies of Mecklenburg, and Pomerania – these disputes over the overlordhip of the Rugian principality had been intermittently breaking out between Denmark, Mecklenburg, and Pomerania from 1326 onwards. Rügen was a Danish principality from 1168 to 1325, consisting of the island of Rügen and the adjacent mainland.

TREATY OF MANTES 1354

When Charles II of Navarre began negotiations with Edward the Black Prince and his supporter Henry of Grosmont, duke of Lancaster, during the 100 Years' War, Edward's arch-enemy King John II of France opened his own negotiations with Charles and agreed to create him Count of Beaumont-le Roger.

TREATY OF VALOGNES 1355

The peaceable relations agreed between Charles II of Navarre and John II of France in the Treaty of Mantes did not last. Within a year Charles had sought an alliance with Henry of Grosmont and John had invaded Charles's territories in Normandy. Later that year John II, anxious to secure Charles as an ally, made a new agreement of reconciliation, the Treaty of Valognes. Charles repeatedly switched sides during the Hundred Years' War, attempting to advance his own position.

TREATY OF PARIS 1355

Agreed between the count of Savoy and the count of Geneva, this treaty recognized Savoy's annexation of the Barony of Gex, confirming Savoy's control of western Chablais. From the 11th century the counts of Savoy had been attempting, through marriage agreements, debt payments and financial pressures, to gain control of the valley of the Rhône, Lake

1358–1373

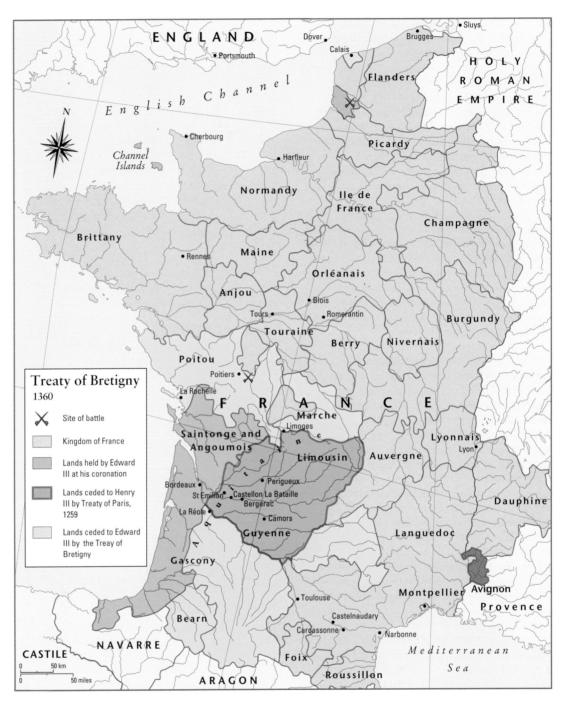

Léman and surrounding areas. The Treaty of Paris confirmed the success of these manoeuvres.

TREATY OF ZADAR 1358
Louis I of Hungary and the Republic of Venice had both been struggling for control of Dalmatia. This treaty forced Venice to cede control of its Dalmatian territories to Hungary, marking the rise of Republic of Ragusa as an independent state.

TREATY OF LONDON 1359
In 1356 the English soundly defeated the French at the Battle of Poitiers, during the ongoing Hundred Years' War. John II of France was captured, and the French were therefore forced to make terms with the English. The treaty was proposed by England and signed by France, and stated that England was permitted to annex much of western France. but the French estates-general, feeling too much land was

being lost, repudiated the concessions made in the treaty. Eventually, the English agreed re-negotiated terms, accepting the territory of Aquitaine.

TREATY OF BRÉTIGNY 1360
Following the defeat and capture of John II of France at the Battle of Poitiers (1356), this treaty was concluded between Edward III of England and John II, temporarily halting the Hundred Years' War, although hostilities broke out again just nine years later. It marked the high point of English hegemony in France. Brétigny was a renegotiation of the Treaty of London, agreed a year earlier – the French position had been further weakened by conflict between the dauphin and Etienne Marcel and a peasant revolt. Edward acquired considerable territories in southwest France. In return Edward gave up his claims to the French throne, forfeiting his suzerainty in Brittany and Flanders and giving up the countships of Anjou and Maine and the duchy of Tourraine. The French agreed to ransom John for the cost of 3 million gold crowns.

TREATY OF STRASLUND 1370
War broke out between the kingdom of Denmark and the Hanseatic League in 1361 when the Danish King Valdemar conquered Scania, Oland, and Gotland as well as the Visby, a major Hanseatic town. Hansa attempts at reconquest failed and they were forced to accept Danish overlordship, losing many of their trading privileges. Unwilling to accept this situation, they raised a fleet in 1367, renewed their alliance with Sweden and defeated the Danes. Under the Treaty of Straslund, Visby was re-established as a Hanseatic centre, and Hanse merchants were guaranteed free trade in the Baltic Sea. With full control of the Skänor fisheries, they had an effective monopoly on the Baltic fish trade. They also obtained a formal veto on the choice of Danish king. The Hanseatic League had reached the apogee of its power.

TREATY OF VINCENNES-EDINBURGH 1371
This treaty renewed the auld alliance between France and Scotland. The signatories agreed that they should bind together in a pact of mutual assistance against any aggression from their old enemy, England. It was also agreed that no truce or peace treaty with England was to be agreed upon by either kingdom in which the other was not included.

ANGLO-PORTUGUESE TREATY 1373
In 1369, an alliance between the kingdoms of France and Castile had caused concern in the English court. The English feared that the French would exploit Castilian sea-power in their continuing struggle with

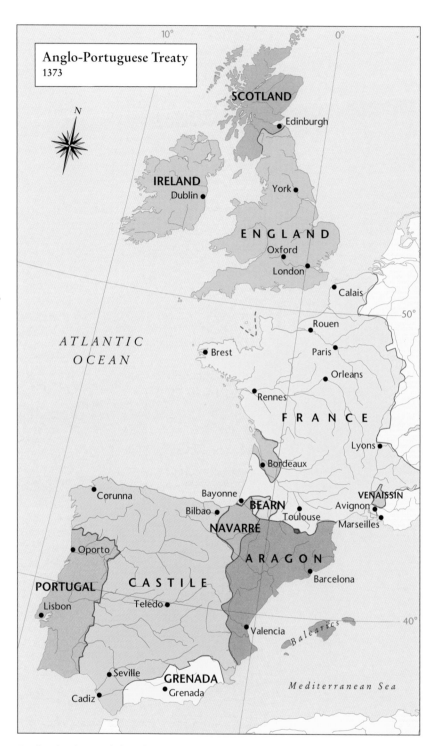

England. The English policy was two-fold: they sent a (failed) military expedition to Iberia in an attempt to push Castile out of the war; at the same time they formed an alliance with Castile's western neighbour, Portugal. The treaty agreed "perpetual friendships, unions [and] alliances" between the two nations, and is the oldest such treaty in the world.

1379–1412

TREATY OF NEUBERG 1379

This treaty, concluded between the Austrian Duke Albert III and his brother Leopold III, divided the Habsburg hereditary lands. Their older brother, Duke Rudolf IV, had been an energetic and expansionist ruler of Austria. Following his death in 1365, his brothers inherited his lands and were named as joint rulers. The brothers soon fell out and the Treaty of Neuberg was agreed to partition their territory: Albert retained Upper and Lower Austria; Leopold became ruler of Styria, Carinthia, Carniola, Tyrol, Further Austria, and parts of Friuli. All Habsburg successors retained the Austrian ducal title, regardless of their territorial possessions.

TREATY OF DOVYDISKES 1380

In 1378 the Teutonic Knights had renewed their campaign against pagan Lithuania. Jogaila and his uncle Kestutis, who many believed should have become Grand Duke, signed a truce the Teutonic Knights. But the truce only covered the Christian south; Kestutis's pagan lands in the north were still vulnerable. In 1380 Grand Duke Jogaila went behind his uncle's back to negotiate a treaty of non-aggression with the Grand Master of the Order of Teutonic Knights. They were free to attack the lands of Kestutis without violating the treaty, and this betrayal eventually led to a civil war in Lithuania (1381–84), in which Jogalia was the victor.

TREATY OF DUBYSA 1382

Signed between Jogaila, Grand Duke of Lithuania, his brother Skirgaila and the Grand Marshal of the Teutonic Order, this treaty never came into effect. Jogaila promised to convert Lithuania to Christianity and give up the territory of Samogitia. He also promised to cooperate with the Teutonic Order, effectively giving up his sovereignty. Ultimately

Jogaila reconciled with his cousin Vytautus, who retained the lands of his father Kestutis.

UNION OF KREWO 1385

This treaty marked a decisive moment in the history of Lithuania, when Grand Duke Jogaila converted to Christianity, married Queen Jadwiga of Poland and was crowned king of Poland (1386). Jadwiga had been crowned queen of Poland, succeeding her father Louis I of Hungary. But the new monarch still needed a suitable husband. The marriage created a union between Lithuania and Poland that was to last until the end of the 18th century. From this point Jogaila was known as King Wladyslaw II Jagiello.

TREATY OF WINDSOR 1386

Ten years after the signature of Anglo-Portuguese friendship in 1373, King Ferdinand of Portugal died. His son-in-law, the Castilian king, was intent on forcing a union between Portugal and Castile. The Portuguese favoured King Ferdinand's half-brother John of Aviz and a civil war ensued. The Portuguese sought help from their English allies and won a victory over Castilian troops at Aljubarrota (1385). Shortly after the coronation of John of Aviz he sent ambassadors to England to negotiate an alliance with Richard II, and raise money for his troops. The English sought Portuguese military assistance for their campaigns in Castile and the Portuguese fleet protected shipping in the Channel. Both countries benefitted from the commercial concessions that were negotiated in the treaty.

TREATY OF KÖNIGSBERG 1390

Königsberg was founded in 1255 by the Teutonic Knights during the Northern Crusades. The treaty signed there in 1390 was between the Samogitian nobles, who had been steadfast in their resistance to the expansion of the Teutonic Order in Lithuania, and the Teutonic Knights during the Lithuanian civil war. The Samogitian nobles pledged loyalty to their king Vytautus, who was in conflict with his cousin Jogaila, Grand Duke of Lithuania. They also guaranteed the Knights trade freedom in their region, in exchange for gifts.

TREATY OF KALMAR 1397

In June 1397 15-year-old Erik of Pomerania was crowned king of Denmark, Sweden and Norway. Scandinavia's Union of Kalmar stated that each country was to be governed by its own laws, but was to give assistance to each other in case of attack. The three countries agreed to be ruled by Erik and his descendants, and to jointly elect a new king should the line of succession fail. The urge to unify the Scandinavian kingdoms was attributable to German

Union of Krewo
1385

expansion northwards into the Baltic; a united front was the best defense. But ultimately the Union did not survive, breaking up in 1523, probably because of the ongoing tension between the monarch's desire for a strong unified state and the Swedish and Danish nobility's resistance to unification.

TREATY OF SALYNAS 1398

This was the peace treaty signed by the Grand Duke of Lithuania Vytautus the Great and the Grand Master of the Teutonic Order of Knights. For the third time Vytautus promised the territory of Samogitia to the Knights – they were keen to acquire it as it physically separated them from their Livonian branch. In 1394, the Knights – enraged by Vytautus's breaching of their original agreement about Samogitia – had invaded Lithuania and besieged Vilnius. They were turned away by Polish and Lithuanian troops, and a truce was negotiated. The treaty laid out spheres of influence, ceding territory to the Knights in exchange for their help with Vytautus's campaign against the Tatars.

PACT OF VILNIUS AND RADOM 1401

Under three acts, passed in the Lithuanian capital Vilnius and ratified in Radom in Poland, it was recognized that Vytautus the Grand Duke of Lithuania was fully in charge of Lithuanian affairs, while his cousin, the Polish king, Wladyslaw II Jagiello, had the rights of an overlord. On the death of Vytautus, Lithuania would be ruled by Wladyslaw II or his legal heir, thus uniting the two kingdoms of Lithuania and Poland. This reaffirmed alliance stabilized a troubled situation, leaving Vytautus free to renew his offensive against the Teutonic Knights.

FIRST PEACE OF THORN 1411

The (first) peace of Thorn (or Toruń) was the treaty that formally ended the conflict between Poland-Lithuania and the Teutonic Knights. Following their decisive victory at the Battle of Grunwald in 1410 Poland-Lithuania failed to capitalize; the Knights restored the territories of Samogitia to Poland-Lithuania, but only temporarily, and it was to take two more wars to resolve some of the outstanding territorial issues between them. However, the Knights did agree to pay substantial reparations to their erstwhile enemies, and never regained their former supremacy.

TREATY OF LUBOWLA 1412

Concluded between King Wladyslaw II Jagiello of Poland and Sigismund of Luxemburg, king of Hungary, this treaty formally recognized the provisions agreed in the Treaty of Thorn, and Hungary agreed to secretly support Poland's rights

to the province of Pomerelia, which had been lost to the Teutonic Knights. In return, the Hungarian crown, desperately short of money because of ongoing wars with the Ottomans, borrowed a huge sum from Poland-Lithuania, offering the salt-producing town in the area of Spisz as surety. In the event, the debt was not repaid and Spisz remained a part of Poland until the 18th century.

COMPROMISE OF CASPE 1412

When King Martin of Aragon died without heirs in 1410, it precipitated a constitutional crisis. There were several possible successors, but the king and his court were unable to resolve the question before his death. The assemblies of the three principal states of Aragon, the kingdom of Valencia, principality of Catalonia and kingdom of Aragon itself, attempted to resolve the question, but the contending factions could not reach an agreement. To resolve the issue nine *compromisarios* (negotiators), representatives of the three states, reviewed the claims of four

The World in 1400

After the expulsion of the Mongols in 1368, the Ming Empire in China, with a standing army of a million troops and a population nearing 100 million, was probably the wealthiest and most powerful dominion worldwide. Periods of isolationism alternated with the expansive maritime tributary missions, undertaken by the Admiral Zheng He (1371–1433), when the countries he visited were persuaded to give tribute in exchange for benefits such as military outposts and trade treaties, thus ensuring peaceful trade would flourish. To the west, Timur, a descendant of Genghis Khan and an outstanding and ruthless warrior, irrupted into Central Asia in 1402, spreading mayhem and conquest. Amongst others he routed the Ottomans and captured their Sultan Bayezid. Intent on looting and conflict, he did not consolidate his victories through diplomacy, and his legacy was squandered. Meanwhile, two of Europe's most powerful unitary states, France and England, were locked in a century of conflict, interspersed with diplomatic negotiations over political prisoners, ransoms, and truces.

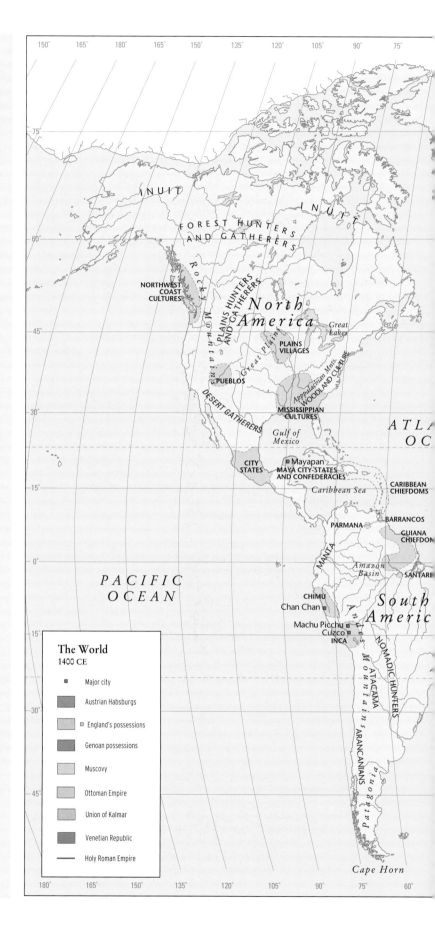

The World
1400 CE

- ■ Major city
- Austrian Habsburgs
- ■ England's possessions
- Genoan possessions
- Muscovy
- Ottoman Empire
- Union of Kalmar
- Venetian Republic
- — Holy Roman Empire

ARCTIC OCEAN

LAPPS

U G R I A N S

S A M O Y E D S

PALAEOSIBERIANS

ICELAND

NORWAY

SWEDEN

NOVGOROD

Siberia

SCOTLAND
DENMARK
IRELAND ENGLAND
London
Cherbourg Calais
Brest
Bordeaux
BEARN
NAVARRE
Bayonne
CASTILE
PORTUGAL
Madrid
GRANADA
ZAYYANIDS
MARINIDS

TEUTONIC
ORDER
HOLY
BOHEMIA
ROMAN
POLAND
EMPIRE
Paris
Venice
Avignon
Genoa
PAPAL
Barcelona STATES
ARAGON
Rome
KINGDOM
OF NAPLES
Tunis
HAFSIDS

PSKOV
MUSCOVY
Moscow
RYAZAN
SMOLENSK
LITHUANIA
MOLDAVIA
WALLACHIA
to Genoa
BOSNIA
SERBIA
Constantinople
OTTOMAN Bursa
EMPIRE
CYPRUS

RUSSIAN
PRINCIPALITIES

KHANATE OF THE
GOLDEN HORDE

Black Sea
TREBIZOND
Caspian
Sea

Samarkand

KHANATE OF
THE OIRATS

Gobi Desert

CHAGATAI
KHANATE

Beijing

TUNGUS

60°

75°

KOREA

JAPAN

Mediterranean Sea
VENETIAN REPUBLIC

MAMLUKS

Ardabil
DULKADIR
Baghdad

EMPIRE
OF TIMUR

KASHMIR

TIBET

Himalayas

MING
EMPIRE

30°

C

BERBERS
BEDUINS
Sahara Desert
TUAREGS
MAGHSHAREN
TUAREG
GHANA
ZAFUNC
WOLOF
SIINE
SALUM
TAKRUR
MALI
MEMA
TENNE
MOSSI
KINGDOMS
BORGU
KINGDOMS

Africa

SONGHAY

BEDUINS

BEDUINS
SHARIFS OF
MEDINA
Mecca
SHARIFS
OF MECCA
Arabian
Peninsula

OMAN

SIND

Delhi

SULTANATE
OF DELHI

KHANDESH
SMALL
STATES

Arabian
Sea

SMALL
STATES
RASULIDS

KANEM
HAUSA
STATES
NUPE
IGALA
BENIN

DAJU

ALWA

ETHIOPIA

IFAT

KWARARAEA
SIDAMA
STATES

CUSHITES

SMALL
STATES

SHARQIS
BAHMANI
KINGDOM
EASTERN
GANGAS

TELINGANA

VIJAYANAGAR

REDDIS

Bay of
Bengal

SMALL
STATES

ARAKAN

SMALL
STATES
SHAN
STATES
AVA
PEGU
SUKHOTHAI
SIAM
Ayutthaya

TOUNGOO
CHIENGMAI

MYANMA
LAOS
CAMBODIA
CHAMPA

PACIFIC
OCEAN

15°

INTERLACUSTRINE
STATES
Lake
Victoria

KONGO

BANTUS PEOPLES

SWAHILI CITY-STATES

MALAYS

GREAT
ZIMBABWE

Kalahari
Desert

KHOISAN
PEOPLES

Cape of
Good Hope

MALAY STATES

PAJAJARAN

Borneo

MAJAPAHIT

M A L A Y S

Philippine
Islands

PAPUANS
New
Guinea

0°

INDIAN
OCEAN

AUSTRALIAN
ABORIGINES

15°

30°

New
Zealand

MAORIS

SOUTHERN OCEAN

45°

1417–1444

candidates. A majority chose the Infante Ferdinand of Castile, by right of his close blood ties with the late king. He was duly proclaimed the next king.

UNION OF HORODLO 1417
The union amended earlier Polish-Lithuanian unions of Krewo and Radom, giving Lithuania more autonomy by allowing the nobility to choose their next Grand Duke, rather than accepting King Wladyslaw II Jagiello as heir. Culturally, Poland and Lithuania drew closer together; 47 Lithuanian nobles were adopted by Polish families and granted Polish coats of arms, a significant step in the modernization and Europeanization of Lithuania.

OTTOMAN-VENETIAN MARITIME TREATY 1416
This was the first maritime treaty to regulate trade between the two countries. The enlarged Ottoman navy in the 14th century had proved to be a threat to Venetian domination of the Aegean. In 1415 the Venetians sent ten galleys, supported by reinforcements from the Aegean Islands, to the Sea of Marmara to hold back the Ottoman fleet. There was a clash on 29 May, during which the Ottoman commander was killed. The victorious Venetians withdrew and a treaty was negotiated: Venice was given trade concessions in the Ottoman Empire; both sides agreed to combat piracy; prisoners of war were released.

TREATY OF TROYES 1420
Ratified by the French king, Charles VI of Valois and King Henry V of England, this treaty enshrined the right of Henry V to be king of France as well as king of England. It was also a marriage treaty, between Henry V and Charles's daughter, Catherine of Valois. The treaty came in the wake of England's resounding victory over France at the Battle of Agincourt (1415). In 1418 John the Fearless, Duke of Burgundy, who favored an agreement with England, had occupied Paris. He was murdered after a year and his son Phillip the Good brokered the agreement with the English. Isabeau of Bavaria the queen of Charles VI, who suffered from intermittent bouts of madness throughout his life, agreed to a treaty disinheriting her son, the dauphin, believing that a union with Henry V would end the bitter conflict of the Hundred Years' War.

TREATY OF MELNO 1422
The Gollub War of 1422 broke out between the Teutonic Knights and Poland-Lithuania because outstanding territorial disputes over the Samogitia region had still not been resolved by the Peace of Thorn. When Sigismund, the Holy Roman Emperor, offered to intervene and handed down a judgement that was unfavorable to the Lithuanians the alliance invaded the monastic state of the Teutonic Knights. Within two months a truce was signed, and the Treaty of Melno was the result. The Teutonic Knights agreed to renounce all territorial claims against the grand duchy of Lithuania, permanently ceding Samogitia to Lithuania. The treaty effectively ended all territorial disputes between Lithuania and the Teutonic Knights.

EDICT OF WIELUN 1424
The Hussite movement, which was a forerunner of the Protestant Reformation, originated in the kingdom of Bohemia, and followed the teachings of Jan Huss, who was condemned to death for heresy and burnt at the stake in 1415. This was the first anti-heretical decree in Poland, which crushed the new Hussite sect. King Wladyslaw II Jagiello signed the decree under pressure from the Catholic Church, and it demonstrated a marked deviation from Poland's tradition of religious toleration. Under the edict, adherents of the Hussite movement were to be punished as if for high treason.

TREATY OF DELFT 1428
The Hook and Cod Wars were a series of battles fought from 1350 over the title of Count of Holland. When William IV, Count of Holland and Hainaut died, both his brother John and his daughter Jacqueline contested the title. The Cods chose the side of John, and after his death Philip the Good, duke of Burgundy. The Hooks supported Jacqueline.

Triple Alliance
1428

Tziuhooac
Tochpan
Metztitlan
Tetzapotitlan
Gulf of Mexico
N
Azcapotzalco
Tliacopan
Texcoco
Tzintzuntzan
Tenochtitlan
Cuauhtochco
Tepeyacac
Cuetlaxtlan
Tepecoacuilco
Teotitlan
Tochtepec
Cihuatlan
Tiaxiaco
Tiapan
Coyolapan
Tehuantepec
PACIFIC OCEAN
Xoconochco

Following her defeat at the battle of Brouwershaven in July 1428 Jacqueline signed the Treaty of Delft, which recognized Philip as her heir in Hainaut, Holland, and Zeeland, where he recognized her as countess. It was agreed that Philip would administer the government in these counties. Jacqueline agreed that if she married again without the consent of her mother, Philip or the Estates of the three lands, her subjects were to cease obeying her and giver their allegiance to Philip. The revenues of Holland, Hainaut, and Zeeland were to be shared between Philip and Jacqueline.

TRIPLE ALLIANCE 1428
This was a military and political alliance between the Aztecs of Tenochtitlan and the city-states of Texcoco and Tlacapan against the city-state of Azcapotzalco, the dominant power in central Mexico. It came about as a result of the alliance's defeat of Azcapotzalco in 1428. When the alliance was forged all three states were equal partners. This changed over the following century, with the Aztecs gaining dominance as their empire expanded and they subjugated many tributary states.

TREATY OF MEDINA DEL CAMPO 1431
This peace treaty between the crown of Castile and the kingdom of Portugal put an end to hostilities between the two kingdoms, which were linked by diplomatic relations and matrimonial and dynastic ties. The treaty marked the end of a long period of confrontations, and the establishment of an economic and political basis for future understanding.

UNION OF GRODNO 1432
This series of acts consolidated the Polish-Lithuanian Union, establishing Sigismund Kestuataitis as the Grand Duke of Lithuania and reaffirming the authority of King Wladyslav II Jagiello, with a clear lord-vassal relationship. After Sigismund's death Lithuania was to return to Poland, with no dynastic rights to Lithuania attributed to his heirs.

TRUCE OF LECZYKA 1433
The Polish-Teutonic War (1431–35) between the Kingdom of Poland and the Teutonic Order took place in two phases (1431–33 and 1435). It started with the invasion of Poland by the Teutonic Knights; they were eventually defeated and a two-year truce ensued. In 1433 the Poles allied with the heretic Czech Hussites against the Teutonic Knights, who had allied with the pope and Holy Roman Emperor and opposed them during the Hussite Wars. The Hussite army captured several castles, and besieged several towns in the summer of 1433, reaching the

Baltic Sea in September. The truce concluded at Leczyca was intended to last twelve years; each side would retain the territory it had occupied during hostilities until a formal peace was signed.

TREATY OF ARRAS 1435
The Congress of Arras took place between France, Burgundy, and England in summer 1435. The English arrived at the congress determined to uphold their claim to the crown of France. Their intractable position led to a breakdown in negotiations. Meanwhile France and Burgundy reached an agreement – England's erstwhile ally Philip the Good of Burgundy reconciled with the French king, Charles VII, recognizing him as king of France in exchange for certain territories.

PEACE OF BRZESC KUJAWSKI 1435
This peace treaty ended the Polish Teutonic War (1431–35), following the defeat of the Livonian Order by Polish-Lithuania forces at the Battle of Pabaiskas. The treaty spelt the end to the power of the Teutonic Knights, who repudiated territorial claims and agreed to pledge their support to Grand Dukes elected by Poland and Lithuania.

TREATY OF COPENHAGEN 1441
The Dutch-Hanseatic War was a conflict over the latter's control of Baltic trade. Signed by the Hanseatic League and the Netherlands, this treaty marked the end of hostilities; the two adversaries guaranteed each other the right to trade freely. This meant that the Netherlands could resume their Baltic trade – a decisive step in their eastwards expansion.

TREATY OF GYEHAE 1443
By the terms of this treaty, signed in 1443, the daimyo of Tsushima, an important Japanese trading center, recognized and obeyed the suzerainty of King Sejong the Great of the Korean Joseon dynasty. In return, the Joseon court rewarded the So clan, which governed Tsushima island, with preferential rights regarding trade between Japan and Korea. The treaty was a way of controlling Japanese piracy.

PEACE OF SZEGED 1444
The Crusade of Varna was initiated in 1443, when Hungarian and Karamanid armies – with the blessing of a papal bull – set out to attack the Ottoman Empire. The Karamanids, an Anatolian Islamic emirate, acted before their Hungarian allies were ready, and were devastated by the Ottomans; the Hungarians were more successful, claiming a Christian victory. This two-part treaty, negotiated in both Edirne and Szeged, was signed between Sultan Murad II of the Ottoman Empire and

1454–1474

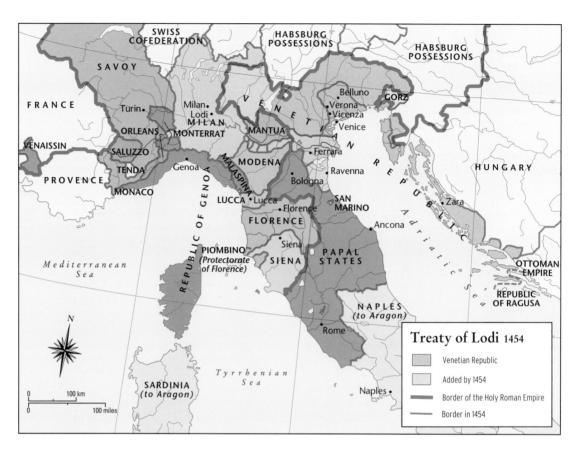

Treaty of Lodi 1454

Venetian Republic

Added by 1454

Border of the Holy Roman Empire

Border in 1454

King Vladislaus of Hungary. The Sultan returned 24 cities, and a ten-year truce was agreed with Hungary. Vlad Dracul, voivode of Wallachia, was no longer obliged to attend Murad's court, though he was still required to pay tribute.

TREATY OF LODI 1454
Five powers dominated the Italian mainland in the 15th century: Venice, Milan, Florence, the Papal States, and Naples. The Treaty of Lodi, signed between Venice and Milan, resolved their long-standing differences, and agreed a border along the River Adda. The treaty pointed the way towards a new balance of power on the peninsula. Later that year Florence joined a defensive league with Venice and Milan, to be joined the following year by Naples and the Papal States. The peace initiated by the Treaty of Lodi lasted only 50 years but the principles of non-aggression and balance of power successfully ended nearly a century of intermittent warfare.

TREATY OF CÖLLN 1454
In February 1454 Poland declared war on the Teutonic Order, initiating the Thirteen Years' War (1454–66). This followed a prolonged period of conflict between the Prussian Confederation

and the Teutonic Order, which had culminated in February 1454, in a formal request by the Prussian Confederation to be brought into the Polish kingdom of Casimir IV. Prussian trading cities objected to the anachronistic government of the Teutonic Knights, which they felt was curtailing their economic growth. The Prussian nobility also felt that they had little say in running their own territory. The Teutonic Knights, who were supported by both conscript and mercenary forces, fought skilfully throughout the summer of 1454, finally inflicting a humiliating defeat on Poland at the Battle of Konitz. The Treaty of Cölln, in February 1454, effectively pawned the Neumark (New March), which was the westernmost territory of the Teutonic Order, to Frederick II, elector of Brandenburg. This deal was completed in order to release funds to the Teutonic Order, following Poland's declaration of war. During the following months Frederick II renewed his efforts to permanently gain the Neumark for Brandenburg. By the Treaty of Mewe, signed in September 1455, Neumark was actually sold to Frederick II for the price of 100,000 Rhenish guilder. The Order was granted the right to buy back the territory after Frederick's death.

TREATY OF RIBE 1460

Alfred von Schauenberg, who had been duke of Schleswig and count of Holstein since 1427, died without an heir in 1450. Nobles of Schleswig and Holstein, aware that the two territories would revert to the Danish crown, wished them to remain united. By the Treaty of Ribe King Christian I of Denmark was elected both duke of Schleswig and count of Holstein, and promised never to separate them, promising that they would remain "forever undivided."

TREATY OF WESTMINSTER 1462

John Macdonald II, Lord of the Isles rose against James II, King of Scotland, in the 1450s. He formed an alliance with William Douglas, 8th earl of Douglas, but stood by when his ally was murdered by the king, who went on to systematically wipe out the House of Douglas, and even acquired some of the confiscated land. When Henry VI of England was deposed by Edward IV in 1461, he fled to Scotland, seeking the protection of the new Scottish King James III. Edward sought an alliance with John Macdonald, who was seen as an enemy of the Scottish crown. The result was the Treaty of Westminster-Ardtornish, in which John severed his links with the Scottish crown and promised his allegiance and homage to Edward. In return Edward promised to support John Macdonald's ambition to control all of Scotland north of the Forth. When, following the treaty, John marched on Inverness, the Scottish king abandoned his protection of Henry VI in order to avoid a war with England.

TREATY OF YORK 1464

During the Wars of Roses the Scottish crown had supported the defeated House of Lancaster, offering protection to the deposed Henry VI of England. Failing to find French support for this foreign policy, and following the devastation of the Borders by the Yorkist earl of Warwick and earl of Douglas, the Scots were forced to abandon their allegiance to the Lancastrians and open negotiations with the Yorkist king, Edward IV. The treaty agreed a truce that would last until 1519, and was ratified by Edward IV.

TREATY OF CONFLANS 1465

The League of the Public Good, established in France in 1464, brought together an assortment of French princes (including, amongst others, the dukes of Berri, Bourbon, Burgundy and Brittany), who jointly defeated King Louis XI at the Battle of Montlhéry. The League concerned themselves with the actions of the French king. He was compelled to negotiate with the League and by the terms of the Treaty of Conflans he restored Normandy to the duke of Berri and the "Somme towns" to Duke Charles "the Bold" of Burgundy.

SECOND PEACE OF THORN 1466

This peace treaty was signed in the Hanseatic city of Thorn by the Polish king, Casimir IV Jagiellon, and the Teutonic Knights, and concluded the Thirteen Years' War, which had begun with a revolt of the Prussian Confederation against their Teutonic overlords. The treaty came after a number of Polish victories; the waning fortunes of the Teutonic Order meant that they could no longer pay for the mercenaries they depended on. They ceded territory in eastern Pomerania to Poland, acknowledging the rights of the Polish crown in western Prussia, which became known as Royal Prussia.

TREATY OF SOLDIN 1466

This treaty, signed by the Elector of Brandenburg Frederick II and the Pomeranian dukes Eric II and Wartislaw X, settled a dispute over the succession of Otto III, duke of Pomerania, who had died without issue. Under the terms of the agreement the Pomeranian dukes took the duchy of Pomerania as a fief of the electorate of Brandenburg. This was one chapter in a long history of disputes between Brandenburg and Pomerania, with Brandenburg regarding Pomerania as its legal fief, and Pomerania rejecting such claims.

TREATY OF PRENZLAU 1472

From 1466–68 a war was fought between Brandenburg and Pomerania for control of Pomerania-Stettin, a splinter realm of the duchy of Pomerania. When Stettin refused to pay homage to the margrave of Brandenburg, as agreed by the Treaty of Soldin, Brandenburg responded by attacking the Pomeranian duchy. A truce was agreed in 1468. In 1472 a peace treaty was signed between Albert III, elector of Brandenburg, and the dukes of Pomerania. The duchy of Pomerania-Stettin was surrendered to Brandenbug; the Uckermark region, with its capital at Prenzlau, became an integral part of Brandenburg, while the rest of Pomerania became a Brandenburgian vassal.

TREATY OF UTRECHT 1474

The Hanseatic-English War of 1470–74 broke out when English authorities confiscated Hanseatic goods and partly destroyed the Hanseatic Steelyard, the main trading headquarters of the League in England. King Christian I of Denmark retaliated by ordering English ships to be taken and the English interpreted this as an act of aggression by the entire Hanseatic League. The war that ensued focussed on merchant shipping and the confiscation of goods.

1478–1485

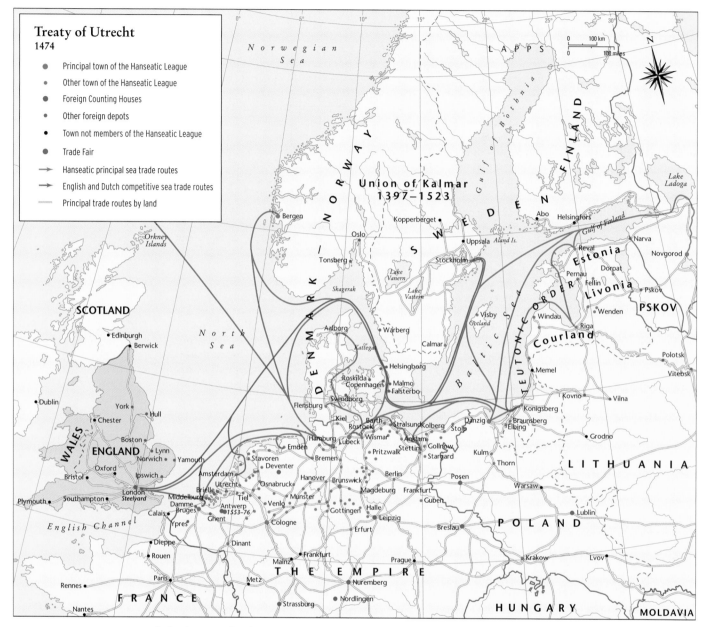

Only the city of Cologne desisted, because English trade was of great importance, and as a result was temporarily excluded from the Hanse in 1471. The Treaty of Utrecht declared peace, restored Hanseatic trading privileges in the Port of London, restored control of the Steelyard to the Hanse, confirmed access to ports of Hull, Lynn, and Boston and granted Hanseatic enterprises immunity from England's tonnage and poundage levy.

TREATY OF BRNO 1478

This division of the lands belonging the Bohemian crown, agreed between Matthias Corvinus of Hungary and King Wladislaw II of Bohemia in Brno

in 1478, ended the Bohemian War of 1468–78. This war broke out when Matthias invaded the kingdom of Bohemia on the pretext of restoring the kingdom to Catholicism. It was agreed that Wladislaw was to retain Bohemia, while a large part of the territory once ruled by Bohemia – Moravia, Silesia, and Lausitz – would remain in Matthias's possession. Wladislaw was entitled to redeem these realms, for the cost of 400,000 florins, after Matthias's death. Both monarchs could use the title king of Bohemia, but only Matthias was required to address his counterpart as king of Bohemia. The treaty was ratified, with great pomp, the following year at Olomouc (1479).

TREATY OF ALCÁCOVAS 1479

The Treaty of Alcacovas was between King Alfonso V, and his son Prince John of Portugal on one side and the Catholic monarchs, Isabella of Castile and Ferdinand of Aragon on the other. It marked the end of the War of Castilian Succession, which the Catholic monarchs had won on the land, while the Portuguese had won at sea. The treaty reflected these outcomes: Isabel was recognized as queen of Castile, while Portuguese maritime dominance was confirmed when all exploration and trading rights along the West African coast and south of the Canary Islands were ceded to Portugal, although the treaty confirmed Spanish ownership of the islands themselves. These terms were later modified by Treaty of Tordesillas.

TREATY OF CONSTANTINOPLE 1479

This peace treaty ended 15 years of warfare between Venice and Ottoman Turkey. It was precipitated by Ottoman raids in Friuli, as well as an advance in Albania, which finally persuaded the Venetian republic to come to the negotiating table. The Venetians ceded to the Ottomans Shkoder and Kruje in Albania, the Aegean islands of Lemnos and Euboea, and the Mani peninsula. The Ottomans agreed to return territory taken from the Venetians in Morea, Albania, and Dalmatia. The Venetians were also allowed to retain a Venetian quarter within Istanbul, with civil authority over Venetians living in the city. The Venetians agreed to pay the Ottomans reparations, as well as an annual payment of 10,000 ducats for the right to trade with the Ottoman Empire without paying import and export duties. The treaty marked a weakening in Venice's domination of the Levant.

TREATY OF FOTHERINGHAY 1482

By the late 1470s the fragile peace between England and Scotland was ceasing to hold and Scottish border raids were becoming frequent. In 1481 English forces, led by Richard of Gloucester, began their offensive in southwestern Scotland. In the following year King James III's brother, the duke of Albany, who had fled to France in 1479, returned to England where King Edward recognized his claim to the Scottish throne. Richard and Albany led a renewed invasion of Scotland and Richard entered the capital city, Edinburgh, which was undefended. The resulting treaty of Fotheringhay restored lands and position to Albany and confirmed that a proposed marriage between the Scottish heir and Cecily, daughter of King Edward IV, should take place. Richard's troops continued to besiege, and eventually capture, Berwick, which has been part of England ever since.

TREATY OF ARRAS 1482

By this treaty, signed by Louis XI of France and the Habsburg Holy Roman Emperor Maximilian I of Austria, it was agreed that Margaret of Austria was to marry the dauphin, while France gained the country of Burgundy and Artois as her dowry and Maximilian acquired the county of Flanders. This was another chapter in the Burgundian succession crisis, precipitated by the death of the Burgundian Duke Charles the Bold in 1477, when the French king seized his territories. Maximilian was married to Charles's daughter Mary, and was intent on defending her heritage. The marriage of Margaret and the dauphin never took place, but the Burgundian lands remained under French control, effectively ending any dreams of an independent Burgundian kingdom.

TREATY OF MÜNSINGEN 1482

Count Eberhard V von Württemberg ("the Bearded") achieved the reunification of two parts of Württemberg – Württemberg-Urach and Württemberg-Stuttgart with the Treaty of Münsingen. He moved the capital to Stuttgart and became the ruler of the united country. The treaty prevented the division of Württemberg, which was elevated to a duchy in 1495.

TREATY OF BAGNOLO 1484

In the early 1480s Duke Ercole of Este and Ferrara began to provoke his northern neighbor, Venice, on a number of political and economic issues, sensing that Venice was losing power after being forced to make concessions to the Ottoman Turks. The pope, who was locked in a struggle with Ercole's father-in-law King Ferdinand of Naples, formed an alliance with Venice and an offensive against Ercole was launched. When the cities of Milan and Florence allied with Ercole, the pope withdrew his support from Venice, and a peace treaty was signed at Bagnolo in 1484. Venice acquired the town of Rovigo and an area of the Po delta known as Polesine.

TREATY OF LEIPZIG 1485

Signed by Elector Ernest of Saxony and his younger brother Albert, this treaty consolidated the division of the Wettin lands into a Saxon and Thuringian part. Since 1464 the territory had been ruled jointly by the two brothers, but in 1484 the lands were partitioned; Ernest, the elder brother, received the electoral lands around Wittenberg. Of the remaining territory, Albert chose the eastern lands of Meissen, while Ernest took Thuringia. Ernest proclaimed himself Landgrave of Thuringia, while Albert became the Margrave of Meissen.

Treaty of Tordesillas 1494

Before the Treaty of Tordesillas, the Portuguese grew accustomed to regarding the Atlantic as their ocean. Prince Henry the Navigator (1394–1460) sponsored a series of expeditions to lay claim to the Azores, Madeira, and the Cape Verde Islands, while exploration of the West African coast was galvanized by discovering supplies of both slaves and gold. The Treaty of Alcáçovas (1479), cemented Portuguese hegemony in the Atlantic; by 1488, Bartholomew Dias had reached the Cape of Good Hope.

Accordingly, when a Genoese called Christopher Columbus appeared at the Portuguese court seeking funding for a trans-Atlantic expedition to the East Indies, he received short shrift (the savvy Portuguese realized his distance computations were hopelessly awry). The Spanish were initially equally reluctant, but, flush from his triumph over the Moors, King Ferdinand relented. When Columbus returned, after making land-fall at the spice islands, he stopped off en route to Spain at Lisbon. This proved the trigger for Tordesillas. John II of Portugal asserted the voyage contravened Alcáçovas, and threatened to send a fleet to claim the new territories. The Catholic Monarchs relied on the papacy to back them. Aragonese by birth, and notoriously corrupt in character, Pope Alexander eschewed any attempt at impartiality. His first Papal Bull Inter Caetera airily assigned "all countries and islands thus discovered… by your envoys" … "100 leagues (345 miles/556 km) to the west and south" of the Azores not owned by "a Christian prince" to the "kings of Castile and Leon."

In an earlier age, the Bull would have been damning to the Portuguese cause, but John II knew his possession of the seas was crucial. He requested the conference at Tordesillas to hammer out a realistic deal. Here the dividing line was moved westward, portentously clipping the coast of Brazil. The effect was galvanizing: within five decades, Spain had conquered the Aztec and Inca, and the Portuguese "Caesar of the East," Afonso de Albuquerque, had won bases controlling the Indian Ocean trade-route "chokepoints" in the Red Sea, Persian Gulf, Goa, and Malacca. The Treaty of Zaragoza (1529) fixed (again imprecisely) the "anti-meridian" to Tordesillas in the Pacific. This became necessary when the Spanish reached the Philippines "backwards" from the Americas, and threatened to contest Portuguese control of the lucrative spice islands. Within a further century, Tordesillas was eclipsed by the rise of new naval powers, but its legacy is profound. America south of the Azores is still Latin, and Portugal's Tordesillas-endorsed perch in Brazil has expanded to house 90 percent of the world's Portuguese-speaking population.

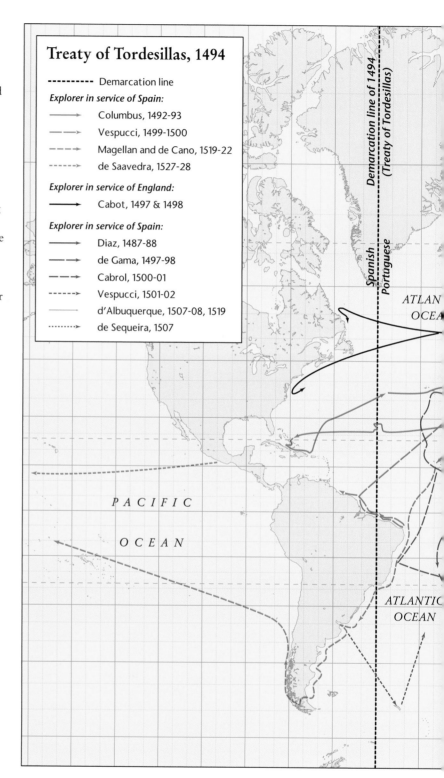

Treaty of Tordesillas, 1494

- - - - - - - - Demarcation line

Explorer in service of Spain:
→ Columbus, 1492-93
→ Vespucci, 1499-1500
→ Magellan and de Cano, 1519-22
→ de Saavedra, 1527-28

Explorer in service of England:
→ Cabot, 1497 & 1498

Explorer in service of Spain:
→ Diaz, 1487-88
→ de Gama, 1497-98
→ Cabrol, 1500-01
→ Vespucci, 1501-02
→ d'Albuquerque, 1507-08, 1519
→ de Sequeira, 1507

Demarcation line of 1494 (Treaty of Tordesillas)

Spanish | Portuguese

ATLAN OCEA

PACIFIC OCEAN

ATLANTIC OCEAN

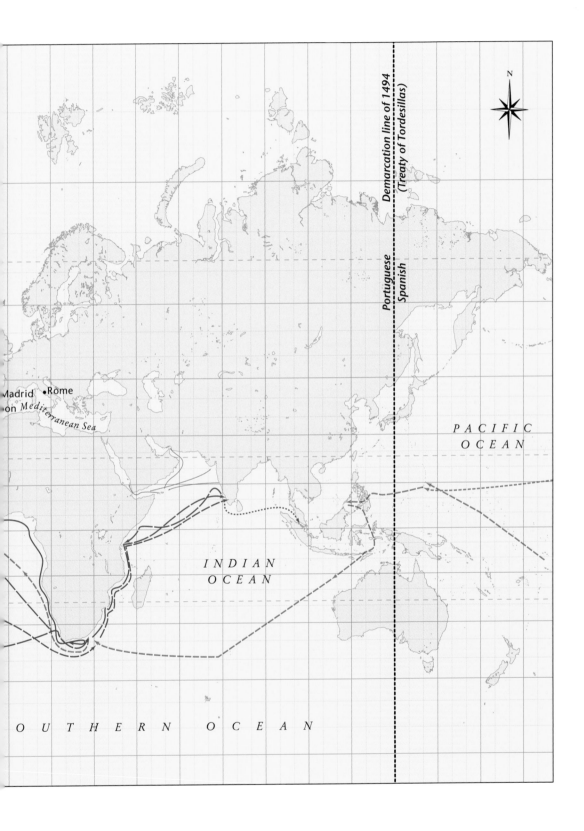

1488–1499

TREATY OF SABLÉ 1488

Proudly independent Brittany refused to accept
French suzerainty. After the death of the French
king, Louis XI, in 1483, disaffected nobles rebelled
against his successor Charles VIII, who was a minor
at the time – his sister Anne and her husband Pierre
de Beaujeu acted as regents. Attempts were made by
the rebellious dukes, amongst them Duke Francis
II of Brittany, to depose Anne, but she held on
to power. In 1486 Louis of Orléans joined forces
with some of Brittany's nobles, following an attack
on northern France by Maximilian of Habsburg.
A series of conflicts ensued between the Beaujeu
faction and the rebels, which led to a decisive defeat
of the rebel lords at Saint-Aubin-du-Cormier. This
was followed by the Treaty of Sablé (sometimes
called Le Verger). Duke Francis II acknowledged
himself as a vassal of the French king, agreed to rid
Brittany of foreign troops, and promised to marry
off his daughters only with the king's consent. The
French king withdrew his troops from Brittany.

TREATY OF MEDINA DEL CAMPO 1489

The first Tudor king, Henry VII of England, was
weakened by his protracted struggles against Richard
III and needed a strong European ally. The Treaty of
Medina del Campo cemented an alliance between
England and Spain. The two countries agreed to
maintain a common policy in relation to France
and to come to each other's aid in the event of war
with France. In addition there would be a reduction
on the tariffs on trade between the two countries.
Finally, a marriage agreement was sealed between
Henry's son Arthur and Katherine, the daughter of
Ferdinand of Aragon and Isabelle of Castille. Arthur
was just three years old at the time of the treaty.

TREATY OF DORDRECHT 1489

In 1489 Henry VII of England further consolidated
his European position by signing this treaty with
Maximilian I of Austria. It signalled the revival of
the Anglo-Burgundian alliance, dedicated to helping
Brittany, and represented a threat to the French in
Flanders, Artois and Picardy.

TREATY OF REDON 1489

Signed between representatives of the rulers of
France and Brittany, this treaty was intended to
assure Anne of Brittany and her fiancé Maximilian
of Austria of English support for Brittany in the
struggle against French hegemony. The treaty
formalized the terms of English support for Brittany;
a clause required Duchess Anne and her heirs to
assist the English if they invaded France.

TREATY OF FRANKFURT 1489

In this treaty, signed between Maximilian I of
Austria and envoys of King Charles VIII of France,
King Charles promised to promote reconciliation
between Maximilian and the Flemish rebels and to
surrender some French-occupied towns in Brittany
to Duchess Anne of Brittany, on condition that she
removed English troops from the duchy. Maximilian
I was the regent for Philip I of Castile, count of
Flanders, where several cities had been in revolt.

TREATY OF WOKING 1490

Following the *rapprochement* of the Treaty of
Frankfurt, King Henry VII renewed his defensive
alliance with Anne of Brittany, sending troops to
the duchy and raiding La Hague in Normandy. The
alliance between France and Maximilian collapsed
and a new defensive and offensive alliance between
Maximilian I and Henry VII was signed at Woking
in 1490. This treaty effectively revived the Anglo-
Burgundian-Breton alliance against France.

PEACE OF PRESSBURG 1491

This was the treaty that marked the end of the
Austrian-Hungarian War (1477–88), signed between
Maximilian I of Austria and King Wladislaw II of
Bohemia and Hungary. Wladislaw renounced his
claim to Lower Austria, agreeing that Maximilian
would succeed to Bohemia and Hungary if he
died without an heir. This was the culmination of
over ten years of warfare, which had been mainly
conducted by the signatories' predecessors, the
Holy Roman Emperor Frederick III and Matthias
Corvinus, king of Hungary.

TREATY OF GRANADA 1491

Boabdil (Abu Abdullah Muhammad XII), had
revolted against his father and gained control of

The Treaty of Granada 1491

   Christian 1481

   Muslim 1481

→ Advances of Christians

✕ Battle site of Christian victory

✕ Battle site of Muslim victory

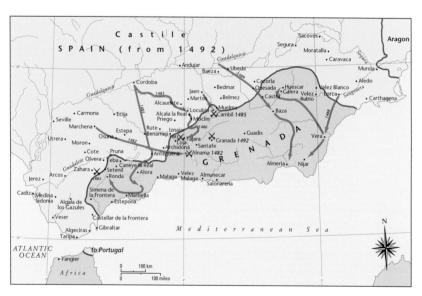

Granada, with the support of the Catholic monarchs, King Ferdinand and Queen Isabella. However, the Granada War broke out in 1482, culminating in the siege of Granada in 1491. The Treaty of Granada recognized the final expulsion of the Muslims from Spain, stipulating that Muslims in Granada would be allowed to keep their property and to worship as, and where, they wished. They were guaranteed safe passage to North Africa if they chose to leave; if they chose to stay they were subject to Islamic, not Spanish, law. There were to be no forced conversions to Christianity. The tolerant terms of the treaty were not destined to last.

PEACE OF ÉTAPLES 1492
In 1492 King Henry VII of England initiated a more aggressive foreign policy against France, which was supporting Perkin Warbeck, a pretender to the English throne. Henry decided to assert his claim to the French throne, crossed the Channel in October 1492 with a substantial force of 26,000 men and besieged Boulogne. Charles VIII of France needed to concentrate all his resources in north Italy; the result was the Peace of Étaples. Henry received a promise from Charles that he would no longer provide support to pretenders to the English throne. The English accepted France's control of Brittany, repudiating the Treaty of Redon. Henry was also to receive a payment of 745,000 crowns, at the rate of 50,000 crowns per year, which accounted for 5 percent of his total annual income.

TREATY OF BARCELONA 1493
In 1462–63 the French had acquired Rousillon and Cerdagne, territory to the north of the Pyrenees that had been offered as collateral for a loan from France to Aragon, that was not paid. In 1493 a treaty was signed between France and the crown of Aragon, by the terms of which France returned these territories to Aragon. King Charles VIII of France was planning an invasion of northern Italy and was anxious to appease any potential enemies.

TREATY OF PYRITZ 1493
The rival claims of the House of Hohenzollern and House of Pomerania over the legal status and succession of the duchy of Pomerania were settled by this treaty, in which the elector of Brandenburg renounced Hohenzollern claims to hold the duchy as a fief. Bogislaw X, duke of Pomerania, acknowledged the rights of the Brandenburgs to succeed to his duchy if his own line should die out.

TREATY OF SENLIS 1493
Maximilian I's military engagements in Hungary prevented him from sending troops to the aid of

Anne of Brittany, who was forced to surrender to French troops at the end of 1491, when she broke off her betrothal to Maximilian and instead married Charles VIII of France. Charles in turn broke off his betrothal to Maximilian's daughter the Archduchess Margareta and returned her dowry, which included the French Comté. The Treaty of Senlis ended the conflict between the Habsburgs and France over the Burgundian inheritance. By the terms of the treaty, Margaretha was sent back to the Habsburg Netherlands in 1493. The county of Burgundy, Artois and Charolais were relinquished to Maximilian and Flanders and Artois were annexed by the Holy Roman Empire.

INTERCURSUS MAGNUS 1496
This important commercial treaty was signed by Henry VII of England and Philip IV, Duke of Burgundy. Other signatories included Venice, Florence, the Netherlands, and the Hanseatic League. While the treaty was ostensibly about the English cloth trade, it was in fact a political treaty, rooted in a history of distrust between Henry VII and Margaret, dowager duchess of Burgundy, who had offered her support to Perkin Warbeck, a pretender to the English throne, resulting in a damaging embargo on trade between England and Burgundy. The Intercursus Magnus restored the trade; the Burgundians offered English merchants favorable conditions, while reciprocal trade privileges were granted to the English and Flemings.

TRUCE OF AYTON 1497
The Scottish offered their support to the English pretender Perkin Warbeck, and the marriage between Warbeck and a cousin of James III of Scotland was seen as a major threat by King Henry VII. He realized that the Scottish border was vulnerable and therefore negotiated the Truce of Ayton. Following the capture of Warbeck, who led a Cornish uprising, and his execution in 1499, it became a full treaty.

TREATY OF BASEL 1499
This was the treaty that marked the end of centuries of conflict between Swiss communities and the Habsburgs, who dominated the region. The Swiss Confederation had been founded in 1291, when three mountain communities allied themselves in a League of Perpetual Defense, soon to be joined by other cantons. Emperor Maximilian I, who already dominated Burgundy, Netherlands and Spain through a series of brilliant marriage alliances, set out to assert power in his family's traditional heartland, allying with the Swabian League of southern Germany against Switzerland. The Swabian

1500–1526

War raged for nine months in 1499, but the Swiss prevailed and Maximilian was forced to sign a peace treaty at Basel in which the Empire formally acknowledged the existence of the League and accepted Swiss independence.

TREATY OF GRANADA 1500

This agreement between Louis XII of France and Ferdinand II of Aragon divided the kingdom of Naples between them. This treaty followed the Italian Wars of Louis' predecessor, Charles VIII, who had invaded and conquered the kingdom of Naples from 1494–95, following the succession of Frederick IV of Aragon to the Neapolitan throne. Charles, who believed the house of Anjou had historic rights to the kingdom of Naples, captured the city, leaving a French garrison there. Ferdinand sent Spanish troops to join the League of Venice and expel the French occupiers from Italy, where Charles died before he could return to France. His successor, Louis, was determined to press his claim to the thrones of Milan and Naples, and in 1499 he formed an alliance with Venice and invaded again, seizing Milan. Louis, concerned that the Spanish might take advantage of his Italian campaigns and invade France in his absence, reached an agreement with Ferdinand II. The treaty divided the Mezzogiorno into a northern part, which went to France, while the southern part went to Spain. King Frederick IV of Naples was to be removed from the throne.

TREATY OF TRENTE 1501

Holy Roman Emperor Maximilian I recognized French conquests in northern Italy in the Treaty of Trente, finally reconciling the two rulers after the long conflict over Flanders.

TREATY OF PERPETUAL PEACE 1502

Signed by King James IV of Scotland and King Henry VII of England, this was an agreement to end warfare between the two countries in perpetuity. As part of the treaty a marriage contract was agreed between James and Margaret Tudor, Henry's daughter. Henry was anxious to sign the treaty because he needed stability within his kingdom and was fearful of another Yorkist uprising or an invasion from Scotland.

TREATY OF BLOIS 1504

At the heart of this treaty between King Louis XII of France and the Holy Roman Emperor Maximilian was a marriage alliance. Louis agreed to marry his daughter Claude to Maximilian's infant grandson, Charles (who would become Emperor Charles V). Her dowry would comprise the duchy of Milan, the duchy of Burgundy and the county of Blois; she was already the heiress of Brittany. However, the treaty fell apart when Claude was betrothed to her second cousin, the future Francis I of France.

TREATY OF LYONS 1504

Following the agreements made at the Treaty of Granada in 1500, the French entered Rome in 1501 and went on to take Naples, while the Spanish took Taranto. The two allies were soon squabbling over the division of the spoils; in 1503 the Spanish defeated the French at Cerignola (believed to be the first battle in history at which firearms were decisive) and the Garigliano River. In 1504 the French surrendered their last stronghold, at Gaeta on the south coast, and Louis XII, ill with malaria, signed the Treaty of Lyons, which conceded Naples to Ferdinand of Aragon. The two signatories also agreed on their Italian territories, with France taking control of northern Italy from Milan, and Spain controlling Sicily and southern Italy.

TREATY OF WESTMINSTER 1511

The War of the League of Cambrai (or Holy League) was fought between 1508 and 1516. The main combatants were France, the Republic of Venice, and the Papal States, but at various times the war drew in contenders from all over Europe, including Spain, England, the Holy Roman Empire, Scotland. The League of Cambrai was an anti-Venice alliance, joined by Louis XII, Maximilian I, Ferdinand II of Aragon and Pope Julius II. Soon friction developed amongst the members of the League, and Pope Julius switched his allegiance to Venice. The Veneto-Papal alliance rapidly grew into the Holy League, which included Spain, the Holy Roman Empire (which had also abandoned the League of Cambrai), and England, intent on using this opportunity to expand its holdings in northwest France. The Treaty of Westminster was a pledge of mutual aid against the French, signed by Henry VIII of England and Ferdinand II of Aragon.

PEACE OF NOYON 1516

Ferdinand II of Aragon, who died in 1516, was succeeded by his grandson Charles, later to become Emperor Charles V. Francis I of France had won control of Milan, following his victory at Marignano in 1515. By the Peace of Noyon Charles recognized Francis's claims in Italy and Francis agreed to pass Naples to Charles through a marriage alliance to France's daughter Louise. Until the marriage could take place Charles was to pay 100,000 crowns a year as rent for Naples. The treaty effectively removed Spain and the Spanish Netherlands from the Italian conflict, leaving Maximilian I, the Holy Roman Emperor, isolated.

TREATY OF ROUEN 1517

James V of Scotland succeeded to the crown after his father James IV was killed at the Battle of Flodden Field in 1513. He was only 17 months old when his father died, and for much of his childhood the pro-French cousin of his father, the duke of Albany, acted as regent. In 1517 he negotiated the Treaty of Rouen between Scotland and France, which stipulated that James V would marry one of the daughters of the king of France, Francis I. It also renewed the Auld Alliance, promising mutual military assistance and aid.

TREATY OF LONDON 1518

This treaty of universal peace, masterminded by Henry VIII's lord chancellor Cardinal Wolsey, united the various warring parties of Europe – France, Spain, the Holy Roman Empire, the papacy, England – under a Christian banner to act against the Ottoman Turks, who were penetrating into the Balkans. The signatories of the treaty – Burgundy, France, England, the Holy Roman Empire, the Netherlands, the Papal States, Spain – agreed to come to each other's aid if attacked, and undertook not to make war on each other. The treaty committed states to a policy of non-aggression but also made them promise to make war on any state that broke the terms of the treaty. The treaty greatly enhanced the standing of Cardinal Wolsey and King Henry VIII in European politics, ensuring that England was seen as a major power.

TREATY OF BRUGES 1521

Negotiated by Cardinal Wolsey, this was a secret treaty between the Holy Roman Emperor Charles V and King Henry VIII providing for a joint invasion of France before March 1523.

TREATY OF WINDSOR 1522

In May 1522 the English ambassador presented Francis I with an ultimatum, accusing the French of – amongst other offenses – conspiring with the duke of Albany in Scotland. Shortly after this the Treaty of Windsor was signed between Holy Roman Emperor Charles V and Henry VIII of England, agreeing on joint military operations against France, with each party providing at least 40,000 men. To consolidate the agreement, Henry's daughter Mary Tudor was promised to the Emperor. In July, English troops attacked Brittany and Picardy from their base in Calais, burning and looting the countryside.

TREATY OF MALMÖ 1524

During the war against Denmark (1523–24) the Swedish nobleman Gustav Vasa led a rebellion against the Kalmar Union under the regency of the Danish-Norwegian king, Christian II. The Hanseatic city of Lübeck, which enjoyed a virtual monopoly on Swedish foreign trade, allied with the rebels, and Stockholm was liberated in 1523 when Gustav Vasa was crowned king of Sweden. Under the mediation of Lübeck the Treaty of Malmö was signed in 1524, and Sweden seceded from the Kalmar Union. In return for a recognition of its independence, Sweden renounced claims to Scania and Blekinge. The question of Gotland was deferred.

TREATY OF MADRID 1526

When Charles V was elected Holy Roman Emperor in 1519–20, France reacted with animosity. War broke out in Europe, sometimes called the Four Years' War, between France and the Republic of Venice on one side and the Holy Roman Empire, England and the Papal States on the other. Hostilities took place all over western Europe – in the Pyrenees, the Low Countries, Northern France, and the Italian peninsula. The imperial alliance took Lombardy from France in 1522. In 1523 Francis's fortunes plunged further when he faced an imperial invasion through the Pyrenees, an English invasion in the north, and a betrayal by the duke of Bourbon who defected to the imperial side. However, the English-imperial alliance did not materialize and Francis turned his attention back to the Italian peninsula. The disastrous defeat of Francis I at the Battle of Pavia in 1525 was a turning point, when Francis was taken prisoner. After many months of diplomatic manoeuvring Francis I and Charles V signed the Treaty of Madrid in January 1526, by which the French king renounced his claims in Italy, Flanders and Artois and surrendered Burgundy to Charles. He surrendered his two sons as hostages to Charles and was released from captivity. However, on 22 March he announced that he would not be bound by the Treaty of Madrid, which had been signed under duress. He was supported by Pope Clement VII, who was threatened by Charles's growing power.

TREATY OF HAMPTON COURT 1526

Signed by Cardinal Wolsey, on behalf of Henry VIII, and the French ambassador, on behalf of Francis I, this treaty agreed that neither ruler should unite with the Emperor against the other. The king of England undertook to procure the liberation of Francis's sons, then held hostages in Spain, as part of the terms negotiated by Francis I in the Treaty of Madrid. This treaty came after five years of war on the European continent when Francis I, supported by the Venetian Republic, was pitted against an alliance of the Holy Roman Empire, England, and the Papal States.

1526–1543

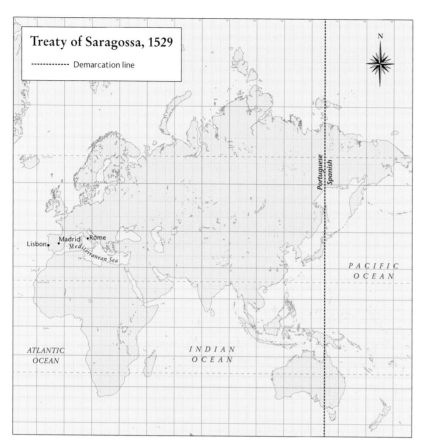

Treaty of Saragossa, 1529

------------ Demarcation line

TREATY OF BERWICK 1526
Archibald Douglas, 6th earl of Angus, was the estranged husband of Henry VIII's sister Margaret Tudor. He allied with Henry VIII and represented him in Scotland, where he was pitted against his estranged wife and the duke of Albany. In 1526 Henry VIII appointed him Lord of the Marches, and charged with suppressing the disorder of the border regions. The treaty signed at Berwick upon Tweed in 1526 agreed on abstinence from war, safe conduct for travellers, redress for cross-border raids, and exchange of prisoners. The treaty was in force for three years.

TREATY OF WESTMINSTER 1527
Negotiated by Cardinal Wolsey, this treaty acknowledged that Henry VIII of England and Francis I of France both shared a goal, to reduce the growing power of Charles V, which was demonstrated all too clearly when his army sacked Rome in May 1527. The two signatories pledged to combine their armies against Charles, and Henry's daughter, Mary Tudor, born in 1516, was used as a bargaining chip in the negotiations. She was promised to Francis I as his wife, despite the fact that she had previously been promised to the dauphin.

The following year France and England declared war on Charles, though Henry withdrew from hostilities because of economic unrest at home.

TREATY OF GORINCHEN 1528
The Guelders Wars were a series of conflicts in the Low Countries between the duke of Burgundy, who controlled Holland, Flanders, Brabant and Hainault, and Duke Charles of Guelders, who controlled Guelders, Groningen, and Frisia. In 1528 Emperor Charles V signed a treaty acknowledging Duke Charles's control of his territories, but on the agreement that they were considered fiefdoms of the Empire.

TREATY OF BARCELONA 1529
Following the imperial sack of Rome in 1527 and an insurrection in Florence, which led to the expulsion of the Medici and the founding of a short-lived republic, this agreement was reached between Emperor Charles V and Pope Clement VII. Under the terms of the treaty Charles V endorsed the supremacy of the Habsburgs in Italy, upholding the rule of the Medici in Florence and granted Milan to its duke, Francesco Sforza. Clement VII agreed to crown Charles V as Holy Roman Emperor and to grant him the kingdom of Naples.

TREATY OF CAMBRAI 1529
Known as Paix des Dames (the Ladies' peace) this treaty was negotiated by Charles V's aunt, Margaret, and Francis I's mother, Louise of Savoy. Francis I agreed to renounce all claims in Italy and as an overlord in Flanders and Artois and to pay a ransom for his two sons, held captive by Charles V, who agreed not to advance his claims in Burgundy. The treaty ended one phase of the War of the League of Cognac (1526–30), in which an alliance of France, Pope Clement VII, the Republic of Venice, England, Milan, and Florence had been pitted against the Habsburg dominions of Charles V – the Holy Roman Empire and Spain.

TREATY OF SARAGOSSA 1529
This treaty, signed between King John III of Portugal and the Holy Roman Emperor Charles V, king of Spain, completed the worldwide division of Iberian colonial interests started with the Treaty of Tordesillas. The Treaty of Saragossa settled a dispute about who would control trade and settlement in eastern Asia. Under the terms of the Treaty of Tordesillas the Portuguese had found themselves with exclusive rights to the undreamt-of wealth of the spice islands. Following Magellan's round-the-world voyage the Spanish laid claim to the Moluccas, and a decade long tug-of-war ensued. The Treaty of

Saragossa proclaimed the boundary near 142 degrees east of longitude, consolidating Portugal's claim to the Indian Ocean and Asia and recognizing Spain's dominion over the Americas and Pacific.

TEATY OF GRIMNITZ 1529
This was the final settlement of a long-running dispute between the House of Hohenzollern and the House of Pomerania over the duchy of Pomerania. It renewed the earlier Treaty of Pyritz (1493). By the terms of the treaty the House of Pomerania received the duchy as an "immediate imperial fief," which placed it under the direct authority of the Holy Roman Emperor. The electors of Brandenburg, from the House of Hohenzollern, were granted rights of succession.

TREATY OF CONSTANTINOPLE 1533
Following the Ottoman victory at the Battle of Mohács (1526) the Hungarian throne was left vacant, with two candidates – Ferdinand I, duke of Austria, and John Zápolya, the voivode of Transylvania. Zápolya was backed by the Hungarian elite and the Ottomans, but Ferdinand declared himself king of Hungary, with the support of his brother, the Holy Roman Emperor Charles V. In response, Emperor Suleiman launched two military campaigns against Austria in 1529 and 1532. Fearing another Ottoman invasion, the Habsburgs sought a negotiation and the Ottomans – preoccupied with rising Persian power in the east – agreed. Under the terms of the Treaty of Constantinople, Ferdinand made his peace with the Ottomans, splitting Hungary into a Habsburg domain in the west, with Zápolya became king of Hungary under Ottoman suzerainty. Austria agreed to pay the Ottomans an annual tribute of 30,000 guldens.

TREATY OF BASSEIN 1534
This treaty, signed between Sultan Bahadur of Gujarat and the kingdom of Portugal gave control of the city of Bassein and its territories, located in Maharashtra, to Portugal. The territories included the islands of Mumbai, then a town of minor importance, although some 100 years later it was to become a major trading centre. This treaty followed a bombardment by the Portuguese fleet in 1531.

TREATY OF NOVGOROD 1537
Towards the end of the 15th century there had been clashes between Sweden and Muscovy on the eastern borders of Finland. Swedish-Finnish settlements had penetrated as far as Nöteborg, in contravention of the treaty agreed there in 1323. Following the death of Grand Prince Vasiliy Ivanovich III in 1533 a new agreement was negotiated, agreeing a 60-year truce.

TREATY OF NAGYVÁRAD 1538
Following the Treaty of Constantinople (1533) the Treaty of Nagyvárad between Emperor Ferdinand I and John Zápolya confirmed Zápolya as King John I, ruler of two-thirds of the kingdom of Hungary; Ferdinand gained western Hungary and was recognized as heir to the Hungarian throne if Zápolya died without heirs.

TRUCE OF NICE 1538
The Italian War of 1536–38 was a conflict between Francis I of France and Charles V, king of Spain and Holy Roman Emperor, during which French troops invaded northern Italy and Spanish troops invaded France. The Truce of Nice left Turin in French hands, but agreed no significant territorial changes in Italy.

FIRST TREATY OF BRÖMSEBRO 1541
This treaty was agreed between arch-enemies Sweden-Norway, ruled by King Christian III, and Sweden, ruled by King Gustav I. The two sides agreed to a joint stance against the Hanseatic League and promised to come to each other's assistance if under attack by foreign or domestic enemies. The treaty was to planned to run for 50 years.

TREATY OF GREENWICH 1543
In 1542 King Henry VIII asked his nephew, the Scottish King James V, to repudiate the "auld alliance" with France and turn Protestant. Henry sent 3,000 men north and met an much larger Scottish army at Solway Moss in the Borders. The Scots were routed and fled, and James – on hearing of the disaster – died, leaving his infant daughter, Mary. Henry was determined to marry Mary to his own son Edward. He released many of the Scottish nobles taken captive at Solway Moss, and the Treaty of Greenwich confirmed the proposed marriage alliance, which would unite the crowns of Scotland and England. Mary was to live in England until her marriage. But the regent of Scotland, the earl of Arran, assisted by the cardinal of St Andrews, took the young queen to Stirling Castle out of the reach of Henry who, furious, repudiated the treaty and seized Scottish merchant ships. The Scottish parliament voted to renew the Auld Alliance.

TREATY OF VENLO 1543
The Truce of Nice (1538) had not resolved the long-standing conflict between Charles V and Francis I, especially over the issue of the duchy of Milan. In 1542 Francis I declared war on Charles V, who had formed an alliance with Henry VIII of England, and fighting broke out in the Low Countries and Spain. Wilhelm of Cleves joined the war on Francis's side,

1544–1556

**Luso-Chinese Agreement
1554**

invading Brabant, and fighting broke out in Artois and Hainaut. Charles in turn attacked Wilhelm of Cleves, invading the duchy of Jülich and capturing Düren. Deserted by his French and German allies, Wilhelm surrendered and signed the Treaty of Venlo with Charles, conceding overlordship of the duchy of Guelders and county of Zutphen to Charles and promising to aid him in suppressing Protestantism. Guelders (Gelderland) became one of the 17 provinces of the Netherlands.

TREATY OF SPEYER 1544
In 1544 Denmark and the Holy Roman Empire signed the Treaty of Speyer, which agreed that Denmark would maintain peace with the Holy

Roman Empire. Charles V recognized Christian III as the rightful king of Denmark and Christian agreed to exempt Dutch ships from trading tolls and facilitate their access to the Baltic Sea.

TREATY OF WEISSENBURG 1551
The Ottoman sultan Suleiman had allocated Transylvania and eastern Hungary to John II Sigismund, the son of the Ottoman vassal John Zápolya. The Eastern Hungarian kingdom was ruled over by John II Sigismund's mother and regent, Isabella Jagiello. In 1549 Imperial armies marched into Transylavania, and Isabella agreed to abdicate on the behalf of her son. Royal Hungary and Transylavania went to Ferdinand I, Charles V's

younger brother, who agreed to recognize John II Sigismund as vassal prince of Transylvania.

TREATY OF CHAMBORD 1552

Signed in January 1552, this was a treaty between King Henry II of France and three Lutheran princes, led by Elector Maurice of Saxony. Maurice ceded control (the vicariate) over the three bishoprics of Toul, Verdun, and Metz to King Henry, who in turn promised to give the princes military support in their struggle again Charles V. The princes actually had no right to expropriate territory that came under imperial control; the French saw the treaty as a pretext to acquire new territory.

PEACE OF PASSAU 1552

The Schmalkaldic War was an eruption of violence between 1546 and 1547 between the forces of Emperor Charles V and the Schmalkaldic League, an alliance of several Lutheran German states that were united against the Catholic Habsburgs. In August 1552 Charles V's younger brother Ferdinand I guaranteed Lutheran religious freedoms in the Peace of Passau. Protestant prisoners captured during the Schmalkaldic War were released.

LUSO-CHINESE AGREEMENT 1554

This agreement legalized trade between China and Portugal by introducing a tax regime. It was signed by Captain-Major Leonel de Sousa and the Provincial Admiral of Guangzhou, Wang Bo. The agreement followed several years in which the Portuguese had been banned from legitimate trade with China and had had recourse to piracy. By the terms of the agreement the Portuguese agreed to pay customs fees and undertook not to construct fortifications.

PEACE OF AUGSBURG 1555

Promulgated by the Diet of the Holy Roman Empire in September 1555, the Peace of Augsburg created the legal conditions for Protestants and Catholics to co-exist within the Holy Roman Empire. Princes were allowed to choose between Lutheranism and Catholicisim as the religion of their domain. Their decision applied to their citizens as well and any dissenters were allowed to migrate to a more sympathetic realm if they chose. No prince would make war on another prince on religious grounds. No provision was made for other Protestant denominations. The free imperial cities were exempt from the general ruling, and citizens could practice the religion of their choice. Charles V, who was resistant to the religious division of his Empire, empowered his younger brother Ferdinand to preside on his behalf.

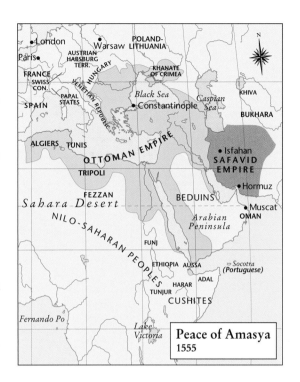

Peace of Amasya
1555

PEACE OF AMASYA 1555

The war between the Ottoman Empire and Safavid Persia started in 1532, triggered by territorial disputes between the two empires, and two decades of incursions and guerrilla warfare had ensued. By 1554 both sides were exhausted and depleted and ready to negotiate. In August 1554 the Safavids sent a peace offering to the Ottoman camp. The Ottomans, who were fighting a war on their western front with the Habsburgs, agreed an armistice. In 1555 a peace treaty was signed that agreed the borders between the two empires, dividing Armenia and Georgia between them. The Ottomans obtained most of Persia, and access to the Persian Gulf. Buffer zones were established in eastern Anatolia, Kars was declared neutral, and its fortress was destroyed. The Ottomans agreed to allow Persian pilgrims free passage to Mecca, Medina, Karbala and Najaf.

TREATY OF VAUCELLES 1556

The Italian War of 1551–59 began when the newly-crowned king of France Henry II declared war on Emperor Charles V, intendingn to recapture Italy and exercise French domination over European affairs. Henry agreed with Suleiman the Magnificent to cooperate against the Habsburgs in the Mediterranean. He also allied with three German princes at the Treaty of Chambord (1552). After initial success in Lorraine, a French invasion of Tuscany in 1553 was defeated by an Imperial-Tuscan army. The Treaty of Vaucelles was signed between

1557–1566

Philip II, the Habsburg king of Spain and son of Charles V, and Henry II of France. Henry agreed to relinquish the territory of Franche-Comté to Spain, but the treaty was broken shortly afterwards.

TREATY OF NOVGOROD 1557

The Russo-Swedish War of 1554–57, the First Northern War, arose out of a series of border skirmishes, starting with a Russian attack on Swedish-Finnish territory, followed by a Swedish counterattack. Both sides used a scorched earth policy; while the Russians could have captured the city of Vyborg in 1556, they contented themselves with ravaging the surrounding area. The Treaty of Novgorod preserved the status quo, agreeing a 40-year truce. Sweden agreed not to support Livonia or Poland-Lithuania in the event of a war with Russia.

TREATY OF POZVOL 1557

The Grand Master of the Teutonic Knights had embraced Protestantism, creating Europe's first Protestant state in the duchy of Prussia under Polish protection. The Livonian territories, however, resisted his attempts to introduce Protestantism and ultimately the Catholic estates rebelled against their Teutonic masters. Under threats of war from Sigismund II Augustus, king of Poland and Grand Duke of Lithuania, the Livonians signed three treaties at Pozvol, which agreed a defensive-offensive pact between Livonia and Lithuania. Wilhelm, archbishop of Riga, who had been arrested by the Livonians when he espoused Lutheranism, was reinstated. Tsar Ivan the Terrible responded to the treaty by declaring war on Livonia.

PEACE OF CATEAU CAMBRÉSIS 1559

This treaty marked the end of the struggle between France and Spain for control of Italy, raging since the end of the 15th century. France was pushed to the negotiating table by defeats at Saint Quentin (1557) and Gravelines (1558), as well as bitter struggles with the French Huguenots and financial difficulties. It was agreed that Henry II of France would restore Piedmont and Savoy to Emmanuel-Philibert of Savoy, an ally of Spain. Henry also restored Corsica to Genoa and gave up his hereditary claims to Milan. Spain became the dominant power in Italy, and would remain so for 150 years. France retained five fortresses in Italy, including Turin, and retained the bishoprics of Metz, Verdun, and Toul, which it had taken from Charles V in 1552. France also retained Calais, captured from the English in 1558.

TREATY OF VILNIUS 1559

The Livonia War (1558–83) was fought for control of Livonia, ranging the Russian tsar against a shifting coalition of Denmark-Norway, Sweden, and Poland-Lithuania. The Russians, who saw Livonia's treaty for Poland-Lithuania in 1557 as a *casus belli*, had early success following their invasion of Livonia, taking Dorpat and Narva in 1558. The estates of Livonia sought protection from Poland-Lithuania and the Treaty of Vilnius (1559) confirmed the offer of Polish-Lithuanian protection. The Polish parliament refused to agree to the treaty, regarding it as a purely Lithuanian matter.

THE TREATY OF BERWICK 1560

Mary Stuart, Queen of Scotland, was the prime Catholic candidate for the English throne. But many Scots espoused Protestantism and were resistant to the Catholic, French-influenced monarchy. In February 1560 Elizabeth I of England capitalized on the divisions and made the Treaty of Berwick with the Lords of the Congregation, the Protestant Scottish nobles who were opposed to the Regency of Mary of Guise, who ruled as Queen Regent while her daughter Mary Queen of Scots was in France with her husband, the dauphin, François. In March Elizabeth sent troops north, and Scotsmen and Englishmen fought alongside each other to expel the French who were defending the Regency.

THE TREATY OF EDINBURGH 1560

When Mary of Guise, the Scottish regent, died in June 1560, the figurehead of the Roman Catholic faith in Scotland was removed. Drawn up between the French, Scots, and English, the Treaty of Edinburgh agreed that the French and English armies would withdraw, leaving the Scottish Protestant nobles in charge. Later that summer the "Reformation Parliament" prohibited the Latin mass and repudiated the authority of the pope, in effect initiating the Reformation in Scotland.

TREATY OF VILNIUS 1561

Russian successes in the Livonian War continued through 1560, following the Treaty of Vilnius in 1559, with a number of small campaigns directed at important fortresses, culminating in the Russian defeat of the Livonian Knights at the Battle of Ergeme in 1560. King Eric XIV of Sweden refused to come to the assistance of Gotthard Kettler, the Grand Master of the Teutonic Order, as did Poland. In 1561 the Second Treaty of Vilnius dissolved the Livonian Order, and its lands were assigned to Lithuania, as the duchy of Livonia and the duchy of Courland and Semigallia. Grand Duke Sigismund Augustus of Lithuania granted the Livonian estates privileges, including religious freedom, which forbade the regulation of the Protestant order by secular authorities.

EDICT OF SAINT-GERMAIN 1562

This royal decree was signed by Catherine de Medici, the mother of ten-year-old Charles IX of France, and his regent. Its intent was to reconcile the Catholics and Huguenots, the French Protestants, by ending the persecution of the Huguenots. They were given the right to preach anywhere outside towns, and Huguenot noblemen were allowed to run Protestant congregations on their estates. The Catholic's reluctant agreement was secured as the first shots of the Wars of Religion were fired, when the Duke of Guise's men attacked a Protestant congregation, killing several. In March 1562, the prince of Condé offered his protection to the Huguenots, and called on his fellow-Protestants to raise an army against Guise and his supporters.

TREATY OF HAMPTON COURT 1562

By this treaty, Elizabeth I of England promised to provide support for the French Huguenots during the First War of Religion. Elizabeth wanted to recover Calais, the last English foothold in France, which had fallen in 1558. She offered 3,000 men to occupy Le Havre and Dieppe and promised the Huguenots economic aid. Once peace was restored, she refused to remove her men, claiming that they had occupied the French ports to indemnify her against her loss of Calais. Catherine de Medici sent combined Catholic and Huguenot forces against Elizabeth and the forts were restored in July 1563.

TREATY OF MOZHAYSK 1562

Russia saw Denmark as the most powerful Baltic trading nation and sought an alliance with the Danes. In 1562 the Treaty of Mozhaysk sealed a Russian-Danish alliance. Tsar Ivan the Terrible recognized Denmark's Livonian possession of Ösel-Wiek, located on the islands and coast in the northern part of the Gulf of Riga. Both sides agreed that neither would support Sweden or Poland-Lithuania, and recognized each other's sphere of influence in the Baltic. Merchants from each country were allowed free passage in both realms.

EDICT OF AMBOISE 1563

The first chapter of the French War of Religion (1562–63) ended with this truce. In 1562 there had been massacres of Huguenots at Toulouse, Sens, and Tours, as well as major engagements at Rouen, Dreux, and Orléans. The Edict allowed open and unregulated Protestant services in private households of Protestant nobles.

TREATY OF DORPAT 1564

The Northern Seven Years' War (1563–70) was fought between Erik of Sweden and a coalition of Denmark-Norway, Lübeck, and Poland. It was motivated by Erik's desire to break Danish dominance in the region. Since Erik was pursuing a war against Denmark, he needed Russian good will and the Treaty of Dorpat was the result. Russia recognized Erik's right to Reval and some other castles, while Erik recognized that the rest of Livonia was the patrimony of Ivan the Terrible.

TREATY OF ACOBAMBA 1566

The mighty Inca civilization of Peru had reached the size of western Europe, some 2,485 miles (4,000 km) north to south at its greatest extent. In 1532 the Spanish began their conquest of the Inca, with just 180 soldiers under the command of the conquistador Francisco Pizarro. The process was to

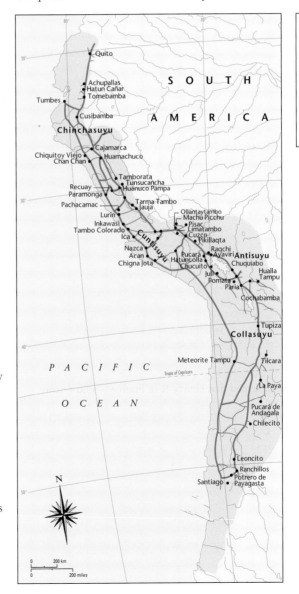

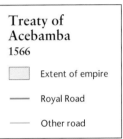

Treaty of Acebamba 1566

Extent of empire

Royal Road

Other road

1568–1579

take 40 years, with the creation of the Viceroyalty of Peru finally taking place in 1572. In 1537, the remnants of the Inca Empire were formed into the Neo-Inca state of Vilcabamba, established by Manco Inca, and then ruled by his son Sayri Tupaq, with the aid of regents. When Sayri Tupaq died in 1561 his half-brother Titu Cosi took control of Vilcabamba and resistance to the Spanish. In 1565 the Spanish viceroy was informed that Titu Cosi was planning another rebellion against the Spanish. Alarmed, he dispatched Spanish envoys to negotiate with the Inca who, aware that a Spanish invasion of Vilacamba province would be disastrous, agreed to negotiate. Under the terms of the Treaty of Acobamba, he agreed to end action against Spanish settlers and consented to an act of submission to the king of Spain by all of the members of the royal family. Titu Cosi was baptized, given the estates of Sayri-Tupac at Cuzco, and allowed to have his son's marriage to Sayri-Tupac's daughter officially consecrated by the Church, consolidating his position as ruler. The signing of the treaty brought 14 years of peaceful co-existence with the Spanish. The Inca balanced tradition with Spanish customs in Vilcabamba, allowing Augustinian missionaries to enter his territory, while still permitting sun worship.

PEACE OF LONGJUMEAU 1568
This edict, signed by Charles IX of France and Catherine de Medici, ended the Second War of Religion in France (1567–68), restoring the rights to

the Huguenots that had originally been granted by the Edict of Amboise. Huguenots were allowed to worship in the suburb of one town in each bailiwick and on noble estates. Huguenot noblemen could let strangers, as well as their own vassals, worship on their estates. Leading Huguenots, such as the prince of Condé, were pardoned for acts committed during the war, and required to surrender their fortresses and renounce foreign alliances.

UNION OF LUBLIN 1569
Poland and Lithuania had been united under the same sovereign since the Treaty of Krewo in 1385, but the Poles feared that – as Sigismund II Augustus of Poland had no heirs – the personal union between the states was in jeopardy, and should be formalized through the Union of Lublin. Many members of the Lithuanian nobility had in any case been drawn into a closer union with Poland, following the outbreak of the Livonian War against Russia (1558), although the dominant Lithuanian magnates had resisted the proposal, fearing it would erode their own powers. When representatives of both countries met in Lublin and failed to agree, Sigismund Augustus annexed Podlasie and Volhynia. The Lithuanian gentry were not prepared to enter a new war against Poland and negotiations resumed. In July the Union of Lublin was agreed, uniting Poland and Lithuania into a single federation, to be ruled by a single, jointly-selected sovereign. Each country retained its own army, bureaucracy, and laws, and participated in a joint Diet. The two nations agreed to cooperate on foreign policy.

TREATY OF STETTIN 1570
Following the break-up of the Union of Kalmar in 1523, King Frederick II of Denmark had sought to restore the Union under his rule. When Frederick invaded Sweden in 1563 he started the Seven Years' War. In July 1570 the Holy Roman Emperor Maximilian II called a peace conference in Stettin. According to the terms of the treaty, the Danish king renounced all claims upon Sweden, while the Swedish kings renounced claims to Norwegian-Danish provinces and Gotland. Sweden was forced to pay a substantial ransom for Alvsborg Castle, which the Danes had captured.

PEACE OF ST GERMAIN-EN-LAYE 1570
During the Third War of Religion (1568–70) Huguenots had taken control of much of southwestern France, advancing up the Rhône to threaten Paris, convincing King Charles IX to make peace. The terms of the peace treaty reinforced the rights the Huguenots had held at the beginning of the conflict, but also gave them control of four

The Union of Lublin
1569

- Polish fief from 1466
- Polish land pledged to Pomerania 1466–1637
- Added to Prussia 1560 (to Courland 1609)
- Polish fief from 1561
- Added to the Polish-Lithuanian state 1561–85
- Lithuania 1562
- Poland before 1569
- Added to Poland under the Union of Lublin 1569
- Western limit of Russian control within Poland-Lithuania 1570
- Lithuania in the Polish-Lithuanian state 1582
- Borders 1585
- Holy Roman Empire

"fortified" towns for two years: La Rochelle, Cognac, Montauban, and La Charité. Nobles' rights to hold Protestant acts of worship on their own estates were reaffirmed. Protestants were allowed to hold public office in France and Catherine de Medici promised her daughter Marguerite de Valois to the Huguenot leader Henry of Navarre.

TREATY OF BLOIS 1572

In the early 1570s both England and France were drawn together by the threat of Spanish invasion from the Netherlands, which fell under the hereditary rule of King Philip II of Spain, and put aside their differences to sign the Treaty of Blois. This provided for a defensive alliance and made provisions for new economic arrangements that would have made Rouen, rather than Antwerp, the main continental market center for English cloth.

EDICT OF BOULOGNE 1573

The fourth phase of the French Wars of Religion was set in motion by the St Bartholomew's Day Massacre (1572), which unleashed a wave of Catholic mob violence against the Huguenots. Attempts by the Catholics to gain control of the Huguenot-held city of La Rochelle led to a six-month siege, followed by the negotiations that led to the Edict of Boulogne. Under the terms of this edict French Huguenots lost many of the rights they had gained earlier; they were only allowed to worship freely in private homes, in the towns of La Rochelle, Montauban, and Nîmes. Protestant nobles with the right of high-justice were permitted to celebrate marriages and baptisms according to the Protestant rites, but only ten people beyond their immediate family were allowed to attend. A general amnesty was granted to the Huguenots for all the actions taken thus far in the Wars of Religion and they were granted freedom of belief.

EDICT OF BEAULIEU 1576

Following the Fourth War of Religion in France, King Charles IX's younger brother, the duke of Alençon, led a movement made up of moderate Catholics and Protestants (the "Malcontents"), who believed that greater tolerance for Protestants was politically expedient. Charles IX died in May 1574 and was succeeded by Henry III. At first he refused the Malcontents' demands, but he succumbed to military pressure and the Protestant siege of Paris in spring 1576 and signed the Edict of Beaulieu (known as "the Peace of Monsieur"), which allowed freedom of worship except in Paris and an area of two leagues (five miles) around the city. In eight *parlements* chambers were established which were divided between Protestants and Catholics.

PACIFICATION OF GHENT 1576

In 1568 the seven northern provinces of the Netherlands rebelled against their Habsburg ruler King Philip II of Spain. After initial success in repressing the rebellion, the uprising resurged in 1572, leading to the de facto independence of the northern provinces in 1581. The southern Netherlands remained under Spanish rule, but the two most important southern provinces, Flanders and Brabant, remained unstable. A mutiny of Spanish soldiers, protesting at non-payment and the sack of Antwerp in November 1576 (the "Spanish fury"), drew all the provinces of the Low Countries together against the marauding Spanish. The Pacification called for the expulsion of Spanish troops, and for religious freedom throughout the Low Countries, ending the persecution of Calvinists. The Pacification asserted the rights of the largest provinces, Holland and Zeeland, to espouse Calvinism as their religion; the largely Catholic southern provinces would not attempt to interfere with their freedom of religious belief. The new governor of the Netherlands, Don John of Austria, swore to uphold the terms of the Pacification and order Spanish troops out of the country.

TREATY OF BERGERAC 1577

The Edict of Beaulieu (1576) proved to be difficult to apply and aroused great hostility amongst French Catholics, who formed into defensive leagues. The States General was summoned and met in Blois, where the atmosphere became very anti-Catholic and the Edict of Beaulieu was revoked. Hostilities between both sides resumed and negotiations led to the signing of the Treaty of Bergerac in September 1577, which was ratified three days later by the Edict of Poitiers. The Huguenots were only allowed to practice their faith in the suburbs of one town in each judicial district.

UNION OF ARRAS 1579

The Low Countries, a remote part of the mighty Spanish Empire, grew ever more resentful of Spanish demands for taxation, while Calvinist ideas spread across the borders from France and the northern German states. The depredations and terror brought to the region by Philip's emissary the duke of Alba and his Spanish army inevitably led to a revolt in Holland and Zeeland, led by William of Orange, and a prolonged war between Spain and the northern provinces. The Pacification of Ghent brought together the entire region against the Spanish, but religious differences led to sectarian violence. Calvinists sacked Ghent in 1579; the Catholic riposte was for three of the southern provinces to form the Union of Arras (Atrecht) in 1579.

1579–1598

UNION OF UTRECHT 1579

Following the Union of the Catholic provinces of the Netherlands with Spain at Arras, the northern provinces of Holland, Zeeland, and Utrecht formed the Union of Utrecht, committed to religious toleration and independence from Spain. During the following months other provinces signed the treaty, including: Ghent, Guelders, Friesland, Groningen, Flanders, and Brabant. These United Provinces still recognized Spanish rule but the Union is seen as a step towards independence and the foundation document of the Seven United Provinces.

TREATY OF FLEIX 1580

The main purpose of the treaty, signed by Henry III of France, was to end the seventh phase of religious wars in France. Huguenots were given the right to reside anywhere in France, and Catholic clergy were forbidden from creating sedition and disturbance from their pulpits. Huguenots were still allowed to practice their faith in the suburb of one town in each judicial district.

TREATY OF PLESSIS-LES-TOURS 1580

This treaty, signed between the Dutch States General and François, Duke of Anjou, proclaimed François as "Protector of the Liberty of the Netherlands" and he became sovereign of the Dutch Republic. François was the youngest son of King Henry II of France and Catherine de Medici. Despite adhering to the Catholic faith, he had fought with the Huguenot rebels, under the prince of Condé, and been rewarded with his dukedom as part of the settlements following the Edict of Beaulieu.

THE PEACE OF JAM-ZAPOLSKI 1582

Jam-Zapolski was one of the treaties that concluded the Livonian War (1558–83) and it was signed after Polish-Lithuanian forces, led by their monarch Stephen Báthory, fought successfully against Tsar Ivan the Terrible. In 1581-82 Polish-Lithuanian forces had besieged Pskov, and the Russians were facing a growing threat from Sweden, who had taken Narva in 1581. The peace treaty, concluded between Russia and Poland-Lithuania, agreed a ten-year truce, and Ivan the Terrible abandoned Livonia and Estonia to Poland, with Bátory returning the Russian territories that his army had occupied.

TREATY OF PLUSSA 1583

This truce between Sweden and Russia put an end to the Livonian War. Under the terms of the truce Sweden kept control of a number of Russian towns and Ingria. Russia retained a narrow passage to the Baltic Sea at the estuary of the River Neva. The truce expired in 1590, with renewed hostilities.

TREATY OF NEMOURS 1585

Henry III of France had no heirs so when his younger brother, the duke of Anjou, died in 1584 the rightful heir to the throne was the king's distant cousin and leader of the Protestants, Henry of Navarre. The following year the Catholic League, headed by Henry, duke of Guise, took control of many of the northern cities in protest. Henry III signed the Treaty of Nemours with the House of Guise in order to gain control of the Catholic League. The treaty forced Henry to retract all the previous tolerant measures agreed in the treatment of Huguenots and to capitulate to the wishes of the Catholic League. This step led to the War of the Three Henrys, between Henry III, Henry of Guise and Henry of Navarre, for the French throne.

TREATY OF NONSUCH 1585

Signed between Elizabeth I of England and the Dutch Rebels, this treaty promised the rebels support, both militarily and financially. As a surety for this assistance the Dutch gave the towns of Brill and Flushing to England, and they were garrisoned at English expense. Elizabeth was also given the right to appoint two councillors to the council of state of the United Province. The support Elizabeth gave to the rebels was seen as a provocation by Philip II of Spain.

TREATY OF BERWICK 1586

This peace treaty, signed between James VI of Scotland and Elizabeth I of England, asserted the friendship between the two Protestant realms of England and Scotland and outlined the mutual support they would provide against Catholic aggression from France and Spain. James VI was agreed as the successor to the English throne.

TREATY OF FERHAT PASA 1590

Named after the Turkish commander and also known as the Treaty of Constantinople, this agreement concluded the Ottoman-Safavid War of 1589–90. The Ottomans had taken advantage of a Safavid succession crisis to push eastwards into Persian territory. When the Ottomans captured Tabriz in 1590 Shah Abbas I opened peace talks with the Turks. The treaty gave the Ottomans control of Azerbaijan, Georgia, Armenia, most of Qarabagn, most of Iranian Kurdistan, Luristan, and Daghestan.

TREATY OF TEUSINA 1595

In 1590 the Russians resumed their war against Sweden, retaking Ivanagorod and Koporye. Guerrilla warfare broke out on the Karelian-Finnish border, and a truce of 1595 eventually led to the Treaty of Teusina. Russia abandoned claims to

Narva and Estonia, but Sweden returned Kexholm and Ingria. A frontier was drawn between Finland and Karelia; Swedish claims to the Kola peninsula were abandoned but the treaty confirmed that much of Lapland was now Swedish territory.

PEACE OF VERVINS 1598

Signed between Henry IV of France and Philip II of Spain, this – along with the Edict of Nantes – was the treaty that effectively ended the French Wars of Religion. Philip had interfered repeatedly in the Wars of Religion, in support of the Catholic League.

Henry, who had converted to Catholicism and been crowned in 1594, had declared war on Spain in 1595 and had won a victory at the Siege of Amiens in 1597. By the terms of this treaty Philip recognized Henry as king of France and withdrew his forces from French territory, effectively depriving the Catholic League of their remaining support.

EDICT OF NANTES 1598

Signed by Henry IV of France this was the treaty that ended the French Wars of Religion. The French Huguenots now held many fortified towns,

The Edict of Nantes 1598

Extent of Catholic League
Governed by Huguenots
Lands of Henry of Navarre 1585
Huguenot centres 1598–1629
● Towns with reformed government
○ Courts for trying Huguenot cases
+ Important battles or treaties

1601–1616

creating a virtual state within a state. The Edict contained 92 articles that granted them religious toleration, as well as a equal status within French society. From now on, Huguenots were to be allowed to worship where they chose in private. In public, they were allowed to worship on the estates of Protestant landowners and in some 200 publicly named towns. They were to be accorded the same rights of inheritance, education, and hospital treatment as the rest of the population and were permitted to engage in trade. The government agreed a general amnesty for all war crimes and agreed to subsidize the garrisons of some 50 Huguenot towns as well as paying Protestant pastors. Catholic opposition to the Edict was contained and the Edict served to consolidate the position of Henry IV, the first Bourbon monarch.

TREATY OF LYON 1601
The Franco-Savoyard war of 1600–1601 was a conflict between the kingdom of France and the duchy of Savoy. This dispute was over the marquisate of Saluzzo, a French enclave in the Piedmontese Alps, which was contested by the duke of Savoy, Charles Emmanuel I. He resisted French diplomacy, but was overcome by superior French forces when conflict finally broke out in 1600. The threat of Spanish intervention on Savoy's side hastened King Henry IV to the negotiating table. Under the treaty Savoy ceded most of its territory on the west side of the Rhône to France, and paid France a sum of 300,000 livres. France granted Saluzzo to Savoy, giving up its holdings on the far side of the Alps.

TREATY OF VIENNA 1606
Signed between the rebellious Stephen Bocskay, a Hungarian nobleman and elected prince of Transylvania, and Matthias, archduke of Austria, this treaty granted constitutional and religious rights and privileges to Hungarians living in both Transylvania and Royal Hungary. Royal Hungary was created following the Ottoman victory at Mohács and the partition of the country; it was the portion of the kingdom where Habsburgs were recognized as kings of Hungary. Bocskay was recognized as the prince of Transylvania, and Transylvanians were given the right to elect their own princes in the future.

PEACE OF ZITAVA 1606
The 15-year-long war between the Habsburg monarchy of Hungary and the Ottoman Empire ended in 1606. The Treaty of Zitava was just one of the peace treaties that ended the anti-Habsburg uprising of Stehphen Bocskay (1604–06), who was elected prince of Transylavania, with Ottoman support, in 1605, leading a coalition of noblemen

and burghers who resented the tyranny of Rudolf II, Holy Roman Emperor. The territorial status quo was accepted, with the exception of Eger and Kanizsa, which were ceded to the Turks. In exchange for an indemnity of 200,000 florins, the sultan agreed to recognize Rudolf as emperor and as king of Hungary. The treaty stabilized the Ottoman-Habsburg frontier for the next 50 years.

TREATY OF ANTWERP 1609
This twelve-year armistice was signed by Spain and the Netherlands, creating an interlude of peace in the protracted war for independence from Spain conducted by the Seventeen Provinces in the Low Countries. The Spanish consented to a proposal from the Netherlands regarding trade in the East Indies, accepting that if peace in Europe was agreed the Netherlands would be granted the right to trade overseas within territories controlled by the Spanish Empire. Outside the Spanish Empire, the Dutch were permitted the right to trade freely, with the permission of the natives.

TREATY OF BRUSSOL 1610
This was an alliance between the duke of Savoy, Charles Emmanuel I, and King Henry IV of France. Both agreed to join their forces together to eject the Spanish from Italy. Various other provisions were made concerning territories: the duke of Mantua was to exchange the province of Casale Monferrato for the province of Cremona; Montferrato and Milan would fall under the control of Piedmont. Charles Emmanuel would be restored to the throne of Lombardy, and would be guaranteed the title of king of Lombardy by France, Venice, and the pope. Henry's death shortly after the treaty was signed meant that it was voided, although Charles Emmanuel went on to seize Montferrato from the Spanish in 1613.

TREATY OF NASUH PASHA 1612
Following the Treaty of Farhad Pasha (Treaty of Constantinople) in 1590, the Ottoman Empire had annexed vast areas from Safavid Persia. However, Shah Abbas I had chosen the moment when the Ottoman Empire was weakened by a long war with the Holy Roman Empire (1593–1606) and a series of revolts in Anatolia to regain many of his losses (1603–12). Under the terms of the treaty the Ottomans agreed to restore all the territory gained by the Treaty of Constantinople, settling the border at the line drawn in the Peace of Amasya (1555). The Persians agreed to pay an annual tribute amounting to some 59,000 kg of silk. Persian Haj pilgrims were now allowed to pass over Syria, rather than Iraq. Shah Abbas had restored Persian prestige.

TREATY OF KNÄRED 1613

Mediated by King James I of England, this treaty
ended the Kalmar War between Denmark-Norway
and Sweden. This war had been precipitated by
Sweden's refusal to pay "Sound Dues," a toll exacted
by Denmark for all shipping passing through the
strait between the Baltic and North Seas. Sweden
established alternative trade routes through Lapland,
and Denmark – deprived of its main source of
income – declared war on Sweden in 1611. Danish
troops besieged the city of Kalmar, taking it in 1611.
The following year the Danes took two fortresses in
Gothenburg, but Swedish guerrilla tactics prevented
them penetrating deeper into Swedish territory.
Under the terms of the treaty Denmark restored
Norway's control of the Swedish land route through
Lapland. Sweden paid a high ransom for its two
captured fortresses, but gained the right of free trade
through the Strait, exempt from the Sound Dues.

TWO ROW WAMPUM TREATY 1613

One of the earliest treaties between American
Indians and European colonists, this treaty was
made between the Dutch and Haudenosaunee (Five
Nations of the Iriquois) as fur-trading Dutch settlers
moved up the Hudson River in present-day New
York state. Rejecting a patriarchal relationship with
the Dutch, the Haudnosaunee insisted that they
should be recognized as brothers, and that neither
party should make compulsory laws or interfere in
the internal affairs of the other. As was customary,
the Haudenosaunee created a wampum belt out of
purple and white quahog shells to commemorate the
agreement. The principles of the Two Row Treaty
agreement were reiterated in other Haudanosaunee
negotiations with French, British, and American
settlers. It was understood to last for ever "as long
as the grass is green, as long as the water flows
downhill…".

TREATY OF XANTEN 1614

The War of the Jülich Succession was a dispute about
the rights of succession to the United Duchies of
Jülich-Cleves-Berg. It broke out in 1610, resulting
in the defeat of the Catholic Archduke Leopold V by
the combined Protestant forces of the Margraviate
of Brandenburg and Palatinate-Neuberg. In 1614
the victors entered into direct combat with each
other, with the Dutch allied with Brandenburg and
the Spanish with Neuberg, further complicating the
situation. The Treaty of Xanten was agreed between
Wolfgang Wilhelm, count palatine of Neuberg,
and John Sigismund, elector of Brandenburg. The
territories of Jülich-Berg and Ravenstein went to
Wolfgang Wilhelm, while the territories of Cleves
and Ravensberg went to John Sigismund.

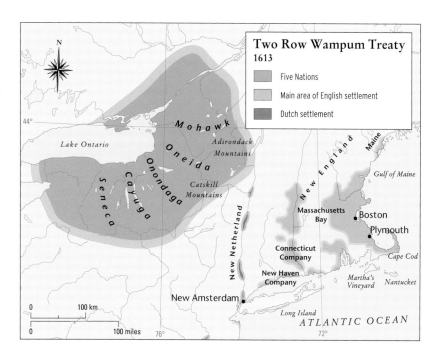

PEACE OF ASTI 1615

Charles Emmanuel I, duke of Savoy, was dissatisfied
with the provisions of the Treaty of Brussol (1610).
When the prince of Monferrato died in 1612, the
principality became an object of conflict. Both
Spain and Savoy claimed the principality; Charles
Emmanuel occupied Trino, Alba, and Moncalvo,
and in 1613 declared war on Spain. In 1615 the
Spanish threatened Turin, the Piedmontese capital,
and the Peace of Asti was concluded, in which
Charles Emmanuel renounced his claims on
Monferrato.

TREATY OF SERAV 1618

According to the terms of the Treaty of Nasuh
Pasha, Shah Abbas, the ruler of Safavid Persia,
had agreed to pay an annual tribute of silk to the
Ottomans as part of reparations. When Shah Abbas
I refused to pay the tribute war broke out again in
1615. The Ottomans besieged the city of Yerevan,
lifting the siege after 44 days, seized Tabriz, and
then threatened Ardabil. Abbas was forced to sue for
peace. The agreement reiterated most of the terms
of the Treaty of Nasuh Pasha, but with some minor
border modifications. The annual Persian tribute of
silk was halved.

TREATY OF LOUDUN 1616

Civil war broke out in France because of a power
struggle between Concino Concini, marquis
d'Ancre – supported by the king's mother Marie de
Medici – and Henry II de Condé, heir-presumptive
to the French throne. Rebellious Huguenots joined

1617–1623

Condé, reawakening religious conflicts. Negotiations took place between the court and Condé and, at the cost of royal concessions, ended the revolt by many French nobles. The treaty paid Condé reparations, granted him amnesty and made him Head of the Council of State.

TREATY OF PAVIA 1617
Following the Peace of Asti (1615), the Treaty of Pavia was concluded between the Spanish Empire and Savoy. The principality of Monferrato, seized by Charles Emmanuel I, duke of Savoy in 1613, was returned to Mantua. An unstable peace was established between Monferrato and Milan.

TREATY OF STOLBOVO 1617
This was the treaty that ended the Ingrian War between Sweden and Russia, which began in 1611. During the course of the war King Gustavus Adolphus of Sweden captured Novgorod, besieged Pskov and pressed the claim of his brother to the Russian throne, envisaging the creation of a vast trans-Baltic domain. Under the terms of the treaty Gustavus Adolphus acknowledged the new House of Romanov had the right to the Russian throne. Russia regained the whole Novgorod patrimony and renounced all claims to Estonia and Livonia, but lost access to the Baltic Sea and was obliged to pay Sweden a sum of 20,000 silver rubles. The Swedes were awarded the province of Ingria – their natural border with Russia was now partly defined by Lake Ladoga and Lake Peipus.

TRUCE OF DEULINO 1618
Between 1609–18 there was a war between the Polish-Lithuanian Commonwealth and the tsardom of Russia. Russia's enemies were exploiting the "Time of Troubles," a period of internal chaos and dynastic crises. In 1610 the Poles entered Moscow, and the son of the Polish king, Sigismund III Vasa, was briefly elected tsar, supported by rebellious boyars. The Poles were expelled from Moscow in 1612, but captured the important city of Smolensk. Hostilities resumed in 1617, culminating in a renewed siege of Moscow in 1618, during which the Poles failed to take the city. Negotiations began and, according to the truce, Russia was obliged to cede to Poland the lands of Smolensk and the Chernihiv Voivodeships, expanding Polish territory to its greatest extent until 1629, when the Commonwealth lost Livonia. Polish claims to the Russian throne remained open.

TREATY OF ANGOULÊME 1619
The French civil war, between supporters of Queen Marie and her son Louis XII, came to an end with the Treaty of Angoulême. In 1617 the royal bodyguard had been charged with task of seizing Marie's favourite, Concini, the marquis d'Ancre. He was murdered during the arrest, and his wife was tried for witchcraft and executed. Many of Concini's possessions, including the governorship of Normandy, went to Charles, duke of Luynes, and Louis XIII's favorite, who had masterminded the plot against Concini. The king refused to receive his mother and she retreated to the château at Blois. In February 1619 the duc d'Épernon, one of her husband's trusted lieutenants, rescued Marie from the château. He took her to Angoulême where they raised an army; it appeared civil war was imminent. It was agreed that the only person who could persuade her to negotiate, and avoid civil war, was Cardinal Richelieu. Acting on her behalf, he negotiated the Treaty of Angoulême in April 1619 with Luynes. By its terms Marie was permitted freedom of movement, and she was awarded the governorships of Anjou and Normandy.

TREATY OF MUNICH 1619
This treaty was signed between Holy Roman Emperor Ferdinand II and Duke Maximilian of Bavaria, leader of the German Catholics. Maximilian had rallied the Catholic League as a counterweight to the Protestant Union, led by the elector palatine. He was willing to help the Emperor Ferdinand in the defense of their shared Catholic faith. Under the terms of the Treaty of Munich, Maximilian made his Bavarian forces available to the penurious Emperor Ferdinand, who was persuaded by the Spanish ambassador, Oñate, to grant Maximilian any part of the palatine that he could occupy, as well as the electoral title of Frederick V. Oñate also guaranteed Ferdinand Spanish support in dealing with the Bohemian rebels.

TREATY OF ULM 1620
Over the autumn and winter of 1619/20 the Protestant Union and Catholic League had both raised armies and their forces were engaged in a tense stand-off in southern Germany, near Ulm. As the two sides began to negotiate, they were joined by a French embassy sent by Louis XIII, in lieu of the army he had originally promised. The treaty signed at Ulm agreed that neither the League or Union would attack within the Empire, although they remained free to make war outside it, in particular in Bohemia.

TREATY OF MADRID 1621
Grisons is the largest and easternmost canton of Switzerland. It became a battleground during the Bündner Wirren (1618–39), a conflict between

France, allied with Venice, and the Spanish-Austrian Habsburg monarchy, over control of the Alpine passes. The conflict also became part of the Thirty Years' War, with the Protestants supported by France and Venice, and the Catholics by the Habsburgs. In July 1620 a force of Catholic rebels from Valtelline, a valley in the Lombardy region of northern Italy, supported by Austrians and Italians, began slaughtering Protestants. A poorly organized Protestant army embarked on a campaign of reprisal, and the Treaty of Madrid was signed in April 1621. Valtelline was restored to the Grisons and the Spanish were allowed to reoccupy Chiavenna in the Lombardy region. Protestants were to be allowed to practice their faith freely in Valtelline.

TREATY OF KHOTYN 1621
The town of Khotyn is in modern-day Ukraine, though in the 17th century it was part of Moldavia. In the Battle of Khotyn an army of 160,000 Ottoman Turks advanced from Adrianople towards the Polish frontier, intent on conquest. The Polish commander stood his ground at Khotyn fortress, holding the Ottomans at bay for a month, until the first snows of autumn forced them to retreat. The Treaty of Khotyn ended the Polish-Ottoman War (1620–21). The treaty was favorable to the Polish-Lithuanian Commonwealth, whose border was confirmed at the Dniester River. Ottoman control over Moldavia was acknowledged and the huge Ottoman army had been prevented from advancing into Poland.

PEACE OF NIKOLSBURG 1621
The principality of Transylvania was ruled by Gabriel Bethlen (1613–29). He invaded Habsburg-controlled Royal Hungary in 1618, taking advantage of Emperor Ferdinand II's preoccupation with the Bohemian Revolt at the beginning of the Thirty Years' War. By 1620 he had conquered all of modern-day Slovakia, although just a year later Ferdinand had defeated the Bohemians at the Battle of the White Mountain and was able to concentrate on the reconquest of most of Royal Hungary. The Treaty of Nikolsburg guaranteed Protestants freedom of worship in Transylvania. Bethlen gained territory around the Upper Tisza River, and was given the title of "Imperial Prince of Transylvania."

TREATY OF MONTPELLIER 1622
In 1617 a royal council demanded the restitution of Roman Catholic property in Navarre and Bearn, the Huguenot strongholds. Owners of confiscated property refused to cooperate, and Louis XIII, king of France, decided that he must assert his authority. In 1619 he occupied both areas with a

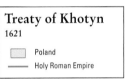

Treaty of Khotyn
1621

☐ Poland
— Holy Roman Empire

royal army, forcing Huguenot leaders to leave, and forcibly handing back confiscated Roman Catholic property. Huguenot cemeteries were desecrated. The remaining Protestant community united under the leadership of the duke of Rohan. Louis embarked on a campaign against Rohan, but was not able to bring the two main Huguenot towns to surrender. The Treaty of Montpellier upheld the rights asserted in the Edict of Nantes (1598). Rohan was pardoned and the Huguenots were allowed to maintain their forts and garrisons.

TREATY OF PARIS 1623
In 1621, under the Mainz Accord, the princes and cities complied with Emperor Ferdinand's demands and the Protestant Union was formally dissolved. Three important princes refused to sign: the margrave of Baden, Duke Christian of Brunswick and the Count von Mansfeld, who commanded the remnants of the Protestant Union's army and fought a series of campaigns against Tilly, the commander of the Catholic's Leagues forces, throughout 1622. In February 1623 Ferdinand formally bestowed the electoral title of the palatinate on Maximilian I, elector of Bavaria. France was suspicious of Habsburg ambitions and was still intent on regaining her position in Italy, following the Habsburg-Valois

1624–1630

War. In 1623 France signed the Treaty of Paris with Savoy and Venice to eject Spanish troops from the Valtelline valley in Lombardy, northern Italy, on the route of the so-called Spanish Road, which was used to supply troops to Germany and the Low Countries. Fearing that war was imminent the Spanish turned to Pope Urban VIII for protection and papal troops were sent to Valtelline, giving the region a temporary reprieve.

TREATY OF COMPIEGNE 1624
This alliance against the Habsburgs was signed by France and the Netherlands. The French were clearly motivated by a desire to reduce the power of the Habsburgs by subsidizing the Dutch struggle against Habsburg Spain in the Dutch War of Independence. In return for French support against Spain, the Dutch provided naval support to France, even agreeing to help the French struggle against the Huguenots, their co-religionists.

TREATY OF THE HAGUE 1625
Signed between England and the Dutch Empire, both sides agreed to provide support to Christian IV of Denmark during his military campaigns in Germany. The original plan had been to enlist the support of Sweden as well as France, Venice, Savoy, and the Protestant German states. However, Sweden could not agree on French support and the Danes entered the war prematurely, thereby excluding key players and reducing the impact of the proposed grand alliance.

PEACE OF PRESSBURG 1626
Gabriel Bethlen had led an uprising against the Habsburg monarchy from 1619–26. The Peace of Nikolsburg (1621) had granted him religious freedoms and the title of prince of Transylvania, but he had gone on, in 1623, to ally with anti-Habsburg Protestants and campaign against Emperor Ferdinand II in Upper Hungary. The Peace of Pressburg followed these campaigns, re-confirming the terms of the Peace of Nikolsburg, with Bethlen agreeing to cease hostilities against Ferdinand, and promising not to ally with the Ottoman Turks.

TREATY OF MONZÓN 1626
This was the treaty that concluded the First Genoese-Savoyard War. Spain, occupying the strategic area of Valtelline in Lombardy, had enlisted the support of papal troops when threatened by France in 1623. The French then claimed that, because of their prior alliance with the duke of Savoy, they must come to the aid of Savoy, which was engaged in an attack on Spanish troops in Valtelline in an attempt to divert them from

providing support to Genoa, Savoy's enemy. In 1624 the French expelled Spanish troops from the valley. The treaty provided for the Grison League, which was Protestant, to rule Valtelline, but at the same time the only religion to be allowed in the valley was Roman Catholicism. The people of Valtelline would pay tribute to the Grisons and appoint their own magistrates and judges, with Grison approval. Both the French and Spanish were given equal access to the mountain passes.

CAPITULATION OF FRANZBURG 1627
The duchy of Pomerania, which had adopted Protestantism in 1534, was a member of the Upper Saxon Circle. The duchy resisted the demands of the Emperor and the victorious Catholic League, but refused an alliance with Protestant Denmark. In 1625/6, Denmark was neutralized and the forces of the Catholic League, under the command of Albrecht von Wallenstein, devastated the Upper Saxon states. Sweden, at war with Poland, an imperial ally, recruited troops in Pomerania and von Wallenstein ordered the occupation of Pomeranian ports and the confiscation of all vessels, thereby securing the southern coastline of the Baltic Sea. Pomeranian towns were forced to garrison imperial troops, whose behavior was theoretically controlled by strict regulations, under the terms of the Capitulation. In practice, the province was devastated by the demands and depredations of the occupying troops.

TREATY OF MUNICH 1628
Maximilian of Bavaria was unwilling to compromise during the Thirty Years' War. While he was willing to return his part of the Lower Palatinate, he was not ready to return his part of the Upper Palatinate, nor surrender the electoral dignity conferred upon him by Emperor Ferdinand II. His implacable stance was reinforced by the fact that Ferdinand owed him 13 million gulden of war costs, which he had promised to repay in 1619. By the terms of the Treaty of Munich, Maximilian agreed to accept the Upper Palatinate and the electoral title as compensation for the assistance already provided.

EDICT OF RESTITUTION 1629
Issued in March 1629, the Edict was an ambitious attempt by Emperor Ferdinand II to restore institutions and territories lost to the Catholics during the previous century. The main aim of the Edict was to reaffirm the Peace of Augsburg (1555), meaning that Catholics could take back a number of monasteries, convents, and other property. The Edict had the effect of significantly reducing the wealth and power of the Protestants and creating still

greater religious division within Germany. In north Germany Ferdinand assigned imperial administrators to control cities and states that had been secularized, and free from Imperial authority, for almost a century.

TREATY OF LÜBECK 1629
Signed by Albrecht von Wallenstein and King Christian IV of Denmark, this was the treaty that ended Denmark's involvement in the Thirty Years' War. Danish intervention had begun in 1625, with some success against the Catholic League, but the League commanders, Wallenstein and Tilly, gained control of central and northern Germany, invading Holstein in 1627 and advancing through the Jutland peninsula. Christian IV made an alliance with Gustavus Adolphus of Sweden, supporting Straslund against Wallenstein. But Christian's defeat at the Battle of Wolgast left him ready for negotiations. The treaty restored to Christian his pre-war possessions, and he agreed to cede his claims to the bishoprics of Lower Saxony and undo his allianes with the North German states, staying out of imperial affairs in the future.

TRUCE OF ALTMARK 1629
The Polish-Swedish war had lasted from 1626–29, and had seen Sweden occupy Livonia and much of Prussia, though it had suffered a defeat at the hands of the Polish-Lithuanian alliance at Hongfelde in June 1629. Neither side was in a position to win the unpopular war, which many Poles felt had been prolonged by Sigismund III's refusal to give up his claim to the throne of Sweden. Under the terms of the Truce, Sweden gained possession of Livonia north of the River Dvina, and was to receive part of the toll charged on the Danzig trade. Sweden evacuated the duchy of Prussia, but retained the coastal cities. Other Swedish gains, made since the 1625 invasion, were restored to Poland-Lithuania.

PEACE OF ALAIS 1629
This treaty was negotiated by the Chief Minister, Cardinal Richelieu, and the Huguenot leaders, bringing to an end religious conflict in France. It deprived Protestants of safe havens, demanding that they relinquish their cities and fortresses, but confirmed their right to practice their religion according to the principles of the Edict of Nantes. The Huguenots were granted amnesty and tolerance was guaranteed.

PEACE OF REGENSBURG 1630
The War of Mantuan Succession (1628–31) took place following the extinction of the ruling Gonzaga line, and pitted France against the Habsburgs in pursuit of control of northern Italy. The French were alarmed by the participation of Imperial troops in the conflict, and sought to prevent this military assistance. The Spanish needed Imperial troops to turn their attention to assisting them in their war against the Dutch. The French had suffered a series of military setbacks in northern Italy, and Mantua had been taken by the Spanish and Imperial armies in July 1630. The treaty allowed the French to maintain their garrison in Grisons, while the Habsburgs agreed to reduce their troops in the region. The French candidate for the Mantuan duchy was confirmed. The treaty included an agreement that the French would not meddle in Imperial affairs, which Louis XIII of France refused to sign, prolonging the war.

TREATY OF STETTIN 1630
This treaty was the legal confirmation of Sweden's occupation of Pomerania during the Thirty Years' War. Following the Capitulation of Franzburg (1627) the Imperial forces had occupied Pomerania. Sweden had intervened, assisting the Hanseatic port of Straslund in its successful resistance to occupation. In 1630 Gustavus Adolpus of Sweden landed with a large invasion force near Peenemünde and faced the troops of Albrecht von Wallenstein, who were defeated, with the Swedes taking Stettin. The Treaty of Stettin confirmed an "eternal" alliance with Pomerania. The Swedish king was given control over Pomeranian military affairs, leaving political and ecclesiastical matters to the nobles and town councils. The duchy made military contributions to Sweden and supplied four Swedish garrisons.

THE TREATY OF MADRID 1630
The Anglo-Spanish War was a conflict between England, allied with the United Provinces, and Spain. English participation had not been noted for its military success: the Spanish had captured the Dutch city of Breda after an 11-month siege; an English naval expedition to Cadiz had failed miserably. The Treaty of Madrid, signed by Charles I of England and Philip IV of Spain, terminated the hostilities. The costs of the war and failures by England's monarchy did much to fuel the disputes that would ultimately lead to the Civil War.

THE TREATY OF BÄRWALDE 1630
This treaty made Gustavus Adolphus of Sweden's ambition – to protect Protestantism in north Germany – easier, because it offered French support to the Protestant monarch, consolidating an alliance against Emperor Ferdinand, rather than a union of co-religionists. Cardinal Richelieu, France's Chief Minister, guaranteed Sweden one million livres a

1631–1645

year for five years to advance into Germany and fight the Imperial forces, while Sweden would provide 35,000 troops. Sweden promised to protect France's commercial interests and not to interfere in Saxony and Bavaria.

TREATY OF MUNICH 1631

Cardinal Richelieu, France's chief minister, wanted to bring about a defensive alliance between King Louis XIII and Maximilian of Bavaria. This alliance would deprive the Emperor Ferdinand of Bavarian support; in addition, Louis and Maximilian shared a devotion to the Catholic cause. In May 1631 the two parties signed a treaty, at Munich and Fontainebleau, promising not to assist each other's enemies, directly or indirectly. Louis XIII promised to defend Maximilian's electoral title, but the elector reserved his right to satisfy his obligations to the Emperor.

TREATY OF SAINT-GERMAIN-EN-LAYE 1632

In 1627 war broke out between France and England, over English support for the French Huguenots in their struggle against Cardinal Richelieu. In 1629, the Kirke brothers, Scottish adventurers and supporters of the Huguenots, commanded a Scottish fleet that intercepted supplies to Quebec, forcing its surrender. At the same time Acadia, a French colonial possession in northeastern Canada, was raided by Scotland. The Treaty of Saint-Germain-en-Laye returned New France (Quebec, Acadia and New Breton Island) to French control.

TREATY OF POLYANOVKA 1634

The Smolensk War was fought between Poland-Lithuania and Russia from 1632–34. Sweden had originally suggested that a joint force of Swedes, Ottomans and Russians attacked the Polish-Lithuanian Commonwealth, but the Russians went ahead unilaterally, seeking to gain control of Smolensk. The Russians began the siege of Smolensk in October 1632, but the city held out throughout 1633, while the new ruler of the Commonwealth, King Wladyslaw IV, organized a relief force. The siege was broken in October 1633, and the Russians retreated, surrendering in February 1634. The treaty confirmed the pre-war status quo and the Russians paid a substantial war indemnity, while Wladyslaw agreed to forfeit his claim to the Russian throne.

PEACE OF PRAGUE 1635

Signed between Emperor Ferdinand II and Elector John George I of Saxony, this treaty brought to an end the internal disputes of the Thirty Years' War. However, the hostilities brought to German territory by other nations, such as Spain, Sweden, and France,

were to continue until 1648. Faced with Swedish intervention, the Emperor had invested sweeping powers in his commander, Albrecht von Wallenstein. After years of savage fighting, Wallenstein had still not managed to reimpose Catholicism by force and was assassinated in 1634. The Emperor was ready to come to terms. The Peace of Prague re-established the Peace of Augsburg (1555); the states within the Empire were forced to renounce formal alliances and leagues, which were dissolved; the various armies were unified as the Army of the Holy Roman Empire, which would defend German territory against foreign invaders; amnesty was granted to princes who had fought against Imperial troops.

TREATY OF STUHMSDORF 1635

Signed between Poland-Lithuania and Sweden in the Prussian village of Stuhmsdorf (Sztumska Wies), this treaty was a re-negotiation of the terms agreed in the Truce of Altmark (1629). Sweden, weakened by its involvement in the Thirty Years' War, was not in a strong negotiating position and Poland-Lithuania regained much of the territory it had lost during the Polish-Swedish War. The Swedes retreated from some of the Baltic ports and stopped collecting the 3.5 percent tax on Baltic trade. The truce satisfied Sweden's allies, France, England, and the Dutch Republic, who needed Swedish support for their opposition to the Holy Roman Empire in the Thirty Years' War.

TREATY OF WISMAR 1636

Concluded between France and Spain, formalizing their alliance in the conflict with the Habsburg Holy Roman Emperor, this treaty delineated geographical spheres of interest. France was to lead the conflict on the left bank of the Rhine, while Sweden – subsidized by France – was to take the conflict to Silesia and Bohemia. It was two years before the treaty was ratified.

TREATY OF HAMBURG 1638

This ratification of the Treaty of Wismar agreed that France would pay Sweden a sum of 1 million livres for giving military assistance to the French against the Habsburgs.

TREATY OF HARTFORD 1638

The Pequots were a powerful tribe who dominated trade with the English and Dutch, and the Pequot Wars (1636–37) broke out after the murder of one of the colonists, John Stone. The wars eliminated most of the Pequot population; the English settlers of the Massachusetts Bay, Plymouth, and Saybrook colonies, allied with the Narrangasett and Mohegan tribes, agreed to divide up the spoils. Women and children were given as slaves to the Narrangasetts and Mohegan, while other survivors were sent as slaves to the West Indies. The Pequot towns went to the Connecticut River colonies, and the Pequot name was outlawed.

TREATY OF BERWICK 1639

The Scottish National Covenant became the leading religious force in Scotland after they threw out the king's bishops. King Charles raised an army to assert his authority and the Covenanters united in the defense of their own beliefs. The resulting First Bishops' War ended in a stalemate and Charles was obliged to call on the English Parliament to raise revenue for further conflict. The Treaty of Berwick was therefore an inconclusive, temporary truce.

TREATY OF ZUHAB 1639

Also called the Treaty of Qasr-e Shirin, this agreement was signed between Safavid Persia and the Ottoman Empire. It brought to an end 150 years of intermittent warfare between the two empires and agreed a national boundary that prefigured the modern border between these two states. The Caucasus was divided between the two powers, with eastern Georgia, Dagestan and Azerbaijan staying under the Safavids, while the Ottomans took control of western Georgia and western Armenia. Mesopotamia was ceded to the Ottomans.

TREATY OF ASURAR ALI 1639

From 1615 onwards, the Mughals had attempted to drive into Ahom territory in the Brahmaputra Valley of Assam. Following a decisive Ahom victory as Duimunisila in November 1638, the Treaty of Asurar Ali was signed in 1639. The treaty fixed the border between the Ahom kingdom and Mughal territories and permitted trade and commerce between the two kingdoms.

TREATY OF RIPON 1640

Following the indecisive Treaty of Berwick (1639) Charles II was determined to subdue the Covenanters in Scotland. An Irish army was coerced into serving against Scotland, but the so-called Short Parliament, summoned to raise funds for the king's war, was uncooperative. Armies were levied in the south of England, but were ill-disciplined, poorly armed, and unfed. The Covenanter army massed on the English border in August 1640, crossing on 20 August and heading for Newcastle. After a humiliating defeat at the Battle of Newburn, the English army collapsed and King Charles summoned a Great Council of Peers at York. They advised him to negotiate a truce, and the Treaty of Ripon agreed a cessation of hostilities. Negotiations for a

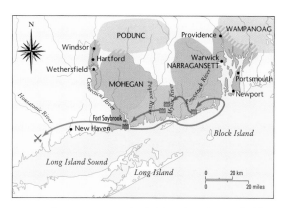

The Pequot War 1636–37
and The Treaty of
Hartford 1638

English punitive expedition
Battles
English settlement attacked by Pequots
British fort
Pequot forts
English settlements by 1636
Hostile Pequot Indians
Tribes unwilling to support Pequots
Other tribes

new settlement were to be initiated, to be ratified by Parliament. Meanwhile, the Scottish army occupied Northumberland and Durham, extracting a payment of £850 a day from the English government.

TREATY OF AXIM 1642

The kingdom of Axim on Africa's Gold Coast had been a Portuguese trading post since the late 15th century, with a fort at St Anthony. The Dutch overwhelmed the Portuguese along the coast and captured the fort in 1642. A treaty was then agreed between the States-General and the Dutch West India Company and the chiefs of Axim, who accepted their status as vassals of the States-General, the Prince of Orange and the West India Company, accepting that Dutch enemies were also their enemies. They agreed not to negotiate without alerting the WIC. Finally, both sides agreed to a military pact, in which each side promised to help the other in times of war.

SOLEMN LEAGUE AND CONVENANT 1643

The English Parliament was anxious to secure military help from the Scots against Charles I's Royalist forces in the Civil War. The Scottish Covenanters were eager to form a religious alliance between the two countries. Both sides swiftly reached an agreement: the Scots would send an army to England on condition that Parliament would uphold Protestantism and eliminate popery; reform of the Anglican church would be carried out according the "word of God," a compromise with the Scottish Covenanters who wanted to both countries to espouse Presbyteriansm.

SECOND TREATY OF BRÖMSEBRO 1645

The Torstenson War (1643–45) between Sweden and Denmark-Norway was a short conflict, provoked by Danish Sound Dues, a toll for passing through the Baltic Sea, and the expansion of Denmark-Norway from the south, which was almost encircling Sweden. The Swedes were victorious and the Peace of Brömsebro was a humiliating disaster for

Treaty of Westphalia 1648

The treaty signed in the Westphalian cities of Osnabrück and Münster between April and October 1648 to end the Thirty Years' War formed the foundation text of modern international relations. Its first innovation was the format of a diplomatic congress at which all parties affected were represented.

The treaty encompassed the normal territorial transactions. The United Provinces of the Netherlands, and the Swiss Confederation, were formally recognized as independent republics for the first time. France and Sweden both made significant acquisitions. Brandenburg-Prussia and Bavaria emerged as the most powerful states in the Imperial Council of Electors of the Holy Roman Empire; Sweden also acquired a seat on the Council through a (disputed) claim for the enclave of Wildeshausen. The wars between France and Spain, and between the nascent Dutch Republic and Portugal continued, while Sweden would clash with both Brandenburg-Prussia and Bremen over contested elements within the treaties. The complex territorial plethora of the German states, and the contentiousness of their relations, contributed to the development of international case law in the Post-Westphalian era.

However, certain tenets of lasting importance were agreed. All parties recognized the principle *cuius regio eius religio*, whereby the ruler of each state would have the freedom to determine the religion of that state (be it Catholicism, Lutheranism or Calvinism). Christians living in states where the official religion was of a different denomination were guaranteed freedom of worship. sovereignty and statehood were neither explicitly referred to, or defined, in any of the treaties, but their terms established both the authority and responsibility of states over their lands, their peoples, and their agents abroad. Pope Innocent X's fulminations against the Treaty ("null, void, invalid, iniquitous, unjust, damnable...") were impotent, underlining Westphalia's net transference of effective power from supranational authorities, both secular and ecclesiastical, specifically, the papacy and Holy Roman Emperor.

1624 was declared the "Standard Year" for determining state religion, and a prince's lands were held to be forfeit if he thenceforth changed his religion, thereby freezing the expansionism of both the Reformation and Counter-Reformation. The principle of "balance of power" was a coincidental by-product of the concerted desire of the counterparties to achieve a resolution. However, it would become a governing political principle over the rest of the century, as rivals tried to curb the threatened domination of Louis XIV's France.

DENMARK

Baltic Sea

• Konigsburg

**Duchy
of
Prussia**

1618 to Brandenburg
under Polish suzerainty
until 1657-60

Bremen-
Verden

Mecklenburg

Hither Pomerania Farther

• Stettin

Brun-
Lüneburg

Brandenburg

• Berlin

abruk

Minden

abruk

Magdeburg

Halberstadt

Walkenried •

POLAND

sse-Cassel

Elbe

Lusatia

Saxony

Silesia

Elbe

Y ROMAN EMPIRE

ippsburg
nch right to garrison

**Upper
Palatinate**

Bohemia

Moravia

Bavaria

Danube

Hungary

Ottoman
Empire

Austria

N

Tyrol

Styria

The Treaty of Westphalia, 1648

To Sweden

To Brandenburg

To Saxony

To Bavaria

To Brünswick-Lüneburg

To Mecklenberg

To Hesse-Cassel

To France

● Ten Imperial cities under French jurisdiction

● Treaty town —— Holy Roman Empire

1648 Date of State Independance

VENETIAN REPUBLIC

AN

1647–1656

Denmark-Norway. The Swedes were exempted from the Sound Dues, and Denmark-Norway ceded Norwegian territory and the Danish islands of Gotland to Sweden, who occupied the Danish province of Halland for 30 years as a guarantee of the treaty.

TRUCE OF ULM 1647
In 1646 the Swedish general Karl Gustav Wrangel invaded Bavaria, causing widespread devastation in the duchy. In March 1647 the onslaught was halted by a general truce, initiated at Ulm, which established peace between Sweden, France, Bavaria and Hessen-Kassel. It was agreed that Bavarian troops would not enter the service of the Emperor, the king of Spain, or any Habsburg allies. Ferdinand von Wittelsbach, the elector of Cologne was required to force the withdrawal of imperialists from territories under his jurisdiction. Any remnants would be expelled by Franco-Swedish forces. Maximilian was to return all occupied towns, castles, and fortresses to the prince of Württemberg. The truce was a preliminary step to the ground-breaking Peace of Westphalia in the following year.

TREATY OF CONCORDIA 1648
The Dutch had begun to settle the Caribbean island of Saint Martin between 1627 and 1631, seeking its salt deposits, and built a fort there. The island fell under Spanish military control in 1638, but it was abandoned after ten years. Later in 1648 the French and Dutch signed the Treaty of Concordia, which divided the island into two parts, with the French occupying the larger northern section and the Dutch the southern part. There would be no physical border and people and goods would travel freely between the two sectors.

PEACE OF RUEIL 1649
The Fronde (1648–53) was a civil war that took place in France during the childhood of Louis XIV, when Cardinal Mazarin was effectively ruling the country. It was a protest against the power of the crown, which came to a head when Mazarin sought to raise taxes from the third estate, the bourgeoisie, to pay for the costs of the Thirty Years' War and ongoing conflict with Spain. When judicial officers of the *parlement* of Paris were taxed, they refused to pay and a revolt broke out, forcing Mazarin to flee Paris. Following the Peace of Westphalia, the French army returned to Paris to fight the insurgents, starting with a siege of Paris. In March 1649 the Peace of Rueil was signed, although it would only last until the end of the year. The Peace effectively returned the status quo, retracted the war of words, and offered unconditional pardons to all concerned.

TREATY OF ZBORIV 1649
The Battle of Zboriv, on 17 August 1649, was a clash between the forces of Poland, led by King John II Casimir, and a combined force of Cossacks and Crimean Tatars. In the treaty the Polish king affirmed Cossack rights and freedoms, increasing the number of Registered Cossacks (special Cossack units of the Polish-Lithuanian army) to 40,000. The Polish army and Jews were banned from the territory of the Kiev, Bratslav and Chernihiv Voivodeships. The Orthodox Church was granted privileges and the Poles agreed to pay the Crimean Khanate a substantial sum of money.

TREATY OF BREDA 1650
Following the execution of King Charles I in 1649, his son Charles, Prince of Wales, was in exile on the continent. The Scottish Parliament proclaimed Charles as his father's legitimate successor, but the Kirk Party was determined that Charles should take the Covenant and impose Presbyterianism on the Three Kingdoms. Negotiations broke down because Charles did not accept the legitimacy of the Kirk Party regime, and finally resumed in Breda in the Netherlands in 1650. The Scots, aware of Charles's desperation, imposed harsh conditions: Charles would sign the Covenant and would impose Presbyterianism throughout the Three Kingdoms; Catholicism would not be tolerated; all members of the royal household were to adopt Presbyterianism; the King was to recognize the authority of the Kirk's General Assembly, and confirm all acts passed since 1641. After much wrangling, Charles agreed to take the oath of the Covenant.

TREATY OF HARTFORD 1650
The Dutch had established a trading post on the Connecticut River in 1633. Three years later English settlers established Hartford, just north of the trading post, and continued to establish new towns along the banks of the river. The Treaty of Hartford, in which the Dutch claims to the Connecticut River Valley were provisionally relinquished, was an attempt to settle their boundary disputes. In effect the Dutch traded land claims in Connecticut in order to agree a clear boundary on Long Island, which was much more densely settled by Dutch colonists.

TREATY OF BILA TSERKVA 1651
Following the Battle of Bila Tserkva, a treaty was signed in 1651 between the Polish-Lithuanian Commonwealth and the Zaporozhian (central Ukrainian) Cossacks. According to the agreement, the number of Registered Cossacks was reduced to 20,000, and they were confined to the Kiev Voivodeship. The Bratslav and Chernihiv palatinates

were given back to Polish administrators, and nobles were permitted to return to their estates.

TREATY OF STETTIN 1653

Brandenburg and Sweden both claimed succession in the duchy of Pomerania, after the last duke of the local House of Pomeraniadied in 1637. While the division of the duchy was agreed in principle under the Peace of Westphalia, the actual border was determined by the Treaty of Stettin, along a line running east of the Oder River. The area to the west of this line was known as Swedish Pomerania, while the land to the east was transferred to Brandenburg. Sweden now controlled the Oder estuary, as well as the lower Weser and Elbe Rivers – all the mouths of Germany's major rivers in the Baltic Sea, with the exception of the Rhine, were in Swedish hands.

TREATY OF PEREYASLAV 1654

This agreement was concluded between the Zaprorozhian Cossacks and representatives of Tsar Alexy I. The Cossacks sought the protection of the Russian state and the treaty was intended as an act of official separation of Ukraine from the Polish-Lithuanian Commonwealth. The Cossacks swore an oath of allegiance to the Russian monarch. The Russians agreed to grant the Cossack state autonomy, preserving the status of the Kiev Orthodox Patriarch. The Cossacks were prohibiting from conducting independent foreign policy, no doubt because the tsar had pledged to defend the Cossacks. Ukraine was now in union with the Russian state, not the Polish-Lithuanian Commonwealth.

TREATY OF WESTMINSTER 1654

As England and the United Provinces of the Netherlands competed for maritime trade, tensions had grown. All over the world, English merchants were losing lucrative trading opportunities to the Dutch and unofficial warfare was breaking out, as English privateers began to seize Dutch ships and cargoes. When Dutch ships traded with Royalists they were contravening an embargo instituted by the English Commonwealth, and were seized. War was officially declared in 1652, and a number of naval battles in the North Sea and English Channel ensued, with the English ultimately defeating the Dutch at the Battle of Scheveningen in July 1653. The Treaty of Westminster recognized Oliver Cromwell's Navigation Acts, which required that imports to the Commonwealth must be carried on English ships, or ships coming from the countries where the merchandise originated. It was also agreed that the Dutch were obliged to salute the Commonwealth flag in open waters, and pay compensation for loss of trade caused by the conflict.

The main aim of the treaty, using a secret clause, was to exclude the pro-Stuart House of Orange from office in the United Provinces. The Act of Seclusion, passed by the States-General, barred William III of Orange from being appointed stadtholder, and British Royalists were expelled from Dutch territory.

TREATY OF KEDAINIAI 1655

The Second Northern War (1655–60) started when Charles X Gustav of Sweden invaded and occupied western Poland-Lithuania; his rapid advance was known as the Swedish Deluge. The Swedes went on to confront Russia, Brandenburg-Prussia (who became Swedish allies in exchange for the receiving the duchy of Prussia as a Swedish fief), the Habsburgs, and Denmark-Norway. The Treaty of Kedainiai, between Poland-Lithuania and Sweden, was signed on 17 August, shortly after the outbreak of the war, and confirmed that the grand duchy of Lithuania was under Swedish protection. The treaty contained a clause stipulating that the two parts of the Commonwealth – Poland and Lithuania – need not fight each other. The Swedes pressed on towards Warsaw and eventually Krakow, which they captured in October. The Polish King, John II Casimir, was exiled to Silesia. On 20 October a second treaty proclaimed the Union of Kediainiai, between Lithuania and Sweden; over the ensuing days most of the Polish army capitulated to Sweden.

TREATY OF RINSK 1655

While Swedish forces were sweeping across Poland-Lithuania, resulting in the fall of Krakow and Warsaw in October 1655, Russian and Cossack forces occupied the east of the Polish-Lithuanian Commonwealth, leaving only Lvov under Polish-Lithuanian control. Nobles in Royal Prussia, the part of the Polish-Lithuanian Commonwealth that had previously been part of the lands of the Teutonic Order, concluded the Treaty of Rinsk with the electorate of Brandenburg. This defensive alliance permitted Brandenburgians to base garrisons in Prussian territory to defend it against Sweden, with the exception of Danzig, Thorn and Elbing (the latter two cities had surrendered to Sweden).

TREATY OF KÖNIGSBERG 1656

Following the Treaty of Rinsk, and the fall of Thorn and Elbling to King Charles X, Frederick William I, elector of Brandenburg, succumbed to the greater force of his Swedish enemy, signing the Treaty of Königsberg. By the terms of this treaty he submitted to the overlordship of Sweden, and undertook to provide a contingent of 1,500 men to assist the Swedes, in event of further hostilities against Poland. He retained control of Pillau and Memel, but half

1656–1658

of the Prussian port-dues went to Sweden. In return Frederick William I received Ermland (Warmia).

TREATY OF MARIENBURG 1656

As Swedish triumphs in Poland began to look more vulnerable, Charles X Gustav sought an alliance with Frederick William I, elector of Brandenburg, and was willing to reward him for his loyalty. This treaty concluded the alliance, which bound both sides to mutually defend their Polish and Prussian acquisitions, and recognized Brandenburg's sovereignty over a large part of Great Poland. The alliance proved its worth during the Battle of Warsaw, 28-30 July 1656, which the alliance won against a greater Polish force.

TREATY OF ELBING 1656

Signed between the Dutch Republic and Sweden, the Treaty of Elbing protected Dutch trading interests in the Baltic Sea, and ended Dutch intervention in the Swedish siege of Danzig, when a relief force of Dutch ships had unblocked Danzig's harbor and taken over the defense of the port. Danzig was the source of grain imports from the Baltic Sea on which the Dutch relied. As one of the terms of the treaty, Sweden recognized Danzig's neutrality, and granted the Dutch Republic "most favored nation" status.

TREATY OF LABIAU 1656

The success of the Swedish-Brandenburg alliance at Warsaw in July 1656 spurred the Habsburgs and Poles to make an alliance. Frederick William of Brandenburg, aware that Sweden was now more than ever anxious to maintain the Swedish-Brandenburg alliance, insisted that its conditions were re-negotiated in his favour. The Treaty of Labiau, November 1656, elevated Frederick William from a Swedish vassal to a full sovereign in the duchy of Prussia and in Ermland, while Sweden renounced her share of the Prussian port-dues.

TRUCE OF VILNA 1656

Signed between Russia and Polish-Lithuanian Commonwealth, this truce ended hostilities in the Russo-Polish War (1654–67), a conflict that had been triggered by the rebellion of Zaporozhian Cossacks against the Commonwealth. The Truce also agreed an anti-Swedish alliance; Alexis of Russia was promised succession to the throne in Poland after the death of John II Casimir in exchange for his military support against Sweden.

TREATY OF VIENNA 1656

This was the formal conclusion of an Austro-Polish alliance, signed on 1 December. The Habsburg emperor, Ferdinand III, agreed to enter the war against Sweden, and to send a contingent of 4,000 soldiers to assist the Polish king, John II Casimir. Ferdinand III died just three days after signature.

TREATY OF RADNOT 1656

This treaty, signed on 6 December, was an alliance between Sweden and Transylvania, which envisaged a partition of the Polish-Lithuanian Commonwealth. George Rákóczi II, the prince of Transylvania, was to take much of Little Poland and Lithuania and to take the title of king of Poland and grand duke of Lithuania. Transylvania's Cossack allies, excluded from the Truce of Vilna, were to take Ukraine. Brandenburg was to retain the parts of Great Poland granted it by the Treaty of Marienburg. Sweden was to receive Royal Prussia. Spurred on by the promised prize, Rákóczi entered Poland with an army of 41,000 in January 1657.

TREATY OF BUTRE 1656

Dutch traders were drawn to West Africa's Gold Coast by the promise of gold. In 1656 the Dutch signed a treaty riendship and cooperation with the West African kingdom of Ahanta at Butre which established a Dutch protectorate. The Dutch built a fort at Butre, called Fort Batenstein.

TREATY OF VIENNA 1657

Emperor Ferdinand III died in 1656 and was succeeded by Leopold, whose election was opposed by George Rákóczi, prince of Transylvania, and an ally of Charles X of Sweden. On 27 May Leopold signed a revised Treaty of Vienna, agreeing to provide 12,000 men, who would garrison Krakow and Poznan, although they would be paid for by his Polish allies. Polish-Lithuanian and Austrian troops occupied Krakow in August.

TREATY OF WEHLAU 1657

Sometimes referred to as the Treaty of Wehlau-Bromeberg or Treaty of Wehlau and Bromberg, this was a treaty between John II Casimir of Poland and Elector Frederick William of Brandenburg-Prussia. By the terms of this new alliance John Casimir renounced the suzerainty of the Polish crown over the duchy of Prussia, making Frederick William duke of Prussia as well as the elector of Brandenburg. In exchange, Frederick William promised Poland military aid in the Second Northern War.

TREATY OF PARIS 1657

The Commonwealth of Oliver Cromwell and Spain were at war between 1654 and 1660, mainly over commercial and colonial conflicts, with maritime clashes taking place in the Caribbean and land actions in the Spanish Netherlands. At the same time the French were involved in the Franco-Spanish War (1635–59), a conflict that had arisen from French involvement in the Thirty Years' War. France had declared war on Spain because, in the wake of the Peace of Prague (1635), the French felt surrounded by Habsburg territory. The Treaty of Paris, signed by England and France, effectively merged these two conflicts. The English agreed to join France in her war against Spain in Flanders, contributing 6,000 men and the English fleet. It was agreed that Gravelines would be ceded to France, and Dunkirk and Mardyck to England.

TREATY OF RAALTE 1657

William of Orange, who was statdholder of Holland, Zeeland, Utrecht, Gelderland, and Overijssel, signed this treaty in 1657. According to the treaty, he relinquished the stadtholdership of Overijssel, resolving a conflict between two opposing groups of towns in Overijssel.

TREATY OF HADIACH 1658

Signed between representatives of the Polish-Lithuanian Commonwealth and Ukrainian Cossacks, this treaty was designed to elevate the Cossacks and Ukrainians (called Ruthenians) to positions of equality, by creating a new entity – the Polish-Lithuanian-Ruthenian Commonwealth (Commonwealth of Three Nations). By the terms of the treaty a new duchy of Ruthenia was created, to be governed by an elected Cossack *hetman* (leader); legal, academic, judicial, and fiscal institutions were to be created in Ruthenia that mirrored those already existing in Poland-Lithuania; all three nations of the Commonwealth were to be connected by a common king and parliament; leading Cossack elders were to be ennobled; a Cossack army was to be established; land and property, previously confiscated by Cossacks, was to be restituted; a general amnesty was to be granted. The Russians saw the treaty as an act of war and immediately sent forces into Ukraine. Ultimately, lack of Commonwealth success against Russian forces undermined waning Cossack commitment to the provisions of the treaty.

TREATY OF TAASTRUP 1658

This preliminary accord, signed by Charles X Gustavus of Sweden and King Frederick III of Denmark-Norway, was agreed after Denmark-Norway was defeated in the Second Northern War. Denmark-Norway had attacked in 1657, aiming to gain territories lost in 1645. The Swedes marched through Pomerania and Mecklenburg, entered Jutland from the south and crossed the frozen seas,

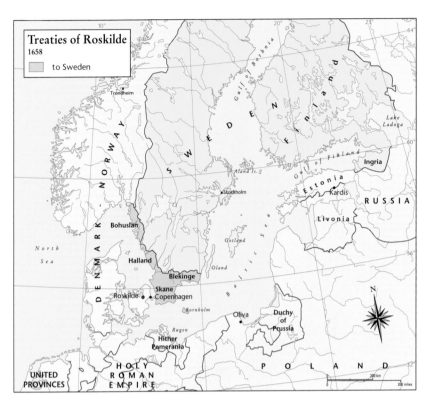

(the "Great Belt" and "Little Belt") separating the Danish islands from the mainland. Their attack on Copenhagen took the Danes completely by surprise and Frederick III was compelled to surrender.

TREATY OF ROSKILDE 1658

The provisional agreement at Taastrup was finalized by the Treaty of Roskilde between Denmark-Norway and Sweden. Denmark relinquished the provinces of Scania, Blekinge, Trøndelag, and the island of Bornholm, as well as her claims to Halland. Denmark-Norway had to agree to forego all anti-Swedish alliances, and to ensure that no warships hostile to Sweden passed through the Baltic Straits. The Danes were called on to pay financial compensation to Sweden for the costs of their occupation forces and to provide troops to help Charles X Gustavus in other wars.

TREATY OF VALIESAR 1658

This was the armistice that ended the Russian-Swedish War of 1656–68. This conflict was initiated by Tsar Alexis of Russia, whose main objective was to reverse the Treaty of Stolvobo (1617), and regain Russian territory on the Baltic coast. By the terms of the treaty Russia was to retain certain territories in Livonia, occupied by Russian forces during the war, for three years. Free trade was restored between the two nations and friendly relations were established between the armies of Russia and Sweden.

1659–1670

TREATY OF THE PYRENEES 1659

This treaty resolved many years of conflict over the border between Spain and France, and in particular the war between France and Spain (1635–59). The Treaty of the Pyrenees finally resolved the issue, fixing the border between France and Spain and bringing Roussillon, Perpignan, and 33 villages in the Cerdagne under the French crown. It also resolved other outstanding problems between France and Spain, with France gaining Montmédy, and parts of Luxembourg, Artois, and Flanders from the Spanish. The French king, in turn, promised to cease supporting Portugal, where a revolt led by the duke of Braganza was underwritten by the French, and to renounce his claim to the county of Barcelona.

TREATY OF COPENHAGEN 1660

The final resolution of the conflict amongst the Scandinavian powers, this treaty was signed by Sweden and Denmark-Norway. Following the Treaty of Roskilde (1658) the Swedish king, Charles X Gustavus, invaded Denmark, seized Fünen, and blockaded Copehnagen. King Frederick III of Denmark-Norway led a heroic defense of his capital. Charles X's sudden death in 1659, leaving his four-year-old son as heir to the Swedish kingdom, put paid to further offensives and the treaty was negotiated. By the terms of the Treaty of Copenhagen, Denmark recovered Fünen and Bornholm and Norway regained Trøndelag. Frederick III was proclaimed hereditary and absolute king and the present-day borders of all three Scandinavian countries were largely agreed.

TREATY OF OLIVA 1660

This was the treaty that ended the Second Northern War of 1655–60, signed between Sweden, Brandenburg, Habsburg Austria, and the Polish-Lithuanian Commonwealth. The main beneficiary of the agreement was Elector Frederick William of Brandenburg-Prussia, who was accepted as sovereign in ducal Prussia, as agreed by the Treaty of Welhau (1657). Sweden's possession of Livonia, won during the course of the war, was recognized by Poland-Lithuania, and John II Casimir, king of Poland, repudiated his claim to the Swedish throne, although he retained the title of hereditary Swedish king for life. Apart from these agreements, all territories reverted to their pre-war status.

TREATY OF CARDIS 1661

Under the terms of this treaty, signed by Russia and Sweden, Russia returned to Sweden all the conquered towns that had been granted to Russia by the Treaty of Valiesar in 1658: Marienburg, Syrensk, Kokenhausen, Dorpt, Anzl, Neinhausen. Both sides agreed not to undertake any further hostilities against each other in the frontier regions. The treaty also endorsed free trade between the two nations, allowing trading representatives to visit a certain number of towns in each other's territories for trading purposes.

TREATY OF MONTMARTRE 1662

By this treaty, Louis XIV of France agreed to extend membership in the royal house of France to the princes of the House of Lorraine. In return for this concession, the long-coveted duchy of Lorraine would be ceded to the French crown.

TREATY OF GHILAJHARIGHAT 1663

Signed between the Ahoms, inhabitants of the kingdom of Assam in the Brahmaputra Valley, and the Mughal forces, this treaty marked the end of the Mughal occupation of the Ahom capital, Garhgaon. Various terms were agreed: a daughter of the house of Ahom was to be sent to the Imperial harem; large quantities of gold, silver and 40 elephants were to be supplied to the Mughal Empire immediately, with an agreement to supply 20 elephants annually; some Ahom territory was ceded to the Emperor of Delhi; six hostages, all of them the sons of the Ahom nobility, were taken hostage until the gold, silver, and elephants agreed upon had been supplied.

PEACE OF VASVÁR 1664

The Austro-Turkish War of 1663–64 had culminated in the Battle of St Gotthard (1664), at which the Turks were defeated. By the terms of this treaty, the Ottoman Empire gained control of Transylvania and Uyvar, and both empires paid tribute to each other. Although the Habsburg Austrians had the upper hand militarily, they were threatened by France in the Holy Roman Empire and Italy, and were eager to turn their attention to these zones, feeling the concessions demanded by the Ottomans were comparatively minor.

TREATY OF PURANDAR 1665

Following the Mughal capture of the city of Pune and several of Shivaji's forts, in retaliation for Shivaji's sacking of the wealthy Mughal trading town of Surat (1664), this treaty was signed between the representative of the Mughal Emperor Aurangzeb and Chhatrapati Shivaji Maharah, a warrior king of Bijapur and member of the Maratha clan. Shivaji agreed to surrender 23 forts to the Emperor; the Emperor, in turn, recognized Shivaji's authority over twelve forts. Shivaji paid Aurangzeb substantial compensation, while 5,000 soldiers were sent to serve in the imperial army under the command of his son, Sambhaji.

TREATY OF BREDA 1667

Fierce competition over commerce led to the Second Anglo-Dutch War (1665–67), with both sides fighting to protect their economic interests. France, committed to aid the Dutch according to a defensive alliance concluded in 1662, tried unsuccessfully to intervene. The Danish joined the French and Dutch Republic, and Brandenburg joined the alliance. The English, in turn, had concluded a defensive alliance with Sweden (1665) against the Dutch. English hopes for victory were undermined by the financial and social pressures of the plague and the Great Fire, making a treaty imperative. The Dutch, French, Danish, and English all attended the peace conference at Breda, with Swedish ambassadors acting as mediators. While English backs were turned, Dutch ships sailed up the Thames and attacked English ships moored in the Medway pre-empting any English attempts to negotiate favorable terms. The Treaty of Breda, signed a month after the Dutch raid, gave the Dutch the right to transport German goods to England, a major unravelling of the much-resented Navigation Act of 1651. None of the property seized during the war was to be restituted and prisoners were freely exchanged.

TRUCE OF ANDRUSOVO 1667

The Thirteen Years' War between Russia and Poland (1654–67) was fought for control of Ukraine. Under the terms of the Pereyaslav Agreement (1654) Russia had annexed Ukraine from Poland-Lithuania, following a revolt against Polish rule by the Zaporozhian Cossacks. This led to war between Poland and Russia, with control of Ukraine frequently shifting between the two contending powers. During the truce negotiations, the outbreak of a new Cossack rebellion weakened the Polish negotiating position. Ukraine was divided along the course of the Dnieper, with Russia retaining the city of Kiev and the provinces of Smolensk and Seversk.

TREATY OF BONGAJA 1667

At Makassar (1666) forces of the Dutch East India Company (VOC) had defeated the army of Sultan Hasanudin of Gowa, in the southern Sulawesi region of Indonesia. By the terms of this treaty Sultan Hasanudin recognized the VOC's influence in Indonesian territories; all traders from Gowa required a license in order to do business in any of the areas controlled by the VOC, which included Makassar, Timor, and the coasts of Java.

FIRST TRIPLE ALLIANCE 1668

This defensive alliance, formed by the Dutch, Swedish, and English, was a reaction to the growing power of Louis XIV's France, which was overrunning the Spanish Netherlands and the Franche-Comté in the War of Devolution. Confronted by the threat of the Triple Alliance and Spain, Louis halted his offensive, leading to the Treaty of Aix-la-Chapelle.

TREATY OF AIX-LA-CHAPELLE 1668

The War of Devolution was the conflict between Louis XIV of France and Spain over control of the Spanish Netherlands. Under pressure from the Triple Alliance of England, Sweden, and the Dutch Republic, Louis XIV sighed the Treaty of Aix-la-Chapelle, by which he agreed to return the cities of Cambrai, Aire and Saint-Omer, along with Franche-Comté, to the Spanish. The French retained a series of fortified towns along the borders of the Spanish Netherlands and the conquests they had made in Flanders in 1667.

TREATY OF LISBON 1668

In 1640 a revolution in Lisbon had ended the 60-year rule of the Spanish Habsburgs in Portugal. Between 1640–68 there was intermittent conflict between Spain and Portugal, as well as more serious alliances with conflicting non-Iberian powers, such as the Dutch, French, and English. A number of Portuguese victories in the 1660s made it clear that Iberia would never be united under Spanish rule and Spain became increasingly over-stretched militarily, and eager to shed some of its commitments. In 1668, by the terms of the Treaty of Lisbon, Spain recognized the sovereignty of the House of Braganza in Portugal and reconfirmed Portuguese sovereignty over its colonial possessions. Portugal ceded the African city of Ceuta to Spain.

SECRET TREATY OF DOVER 1670

Two treaties were signed at Dover in 1670: one was a public, formal assertion of an alliance between Charles II and Louis XIV designed to subjugate the Netherlands; the second, secret, treaty was concerned with the conversion of England to Roman Catholicism, with the support of French troops and French money. The latter clause never came into effect: Louis was more interested in the military aspects of the public treaty, and Charles was satisfied with advancing the Catholic cause in England by promoting religious toleration.

TREATY OF MADRID 1670

This agreement between England and Spain recognized England's possessions in the Caribbean, including Jamaica, which the English conquered in 1655. After the conquest they established a naval base from which they disrupted trade on the Spanish Main. The governor of the island,

1670–1689

lacking any support or funding from London, used untrustworthy privateers to defend the island, and they took to raiding Spanish territories in Mexico and Nicaragua. The Spanish, furious, authorized reprisals and Charles II of England, alarmed at the prospect of outright war, began to negotiate. Both sides continued raiding while the negotiations were ongoing, and there were devastating attacks in Charleston, Panama, and Portobello. By the terms of the treaty, signed in July 1670, the Spanish recognized English ownership of Jamaica and Virginia, the first time that Spain had acknowledged the possessions of any other nation in the new world.

TREATY OF COPEHAGEN 1670
This commercial alliance was signed between King Charles II of England and King Christian V of Denmark and Norway. England promised that its privateers would desist from their attacks on the Danish colony on Saint Thomas in the Virgin Islands, giving the Danes a measure of security. English subjects were not allowed to visit the colonies of Denmark without a licence from the Danish king.

TREATY OF BUCZACZ 1672
A series of irregular border conflicts in Ukraine between the Cossacks and Tatars and the Polish-Lithuanian Commonwealth escalated into the Polish-Ottoman War (1672–76) when the Cossacks enlisted the support of the Ottoman Empire. A large Ottoman army invaded the Polish Ukraine in August 1672 and the Commonwealth, impeded by internal conflict, was unable to raise a large enough army to resist. The Treaty of Buczacz ceded the Commonwealth's possessions in Ukraine, west of the Dnieper, to the Ottomans and agreed to pay tribute.

TREATY OF WESTMINSTER 1674
This treaty officially brought the Third Anglo-Dutch War to a close, although intermittent hostilities continued for several decades. The treaty essentially renewed the Treaty of Breda of 1667. The area known as New Netherland in North America, which had been retaken by the Dutch in 1673, was transferred to the English, while the Dutch were granted Suriname in South America. When the English took over the Dutch territory they renamed it New York, in honor of King James II, duke of York. The treaty also provided for a joint commission for the regulation of commerce, especially in the East Indies.

STRASBOURG AGREEMENT 1675
This was the first international agreement banning the use of chemical weapons, a response to the use of poisoned bullets. The treaty was signed between France and the Holy Roman Empire.

TREATY OF ZURAWNO 1676
Following the unfavorable terms agreed in the Treaty of Buczacz (1672), which galvanized the Polish people, there had been a renewal of hostilities between the Polish-Lithuanian Commonwealth and Ottoman Empire, with Polish forces led by the able commander, John Sobieski, who was elected king of Poland in 1674, and ruled as King John III. By the terms of the treaty Podolia and southern Ukraine were ceded to the Ottomans, but the rest of the Ukrainian frontier was left unresolved. The Commonwealth no longer had to pay tribute to the Ottomans, and had effectively regained one-third of Ukrainian territory.

TREATY OF 1677
Sometimes called the first Treaty of Middle Plantation, this treaty was signed in Virginia between King Charles II of England and representatives of several Virginia tribes, including the Nazatico, Nansemond, Nottoway, Appomattoc, Monocan and Sapponi. It followed the revolt of Virginia settlers, led by Nathaniel Bacon, against Governor William Berkeley. It was agreed that treaty signatories would be subjects of the king of England, holding their reservation land by patent and paying 'rent' (beaverskins) to the governor annually. No English were to settle within three miles of any Indian town. They would be given hunting and fishing rights and the right to bear arms.

TREATIES OF NIGMEGEN 1678
Following the occupation of Nigmegen by French troops in 1674, as part of the long-running conflict between the Dutch Republic, France, Spain, and their various allies, Louis XIV realized that he had failed in his long-term goals – in that year the English, his allies, had made peace with the Dutch Republic, leaving the French exposed. After protracted negotiations, during which the town of Nijmegen hosted an impressive array of ambassadors and diplomats from a wide range of countries, the Dutch and French signed a peace treaty, which fixed the borders of northern France near their modern position, giving the French control over Franche-Comté, as well as certain territories of the Spanish Netherlands. The French ceded control of Maastricht and the principality of Orange to the Dutch stadtholder William III. Further treaties followed: between France and Spain; France and the Holy Roman Empire; Sweden and the Holy Roman Empire; Sweden and the prince-bishopric of Münster; Sweden and the Dutch Republic.

TREATY OF CASCO 1678

This treaty marked the end of a war between English settlers in Massachusetts Bay Colony and the eastern Indians. According to its terms, the Abenaki Indians who, along with their allies, had wiped a 60-mile (95 km) stretch of coast east of Casco Bay clean of English settlements, recognized English property rights, but maintained sovereignty over the state of Maine, which was symbolized by an annual land use tax that had to be paid by every English family. From this point on the fur trade would be subject to closer regulation by the government.

TREATY OF SAINT-GERMAIN-EN-LAYE 1679

Agreed between France and the electorate of Brandenburg, this treaty was considered to be a low point for Elector Frederick William I, who was forced to relinquish much of the territory he had gained from Sweden. Sweden, an ally of France, had demonstrated its support of France by invading Brandenburg in 1674, leading to the Scanian War, during which Brandenburg occupied Swedish domains in northern Germany and Pomerania, and Denmark invaded Scania. Following the various peace treaties agreed at Nigmegen in 1678, France was free to support Sweden again, invading the duchy of Cleves, a Brandenburgian domain. Exposed and lacking allies, Brandenburg sought peace. While much of Pomerania was restored to Sweden, Brandenburg gained the eastern bank of the River Oder, and agreed to accept a fixed sum from France.

TREATY OF FONTAINEBLEAU 1679

This treaty ended the hostilities between Sweden and Denmark-Norway in the Scanian War. Under French pressure, Denmark returned its conquests and Holstein-Gottorp to Sweden. The agreement was ratified by the Peace of Lund later that year.

TREATY OF BAKHCHISARAI 1681

The Russian-Turkish War of 1676–81 ended with the Treaty of Bakhchisarai, agreed between Russia, the Ottoman Empire, and the Crimean Khanate. It was agreed that the Dnieper River would form the boundary between Russian and Ottoman territory; the territory between the Southern Bug and Dnieper Rivers was to be left unsettled. The war had been caused by Ottoman expansionism, which had inevitably followed gains made during the preceding Ottoman-Polish War. The Ottomans strove to gain dominance over "right-bank" Ukraine, the area to the west of the Dnieper, besieging the city of Chyhyryn, and eventually occupying it in 1678, forcing the Russians to retreat over the Dnieper, where they were attacked by Crimean Tatars.

TRUCE OF RATISBON 1684

Louis XIV of France claimed sovereignty over the province of Alsace, and asserted this claim by sending a French army to march on Strasbourg, and demand its capitulation, in September 1681. He went on to capture Courtrai, Dixmude, and Luxembourg (1684). In August 1684 a 20-year truce was signed between France and Spain and the Holy Roman Empire. France continued to hold all the territory that had been held during the conflict (named the War of the Reunions), including the cities of Strasbourg and Luxembourg.

ETERNAL PEACE TREATY OF 1686

Concluded between Russia and the Polish-Lithuanian Commonwealth, this agreement confirmed the Andrusovo Treaty (1667), under which Poland had renounced Kiev, and reaffirmed Russia's possession of left-bank Ukraine (east of the Dnieper), while Poland retained right-bank Ukraine. Both sides agreed not to sign a separate treaty with the Ottoman Empire; Russia had become a member of the anti-Turkish coalition, comprising the Holy Roman Empire, Poland, and Venice. The treaty was opposed in Poland and was only ratified by the Polish Sejm (parliament) in 1710.

TREATY OF NERCHINSK 1689

Russia had been steadily expanding eastwards, with outposts reaching as far as the Amur River Basin, which they reached in the 1640s. The Manchu Emperors of China feared that the Russians were

1691–1701

encroaching on their Manchurian homeland, and the Treaty of Nerchinsk was designed to check this progress. Russia lost access to the Sea of Okhostsk and the markets of the Far East, but secured its claim to the area east of Lake Baikal. Russian trade caravans were also given access to the markets of Beijing. The borders between Russia and China were agreed as lying along the Argun River and the Stanaovoy Range. The language used for the treaty was Latin; this was the first time that a European power had negotiated a treaty with the Chinese on equal terms.

TREATY OF LIMERICK 1691

The Williamite War in Ireland (1688–91) was fought between the Jacobite supporters of the Catholic king of England, Ireland, and Scotland, James II, and the

Williamites, who supported the Dutch Protestant Prince William of Orange. James had been deposed in the Glorious Revolution of 1688, and saw Ireland as a base from which, with French support, he could regain the throne of the three kingdoms. Irish Protestant supporters of William of Orange were based in the north of the country. They joined William when he arrived in Ireland with a multi-national Protestant force, which culminated in his victory over the Jacobites at the Battle of the Boyne (1690) and Battle of Aughrim (1691). The treaty contained both military and civil articles. The military articles agreed that Irish members of the Jacobite army could migrate, with their families, to France; alternatively they could join the Williamite army. The civil articles decreed that Jacobites remaining in Ireland were to be left in peace as long as they pledged allegiance to King William. They were allowed to keep their estates and property and Catholic nobles were permitted to bear arms.

TREATY OF RYSWICK 1697

The Nine Years' War (1688–97) had pitted France against a coalition of Austria and the Holy Roman Empire, Spain, the Dutch Republic, Britain, and Savoy. It was a wide-ranging conflict, fought on continental Europe, in Ireland, on the surrounding seas, and in North America. Louis XIV sought political dominance in Europe and was prepared to use force to assert his territorial claims. The prolonged conflict exhausted all the contenders, both militarily and financially, and by 1697 they were eager for a settlement. Under the terms of the treaty Louis XIV recognized William III as king of England, and agreed to relinquish his attempts to gain control of Cologne and the Palatinate, end the French occupation of Lorraine and restore Barcelona, Luxembourg, Mons, and Courtai to Spain. France retained Strasbourg and some towns in Lower Alsace. The Duch were allowed to garrison fortresses in the Spanish Netherlands to protect themselves against incursions from France.

TREATY OF DEN HAAG 1698

Signed between England and France, this treaty was an attempt to resolve the question of the succession to the Spanish throne, and proposed that the heir should be Joseph Ferdinand of Bavaria. This agreement would then lead to a whole series of bequests: the Grand Dauphin, Louis, would get Naples and Sicily; Archduke Charles would get the Spanish Netherlands; Leopold, Duke of Lorraine, would take Milan. The treaty was invalidated when Joseph of Bavaria died. In the following year a second partition treaty was mooted, but Archduke Charles refused to sign it because it did not grant

Treaty of Limerick
1690–91

● Towns held by Protestants on the arrival of William III

→ Campaigns of 1690

→ Campaigns of 1691

→ James II advances to meet William III

✕ Major battle

Italy to Austria. In the event King Charles II of Spain rejected these suggestions, which would have divided the Spanish Empire, and bequeathed all his possessions to the dauphin's second son Philip, the Duke of Anjou. The will was contested, leading to the War of the Spanish Succession.

TREATY OF KARLOWITZ 1699
Hostilities between the Ottoman Empire and the Holy League (Austria, Poland, Venice, and Russia), which had begun in 1683, reached a turning point in September 1697, when Sultan Mustafa II was defeated at the Battle of Zenta. For the first time the Ottomans agreed to negotiate with a coalition of European nations at Karlowitz, overseen by neutral powers, and to admit defeat. The Ottomans signed peace treaties with Austria, Poland, and Venice. By the terms of these treaties, Austria received most of Hungary, Transylvania, Croatia, and Slovenia; Venice received the Peloponnese and most of Dalmatia; Poland regained Podolia and part of western Ukraine. The Russians and Turks signed an armistice, but did not agree a treaty until 1700. Austrian influence in central Europe was now secure, while Turkey's dominance had diminished.

TREATY OF PREOBRAZHENSKOYE 1699
The treaty that gave impetus to the Great Northern War, this was the agreement to partition the Swedish Empire between the Polish-Lithuanian Commonwealth, Denmark, Saxony and Russia.

PEACE OF TRAVENDAL 1700
Hostein-Gottorp, just to the south of Denmark, was tied to Sweden because its duke was Charles XI of Sweden's son-in-law. Sweden had enlisted the maritime powers of England and the Netherlands, which had assisted the Swedish fleet in threatening Copenhagen. Under the terms of the Peace, agreed between the Swedish Empire and Denmark-Norway, Denmark agreed to return Holstein-Gottorp, which it had seized, to its duke, effectively withdrawing from the Great Northern War and enabling Charles XI to concentrate on the Baltic theater of operations.

TREATY OF LONDON 1700
The death in 1699 of Joseph Ferdinand of Bavaria – designated by the Treaty of Den Haag as heir to the Spanish throne – had reopened the issue of the Spanish succession. The Treaty of London (the Second Partition Treaty), signed by England and France, assigned the Spanish throne and the remainder of the Spanish Empire to the Archduke Charles, while the Italian territories would go to France. Archduke Charles refused to sign the treaty because he wanted the whole of Spain and the Italian

territories. King Charles II of Spain also refused as it would divide the Spanish Empire and, by his will, left all his possessions to the dauphin's second son Philip, the duke of Anjou. On Charles II's death in 1700, King Louis XIV of France renounced the treaty, contested the will, and Anjou was proclaimed King Philip V of Spain and ruler of the entire Spanish Empire, contrary to the provisions of the Second Partition Treaty.

TREATY OF CONSTANTINOPLE 1700
Russia had refused to sign the Treaty of Karlowitz as it completely ignored its interests. Further negotiations between the Russians and the Turks led to the signing of the Treaty of Constantinople which agreed to a 30-year truce, confirmed Russia's possession of the Azov region and the dropping of her claims to the Kerch Strait. The Turks also agreed that the Tatars would not attack Russia, while the Russians guaranteed the Cossacks would not attack Turkey. But before the treaty was concluded, the Swedes occupied Karelia, Ingria, Estonia and Livonia, thereby blocking Russia's way to the Baltic coast. To curb Sweden's power, and taking advantage of the fact that it was ruled by the 18-year-old Charles XII, Tsar Peter I of Russia formed secret alliances with Saxony, Poland, and Denmark–Norway, setting in motion the Great Northern War (1700–21). In this conflict the Russian-led coalition contested the supremacy of the Swedish Empire in central, northern, and eastern Europe.

GREAT PEACE OF MONTREAL 1701
In order to put an end to 100 years of conflict centered on the fur trade, the rivalry between the French and the Iroquois League, and the hostilities between the French, British and the Dutch, more than 1,300 delegates from 39 different "First Nations" (the predominant Aboriginal peoples of Canada south of the Arctic) met at Montreal to negotiate a peace treaty with France. Leading the negotiations were Huron-Wendat Grand Chief, Kondiaronk, and Louis-Hector de Callière, governor of New France. The terms of the treaty benefitted the First Nations as it settled most of their long-standing quarrels over the use of traditional hunting and trapping lands, while the French gained the right to found Detroit in Iroquois territory. The Iroquois undertook to remain neutral in the event of a war between France and England. The treaty introduced a new era of peace between the French, their First Nations allies, and the Iroquois.

TREATY OF THE HAGUE 1701
The Treaty of London (1700) had led to the declaration by France's King Louis XIV of his

1703–1713

grandson as Philip V of Spain and ruler of the Spanish Empire. With Philip ruling in Spain, Louis secured great advantages for his dynasty. Furthermore, in an aggressive move, he cut off England and the Netherlands from Spanish trade. England's king, William III, responded by negotiating the Treaty of The Hague with the United Provinces and Austria. By the terms of the agreement, Philip V was recognized as king of Spain, while England and the Netherlands retained their commercial rights in Spain. Austria acquired the Spanish territories in Italy, but was forced to accept the Spanish Netherlands to protect them from French control. To counter Louis's growing dominance, the treaty's signatories formed an alliance against France, formally declaring war, the War of the Spanish Succession, in May 1702.

METHUEN TREATY 1703
This treaty was both a military and commercial agreement between Portugal and England, the latter represented by its ambassador John Methuen. It established the war aims of a European coalition (known as the Grand Alliance) led by England, the United Provinces, and Austria, which had been founded as the League of Augsburg (1686) in an attempt to halt Louis XIV of France's expansionist policies. Portugal, initially an ally of the French, joined the Grand Alliance in 1703, thus providing a base for the Archduke Charles of Austria to conduct his war for the Spanish throne. It was also agreed that Portugal would purchase English wheat, textiles, and manufactured goods in exchange for preferential duties on olive oil and wine.

TREATY OF ILBERSHEIM 1704
After the disastrous defeat of the Franco-Bavarian army by British and Austrian forces, commanded by the duke of Marlborough, at the Battle of Blenheim, the Franco-Bavarians lost 40,000 men killed, wounded or taken prisoner. This treaty, signed by the electress of Bavaria with Austria, forced Bavaria out of the War of the Spanish Succession and placed its forces under Austrian military rule. The first major defeat suffered by France in over 50 years, Blenheim compelled France to retreat behind the Rhine and saved Vienna from a threatening Franco-Bavarian army, thus preventing the collapse of the Grand Alliance.

TREATY OF WARSAW 1705
This was one of several treaties signed during the Great Northern War, a conflict fought between a Russian-led coalition and Sweden for mastery of the Baltic coastal region. Early in the war, Charles XII of Sweden had campaigned in the Polish-Lithuanian Commonwealth to remove his adversary, Augustus the Strong, elector of Saxony, from Poland's throne and for his candidate, Stanislaus Leszczynski, to be accepted as king instead. Augustus's ally, Peter the Great of Russia, was reluctant to engage Charles in a major battle as a consequence of the decisive defeat his army had suffered at Narva in 1700. When Leszczynski was accepted, and crowned in 1705, Sweden negotiated a peace with Poland. By the terms of the Treaty of Warsaw, neither nation was to sign a peace with Augustus without the other's approval; Poland was to support Sweden in the war against Russia; and Swedish troops were to remain in Poland to guarantee the security of the newly crowned King Stanislaus.

TREATY OF GENOA 1705
When Philip V was recognized as king of Spain in 1701, Catalonia – then effectively an independent nation – fearing that its freedoms and institutions would be threatened under Philip's rule, signed the Treaty of Genoa with England. Now allied with England, Catalonia fought for the Habsburg cause against Bourbon Spain in the War of the Spanish Succession. When England withdrew its support for the Habsburgs and signed the Treaty of Utrecht in 1713, Catalonia fought on alone.

TREATY OF ALTRANSTÄDT 1706
The crowning in 1705 of Stanislaus Leszczynski as king of Poland was opposed by a faction of the Polish Commonwealth who remained loyal to the deposed king, Augustus of Saxony. This faction, formed into the Sandomierz Confederation, was determined to reinstate Augustus. In the civil war that followed (1704–06), Augustus's army was defeated at the Battle of Fraustadt. The peace treaty, concluded at Altranstädt between Charles XII, Augustus, and Poland-Lithuania, forced Augustus to renounce his claims to the Polish throne, ended his alliance with Russia and left Charles in control of Poland.

TREATY OF UNION 1707
Although the crowns of England and Scotland were formally united in 1603 when James VI of Scotland became James I of England, Scotland had retained a separate parliament. Deeper political integration had been a key policy of Queen Anne ever since she acceded to the throne in 1702. Under the aegis of the Queen, English and Scottish commissioners began negotiations in 1706, which culminated in the Treaty of Union. The treaty agreed that the two kingdoms of England and Scotland would be united into one kingdom by the name of Great Britain; Scotland would lose its own parliament but was to be represented in the new parliament of Great Britain.

Scotland accepted the succession of the House of Hanover and gained free trade with England. When the treaty was ratified in May 1707, it was known as the Act of Union.

TREATY OF ALTRANSTÄDT 1707

While Charles XII was concluding the Treaty of Altranstädt in 1706, he negotiated a further treaty with the Habsburg emperor, Joseph I. The emperor signed the convention to prevent Charles from entering the War of the Spanish Succession as an ally of France. He also agreed to protect the rights of Protestants in Silesia.

TREATY OF THORN 1709

With the decisive defeat of Swedish forces by Russia at the Battle of Poltava in June 1709, Peter the Great had gained the upper hand in the Great Northern War. Sweden's main army was destroyed and the wounded Charles XII fled into Ottoman territory. Augustus the Strong, who had been forced to renounce the throne of Poland in favour of Charles's candidate, Stanislaus Leszczynski, was restored as king of the Polish-Lithuanian Commonwealth. The territory reconquered by Augustus included the Polish city of Thorn (in present-day Ukraine), where he and Peter met to sign the treaty in October. In a secret article, it was agreed that Swedish Livonia was to be partitioned, with Augustus gaining the southern part and Peter gaining the northern part (Estonia).

TREATY OF COPENHAGEN 1709

In 1699 Frederick IV of Denmark-Norway had joined Russia and Poland in a pact of aggression against Sweden. Denmark's goal was to reclaim territories, especially Scania, which had been lost to Sweden in 1658. But when Denmark's attempt to remove Swedish troops from the duchy of Holstein-Gottorp was repulsed, and the safety of Copenhagen threatened, Denmark had withdrawn from the Great Northern War in 1700. However, following Sweden's decisive defeat at Poltava, Denmark-Norway re-entered the war, renewing its alliance with Russia in the Treaty of Copenhagen. Under the treaty's terms, Denmark was to conduct an offensive war against Sweden and help to reinstate Augustus as king of Poland.

CAPITULATION OF ESTONIA AND LIVONIA 1710

Peter the Great of Russia followed up the advantage he had gained over Sweden at Poltava by continuing his campaigns in the Baltics. In 1710 his forces captured Riga – at the time the most populated city in the Swedish realm – Tallinn and Pernau, thus evicting the Swedes from the Baltic provinces. With the capitulation of Estonia and Livonia, Peter integrated them into the Russian Empire and confirmed their local laws and privileges, especially with regard to the Protestant faith.

TREATY OF HANOVER 1710

Concluded during the Great Northern War, this treaty allied the Russian Empire with Brunswick-Lüneburg (Hanover). Though Hanover was not among the most prominent states of the Holy Roman Empire, the alliance was important since the Hanoverian duke, with whom the alliance was concluded, would later become King George I of Great Britain.

TREATY OF SZATMÁR 1711

The Treaty of Karlowitz (1699) resulted in the transfer of most of Ottoman Hungary to the Habsburgs. But the harsh rule of the Austrians provoked rebellion from the Hungarian peasants and nobility. Led by Ferenc Rákóczi, the uprising spread throughout Upper Hungary. After eight years of indecisive and fruitless fighting against the Habsburg armies, a peace was concluded at Szatmár (present-day Satu Mare, Romania). The treaty provided for the cessation of hostilities and for a general amnesty, and it continued in general terms the rights and liberties of Hungary (including Croatia) and of Transylvania.

TREATY OF PRUTH 1711

Following Sweden's defeat by Russia at Poltava in 1709, Charles XII of Sweden fled into Ottoman territory. Repeated demands by Peter the Great of Russia for Charles's eviction were refused by the Turks, prompting Peter, with Moldavia as an ally, to invade Ottoman territory. When the Russian army was surrounded and trapped by the Turks, Peter negotiated this treaty on the banks of the River Pruth. The treaty dictated that Russia would give up the fortresses of Azov and Tagonrog and dismantle both its forts on the lower Dnieper and its Black Sea fleet. In addition, Russian troops were to leave Poland and Charles would be permitted to return to Sweden without Russian interference. In return, the defeated Russian army was allowed to retreat unhindered to Russian territory. Satisfied with the treaty's terms, the Turks withdrew, bringing to an end the Russo-Turkish War of 1710–11. The treaty nullified the military gains Peter had accrued against the Ottomans throughout his reign.

TREATY OF PORTSMOUTH 1713

The land between British territory in North America (coastal Massachusetts, New Hampshire,

Treaties of Utrecht 1713–14

The "Glorious Revolution" of 1689 brought the Dutch prince William of Orange to the British throne. William had been instrumental in the formation of the League of Augsburg, designed to protect the enfeebled Holy Roman Empire from French aggrandizement. He promptly enrolled Britain in the League, thereby upgrading it to the Grand Alliance, whose nine-year war gained the better of France without achieving decisive victory. An uneasy peace prevailed at the turn of the century, before a dispute over the Spanish Succession between rival claimants proposed by Louis XIV and Emperor Leopold I reignited the conflict. The childless Spanish king, Charles II, had signed successive treaties of Partition in 1698–99, each dividing his empire between French and Habsburg nominees. He then recanted, awarding his entire inheritance to the grandson of Louis XIV. The Grand Alliance was swiftly resurrected, and its armies achieved a series of decisive victories in the Low Countries and Italy, driving the French back to their own soil. However, Louis's grandson Philip V kept a stubborn grip on Spain, and when the Alliance's nominee, Archduke Charles of Austria, became Holy Roman Emperor, Britain and the Dutch decided his additional acquisition of Spain would be worse for the balance of power than the status quo and the Grand Alliance collapsed.

In 1713 at Utrecht Britain secured the all-important renunciation by Philip V of any claim to the French throne, averting any union with Spain. Britain also obtained cessions in North America and the Caribbean, together with Gibraltar and Minorca. Savoy received Sicily and a portion of the duchy of Milan. Austria and the Holy Roman Empire reached terms with France the following year, respectively at Rastatt and Baden. Austria collected the Spanish Netherlands, the Kingdom of Naples and Sardinia, while the Holy Roman Emperor's querulous demand to retain the empty title of king of Spain was humored. The Dutch gained only the confirmation of the line of defensive fortifications on their French border in the Barrier Treaty (1715).

In terms of the European balance of power, the treaties of Utrecht saw Habsburg Austria at its zenith, crowning its defeat of the Ottomans (1683–99). Equally important was the rise of Britain. The Dutch, heretofore their main maritime rival, were crippled by the costs of the war, leaving Britain Europe's foremost naval and commercial power. Ironically, Emperor Charles also failed to produce a male heir and his Pragmatic Sanction (1713), to obtain recognition for the succession of his daughter Maria Theresa, would be touted round Europe with increasing desperation: its flouting would lead to a series of European conflicts from 1740.

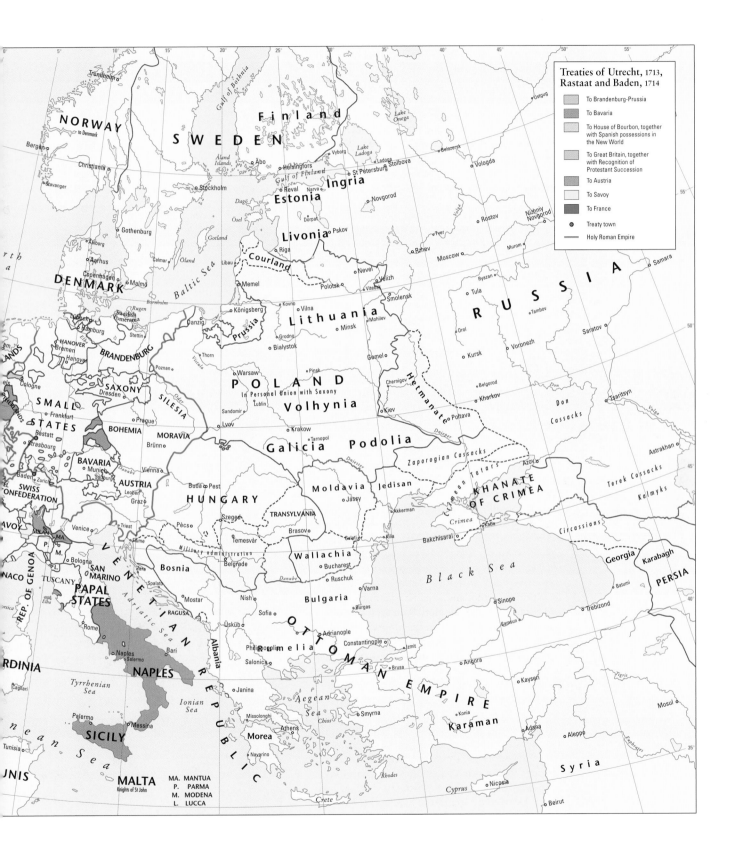

Treaties of Utrecht, 1713, Rastaat and Baden, 1714

- To Brandenburg-Prussia
- To Bavaria
- To House of Bourbon, together with Spanish possessions in the New World
- To Great Britain, together with Recognition of Protestant Succession
- To Austria
- To Savoy
- To France
- ● Treaty town
- — Holy Roman Empire

NORWAY
to Denmark
Trondheim
Bergen
Stavanger
Christiania

SWEDEN
Finland
Gulf of Bothnia
Åbo
Åland Islands
Helsingfors
Stockholm
Gothenburg
Calmar
Öland
Gotland
Aalborg
Bornholm

DENMARK
Aarhus
Copenhagen
Malmö

Baltic Sea

Gulf of Finland
Reval
Narva
St Petersburg
Stolbova
Estonia
Ingria
Dagö
Dorpat
Ösel
Pskov
Livonia
Riga
Libau
Courland
Memel

Lake Ladoga
Ladoga
Vyborg
Lake Onega
Belozersk
Vologda
Ustjug

RUSSIA
Novgorod
Tver
Rzhev
Moscow
Murom
Nizhniy Novgorod
Rostov
Samara
Saratov
Volga

Swedish Pomerania
Rügen
Lübeck
Hamburg
Stralsund
Stettin
HANOVER
Bremen
Hanover
BRANDENBURG
Poznan
Königsberg
Danzig
Prussia
Thorn
Vistula
Warsaw

LITHUANIA
Kovno
Vilna
Grodno
Bialystok
Minsk
Polotsk
Nevel
Velizh
Vitebsk
Mohilev
Smolensk
Tula
Orol
Tambov
Ryazan

SAXONY
Dresden
SILESIA
Oder
POLAND
In Personal Union with Saxony
Pinsk
Gomel
Kursk
Voronezh
Belgorod
Don

SMALL STATES
Frankfurt
Cologne
Restatt
Strasbourg
Prague
Brünn
MORAVIA
Lublin
Sandomir
Volhynia
Chernigov
Hetmanate
Kiev
Pottava
Kharkov
Tsaritsyn
Astrakhan

NETHERLANDS
BOHEMIA
BAVARIA
Munich
Salzburg
Danube
Leoben
AUSTRIA
Vienna
Buda Pest
Lvov
Tarnopol
Krakow
GALICIA
PODOLIA
Dniester
Zaporogian Cassacks
Don Cassacks
Terek Cassacks
Kalmyks

SWISS CONFEDERATION
Baden
Zurich
Graz
HUNGARY
Szeged
Temesvàr
TRANSYLVANIA
Brasov
Moldavia
Jassy
Jedisan
Akkerman
Crimean Tatars
KHANATE OF CRIMEA
Azov
Circassians
Georgia
Karabagh

SAVOY
MILAN
MA.
P.
M.
Venice
Triest
Fiume
Military administration
Belgrade
Pècs
Galati
Kilia
Bakchisarai
Kaffa
Crimea
PERSIA

REP. OF GENOA
TUSCANY
Bologna
SAN MARINO
Zara
Spalato
VENETIAN REPUBLIC
Bosnia
Mostar
RAGUSA
Nish
Wallachia
Bucharest
Ruschuk
Danube
Varna
Black Sea
Sinope
Batumi
Trebizond
Karaman

MONACO
PAPAL STATES
Rome
Elba
Adriatic Sea
Albania
Bulgaria
Sofia
Üsküb
Burgas
Angora
Brusa
Kayseri

Corsica
SARDINIA
Cagliari
Naples
Salerno
Bari
NAPLES
Tyrrhenian Sea
Ionian Sea
Janina
OTTOMAN EMPIRE
Adrianople
Philippopoli
Rumelia
Constantinople
Izmit
Salonica
Mosul
Aegean Sea
Chios
Smyrna
Konia
Adana
Aleppo
Tigris

Palermo
Messina
SICILY
Missolonghi
Athens
Navarino
Morea
Crete
Rhodes
Cyprus
Nicosia
Syria
Beirut
Euphrates

TUNIS
Tunisia
MALTA
Knights of St John
MA. MANTUA
P. PARMA
M. MODENA
L. LUCCA

1713–1721

Maine and Acadia, renamed Nova Scotia) and the French-controlled St Lawrence River valley around Quebec was Wabanaki territory and both France and England agreed to respect the other's "First Nations" allies. But when the Wabanaki realized they could no longer depend on the French for protection, they proposed a peace conference, which took place at Portsmouth, New Hampshire. The treaty agreed that the British would respect the Wabanaki's hunting rights and limited British settlements to the west of the Kennebec River. Both sides accepted the treaty as a symbol of friendship. The British, however, failed to fulfil their obligations under the treaty by encroaching on Wabanaki land. The Wabanaki responded by resuming raids on the British settlements.

TREATY OF SCHWEDT 1713
This treaty was concluded between Brandenburg-Prussia and Russia during the Great Northern War with the intention of forming a new anti-Swedish alliance. Brandenburg-Prussia was promised southern Swedish Pomerania up to the Peene River, which had just been conquered by Russia. In turn, Brandenburg-Prussia accepted Russia's annexation of Swedish Ingria, Estonia, and Karelia and agreed to pay a sum of money to Russia.

TREATY OF RASTATT 1714
The Treaty of Rastatt ended hostilities between France and Austria. By the terms of the treaty, Austria received from Spain the Spanish territories in Italy: Naples, Milan, Sardinia, and the southern Netherlands. Austria received from France Freiburg and several small areas on its eastern borders. The Habsburg Empire had now reached its greatest territorial extent and had become a major European power. However, Emperor Charles VI was outraged at the loss of Spain and considered the treaty an unacceptable failure. The Utrecht and Rastatt Treaties confirmed the throne of Spain for the House of Bourbon, but also denied France the additional territorial gains it had sought, and affirmed that the thrones of France and Spain could not be united.

TREATY OF BADEN 1714
Complementing the Treaties of Utrecht and of Rastatt, the Treaty of Baden agreed the terms of peace between France and the Holy Roman Empire, ending the many conflicts within the War of the Spanish Succession. The treaty allowed France to retain Alsace and Landau, but returned the east bank of the River Rhine (the Breisgau) to Austria. France's allies, the electors of Bavaria and Cologne, were allowed to recover their possessions. Emperor Charles VI of Austria renounced his claims to the

Spanish throne but did not actually make peace with Spain and did not recognize the Bourbon Philip V as king of Spain. A technical state of war with Spain existed until 1720.

TREATY OF STETTIN 1715
The treaty was concluded between Hanover and Brandenburg-Prussia during the Great Northern War. Signed in the Prussian camp at Stettin (now Szczecin, Poland), the treaty allied George I of Great Britain as elector of Hanover with the kingdom of Prussia against the Swedish Empire.

TREATY OF BERLIN 1715
Concluded during the Great Northern War, this treaty allied George I of Great Britain with Denmark-Norway in exchange for the cession of the Swedish dominion Bremen-Verden – then occupied by Denmark – to Hanover. Denmark and Hanover joined the Russo-Prussian coalition established by the Treaty of Schwedt in 1713.

SECOND TRIPLE ALLIANCE 1717
The First Triple Alliance (1668), formed by the Dutch, Swedish, and British, had curbed the growing power of Louis XIV's France. Soon after Louis's death in 1715, France's regent, the duke of Orléans, sought a *rapprochement* with Britain to check the ambitions of Philip V of Spain to retake territories in Italy and to claim the French throne. Together they reached an understanding to guarantee the Protestant succession in France and Britain, and to expel James Edward Stuart, the "Old Pretender" from French soil. By the accession of the Dutch Republic in 1717, the alliance was converted into a Triple Alliance. When Austria joined it in 1718, it became a Quadruple Alliance.

TREATY OF PASSAROWITZ 1718
In 1715 the Ottomans had forced Venice to surrender the Peloponnese, the major Venetian gain under the Treaty of Karlowitz (1699), and had threatened Venetian possessions in Dalmatia and the Ionian Islands. Austria intervened by concluding an alliance with Venice. In the ensuing hostilities, the Ottomans suffered a series of disastrous defeats by the Austrians. In 1718, at the initiation of Britain and the Dutch Republic, whose eastern Mediterranean trade was disrupted by the war, a treaty was concluded at Passarowitz. The treaty, signed between the Ottoman Empire on one side and the Habsburg monarchy of Austria and the Republic of Venice on the other, brought to an end the Austro-Turkish and Venetian-Turkish wars of 1716–18 and provided for a 24-year peace between the Ottomans and Austria. The Ottomans lost substantial territories

in the Balkans to Austria, thus marking the end of their further expansion westward. The treaty stipulated that Venice would surrender the Morea to the Ottomans while retaining the Ionian Islands and making gains in Dalmatia.

TREATY OF BADEN 1718

The Toggenburg War (also known as the Second War of Villmergen) was a Swiss civil war during the Old Swiss Confederacy – a loose confederation of small, independent states (cantons) formed during the 14th century – that took place during 1712. On the one hand there were the Catholic "inner cantons" and the Imperial Abbey of Saint Gall; on the other the Protestant cantons of Bern and Zurich, as well as the abbatial subjects of Toggenburg. The conflict was simultaneously a religious war, a war for the hegemony within the Swiss Confederacy, and an uprising of subjects. The war ended in a Protestant victory and toppled the balance of political power within the Confederacy. Despite the cessation of hostilities in 1712, the refusal of Saint Gall to seek a compromise delayed the signing of the treaty for a further six years.

TREATY OF DEN HAAG 1720

The Treaty of Utrecht, which had ended the War of the Spanish Succession, had divided the Spanish inheritance between Austria and Spain in order to create a balance of power in Europe. But both Austria and Spain objected to some of the treaty's terms. As a result, Spain seized control of Sardinia and Sicily, which the treaty had assigned to Austria and Savoy respectively. With the backing of the Quadruple Alliance (Savoy later joined as the fifth ally), the British fleet brought Austrian troops to Sicily, and the French sent troops to occupy northern Spain. The War of the Quadruple Alliance (1718–20) was concluded with the Treaty of Den Haag, signed between Philip V of Spain and the allies. By its terms, Spain was forced to renounce its claims in Italy and Victor II, duke of Savoy, ceded Sicily to Austria in exchange for Sardinia. Austria assured Philip V that the duchy of Parma would be ceded by his son, Charles, upon the extinction of the Farnese line. Uniquely in the 18th century, this was a war when Britain and France were on the same side.

TREATY OF FREDERIKSBORG 1720

This treaty, concluded between Sweden and Denmark-Norway, renewed four previous treaties signed during the 17th century, the last of which had obliged Denmark to return its conquests and Holstein-Gottorp to Sweden. The Treaty of Frederiksborg ended the Great Northern War between Sweden and Denmark-Norway.

TREATIES OF STOCKHOLM 1719/1720

The death of Charles XII in 1718 at the Siege of Frederikshald during Sweden's invasion of southern Norway heralded the conclusion of the Great Northern War. His successor, Ulrica Leonora and her husband Frederick I of Sweden, began peace negotiations with all Sweden's enemies. By the terms of the two Treaties of Stockholm, Sweden, Saxony, and Poland returned to the status quo before the start of the war in 1700. Denmark gave back its conquests to Sweden in return for a substantial sum of money. Sweden ceded the parts east of the Oder River that had been won in 1648. They also ceded western Pomerania south of the Peene River, and the islands of Wolin and Usedom, to Brandenburg-Prussia.

TREATY OF NYSTAD 1721

This treaty, concluded between Russia and Sweden, was the last peace treaty of the Great Northern War. Under its terms, Sweden formally recognized the transfer of Estonia, Livonia, Ingria, and southeast Finland to Russia in exchange for a large sum of money, while Russia returned the bulk of Finland to Swedish rule. The treaty also enshrined the rights of the German Baltic nobility within Estonia and Livonia to maintain their financial system, their existing customs border, their self-government, Lutheran religion, and the German language. The lasting result of the war was a decisive shift in the European balance of power: the Swedish imperial era had ended while Russia had emerged as a new and powerful empire.

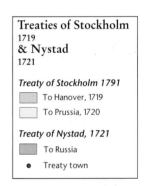

Treaties of Stockholm
1719
& Nystad
1721

Treaty of Stockholm 1791

☐ To Hanover, 1719

☐ To Prussia, 1720

Treaty of Nystad, 1721

☐ To Russia

● Treaty town

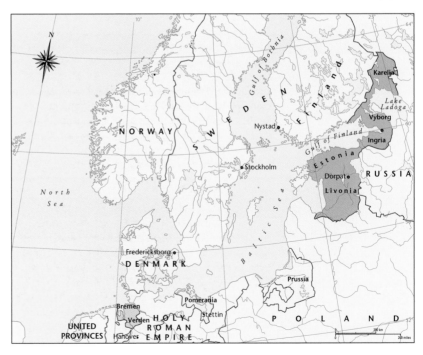

1725–1739

TREATY OF VIENNA 1725

The Pragmatic Sanction was an edict issued by Charles in 1713 to ensure that the Habsburg hereditary possessions could be inherited by a daughter, and it was guaranteed by this treaty, signed between Emperor Charles VI of Austria and Philip V of Spain. The Austrians relinquished all claims to the Spanish throne and vowed to aid Spain in recapturing Gibraltar from the British, who had held it since 1704. The British also exerted diplomatic pressure on Austria to wind up the Ostend Company (a chartered trading company in the Austrian Netherlands) as they feared its effects on their own trade with the East and West Indies.

TREATY OF HANOVER 1725

When Philip V of Spain allied himself with Habsburg Austria after his daughter's engagement to Louis V of France was broken off, George I of Britain grew concerned that Spain would try to recapture Gibraltar. He therefore concluded an accord with France and Prussia against Spain.

TREATY OF KYAKHTA 1727

In 1689 Russia and China had signed the Treaty of Nerchinsk which was designed to check the eastward expansion of Russia into Manchuria, and to regulate the borders between the two countries. The Treaty of Kyakhta confirmed and expanded this treaty, and opened up markets for trade.

TREATY OF SEVILLE 1729

Spain's half-hearted siege, with Habsburg support, of British-held Gibraltar, which began in 1727, was ended with this treaty, which restored Britain's commercial standing. Britain agreed to support Spanish claims to the duchy of Parma. The treaty opened the way for a British alliance with Austria.

TREATY OF VIENNA 1731

In 1717 Britain, France, and the Dutch Republic had signed the Second Triple Alliance with the aim of limiting the ambitions of Spain. In 1731, however, Britain jettisoned the alliance in favour of one with Austria. Britain guaranteed Maria Theresa's succession to the Habsburg dominions under the Pragmatic Sanction, a guarantee previously given by Austria and Spain in the 1725 Treaty of Vienna. Austria also confirmed the commitment it had made to wind up the Ostend Company.

LÖWENWOLDE'S TREATY 1733

In 1732 a secret treaty was signed by Austria, Russia, and Prussia to signal to their common neighbour, the Polish-Lithuanian Commonwealth, their joint policy with regard to the succession to the Polish throne. Following the death of the Polish king, Augustus II, in 1733, Austria and Russia distanced themselves from the treaty and instead signed the Löwenwolde's Treaty with the new elector, Frederick Augustus II of Saxony. In exchange for Russian support, he agreed to give up any remaining Polish claims to Livonia, and promised Empress Anna of Russia to accept her choice of successor to the duchy of Courland. To the Austrian emperor he promised recognition of the Pragmatic Sanction of 1713. Prussia continued to oppose the election of Frederick Augustus, while Austria and Russia refused to recognize Stanisław Leszczynski – who was backed by his son-in-law Louis V of France – if he were to be elected. The interference of these foreign powers in the Polish election led to the War of the Polish Succession (1733–38).

TREATY OF RASHT 1732

Under the terms of this treaty, signed between Russia and the Safavid Empire, Russia waived its claim to any territory south of the Kura River. This included return of the provinces of Giland, Mazandaran, and Astrabad, conquered by Peter the Great of Russia in the early 1720s. The Persian cities of Derbent, Tarki and Ganja, north of the Kura River, would be returned three years later. In return, the Persians, now de facto ruled by the militarily successful Nader Shah, granted trade privileges to the Russian merchants and promised to restore the Georgian king, Vakhtang VI, then residing in exile in Russia, to the throne of Kartli as soon as the Ottoman troops could be expelled from that country. The treaty's provisions were confirmed by the 1735 Treaty of Ganja which stipulated that all the regions north of the Kura River were to be returned as well.

TREATY OF TURIN 1733

This treaty was a secret agreement between Louis XV of France and Charles Emmanuel III, king of Sardinia (primarily in his role of Duke of Savoy). Charles was promised French military support for the conquest of the duchy of Milan in exchange for allowing French troops to use his territory in the conquest of Tuscany, the two Sicilies, and other territories. The treaty paved the way for French military activity on the Italian peninsula in the War of the Polish Succession in which Louis backed the claim of his father-in-law Stanisław Leszczynski, to the Polish throne.

TREATY OF ESCORIAL 1733

Louis XV concluded this secret treaty with his uncle, Philip V of Spain, which cemented their joint support for Stanisław Leszczynski to be crowned as the Polish king in the War of the Polish Succession. This alliance became known as the Family Compact. Philip planned to use the war to win back lost territory in Italy for his sons by his second marriage to Elizabeth Farnese: Mantua for the elder son, Don Carlos, and the kingdoms of Naples and Sicily for the younger son, Don Felipe.

TREATY OF CONSTANTINOPLE 1736

This treaty was preceded by the Treaty of Ahmet Pasha, signed between the Ottoman Empire and Safavid Persia in 1732 to end seven years of hostilities over their national boundaries. But the terms of the treaty had not satisfied either party: Ottoman Sultan Mahmut disapproved of the abandonment of Tabriz, while Nader, the future shah of Persia, dethroned Tahmasp II for accepting Ottoman control of the Caucasus. In the ensuing war, Nader forced the Ottomans to abandon both Tblisi and Yerevan. When the Russians threatened to attack Crimea and Ukraine, the Ottomans were forced to sign the Treaty of Constantinople by which they recognized Nader as the shah of Persia, conceded the Caucasus

to Persia, and agreed to allow Iranian *hajis* (pilgrims) to go to Mecca, then under Ottoman control.

TREATY OF EL PARDO 1739

For several decades, the Spanish had been trying to enforce a ban on foreign ships trading with their colonies in the West Indies and South America. The Treaty of Utrecht (1713) gave Britain a 30-year *asiento*, or contract, to supply slaves to these colonies. But the Spanish became suspicious that British traders were abusing the *asiento* and began to board ships and confiscate their cargoes. The claim by one of the ship's captains, Robert Jenkins, that one of his ears had been cut off by Spanish coastguards, fostered longstanding Anglo-Spanish antagonism over the issue. The Treaty (or Convention) of El Pardo provided compensation for vessels lost by Britain, but avoided the crucial issue: Spain's continued determination to suppress all smuggling attempts. Amidst growing indignation, Britain finally declared war in 1739. Known as the War of Jenkins' Ear, the war later became subsumed into the wider War of the Austrian Succession.

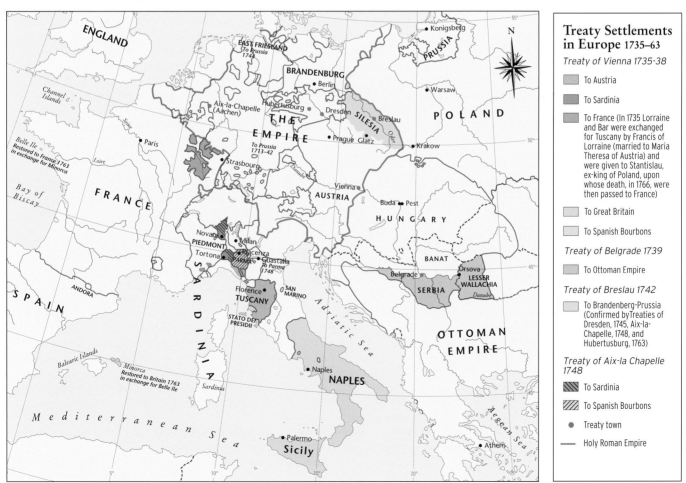

Treaty Settlements in Europe 1735–63

Treaty of Vienna 1735-38

- To Austria
- To Sardinia
- To France (In 1735 Lorraine and Bar were exchanged for Tuscany by Francis of Lorraine (married to Maria Theresa of Austria) and were given to Stanislau, ex-king of Poland, upon whose death, in 1766, were then passed to France)
- To Great Britain
- To Spanish Bourbons

Treaty of Belgrade 1739

- To Ottoman Empire

Treaty of Breslau 1742

- To Brandenberg-Prussia (Confirmed byTreaties of Dresden, 1745, Aix-la-Chapelle, 1748, and Hubertusburg, 1763)

Treaty of Aix-la Chapelle 1748

- To Sardinia
- To Spanish Bourbons
- Treaty town
- Holy Roman Empire

1739–1745

TREATY OF BELGRADE 1739

Austria's entry into the Russo-Turkish War as an ally of Russia ended in failure. Following several defeats, including the loss of Belgrade, Austria was forced to make a separate peace with the Ottomans. Under the terms of the treaty, Austria ceded northern Serbia, including Belgrade and Little Wallachia (in southern Romania) to the Ottomans, thus renouncing the strong position in the Balkans that it had obtained under the Treaty of Passarowitz (1718). In return, the Turks acknowledged the Habsburg Emperor as the official protector of all Ottoman Christian subjects, a position also claimed by Russia. The Treaty of Belgrade effectively ended the kingdom of Serbia, which had existed since 1718.

TREATY OF NIŠ 1739

This peace treaty concluded the Russo-Turkish War of 1735–39. Disputes arising from ill-defined frontiers between Russian-ruled Ukraine and the Ottoman-dominated Crimean Tatars had provided the pretext for Russia's continuing struggle for access to the Black Sea. On the eve of the war the Russians had made peace with Persia, returning all the remaining territory conquered during the Russo-Persian War (1722–23). In 1737, Austria entered the war as Russia's ally but, following several military failures, was forced to withdraw. With Austria's defection, the Russians had to make a disappointing peace with the Ottomans. Under the terms of the Treaty of Niš, Russia gave up its claim to the Crimea and Moldavia but was allowed to build a port at Azov, though without fortifications and without the right to maintain a fleet in the Black Sea.

TREATY OF FRIENDSHIP AND ALLIANCE 1740

This treaty was signed between the British and King Edward I of the Miskito Nation, a Native American ethnic group in Central America, of primarily African-Native American ancestry. English privateers made informal alliances with the Miskito and began to crown Miskito leaders as kings; their territory was called the Mosquito kingdom. In the late 17th and early 18th centuries, the Miskito began a series of raids, reaching as far north as the Yucatan, and as far south as Costa Rica, attacking Spanish-held territories and the still independent indigenous groups in the area. They sold many of their captives as slaves to English merchants. Based on the terms of the treaty, King Edward relinquished his kingdom to King George II in return for British military protection, and agreed to adopt English laws throughout his territories.

TREATY OF BRESLAU 1742

This preliminary peace agreement, negotiated between Archduchess Maria Theresa of Austria and King Frederick II of Prussia (later called 'the Great'), would lead to the conclusion of the First Silesian War (1740–42). The cause of the war was Frederick's violation of the Pragmatic Sanction (1713) by his invasion of the Habsburg province of Silesia. This invasion threatened not only to conquer the wealthiest of the Habsburg lands but also to challenge Maria Theresa's right to rule the remainder. Maria Theresa responded by sending an army to meet Frederick's forces, but it was defeated at the Battle of Mollwitz (1741). This defeat prompted the formation of an alliance of France, Bavaria, and Spain – joined later by Saxony – with the aim of dismembering the Habsburg monarchy. Faced by this threat, Maria Theresa made peace with Frederick. Under the treaty's terms, Austria ceded most of the Silesian duchies to Prussia, except for the duchy of Troppau and Krnov and the southern part of the duchy of Nysa, which would become the province of Austrian Silesia. In addition, Frederick annexed the Bohemian county of Kladsko.

TREATY OF BERLIN 1742

Signed in July 1742 by Maria Theresa of Austria and Frederick the Great of Prussia, this was the formal peace treaty that confirmed the Treaty of Breslau,

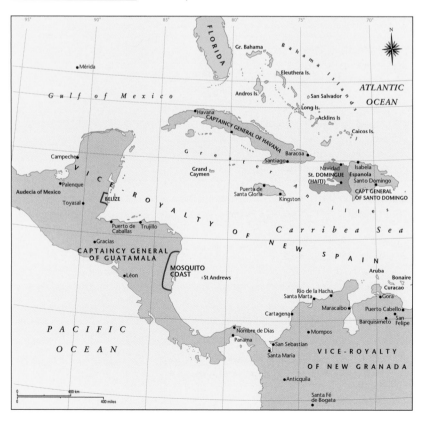

Treaty of Friendship and Alliance 1740

- Spanish possessions
- British possessions
- Portuguese possessions
- Dutch possessions
- French possessions

signed a month earlier, that had ended the First Silesian War. Peace was short-lived as both sides prepared for the Second Silesian War (1744–45), precipitated by Frederick marching against Prague in Bohemia. The two Silesian Wars formed part of the War of the Austrian Succession (1740–48).

CONVENTION OF TURIN 1742

Signed between Austria and Sardinia, this treaty created a military alliance between the two countries, directed principally against Spain. Following the outbreak of the War of the Austrian Succession, and the attack by a coalition of states, including France, Prussia, Bavaria, and Saxony, the Italian territories of Austria and Sardinia began to look vulnerable. Spain's ambitions in the area were driven by the Spanish queen, Elizabeth Farnese, who wanted to secure Italian kingdoms for her sons. Sardinia was also threatened by a large Spanish force that had crossed the Mediterranean and was poised for offensive operations in Italy. Sardinia responded by negotiating agreements with both the British and the Austrians. They initially requested specific Austrian territories in payment for their cooperation, but later settled for vaguer promises for new territory in Lombardy.

TREATY OF ÅBO 1743

In 1741 Sweden declared war on Russia in an attempt to regain some of the territories it had lost in the Treaty of Nystad (1721), which had concluded the Great Northern War. But the Swedish forces that invaded eastern Karelia were quickly defeated. By the end of the Russo-Swedish War (1741–43), the Russian army had occupied most of Finland. Russia, taking advantage of a succession crisis in Sweden, offered to return most of Finland if Sweden would accept the Russian-supported candidate, Adolf Frederick of Holstein-Gottorp as heir apparent to the Swedish throne. The Swedes agreed, and signed the Treaty of Åbo with Russia. By the terms of the treaty, Sweden ceded to Russia the areas east of the Kymi River with the fortress of Olavinlinna and the cities of Lappeenranta and Hamina. Thus the Swedish border was moved further north, which reduced the danger of a Swedish attack on the Russian capital, Saint Petersburg.

TREATY OF WORMS 1743

The British sought to split the Holy Roman Emperor, Charles VII, from French influence and this treaty was a political alliance formed between Britain, Austria, and Sardinia. It was also an attempt to resolve the differences between Charles VII, Maria Theresa of Austria, and Charles Emmanuel III of Sardinia. Under the terms of the treaty, Maria

Theresa agreed to transfer to Sardinia the city, and part of the duchy, of Piacenza, part of the duchy of Pavia, the County of Anghiera, and claims to the marquisate of Finale. She also engaged to maintain 30,000 men in Italy, to be commanded by Savoy-Sardinia. Britain agreed to pay the sum of £300,000 for the ceding of Finale, and to furnish an annual subsidy to Savoy-Sardinia. Additionally, Britain agreed to send a fleet into the Mediterranean, and to pay Maria Theresa an annual subsidy of £300,000 for as long as she needed it.

TREATY (or PEACE) OF FÜSSEN 1745

After the conquest of Prague by Bavarian and French troops in 1741, Elector Charles Albert of Bavaria, supported by France and Prussia, declared himself king of Bohemia and was crowned Emperor Charles VII in January 1742. On the day of his coronation, Austrian troops occupied Bavaria and Hungarian hussars plundered Munich. The Bavarians were forced to evacuate Bohemia, which they had only just occupied. With French assistance, Charles fought Austria for three years, but without success. When Charles died in January 1745, his son and successor Elector Maximillian III Joseph of Bavaria signed the Treaty of Füssen with Austria by which he abandoned his father's claim on Bohemia and recognized the Pragmatic Sanction. The treaty ended Bavaria's participation in the War of the Austrian Succession.

TREATY OF DRESDEN 1745

The First Silesian War (1740–42) had been concluded with the Treaty of Berlin (1742), signed between Maria Theresa of Austria and Frederick the Great of Prussia. The Second Silesian War (1744–45) was caused by Austria's attempt to regain control of Silesia. The war, climaxed by a series of Prussian victories won against Austria and its ally Saxony, again confirmed Frederick's conquest of Silesia. Austria and Saxony were obliged to sign the Treaty of Dresden with Prussia, in which Maria Theresa recognized Frederick's sovereignty over Silesia and the duchy of Glatz in return for his agreement to support the election of her consort, Francis Stephen of Lorraine, as Holy Roman Emperor. In return, he maintained control over Silesia. Saxony had to pay Prussia a large sum of money in reparations.

TREATY OF FONTAINEBLEAU 1745

The Treaty of Fontainebleau was signed between Louis XV of France and the Pretender to the thrones of Great Britain and Ireland, Charles Edward Stuart. Based on the terms of the accord, both signatories agreed to establish a military alliance against George II of Great Britain. Louis also recognized

1746–1762

Charles Edward as king of Scotland and promised to recognize him as king of England as soon as this could be shown to be the wish of the nation.

TREATY OF KERDEN 1746

The Ottoman-Persian War (1743–46) had been precipitated by the ambitions of Nader, founder of the Afsharid dynasty and Shah of Persia, to found an empire that stretched from the Indus to the Bosphorus. With an army of 200,000, which consisted largely of rebellious Central Asian tribesmen, he captured Kirkuk and Arbil from the Ottomans but failed to take Mosul and was forced to retreat. However, Nader Shah's operations in

Ottoman lands were mostly fruitless and he decided to make peace. Under the terms of the Treaty of Kerden, signed between the Ottoman Empire and Afsharid Persia, the boundary between the two countries remained the one agreed by the Treaty of Zuhab (1639); the Ottomans agreed to legitimize the Afsharid dynasty as the rulers of Persia. Nader Shah abandoned his attempt to force the Ottomans to accept Shia as the fifth legal sect of Islam.

TREATY OF AIX-LA-CHAPELLE 1748

The treaty that ended the War of the Austrian Succession was signed at the Free Imperial City of Aachen (Aix-la-Chapelle). It was drawn up by Great Britain and France and Maria Theresa of Austria reluctantly agreed to its terms. Austria recognized Frederick II of Prussia's conquest of Silesia. France withdrew from the Austrian Netherlands, but gained some of its overseas colonies. Maria Theresa ceded the duchy of Parma, Piacenza and Guastalla to Spain. Austria's conquests, the duchy of Modena and republic of Genoa, were restored. The *asiento* slave contract, agreed by the Treaty of Utrecht, was renewed. A temporary truce in the Anglo-French conflict in North America and India was agreed. In general, the treaty reverted to the pre-war situation, restoring territory to its original owners, but left many conflicts unresolved; these would flare up again in the Seven Years' War (1756–63).

TREATY OF MADRID 1750

This treaty, signed by Spain and Portugal, ended armed conflict over the boundaries between their two South American empires. Spain wanted to halt the westward advance of the Portuguese, who had already encroached on much of what was theoretically Spanish territory, while Portugal aimed to secure the greater part of the Amazon basin. The terms of the treaty were based on the principles of *Uti possidetis, ita possideatis* from Roman law ("who owns by fact owns by right") and on the natural boundaries created by mountains and rivers. Thus Portugal retained the Spanish lands they had occupied. The treaty stipulated that Spain would receive the Sacramento Colony, and would cede to Portugal the territory of the seven Jesuit missions on the upper Uruguay River. But the Guarani inhabitants of the missions refused to be forcibly relocated, and Spanish and Portuguese armies joined forces to drive them out in the Guarani War (1754–56). The treaty was significant because it substantially defined the modern boundaries of Brazil. In the face of Spanish objections to the *asiento* contract, granted to Britain in the Treaty of Utrecht, the Treaty of Madrid also required Britain to surrender its claims in return for a sum of £100,000.

Treaty of Madrid
1750

Spanish lands
Portuguese lands
British lands
Dutch lands
French lands
Jesuit Mission States

TREATY OF ARANJUEZ 1752

Austria, Spain, and Sardinia ratified the terms of the Treaty of Aix-la-Chapelle (1748 and all the signatories agreed to acknowledge each of their respective interests in Italy.

TREATY OF GIYANTI 1755

From 1619, when the Dutch East India Company (VOC) established a capital in Jakarta, they had become unwillingly caught up in the struggles for power between rival Javanese rulers, which led to three wars of succession during the 18th century. The Third Javanese War of Succession (1746–55) saw two of the rulers, Prince Mangkubumi and Mas Said, contest the throne of Mataram's King Pakubuwono II. The war dragged on until 1755, when the Treaty of Giyanti was ratified. Based on the terms of the agreement, signed between Mangkubumi, the VOC, and Pakubuwono III, the eastern half of the Sultanate of Mataram in central Java was given to Pakubuwono III with Surakarta as its capital, while the western half was given to Prince Mangkubumi with its capital in Yogyakarta. After the signing of the treaty Mangkubumi took the title of sultan and the name Hamengkubuwono. The VOC's policy of divide and rule brought a measure of peace to Java thereafter.

TREATY OF WESTMINSTER (CONVENTION OF WESTMINSTER) 1756

British fears of French attacks on Hanover instigated this treaty of neutrality, signed between Frederick the Great of Prussia and George II of Great Britain, elector of Hanover. By its terms, Britain agreed that it would not aid Austria in a renewed conflict for Silesia if Prussia agreed to protect Hanover from France. This treaty was part of the Diplomatic Revolution, a dramatic reversal of longstanding European alliances, which saw Austria change from being an ally of Britain to being an ally of France, and Prussia becoming an ally of Britain.

FIRST TREATY OF VERSAILLES 1756

Responding to the Treaty of Westminster, France and Austria concluded the First Treaty of Versailles, in which both sides agreed to remain neutral and to provide 24,000 troops if either came into conflict with a third party. Austria, after securing French neutrality, began to establish an anti-Prussian coalition. Austria's actions alerted Frederick, who struck first by invading Saxony, an action that led to the Seven Years' War (1756–1763). The war was to involve every European great power except the Ottoman Empire, and to span five continents, affecting Europe, the Americas, West Africa, India, and the Philippines.

TREATY OF EASTON 1758

The French and Indian War (1754–63), fought in North America, which became subsumed into the global conflict of the Seven Years' War, pitted the colonies of British America against France and its allies – the chiefs of 13 Native American nations representing tribes of the Iroquois, Lenape (Delaware) and Shawnee. The war began with a dispute over control of the confluence of the Allegheny and Monongahela Rivers, and the site of the French Fort Duquesne. The treaty, negotiated between the British colonial governors of the provinces of Pennsylvania and New Jersey and the chiefs, specified that the Native American nations would not fight on the side of the French against the British in the current war. In return, Pennsylvania returned large blocks of land that the Iroquois had ceded a few years previously. The British promised to recognize the rights of the Iroquois and other tribes to their hunting grounds in the Ohio River valley, and to refrain from establishing colonial settlements west of the Allegheny Mountains.

TREATY OF EL PARDO 1761

By the Treaty of Madrid (1750), the Jesuits had agreed to relocate their missions from the eastern, Portuguese, side of the Uruguay River to the western, Spanish, side. But the 30,000 Guarani Indians within the missions had refused to relocate, which led to the Guarani War (1754–56). With the accession to the throne of Charles III of Spain, the Spanish king decided that a general revision of the treaties made with Portugal was required. The Treaty of Madrid was annulled, and Spain and Portugal signed the Treaty of El Pardo, which restored the Jesuits to their missions.

TREATY OF FONTAINEBLEAU 1762

This secret treaty followed Britain's defeat of the French at the Battle of Signal Hill (1762) during the French and Indian War (1754–63). The battle was the last to be fought in the North American theater of the Seven Years' War. The French defeat confirmed British control of Canada. Having lost Canada, Louis XV of France signed the treaty with Charles III of Spain. Under its terms, France ceded its Louisiana colony to Spain. This agreement covered all of Louisiana: the entire valley of the Mississippi River, from the Appalachians to the Rockies. The treaty was kept secret until April 1764, well after the signing of the Treaty of Paris (1763) that ended the French and Indian War.

TREATY OF SAINT PETERSBURG 1762

This treaty, signed between Prussia and Russia, ended the fighting between the two countries in the

1763–1772

Seven Years' War. The agreement was influenced by the death in 1762 of Frederick the Great's bitterest enemy, Empress Elizabeth of Russia, an event that changed the entire political situation in Europe. Her successor, Peter III, was a fanatical admirer of Frederick and was determined to end Russia's war against Prussia. Under the terms of the treaty, Russia pledged to assist in concluding peace among the individual participants in the war, and to return to Prussia all lands occupied by Russian troops during the conflict. Furthermore, it was agreed that Russia would aid Prussia in negotiating peace with Sweden. Peter also promised Frederick a token force of 18,000 men to be used against the Austrians.

TREATY OF PARIS 1763
This was the treaty that ended the Seven Years' War between Great Britain and France and their various allies. Britain had won many significant battles overseas during the course of the war: in Canada, India, the Caribbean. In March 1762 the French sued for peace, but initial attempts to reach an agreement failed and Spain entered the war on the side of the French. When news reached Europe of the British capture of the Spanish colony of Cuba, the situation changed. The French ambassador proposed a solution that would re-allocate colonial territory between France, Spain and Britain. The French were prepared to forego vast tracts of mainland American territory in order to ensure that they retained the lucrative sugar trade of the Caribbean islands. The treaty therefore confirmed the British conquest of Canada and extended British possessions to the line of the Mississippi River. French territories west of the Mississippi would become Spanish; Spain retained Cuba in exchange for Florida, which was handed over to the British. The British gained huge amounts of territory from the treaty, but were unwilling to expend the necessary resources on maintaining a military presence, and failed to balance the colonists' and natives' interests. The levying of taxes to pay for the expenses of the war was an intolerable drain on the colonists' resources and would ultimately lead to the quest for independence.

TREATY OF HUBERTUSBURG 1763
The Treaty of Saint Petersburg had allied Prussia and Russia, and the Treaty of Hamburg had made peace between Prussia and Sweden. Austria was thus deprived of two of her allies in her fight against Frederick the Great over his occupation of the Austrian province of Silesia. When the Treaty of Paris was signed in early 1763, Austria and Saxony were left facing Prussia alone. The Treaty of Hubertusburg, signed between Austria, Prussia, and Saxony, guaranteed that Frederick maintained his

possession of Silesia, and that the county and fortress of Glatz, which were occupied by the Austrian army, were evacuated and returned to Prussia. Prussia's only concession was to consent to the election of Archduke Joseph as Holy Roman Emperor. Prussia agreed to withdraw its troops from Saxony. The treaty ended the Seven Years' War in Germany.

TREATY OF HAMBURG 1762
The Treaty of Saint Petersburg accelerated peace negotiations between Prussia and Sweden. The two states had been engaged in the Pomeranian War (1757–62), a theatre of the Seven Years' War, during which they had fought in Swedish Pomerania, Prussian Pomerania, northern Brandenburg, and eastern Mecklenburg-Schwerin. Sweden was now nearing bankruptcy, and the Russo-Prussian alliance threatened to make Russia an enemy, not an ally. The peace negotiations that led to the Treaty of Hamburg were facilitated by the mediation of Frederick the Great's beloved sister, Queen Louisa Ulrika of Sweden. The treaty, signed between Sweden and Prussia, re-established the pre-war borders between the two states.

TREATY OF ALLAHABAD 1765
This treaty ended a brief war fought by the East India Company against the combined forces of the nawab of Bengal, the Mughal Emperor Shah Alam II and the nawab of Oudh, Shuja-ud-Daulah over the sovereignty of Bengal. Signed by Robert, Lord Clive for the Company, Shah Alam and Shuja-ud-Daulah, the latter granted the East India Company Diwani Rights – the right to collect taxes on behalf of the Emperor and to decide civil cases in the province of Bengal-Bihar-Orissa. In return, the Company paid an annual tribute of 26 lakhs of rupees. Shah Alam was assigned the districts of Kora and Allahabad, ceded to him by Shuja-ud-Daulah. The accord also dictated that the province of Varanasi would be restored to Shah Alam provided he paid a revenue to the Company. The state of Oudh was returned to Shuja-ud-Daulah, who also had to pay 53 lakhs of rupees as war indemnity to the Company. The treaty marks both the political and constitutional involvement of Britain in Indian affairs and the beginning of British rule in India.

TREATY OF BATTICALOA 1766
The ousting of the Portuguese from Ceylon (Sri Lanka) by the Dutch in 1658 left the Dutch East India Company (VOC) in control of two coastal provinces: the region around Galle and Colombo in the south, and the northern region around Jaffna. The VOC's most important commodity was cinnamon, which grew wild in the territories of the

king of Kandy, Keerthisiri Rajasinghe. In 1760, the VOC's strict regulations on its cultivation created so much resentment that the inhabitants rose in rebellion and a full-scale guerrilla war developed during which the Sinhalese inflicted serious losses on the Dutch. The Dutch retaliated, but by 1766 both sides were exhausted and ready to make peace. The Treaty of Batticaloa was signed between the Dutch and Keerthisiri Rajasinghe. The king had to pay 10 million florins to the Dutch in reparations and to recognize the coastal provinces as Dutch territories. Furthermore, the kingdom of Kandy was forbidden from engaging in relations with foreign traders.

TREATY OF FORT STANWIX 1768

Following the French and Indian War (1754–63), Britain issued the Proclamation of 1763 to keep British colonists from moving west of the Appalachian Mountains. The land that Britain claimed between the Appalachians and the Mississippi River was to become an Indian reserve. But colonists continued to move west, the majority settling along the Kentucky bank of the Ohio River. Hoping to prevent tensions with Native Americans in the Ohio county, Britain negotiated the treaty of Stanwix, which was signed between Britain and representatives of the Six Nations (the Iroquois). The Iroquois ceded land south and east of a line running from Fort Stanwix south to the Delaware River, west and south to the Allegheny River, and downstream to the confluence of the Ohio and Tennessee Rivers. This boundary was called the Line of Property. Iroquois lands ceded to the British in Pennsylvania were known as the New Purchase.

TREATY OF MASULIPATAM 1768

Attempts by the East India Company to check the expansionist policies of the ruler of Mysore, Hyder Ali, had precipitated the First Anglo-Mysore War (1767–69). The Company had originally joined the nizam of Hyderabad against Hyder Ali in return for the cession of the northen Sarkars, but the nizam had abandoned the war in 1768, leaving the British to face Hyder Ali alone. The nizam finally made peace with them at the Treaty of Masulipatam when the British recognized the nizam as ruler of Balaghat. However, at the end of the war in 1769, the British signed the Treaty of Madras, which recognized the sovereignty of Mysore over Hyderabad and contained a clause requiring the British to assist Hyder Ali if he was attacked by his neighbors.

TREATY OF LOCHABER 1770

Under the terms of the Treaty of Fort Stanwix (1768), cessions by the Six Nations (Iroquois) of land in what is now western Pennsylvania, Kentucky,

West Virginia, and New York, had opened vast tracts of territory west of the Appalachian Mountains to white exploitation and settlement. The southern portion of this cession was in fact beyond Iroquois territory, and the British had negotiated the Treaty of Hard Labor (1768) with the Cherokee, which verified the new boundaries in what is now West Virginia. But the British settlers' appetite for land was still unsatisfied and they negotiated the Treaty of Lochaber with the Cherokee. By the terms of the treaty, the new Cherokee land cession extended the western border to the Kentucky River in eastern Kentucky, and to the Holston River in eastern Tennessee. Included in this cession was most of the region of present West Virginia southwest of the line established by the Treaty of Hard Labor.

FIRST PARTITION OF POLAND 1772

This was effectively a land grab by Russia, Prussia, and Austria. It came about because of a shift in the European balance of power, when Russia – victorious in the Russo-Turkish War (1768–74) – was seen as threatening Austrian hegemony in the region. Frederick II of Prussia sought to re-focus Russian attention away from Austria's Balkan territories, towards Poland, already effectively a Russian vassal and weakened by war. In the First Partition, the Polish-Lithuanian Commonwealth signed away about 81,500 square miles of territory.

Partition of Poland
1772

☐ 1772 territory to Poland

1774–1779

TREATY OF KÜÇÜK KAYNARCA 1774

The Russo-Turkish War (1768–74) began after Turkey demanded that Russia should abstain from interfering in Poland's internal affairs. During the war the Russians had inflicted heavy defeats on the Turks. They had captured Azov, Crimea, and Bessarabia, overrun Moldavia, destroyed the Turkish navy in the Aegean Sea and defeated the Turks in Bulgaria. The Turks were compelled to seek peace, which was concluded by the Treaty of Küçük Kaynarca. Signed between Russia and the Ottoman Empire, the treaty granted independence to the Crimean khanate. It also advanced the Russian frontier southward to the Southern Bug River, including Oziv and the fortresses of Kerch, Yenikale, and Kinburn. It gave Russia the right to maintain a fleet on the Black Sea, and assigned Russia vague rights to protect all Orthodox Christians under Ottoman rule. Moldavia and Walachia were returned to Turkey.

TREATY OF WATERTOWN 1776

Signed within days of the adoption of the Declaration of Independence, this was the first treaty to recognize the United States of America as an independent nation. It was a treaty of military alliance and friendship between the United States and the Mi'kmaq and St John's Tribes (the Passamaquoddy and Maliseet), two of the constituent tribes in the Wabanaki Confederacy. The British had signed the Treaty of Portsmouth (1713) with the Confederacy, agreeing to respect their lands and hunting rights, but had continued to encroach on Wabanaki territory. Under the terms of the Treaty of Watertown, the Mi'kmaq and Passamaquoddy agreed, in principle, "to supply and furnish 600 strong men" for service in the Continental Army to fight against the British in the American Revolutionary War (1775–83). Although the tribes were briefly involved in some of the fighting in the war, the treaty was never fully ratified by the Mi'kmaq chiefs.

TREATY OF PURANDAR 1776

After the death of the *peshwa* (chief minister) Narayan Rao of the Marathas in 1773, his uncle Raghunath Rao, although not the legal heir, tried to secure the succession. The East India Company's Bombay government supported his claim in the Treaty of Surat (1775) in return for Salsette Island and Bassein (Vasai-Virar), together with part of the revenues from Surat and Bharuch districts. In return, the British promised to provide Raghunath Rao with 2,500 soldiers. But the political asylum offered by the British to Raghunath Rao precipitated a series of battles and skirmishes between the British and the Marathas known as the First Anglo-Maratha War (1775–82). The British Calcutta Council (consisting of three members representing the British Parliament and two Company members) condemned the treaty and sent its own agent to renegotiate. The resulting Treaty of Purandar annulled the Treaty of Surat; Raghunath Rao was pensioned and his cause abandoned, but the revenues of Salsette and Bharuch districts were retained by the British.

FIRST TREATY OF SAN ILDEFONSO 1777

The Spanish-Portuguese War (1776–77) had been fought on land and at sea to settle the border between Spanish South America and Portuguese South America. This treaty concluded peace between Spain and Portugal, settling territorial disputes in the Rio de la Plata region. Based on the terms of the treaty, Spain ceded territories in Brazil to Portugal (the Amazon basin) in return for maintaining control over the Banda Oriental (Uruguay). The treaty partly reaffirmed the Treaty of Madrid (1750) since Spain retained both the Jesuit missions and the Sacramento colony.

TREATY OF ARANJUEZ 1777

The division of the Caribbean island of Hispaniola into the Spanish-speaking Dominican Republic and French-speaking Haiti had been decided by the Treaty of Ryswick (1697), under which Spain transferred the western third of what was then the Spanish colony of Santo Domingo to France. Under the terms of the Treaty of Aranjuez, France and Spain defined precisely the border between their respective territories on the island. Spain made substantial gains in the upper Artibonite Valley in the center of the island. The new border was to be marked by border stones.

TREATY OF AMITY & COMMERCE 1778

Early in 1776, as the American Continental Congress (a convention of delegates from the Thirteen Colonies) moved closer to declaring independence from Britain, leading American statesmen began to consider the benefits of forming foreign alliances to assist in their rebellion against Britain. The most obvious potential ally was France, which was resentful over the loss of its North American Empire after the French and Indian War (1754–63). Covert French aid had begun filtering into the colonies soon after the outbreak of the American War of Independence in 1775, but it was not until the American victory at the Battle of Saratoga (1777) that the French became convinced that the Americans were worth backing in formal treaties. The Treaty of Amity and Commerce, the first of two treaties signed between the United

States and France, recognized the United States as an independent nation and promoted trade and commercial ties between the two countries.

TREATY OF ALLIANCE 1778

In addition to the Treaty of Amity and Commerce, the Treaty of Alliance created a military alliance between the United States and France against Britain. Negotiated by the American diplomats, Benjamin Franklin, Silas Deane, and Arthur Lee, the treaty stipulated that neither France nor the United States would agree to a separate peace with Britain; that American independence would be a condition of any future peace agreement; and that France would renounce all territorial claims in North America east of the Mississippi River and in Bermuda. France also agreed to guarantee the American boundaries that existed at the end of the war in exchange for America's guarantees of French possessions in the West Indies. The two treaties, both signed on 6 February, formalized France's commitment to assist the American colonies in their struggle against Britain. One month later, war between Britain and France formally began when a British squadron fired on two French ships.

TREATY OF EL PARDO 1778

This treaty, signed between Portugal and Spain, aimed at resolving long-standing territorial disputes arising from non-observance of the terms of the Treaty of Tordesillas (1494), which had established the border between the Spanish and Portuguese empires in South America. Two subsequent treaties, the Treaties of Madrid (1750) and El Pardo (1761) had attempted to resolve the matter. But renewed disputes led to the Spanish-Portuguese Wars of 1761–63 and 1776–77. Hostilities were concluded by the Treaties of San Ildefonso (1777) and El Pardo of 1778. The latter reaffirmed the Treaty of Madrid and confirmed Portuguese control of Brazil (in particular, Rio Grande do Sul), and Spanish control of the Banda Oriental (Uruguay), including the Sacramento colony. In exchange, Portugal agreed to cede territories in West Africa to Spain. These included the islands of Annobón and Fernando Pó, as well as the Guinea coast between the Niger River and the Ogoue River.

TREATY OF FORT PITT (TREATY WITH THE DELAWARES) 1778

This was the first written, formal treaty between the United States and Native Americans – in this case, the Lenape (Delaware Indians). Essentially a treaty of alliance, it gave the United States permission to travel through Delaware territory and called for the Delawares to aid American troops in their war against Britain, including the use of their own warriors. In exchange, the United States promised "articles of clothing, utensils and implements of war," and to build Fort Laurens in Delaware country to protect their people from the British. The treaty also recognized the Delawares as a sovereign nation and guaranteed their territorial rights.

TREATY OF ARANJUEZ 1779

This treaty, signed between France and Spain, agreed that France would aid Spain in the capture of Gibraltar, the Floridas, and the island of Minorca. In return, the Spanish agreed to join France against Britain in the American War of Independence. The treaty succeeded three earlier Bourbon Family Compacts that allied Spain with France: the Treaties of the Escorial (1733), Fontainebleau (1743), and Paris (1763). The clause in the Treaty of Aranjuez that committed France to continue fighting until Spain had gained Gibraltar almost led to the war continuing into 1783. Spain, however, agreed to accept Minorca and West Florida in lieu of Gibraltar.

TREATY OF TESCHEN 1779

When the Elector Maximillian III Joseph of Bavaria died childless in 1777, the Habsburg emperor Joseph II sought to acquire most of the electorate of Bavaria and the Upper Palatinate. Maximillian's direct heir, his cousin Charles Theodore, agreed with Joseph to exchange parts of the Austrian Netherlands for parts of his Bavarian inheritance. But Charles Theodore's heir, Charles II August, objected strongly to this arrangement. His cause was taken up by Frederick the Great of Prussia and by Saxony. The Prussian army's subsequent invasion of Bohemia precipitated the War of the Bavarian Succession (1778–79). The war soon became a stalemate and Maria Theresa, who was against the war, intervened directly with Frederick and together they concluded the Treaty of Teschen. Under the terms of the treaty, Austria returned Lower Bavaria to Charles Theodore, but kept the so-called Innviertel, a region east of the Inn River. Furthermore, Austria recognized Prussian claims to the Franconian margravates of Ansbach and Bayreuth. Saxony received a financial reward of six million gulden from the principal combatants for their role in the intervention.

TREATY OF AYNALIKAVAK 1779

The Ottoman Empire had lost the Crimean khanate in the Treaty of Küçük Kaynarca (1774). The Crimean khan, Devlet IV, appealed to the Ottomans to renew the region's dependency, a proposal that was impossible under the terms of Küçük Kaynarca. When the Russians heard of Devlet's appeal, they forced him to abdicate and replaced him with

1780–1784

Sahin Giray. The Ottomans declared that Russia's intervention in the Crimea was against the terms of Küçük Kaynarca. To resolve further tensions in the Crimea, the Ottomans and Russians signed the Treaty of Aynalikavak. Under its terms, the two empires agreed to ratify Küçük Kaynarca and to cease interfering in Crimean politics. The Russians also promised to withdraw their troops from the khanate, and their ships were granted the right to free passage in the Mediterranean Sea. The Ottomans acknowledged Sahin Giray as the Crimean khan.

TREATY OF ARANJUEZ 1780

Under this treaty, Morocco gained territories ceded by Spain. In return, Morocco recognized Spanish imperial rule over the remainder of Melilla, a Spanish fortress on the Moroccan Mediterranean coast which had been besieged by a British-backed Moroccan force in 1774. The treaty defused tensions, lessening the chance that Morocco would agree to British requests to declare war on the Spanish.

EDICT OF TOLERANCE 1782

During his reign as Holy Roman Emperor, Joseph II issued a series of drastic reforms with the aim of remodelling Austria in the form of the ideal enlightened state. In 1781 he issued the Patent (or Edict) of Toleration, which granted religious freedom to the Lutherans, Calvinists and Serbian Orthodox, giving them near equality with Roman Catholics. In 1782 he issued the Edict of Tolerance, which regulated the status of Jews in the Habsburg territories, freeing them from the many discriminatory restrictions imposed upon them by Maria Theresa who regarded Protestants as heretics and Jews as the embodiment of the Antichrist.

TREATY OF SALBAI 1782

The Treaty of Purandar (1776) had been rejected by the British Calcutta Council. In 1777 Nana Phadnavis, leader of the twelve Maratha chiefs, violated the treaty by granting the French a port on India's west coast. The British responded by sending a force towards Pune. This was another stage in the First Anglo-Maratha War (1775–82). After long negotiations, the East India Company and the Maratha Empire signed the Treaty of Salbai which ended the war, and ushered in a period of relative peace between the East India Company and the Marathas. Under its terms, the Company retained control of Salsette and Bharuch and obtained guarantees that the Marathas would defeat Hyder Ali of Mysore, retake territories in the Carnatic (the region of South India lying between the Eastern Ghats and the Coromandel Coast), and prohibit

the French from establishing settlements on their territories. The British agreed to acknowledge Madhavrao II as *peshwa* of the Maratha Empire. The British also recognized the territorial claims of the Mahadji Sindhia west of the Jumna River. All the territories occupied by the British after the Treaty of Purandar would revert to the Marathas. British dominance had now become the controlling factor in Indian politics.

TREATY OF AMITY AND COMMERCE 1783

Signed in Paris between the United States and Sweden, this treaty established a commercial alliance between the two nations. The United States was represented by Benjamin Franklin, America's ambassador in Paris, who both negotiated and signed the treaty.

TREATY OF PARIS 1783

This was the treaty, considered to be highly favorable to the United States, that ended the revolutionary war between the United States and Great Britain and recognized American independence. Negotiations on the American side were conducted by John Adams, Benjamin Franklin, and John Jay and commenced after the British defeat at Yorktown. The Americans were wary of attempts by their erstwhile allies, the French, to join the diplomatic process, preferring to conduct independent negotiations. In addition to recognizing American independence, the Americans secured fishing rights off the Grand Banks of Newfoundland. The British also ceded them all the territory between the Allegheny Mountains and the Mississippi River, north of Florida and south of Canada, doubling the size of the new nation. In separate agreements with France and Spain, Britain ceded Florida to Spain, as well as Minorca. The Bahamas, Minorca, and Grenada were returned to Britain. There were exchanges of captured territory with the French, who also gained Tobago and Senegal in western Africa.

TREATY OF GEORGIEVSK 1783

This was a bilateral treaty concluded between Russia and the east Georgian kingdom of Kartli-Kakheti. The treaty established Georgia as a protectorate of Russia, which guaranteed Georgia's territorial integrity and the continuation of its reigning Bagrationi dynasty in return for prerogatives in the conduct of Georgian foreign affairs. Furthermore, Georgia agreed to support Russia in any war, and to have no diplomatic communications with other nations without Russia's prior consent. Georgia also agreed that its future monarchs would be obliged to swear allegiance to Russia's emperors.

SECOND TREATY OF FORT STANWIX 1784
Under the terms of the first Treaty of Fort
Stanwix (1768), signed between the British and
representatives of the Six Nations (or the Iroquois
Confederacy), the Iroquois had ceded vast tracts of
their territory west of the Appalachian Mountains.
During the American War of Independence the

powerful Iroquois, now considerably weakened by
the American frontier campaign, reluctantly agreed
with the United States to redraw their eastern
boundaries. Under the terms of the second Treaty
of Fort Stanwix, the Iroquois were persuaded to
yield a small section of western New York and a
vast region in western Pennsylvania. However, their

1784–1789

relinquishment of claims to additional territory west of the Ohio River was disputed by adjacent tribes, especially the Shawnee. The Ohio country became a violent place as Anglo-American settlers, emboldened by the treaty, began to arrive in the region in the mid-1780s.

TREATY OF MANGALORE 1784

The Treaty of Madras (1769), which had ended the First Anglo-Mysore War (1767–79), fought between the British East India Company and the kingdom of Mysore, contained a clause requiring the British to assist Mysore's ruler, Hyder Ali, if he was attacked by his neighbors. Convinced that the British were in breach of the treaty, Hyder Ali, with an army of some 90,000 men, invaded the Carnatic (the region between the Eastern Ghats and the Coromandel Coast) and the British strongholds of Vellore and Madras (Chennai). This invasion precipitated the Second Anglo-Mysore War (1780–84). The British suffered defeats by a force led by Hyder Ali's son, Tippu Sultan. The British counterattack, though successful, led to a stalemate. The war was concluded by the Treaty of Mangalore, signed between the East India Company and Tippu Sultan, which agreed both sides should return conquered territories.

TREATY OF FONTAINEBLEAU 1785

This treaty, signed between the Dutch Republic and Austria, permitted the Dutch to maintain sovereignty over the Scheldt estuary. However, they had to make several concessions to Austria, including payment of ten million Dutch florins and the dismemberment of certain military fortifications. This treaty confirmed and reinforced the tenets of the Treaty of Munster, one of several treaties that formed part of the Peace of Westphalia (1649).

TREATY OF AMITY AND COMMERCE 1785

Following the second Treaty of Paris (1783), the newly independent United States sought to conclude treaties with various European nations in order to offset its severed trade relations with Britain. Accordingly, the Continental Congress instructed its commissioners in Europe, Thomas Jefferson, Benjamin Franklin, and John Adams, to negotiate the Treaty of Amity and Commerce with Prussia. Signed by Frederick the Great and George Washington, the treaty promoted free trade and commerce between the two nations. It also, for the first time in international law, defined precisely how prisoners of war should be treated by their captors.

TREATY OF HOPEWELL 1785

After the War of American Independence, the newly constituted federal government of the United States decided to employ a peaceful treaty process to order its relations with Native Americans rather than subduing them outright through conquest. Signed between the United States and the Cherokee, the first Treaty of Hopewell specified a western boundary and prohibited American citizens from settling on Indian lands. The exchange of prisoners was agreed; the Cherokee acknowledged American protection and the supremacy of the federal government to regulate trade. Both parties agreed to perpetual peace and friendship.

TREATY OF FORT McINTOSH 1785

This treaty was signed between the United States and representatives of the Wyandotte, Lenape (Delaware), Chippewa, and Ottawa nations of Native Americans. Under the terms of the treaty, the tribal leaders agreed that they lived under the protection of the American government and could not form alliances with any other powers. They also agreed to relinquish their lands in southern and eastern Ohio, and were to be confined to its western corner. In addition, the prisoners they had taken in raids along the frontier would be returned. Most Indians rejected the validity of the treaty and, rather than improving relations, it only intensified the tensions that existed between the American settlers and the Ohio Country Indian tribes.

EDEN AGREEMENT 1786

Signed between Britain and France, the treaty put a temporary end to almost a hundred years of Anglo-French commercial rivalry. Britain's main incentive was its need to explore trading opportunities in Europe following the loss of its 13 American colonies; France was motivated by the loss of both their Canadian and Indian colonies. Under the terms of the treaty the British agreed to allow French silks into their markets, to reduce English duties on certain commodities, and to abolish their preference for Portuguese wines over French. The treaty also gave each state "most favored nation status" with respect to certain goods, such as French olive oil, and it opened up the French market to British textiles with only low import duties levied. The treaty was almost wholly beneficial to the British, while the unequal protection on certain industries proved damaging to the French economy.

MOROCCAN–AMERICAN TREATY OF FRIENDSHIP 1786

Prior to the reign of Sultan Muhammad III (1757–90), Morocco had suffered 30 years of internecine battles, instability, and turmoil. During his reign, Muhammad transformed Morocco's politics, economy, society, and overseas trade. Central to his pursuit of international trade was the negotiation of agreements with foreign commercial powers. Formal relations between Morocco and the United States began in 1777, when Morocco became the first country to recognize the American colonies as a nation. Signed between Muhammad, John Adams, and Thomas Jefferson, the treaty established the framework for diplomatic relations, assurances of non-hostility, access to markets on a "most favored nation" basis, and protection of American ships from attack by foreign vessels in Moroccan waters. Renegotiated in 1836, the treaty is still in force, constituting the longest unbroken treaty relationship in American history.

TREATY OF HARTFORD 1786
The colonial charters for New York and Massachusetts both described their boundaries as extending westward to the Pacific Ocean, but as they used distances from coastal rivers as their baselines, they could both claim the same land. The disputed area included much of the Finger Lakes region in western New York State, extending to Lake Ontario. The two states agreed that all of this land – about 6 million acres – would be recognized as part of New York state. In return, Massachusetts obtained the right of preemption, giving it the exclusive right to extinguish by purchase the possessory rights of the Indian tribes (except for a narrow strip of land along the Niagara River, belonging to New York). It was also agreed that Massachusetts could sell or assign its preemptive rights. In 1788 the remaining 6 million acres were sold to Oliver Phelps and Nathaniel Gorham for $1,000,000, the money used to repay some of the state's debt incurred during the American Revolution.

SECOND TREATY OF HOPEWELL 1786
Signed between the United States and the Choctaws, the terms of the second Treaty of Hopewell were identical to the first Treaty of Hopewell of 1785. A separate, and identical, treaty was signed between the United States and the Chickasaw. These treaties ended years of participation in the American War of Independence for the Native Americans who had befriended the British.

CONVENTION OF LONDON 1786
Both Treaties of Paris (1763 and 1783) had decreed that the British settlements on the Mosquito Coast of Central America should be evacuated. But the settlers had resisted on the grounds that the Spanish had never actually controlled the area, and that it therefore did not belong to them. When both sides increased military activity in the area of the Black River Settlement, they decided to negotiate.

By the terms of the Convention, Britain agreed to evacuate all their settlements on the Mosquito Coast. In exchange, Spain agreed to expand the territory available to British loggers on the Yucatan Peninsula and to allow them to cut the valuable mahogany. Despite their opposition, over 2,000 settlers evacuated the area, the majority moving to Belize.

TREATY OF BEAUFORT 1787
In 1732, Britain chartered the colony of Georgia, setting the boundary between Georgia and South Carolina as the most northern part of the Savannah River. However, the precise location of parts of the boundary was disputed by the two colonies. Much of the controversy originally concerned navigation rights on the river. The precise boundary was still in dispute when the colonies became states. Signed between the United States, Georgia, and South Carolina, the Treaty of Beaufort agreed that the northernmost branch of the Savannah River should be the boundary between them. In an effort to make clear what that meant with regard to islands in the river, the treaty gave all of them to Georgia. Over time, the river has altered its shape, giving rise to further disputes over the boundary.

THIRD TRIPLE ALLIANCE 1788
Signed between Britain, Prussia and the United Provinces, this treaty was essentially a defensive alliance. In April Britain signed a treaty with the Dutch by which each country agreed to guarantee the possessions of the other and to assist in case of an attack. In August, the Anglo-Prussian alliance was signed. This marked the formation of the Triple Alliance. Britain's aim was to maintain the balance of power in Europe, particularly with regard to France and Russia, and the potentially unstable regions of the Baltics, the Balkans and the United Provinces. Prussia's aim was to secure an ally to offset the dangers of the entente of Joseph II of Austria and Catherine the Great of Russia. Under the terms of the treaty, each state agreed to help each other, and both pledged themselves to defend the Dutch and to uphold their Constitution.

JAY-GARDOQUI TREATY 1789
This treaty was negotiated in an attempt to solve problems regarding the southwest boundary between the newly established United States and Spanish America, and American rights to navigate the Mississippi River between Natchez and New Orleans. After a year of negotiations the treaty stipulated that Spain would grant America commercial privileges for its European and West Indian ports. However, Spain still refused American rights on the Mississippi River. The American

1789–1795

negotiator then proposed to Congress that the United States should accept the restrictions on navigation on the Mississippi for 25 to 30 years in exchange for the immediate benefit of the trade agreement. This proposal failed through lack of votes in Congress and the treaty was never ratified.

TREATY OF FORT HARMAR 1789
The aim of the treaty was to address issues remaining unresolved by the Treaties of Fort Stanwix (1784) and Fort McIntosh (1785) over who controlled the Ohio country: American settlers or Native Americans. The Indians hoped that the United States would agree to establish a reservation for them consisting of land west of the Muskingum River and north of the Ohio River. But the Americans demanded that the Indian chiefs agree to the reservation boundary established in the Treaty of Fort Stanwix and threatened them with attack if they refused, then bribed them with presents. The chiefs signed the Treaty of Fort Harmar, which merely reiterated the terms of the previous treaties. But, rather than settling the Indians' claims, the treaty provoked them to further resistance.

TREATY (or CONVENTION) OF REICHENBACH 1790
Signed between Frederick William II of Prussia and Leopold II of Austria, this treaty aimed to settle differences between the two powers. Following the death of his brother Joseph II, Leopold took immediate steps to avert the threats posed by Prussia and Catherine the Great's ambitions for territorial gains in Poland and Turkey. Under the terms of the treaty, Austria agreed to restore all conquered territories to Turkey; to grant amnesty to the Austrian Netherlands; and to refrain from supporting Russia in its campaigns against Turkey. Prussia had won a superficial diplomatic victory at the price of temporarily sacrificing its expansionist ambitions. But Leopold had secured his essential objective: peace on reasonable and honourable terms.

TREATY OF VÄRÄLÄ 1790
The Russo-Swedish War (1788–90) began as a result of Sweden's aim to regain territory along Finland's eastern frontier, which it had lost during two previous wars with Russia. The war's unsuccessful outcome, and its unpopularity in Sweden, forced Gustav III of Sweden to make peace. Under the terms of this treaty, the borders remained as they were before the war. However, Russia's right to interfere with Swedish interior affairs, contained in the Treaty of Nystad (1721) was revoked. The provisions of the Treaty of Åbo (1743) were confirmed. The treaty's chief significance lay in

Sweden's renunciation of its alliance with Turkey. The treaty contributed to the growth of Russia's international prestige.

TREATY OF NEW YORK 1790
Signed between the United States and the Creek Nation, this treaty pledged lasting peace and friendship. The Creeks would be subject to federal laws, rather than Georgia state laws. They also ceded a significant portion of their hunting grounds to the United States, including land stretching to the Oconee River. In addition, Creeks within American territory and Americans in Creek territory would be subject to United States law, but Americans settling in Creek territory would forfeit federal protection. The right of the British to pass through Creek lands was also restricted, and Creek prisoners were to be returned from American custody.

TREATY OF HOLSTON 1791
This treaty reaffirmed the conditions of the earlier Treaty of Hopewell (1785), which the United States had made with the Cherokee Nation. In addition, the terms of the treaty stated that the Cherokees could not treat with any foreign power or another state. For a $1,000 annuity (raised to $1,500 in 1792), the Cherokees ceded all claims to the area east of the Clinch River, and north of a line through Kingston to the North Carolina border. For the first time, the US Government's desire for Native Americans to settle down and become farmers was made clear. To help them to do so, the Cherokees were promised "useful implements of husbandry."

TREATY OF SISTOVA 1791
Negotiated by Britain, Prussia, and the Dutch, the treaty ended the Austro-Turkish War of 1787–91. The war was launched by Joseph II of Austria who, having concluded an alliance with Catherine the Great of Russia in 1781, was obliged to come to Russia's aid when Turkey declared war on Russia in 1788. Although Austrian and Russian forces made gains, Joseph's successor, Leopold II, was compelled to end the war due to the threat of Prussian intervention in support of the Turks, and to the evolving French Revolution. Austria returned its recent conquests in Bosnia and Serbia. The Russians gained new territory along the Black Sea and forced the Turks to acknowledge previous conquests.

TREATY OF JASSY 1792
The treaty ended the Russo-Turkish War (1787–92), an unsuccessful attempt by Turkey to regain lands, including the Crimean khanate, lost to Russia during the previous Russo-Turkish War (1768–74). Following several Russian victories that gave Russia

control of the lower Dniester and Danube Rivers, the Turks were compelled to sign the Treaty of Jassy. Under the terms of the treaty, the annexation of the Crimean khanate was confirmed, and the Russian frontier was advanced to the Dniester River, including the fortress of Ochakov. Bessarabia, Moldavia, and Walachia were restored to the Turks.

TREATY OF SERINGAPATAM 1792

The Third Anglo-Mysore War had broken out in late 1789 when Tippu Sultan, the ruler of Mysore, attacked the kingdom of Travancore as part of the Mysorean invasion of Kerala (1766–92). As an ally of Travancore, the British East India Company came to its aid. For two years the Company's forces, led by Lord Cornwallis, together with forces from the Maratha Empire and Hyderabad, fought the Mysoreans. In 1792, they laid siege to Mysore's capital, Seringapatam. Tippu Sultan was forced to capitulate. Under the terms of the treaty, signed between the Company, the Nizam of Hyderabad, the Marathas and Tippu Sultan, Mysore ceded half its territories to the other signatories. The Company received a large portion of Mysore's Malabar Coast between Travancore and the Kali River; the Marathas acquired territory up to the Tungabhadra River; the Nizam was awarded land from the Krishna to the Penner River. Tippu Sultan, unable to pay an indemnity of 330 lakhs of rupees, had to surrender two of his three sons as hostages.

SECOND PARTITION OF POLAND 1793

Agreed between Russia and Prussia, this was essentially a clampdown on the pro-Constitution movement in Poland, which supported reforms that enfranchised the bourgeoisie. Russia invaded Poland to defeat the reforms; Prussia argued that, because it had supported Russia in the War of the First Coalition against Napoleonic France, it should be compensated with further Polish territory. In 1793 the Polish Sejm, surrounded by Russian troops, approved the agreement, signing away a further 115,000 square miles of territory.

JAY TREATY (TREATY OF AMITY, COMMERCE AND NAVIGATION) 1794

This treaty, signed between Britain and the United States, attempted to diffuse tensions between the two countries that had escalated since the end of the American Revolution and were threatening to lead to war. Under the terms of the treaty, Britain agreed to evacuate the Northwest Territory – the region lying west of Pennsylvania, north of the Ohio River, east of the Mississippi River, and south of the Great Lakes. Britain also agreed to compensate for its depredations against American shipping; to

end discrimination against American commerce; and to grant the US trading privileges in England and the British East Indies. The treaty also declared the Mississippi River open to both countries. Both parties agreed that disputes over wartime debts and the American-Canadian boundary were to be sent to arbitration. This was one of the first major uses of arbitration in diplomatic history and the one that set the precedent used by other nations.

TREATY OF CANANDAIGUA 1794

This was one of several treaties that the US Government concluded with Native Americans to establish firm land boundaries following the American Revolution. The treaty established peace and friendship between the United States and the Grand Council of the Six Nations (the Haudeonosaunee), and affirmed the Six Nations' land rights in the state of New York, and the boundaries established by the Phelps and Gorham Purchase as agreed by the Treaty of Hartford of 1786. It also bound the US to make a one-time payment to the Six Nations of $10,000, plus annual payments of $4,500 in goods, including calico cloth, which the Indians prized for use in regalia.

THIRD PARTITION OF POLAND 1795

Under the terms of this agreement, Poland effectively lost sovereignty until 1918. It was provoked by a series of revolts and a nationwide

Partitions of Poland
1793-95

1793 territories lost to Poland

Final partition of P oland 1795

1795–1796

uprising, the Kosciuszko Rebellion, which reflected Polish nationalism and their repudiation of the preceeding two partitions. Despite initial success against the occupiers, the uprising was crushed by Prussian and Russian forces in Nomber 1794. Representatives of the Austrian Empire, Prussia and Russia met in October 1795 and erased Poland from the map, dividing up its territory between them. Since Poland had literally ceased to exist, no approval process by its government was required. The signatories even agreed to obliterate the name of Poland, stating that it would "remain suppressed as from the present and forever..."

PINCKNEY'S TREATY 1795 (TREATY OF SAN LORENZO)
This treaty established the 31st parallel as the border between the United States and Spanish West Florida. Under the terms of the Treaty of Paris (1763), Spain had ceded that area to Britain, which had moved the boundary from the 31st parallel to a line north of the 32nd parallel. When the British returned Florida to Spain after the American Revolution, this boundary was disputed. Pinckney's Treaty also agreed that Spain would allow the United States free navigation of the Mississippi River to the Gulf of Mexico, and granted it the right to deposit goods in New Orleans. This was of vital importance to the farmers and merchants who lived in Kentucky and Tennessee and to the settlers of the Ohio Valley as they could now ship their goods on the waterways to the eastern seaboard of the United States, to Europe, and to other areas. Additionally, both nations agreed not to incite attacks by Native Americans against the other nation.

PEACE OF BASEL 1795
The First Coalition of European nations (1793–97) was established in an attempt to defeat the forces of the First French Republic following the French Revolution of 1789. The Coalition comprised Spain, the Austrian Netherlands, Austria, Prussia, Britain, and Sardinia. In 1792 the War of the First Coalition (1792–97) began when France pitted its forces against Austria and Prussia. The successes of the French army led to the Peace of Basel, which consisted of two separate treaties. In the first treaty, signed between France and Prussia, Prussia ceded territory on the left bank of the Rhine to France. In the second treaty, signed between France and Spain, Spain ceded two thirds of the island of Haiti; the parts of Catalonia, Navarre and the Basque provinces that were occupied by French troops were returned to Spain. The conclusion of these treaties beween France and members of the Coalition signalled the beginning of the breakdown of the alliance.

TREATY OF THE HAGUE 1795
During the War of the First Coalition, France overran the Austrian Netherlands, established it as a puppet state and renamed it the Batavian Republic. Based on the terms of the peace treaty, the Dutch ceded to France the territories of Maastricht, Venlo, and Zeelandic Flanders (the southernmost region of the province of Zeeland). The treaty also established a defensive alliance between the two nations. Furthermore, the Dutch agreed to pay an indemnity of 100 million guilders for their part in the war and to provide France with a large loan against a low rate of interest. The barrier forts in the former Austrian Netherlands were to be dismantled, and the port of Flushing was to be placed under a co-dominion. Finally, in a secret clause, the Dutch agreed to pay for a French army of occupation of 25,000 until the war was ended.

TREATY OF GREENVILLE 1795
Signed between the United States and a coalition of Native American tribes (known as the Western Confederacy), this treaty followed America's defeat of the Indians at the Battle of Fallen Timbers (1794). The battle ended the Northwest Indian War (1785–95), which had been fought for control of the Ohio country. The treaty established the Greenville Treaty Line, a boundary between Native American territory and lands open to European-American settlers. In effect, the boundary forced the Indian tribes to give up claims to most of what is now the state of Ohio. The treaty also established the "annuity" system: yearly grants of federal money and supplies of calico cloth to Native American tribes.

TREATY WITH TRIPOLI 1796
This treaty was one of several negotiated by the United States government with the Barbary States (Tunis, Morocco, Algiers, Tripoli, and Turkey) to stop attacks on their merchant ships by state-sponsored pirates operating in the Mediterranean Sea and Atlantic Ocean. Before the American Revolution, American shipping had enjoyed the protection of the British navy. This protection, assumed by France during the war, ceased after the Treaty of Paris (1783). America's unprotected ships were attacked, their crews enslaved, and tributes demanded. The Treaty with Tripoli declared peace and friendship between the two countries and payment was made by America in the form of goods and money. The American Senate unanimously approved the treaty in 1797. Article 11 remains the focal point of controversy more than two centuries later: the first sentence begins: "As the government of the United States of America is not, in any sense, founded on the Christian Religion..."

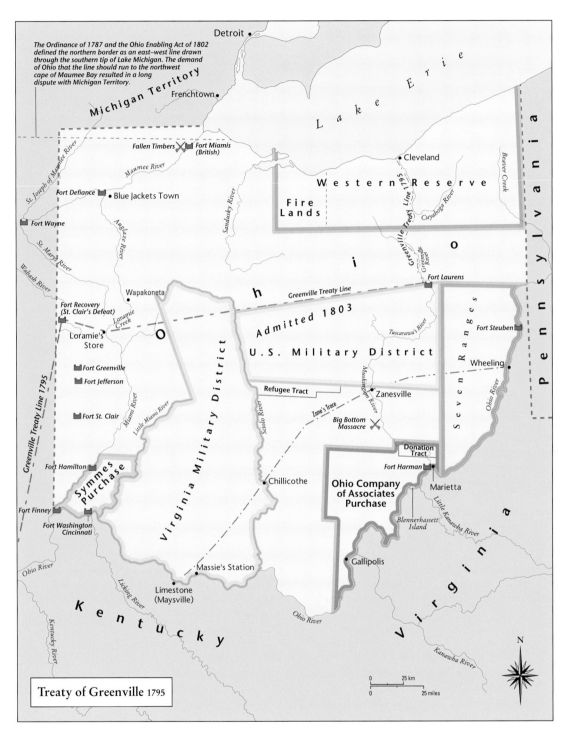

The Ordinance of 1787 and the Ohio Enabling Act of 1802 defined the northern border as an east–west line drawn through the southern tip of Lake Michigan. The demand of Ohio that the line should run to the northwest cape of Maumee Bay resulted in a long dispute with Michigan Territory.

Treaty of Greenville 1795

TREATY OF COLERAIN 1796
Signed between the United States and representatives of the Creek Nation, this treaty affirmed the terms of the Treaty of New York (1790). Furthermore, it bound the Creeks to acknowledge the boundary lines between the Choctaws, Chickasaws, Cherokees, and the United States, established by the two Treaties of Hopewell (1785 and 1786) and the Treaty of Holston (1791). The Treaty of Colerain also established the boundary line between the Creeks and the United States and allowed for the US to establish trading or military outposts. The Creeks agreed to give up American prisoners and return all "citizens, white inhabitants, negroes and property."

1796–1802

SECOND TREATY OF SAN ILDEFONSO 1796

Between 1793 and 1797 a First Coalition of European nations was established in an attempt to defeat the forces of the First French Republic following the French Revolution. Spain had been one of the members of the First Coalition and had fought with its allies in the War of the First Coalition (1792–97). Spain's prime minister, Manuel de Godoy, convinced that Britain, not France, was the real enemy of Spain, signed the Treaty of San Ildefonso, which allied Spain with France against Britain in the French Revolutionary Wars.

TREATY OF LEOBEN 1797

This treaty was an armistice and preliminary peace agreement between Austria and France. It was signed by representatives of Emperor Francis II of Austria and by General Napoleon Bonaparte on behalf of the French Directory. Following his victorious campaign in Italy, Napoleon had proposed the peace to prevent further loss of life in the War of the First Coalition. Receiving no response from the Austrians, he advanced his troops as far as Judenburg, which prompted the Austrians to agree to a truce. Under the terms of the treaty, Francis ceded the Austrian Netherlands to France. The treaty contained secret clauses by which Francis ceded Lombardy in exchange for the eastern part of the Republic of Venice. Except for these personal losses to the ruling Habsburgs, the treaty preserved the integrity of the Holy Roman Empire.

TREATY OF CAMPO FORMIO 1797

The Treaty of Leoben, signed in April, was an armistice, whereas the Treaty of Campo Formio, signed in October, marked the definitive end of the War of the First Coalition. Under the terms of the treaty, Austria ceded Belgium to France and recognized French control of the Rhineland. The Cisalpine and Ligurian republics in northern Italy were established under French influence, and France gained the Ionian Islands in the Adriatic Sea. In compensation for loss of possessions in Lombardy, Napoleon gave Austria the Venetian territory east of the Adige River, including Istria, Dalmatia and the city of Venice. Of the original anti-French coalition, the treaty left only Britain hostile to France.

TREATY OF TOLENTINO 1797

Napoleon's first invasion of Italy in 1796, which took place in the French Revolutionary Wars (1792–1802), had been concluded by an armistice, the Peace of Bologna. His second invasion in 1797 saw the defeat of Austrian forces at the battles of Mantua, Rivoli and Arcola Bridge. His invasion of the Papal Romagna Region left the pope, Pius VI, no choice but to conclude peace with the Treaty of Tolentino. Signed between France and representatives of the pope's Curia, the treaty recognized some of the terms agreed by the Peace of Bologna. The papal city of Avignon and the Comtat Venaissin (territory within the Papal States) were ceded to France, thus ending half a millennium of papal rule. The Romagna region was also ceded to France, including the newly-created Cisalpine Republic. In addition, a further 15 million livres was added to the 21 million livres the Papal States had been required to pay under the terms of the Peace of Bologna. The treaty also formalized the confiscation by France of over 100 paintings and works of art from the Vatican.

TREATY WITH TUNIS 1797

This treaty, signed between the United States and Tunis, was a further attempt by America to curb the costly attacks on its commercial shipping by Barbary pirates in the Mediterranean Sea. In order to ensure the safety of its vessels and seamen, America agreed to an even higher tribute than that promised in the Treaty with Tripoli of 1796. The treaty is notable because of its religious language: the treaty's opening statement recognized the president of the United States as "the most distinguished among those who profess the religion of the Messiah, of whom may the end be happy." The failure of the various Barbary States to prevent piracy led to the first American military actions overseas in the First and Second Barbary Wars of the early 1800s.

THIRD TREATY OF SAN ILDEFONSO 1800

Signed between Spain and France, this secret treaty was actually a draft that was confirmed by two later treaties in 1801 and 1802. Under the terms of the Treaty of San Ildefonso, Louisiana – owned by Spain since the Treaty of Paris (1763) – was to be retroceded to France. Spain would be compensated by the creation in Tuscany of the kingdom of Etruria, which was to be given to the duke of Parma, son-in-law of Charles IV of Spain. Although Napoleon agreed never to alienate Louisiana, he disregarded the treaty and sold Louisiana to the United States three years later. The intention was to create, in the words of French foreign minister Talleyrand, "a wall of brass," impenetrable to both England and America. The Americans were deeply disturbed by the fact that the mouth of the Mississippi, a major outlet for the produce of the western states, was now in the hands of Napoleon.

TREATY OF MORTEFONTAINE 1800

This treaty followed the Quasi War, a dispute between France and America sparked by the French decision to attack American merchant shipping, and ignited by a failure of diplomacy in Paris, when a fee was demanded from the Americans for an audience with the French ambassador. There was outrage back in the US, with anti-French feelings running high, and the US Navy initiated a war in the Caribbean. Napoleon came to power and urged an end to hostility against France. A commission of three diplomats was sent to Paris. The Convention of 1800 agreed the cessation of the alliance between America and France, agreed in 1778, ending any American alliances with foreign countries. The 1800 treaty also ended the Quasi War, providing for the return of captured vessels, the inviolability of neutral flags, and mutual commercial advantages. Bonaparte's focus was on the anti-French coalition headed by Great Britain and it was therefore a priority to prevent an Anglo-American *rapprochement*.

CARNATIC TREATY 1801
The nawab of Arcot in South India was sometimes referred to as the nawab of the Carnatic. The nawabs of the Carnatic trace their origins back to the Mughal Emperor Aurangzeb, who appointed the first nawab in 1692. In the Carnatic Wars of the mid-18th century the Carnatic became a battleground for a proxy war between the French East India Company and the British Empire as well as the Mughal Empire. The Siege of Arcot was a major battle between the British commander Robert Clive and the nawab of the Carnatic, Chandha Sahib, assisted by some French troops. Clive's victory was seen as a turning point for British rule in India. In 1801 the nephew of the late nawab signed a treaty with the British East India Company passing on the entire civil and military governance of the Carnatic to the British; in exchange for this he retained one-fifth of all the country's revenues.

TREATY OF LUNÉVILLE 1801
Following Napoleon's defeat of the Austrian army at the Battles of Marengo in June 1800 and Hohenlinden in December, the Austrians were forced to sign a humiliating treaty, which effectively ended the Second Coalition, leaving Great Britain as the sole nation at war with France. The treaty enforced the terms of Campo Fiorno (1797), by which Austria relinquished certain territories and French control extended to the left bank of the Rhine. The grand duchy of Tuscany was ceded to France, although Austria's possession of Venetia and the Dalmatian coast was confirmed.

TREATY OF FLORENCE 1801
The kingdom of Naples had formed part of the Second Coalition, which was ranged against Napoleon and his Spanish ally. Naples' ally, the Holy Roman Empire, had made its peace earlier in the year with Napoleon, following its defeat at the Battle of Marengo. Naples was left exposed, with no powerful ally. As the French army advanced in January 1801, the Neapolitans sought an armistice. The final treaty was signed nearly two months later. It was agreed that King Ferdinand would be restored to the Neapolitan throne, and Naples would cede the state of Presidi and the principality of Piombino to France. Neapolitan ports were to be closed to British shipping and France would have preferential trading relations with Naples.

TREATY OF ARANJUEZ 1801
By the terms of this secret agreement, which confirmed the Treaty of San Idelfonso, the Spanish possessions of Louisiana and the duchy of Parma in France were transferred to France in exchange for the grand duchy of Tuscany, which was to be named the kingdom of Etruria and given to the Spanish infante Louis Francisco. Louisiana covered a surface area 100 times larger than Tuscany.

TREATY OF BADAJOZ 1801
Portugal's long-standing alliance with England was challenged by Napoleon, who wanted Spain to coerce Portugal into breaking the treaty, and closing their ports to British ships. Napoleon's threats to take the war to Spain if they didn't cooperate were hard to ignore and the Spanish eventually gave the Portuguese an ultimatum, which they refused to accept. An army of some 80,000 French and Spanish troops crossed the Portuguese border, occupying several towns and cities and meeting little resistance (the War of the Oranges). The Portuguese king surrendered and signed the Treaty of Badajoz on 6 June. Most of the Spanish conquests were returned to Portugal, except the disputed territory of Olivença. Portugal closed its ports to Britain; their close alliance would be renewed just four years later, following the Battle of Trafalgar.

TREATY OF MADRID 1801
Signed between John VI of Portugal and representatives of the French Republic on 29 September, this treaty obliged Portugal to adhere to the terms of the earlier Treaty of Badajoz, which followed the War of the Oranges. In addition, the Portuguese were obliged to pay the French an indemnity of 20 million francs and to surrender half of their colony of Guiana to France.

TREATY OF AMIENS 1802
By 1801 Britain was heartily sick of war and ready to start negotiations with the French. A 14-month interregnum in the Napoleonic Wars was brought

The World in 1800

In 1800, Europe was extending its power across the globe, and its its colonial possessions were scattered across the world map. Meanwhile, the power of its rival, the Ottoman Empire, was diminishing. The United States was newly independent, but the southwest remained under Spanish control. Central and South America, in addition to the West Indies, were western European possessions. The Europeans stood on the threshold of a period of even greater colonial expansion. The British controlled much of India, under the aegis of the East India Company and its negotiated trade settlements and military protection deals with local rulers, while the Dutch and French had colonized much of the East Indies. The Chinese Qing dynasty, while still at its apogee, was uneasy about European possessions encroaching on its borders. China provided Europe with silk, tea, and ceramics and was paid in silver and opium, eventually leading to the Opium Wars, the "unequal treaties," and partial colonization by the British and Portuguese. In Europe itself, Napoleon was rampaging throughout the continent, masterfully negotiating diplomatic treaties such as Campo Fiorno (1807) and Tilsit (1807), which brought erstwhile enemies into the Napoleonic fold.

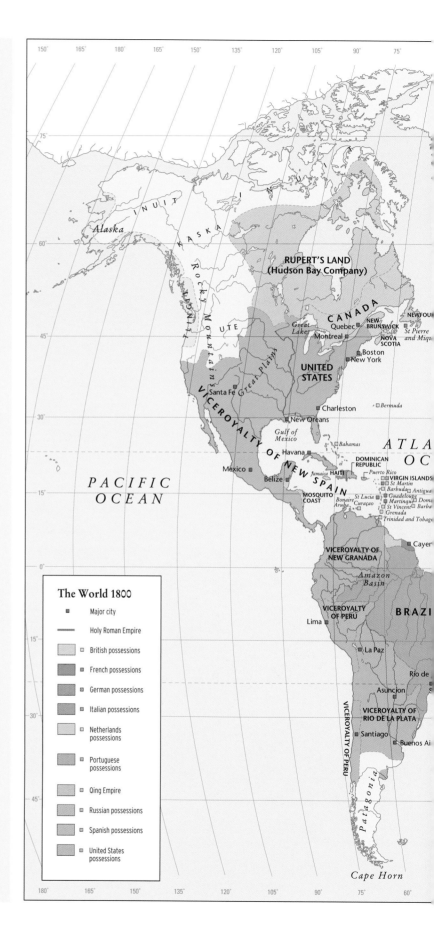

The World 1800

- ▪ Major city
- — Holy Roman Empire
- ▫ British possessions
- ▫ French possessions
- ▫ German possessions
- ▫ Italian possessions
- ▫ Netherlands possessions
- ▫ Portuguese possessions
- ▫ Qing Empire
- ▫ Russian possessions
- ▫ Spanish possessions
- ▫ United States possessions

ARCTIC OCEAN

Iceland

Siberia

CHUKCHI

SWEDEN

NORWAY

St Petersburg

NETHERLANDS
(BATAVIAN
REPUBLIC)

DENMARK

Moscow

IRELAND BRITAIN
London

Berlin

PRUSSIA

GALICIA

Kiev

TRANSYLVANIA

K A Z A K H S

Gobi Desert

Beijing

KOREA

JAPAN

Paris

FRANCE

Vienna

HUNGARY

MOLDAVIA

HELVETIAN REPUBLIC
CISALPINE REPUBLIC
PIEDMONT
LUGURIAN REPUBLIC

WALLACHIA

TUSCANY
PAPAL
STATES

Rome

RAGUSA

Black Sea

Caspian
Sea

KHIVA

KOKAND

BUKHARA

SMALL
TURKMEN
STATES

QING
EMPIRE

Edo

PORTUGAL   SPAIN

Lisbon   Madrid

SARDINIA

Minorca

NAPLES

IONIAN
REPUBLIC

Malta

Constantinople

GEORGIA

BALKH

KUNDUZ
BADAKHSHAN

Med

Ceuta
Melilla

Gibraltar

ALGIERS

TUNIS

anean Sea

Tehran

PERSIA

AFGHANISTAN

Himalayas

Madeira

MOROCCO

OTTOMAN EMPIRE

Cairo

SIKH
STATES

Panipat

NEPAL

BHUTAN

Canary
Islands

C

Sahara Desert

TRIPOLI

EGYPT

FEZZAN

NEJD

Bahrain

BALUCHISTAN

SIND

Delhi

OUDH

BIHAR

CACHAR
MANIPUR

RAJPU-
TANA

ASSAM

Macao

MUGHAL
EMPIRE

MARATHA
CONFEDERACY

BENGAL

Serampore

Arabian
Peninsula

OMAN

Diu Damao

BURMA

LUANG PRABANG
TRAN NINH

*Verde
nds*

FUTA
TORO

St Louis
Goree

KAARTA

MOSSI
KINGDOMS

BORGU
KINGDOMS

BORNU

WADAI

YEMEN

NORTHERN
SARKARS
Yapaon

Bassein
Bombay
Chaul

Rangoon

VIETNAM

PACIFIC
OCEAN

Joal

SEGU

HAUSA
STATES

DARFUR

ETHIOPIA

Goa

MYSORE

Bay of
Bengal

SIAM

Manila

PHILIPPINE
ISLANDS

Portudal
Albreda
James Island

FUTA
JALLON

MAMPRUSI
SAGOMBA

NUPE

IGALA

HARAR

Mahe

Pondicherry
Tranquebar
Karikal

Bangkok

CARNATIC

CAMBODIA

MAGINDANAO

Cacheu

ASANTE

OYO
Whydah
BENIN
DAHOMEY

TRAVANCORE

Penang and
Wellesley Province

MALAY
STATES

SULU

Freetown
SIERRA LEONE

GOLD COAST

KANIOK

KANDY

Ceylon

Nicobar
Islands

ATJEH

SIAK
RIAU

JOHOR

BRUNEI

BULUNGAN

Menado

Fernando Po

BUNYORO

TORO

BUGANDA
BUSOGA

Malacca

Sambas

MALAY
STATES

KUTEI

Tidore

SAO TOME

TEKE

ANKOLE

RWANDA

KARAGWE
BURUNDI

Lake
Victoria

Mombasa
(To Oman)

Batavia

MALAY
STATES

SUKA-
DANA

BAND-
JARMASIN

PAPUANS
New
Guinea

KUBA

KALUNDE
LUBA
KIKONJA

Zanzibar
(To Oman)

*Seychelle
Islands*

DUTCH POSSESSIONS

MATAMBA

LUNDA

KAZEMBE

Kilwa
(To Oman)

MALAY
STATES

PORTUGUESE
TIMOR

ANGOLA
KASANJE

NDULU

MALAVI

INDIAN
OCEAN

MBAILUNDU

LOZI

Australia
ABORIGINAL PEOPLES

KIAKA

BIHE

GALANGI

BUTUA

MOZAMBIQUE

MERINA
KINGDOM

KAKONDA

WAMBU

*Kalahari
Desert*

Madagascar

MALAYS

Mauritius

Réunion

NEW
SOUTH
WALES
(Claimed
by Britain)

Lord Howe
Islands

Cape Town
CAPE COLONY

*Cape of
Good Hope*

Sydney

*New
Zealand*

MAORIS

SOUTHERN OCEAN

1802–1804

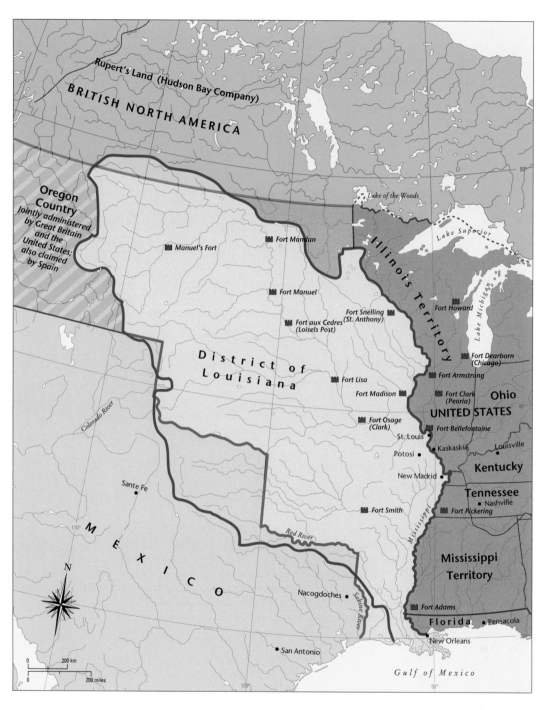

Louisiana Purchase and Border Settlements 1803–1819

~ Louisiana Purchase 1803, natural border of Louisiana, drainage of the Mississippi

▢ Territory of Louisiana from 1805–12, then Missouri Territory

— U.S.-British Treaty line of 1818, the 49th Parallel

~ Adams-Onis Treaty line of 1819

▢ Red River Basin ceded by Great Britain to U.S. in 1818

▢ Area ceded by U.S. to Great Britain 1818

▢ Spanish territory

about by this treaty, signed in January 1802 by France, Spain, Britain, and the Batavian Republic (Netherlands). France regained most of her overseas colonies, although Britain retained Trinidad and Ceylon. France agreed to evacuate the Two Sicilies and the Papal States, retaining the Netherlands, the west bank of the Rhine, Piedmont, and Savoy. Britain agreed to restore Egypt to the Ottoman

Empire and Malta to the Knights of St John. The Treaty of Amiens was really no more than a truce, which allowed both sides to regroup in readiness for the next onslaught.

TREATY OF BASSEIN 1802
The Maratha Confederacy was an alliance of kingdoms in western India, which united to resist

Mughal expansion in the 18th century. From 1761 the Confederacy was an alliance of five chiefs, under the leadership of the peshwa at Poona (Pune). The Treaty of Bassein was a decisive step in the break-up of the Confederacy, leading to the East India Company's annexation of the peshwa's territories in 1818, and effectively making Pune into a client British state. According to the terms of the treaty, the peshwa agreed to maintain a British force of six battalions, to give up his claims on Surat and Baroda, to exclude all foreigners from his service, and to only conduct foreign relations with British approval.

TREATY OF PARIS 1802

Between 1798 and 1802 Napoleon Bonaparte campaigned in Egypt and Syria, intent on disrupting Britain's access to India, defending French trade interests and conducting scientific investigations – indeed, the arrival of his forces in Egypt saw the beginnings of Egyptology, the systematic study and interpretation of Egyptian antiquities. In 1800, Egypt was in the hands of a French garrison – Bonaparte had returned to France in autumn 1799 – and an Anglo-Ottoman offensive in 1800 led to a French capitulation. In 1802 the Treaty of Paris, signed by France and the Ottoman Empire, formally brought to an end the French campaign in Egypt and Syria, restoring Ottoman-French relations to their pre-war status. The Ottomans also assented to the Treaty of Amiens.

THE LOUISIANA PURCHASE 1803

Signed by President Thomas Jefferson in April 1803, the Louisiana Purchase nearly doubled the size of the United States, and cost just 50 million francs ($11.25 million). It was an acquisition of nearly 830,000 square miles, stretching from the Gulf of Mexico to Canada, rich in gold, silver and other ores, fertile land, and huge forests. In 1682 the French explorer de La Salle had taken possession of the whole Mississippi River basin, naming the land Louisiana, in honour of Louis XIV. Since then the territory, considered valueless by the French, had been passed to Charles III of Spain. However, in 1800 Napoleon had negotiated to regain the region, in exchange for the small kingdom of Etruria, in northern Italy. Jefferson realized that the territory would stand in the way of the United States' western expansion; Napoleon, facing renewed war with Britain, was ready to sell.

TREATY OF SURJI-ANJANGAON 1803

The second phase of the Maratha War (1803–05) began when Lord Arthur Wellesley, acting on behalf of the East India Company, decided that he needed to deal with the separate chiefs of the loose Confederacy individually. He turned his attention to the Maratha chief Daulat Rao Scindiah, defeating him at the battles of Argaon and Assaye. Under the terms of the treaty the Company demanded that Scindiah ceded extensive territories: Ganges-Jumna Doab, Delhi-Agra, parts of Bundelkhand, Broach and some districts of Gujarat. He also was to accept that the Mughal Emperor fell under Company protection. He was required to ban Frenchmen serving at his cCourt, and accept an English Resident at court. He was also obliged to accept any treaties that the Company concluded with Scindiah's northern tributary chieftains, who were engaged in conflict with General Lake in Hindustan.

TREATY OF FORT WAYNE 1803

William Henry Harrison, the US superintendent of Indian affairs and commissioner plenipotentiary of the US, negotiated this treaty with representatives of several Native American tribes: Delawares, Potowatomi, Miami, Shawnee, and Kickapoo. The treaty precisely delineated the tract of land surrounding Fort Vincennes, which passed from Britain to the US in 1783, and was agreed to amount to 160,000 acres around the Wabash River. The US relinquished any claims to land abutting the tract. Further clauses ceded a salt spring at the mouth of the Wabash River to the US and allowed the US to build "entertainment" facilities for travelers on the road between Vincennes and Clarksville and Vincennes and Kaskaskia.

TREATY OF ST LOUIS 1804

Four Sauk and one Meswaki representatives signed this treaty, ceding over 50 million acres of land in Illinois, southwestern Wisconsin and northeastern Missouri to the US. The price was a mere $2,234 dollars' worth of goods and an annuity to be paid to the tribes in perpetuity of $1,000. From the md-18th century the Sauk and Meswaki had enjoyed cordial trading relations with the Europeans. The Louisiana Purchase changed the status quo, throwing the tribes into turmoil, which was exacerbated by the arrival of numerous white settlers. In September 1804 four Sauk hunters encountered illegal white settlers on their land and killed three of them. The Sauk and Meswaki were anxious to seek a pardon for what had transpired, and the Americans threatened retaliation if they did not come to the negotiating table. There, they signed away their tribal lands, without the authority of their Tribal Council, and possibly in ignorance of what they were giving away.

TREATY OF FORT INDUSTRY 1804

Following the Louisiana Purchase, President Jefferson was eager to drive American expansion

1805–1808

westward. The Treaty of Fort Industry was signed between the US and representatives of the Wyandot, Ottawa, Chipawa, Munsee and Delaware, Shawanee, and Pottawatima nations. By the terms of the treaty, the tribes relinquished half a million acres of land south of Lake Erie and west of the Cuyahoga River in northeastern Ohio. The US government paid annuities to each tribe, ranging from $1,000–4,000. The tribes still retained the right to hunt and fish on the land.

TREATY OF PRESSBURG 1805
Following Napoleon's victories at Ulm and Austerlitz, Austria signed a treaty with France at Pressburg. Austria relinquished its newly-acquired Venetian territory, and territory in Germany, ceding the Tyrol and Voralberg to Bavaria and Venetia, Istria, and Dalmatia to Italy. Austria agreed to elevate the electors of Napoleon's allies, Württemberg and Bavaria to the rank of kings, releasing them from their semi-feudal relationship with the Holy Roman Empire and thereby reducing Austria's influence in Germany. France's acquisition of Piedmont, Piacenza, and Parma excluded Austria from Italian territory. Austria's war indemnity to France was agreed at 40 million gold francs. The treaty isolated Austria, encircling it with a ring of French client states.

TREATY OF PEACE AND AMITY 1805
Signed in Tripoli in June, 1805, this was an agreement between the US and the Bashaw of Tripoli (Tripolitania). For three centuries shipping in the Mediterranean Sea had been vulnerable to privateers from the North African Muslim states, who captured hostages and sold them into slavery or demanded ransoms for their release. Before the Revolutionary War the British navy had provided protection for American shipping, while the French had taken on a protective role during the Revolution. But after US independence the Americans had to confront the depredations of Barbary (North African) pirates on their own, prompting them to negotiate a series of peace treaties, known as the "Barbary treaties." All of these treaties recognized the religion of the signatories, and in each case the US guaranteed substantial payments to the Barbary states in return for a promise that no further attacks would take place.

TREATY OF POZNAN 1806
The Fourth Coalition fought against Napoleon's French Empire from 1806 to 1807 and was ultimately defeated. Coalition partners included Britain, Russia, Sweden, Prussia, and Saxony. France decisively defeated Prussian and Russian troops at the Battle of Jena-Auerstedt on 14 October 1806, going on to occupy Berlin. Two month later the Treaty of Poznan was signed between Saxony, an erstwhile member of the coalition, and France. Emperor Napoleon Bonaparte had abolished the Holy Roman Empire in 1806, and agreed to establish the Electorate of Saxony as a kingdom, and a member of the newly-founded Confederation of the Rhine. Saxony paid France 25 million francs in reparations and from this point on the newly-elevated King Frederick Augustus III remained loyal to Napoleon.

TREATY OF DETROIT 1807
This was another treaty in President Jefferson's project to acquire Indian lands and push US territory westwards. The governor of the Michigan territory, General William Hull, was commissioned to negotiate with the representatives of the Chippewa, Ottawa, Wyandot, and Potawatamie tribes. By the terms of the treaty the US acquired a huge tract of land comprising southeast Michigan and a small section of Ohio north of the Maumee River. Within this territory the tribes retained small tracts of land and were promised the sum of $10,000 in money, as well as goods and "implements of husbandry."

TREATIES OF TILSIT 1807
Two treaties were signed at Tilsit, on 7 and 9 July, between France and Russia and France and Prussia respectively. The treaties came in the wake of Napoleon's victories at Austerlitz, Jena, and Friedland, defeating the armies of Austria, Prussia, and Russia, and the French Emperor was riding high. When Tsar Alexander I suggested peace talks, Napoleon was eager to consolidate his dominant position in Europe. The treaties agreed that both Prussia and Russia were to join the Continental System, which was a trade blockade aimed at British shipping. Prussia was forced to give up territory for Napoleon's newly-created grand duchy of Warsaw, which was to be given to the French ally, King Frederick Augustus III of Saxony. The kingdom of Westphalia was also confiscated and passed to Napoleon's brother Jerome Bonaparte. These territorial losses, combined with the demand for huge reparations from the Prussians, were a grave humiliation for Prussia. Many Russians also felt that the treaty was a shameful capitulation.

TREATY OF FINCKENSTEIN 1807
Napoleon consolidated his network of alliances beyond European borders with this treaty, signed between Persia and France in Finckenstein Palace, Prussia. He recognized Persian sovereignty over Georgia, Armenia, and Azerbaijan. He also agreed

Treaty of Tilsit
1807

- French Empire
- Allied to France
- Added to the Confederation of the Rhine
- Under French Administration

to supply the Persians with arms and training. The Shah would declare war on Britain and would assist the French if they attacked Britain from the east.

TREATY OF FONTAINEBLEAU 1807
Signed by Charles IV of Spain and the Emperor Napoleon, this treaty agreed the partition of Portugal. By this accord Napoleon secured the Continental Blockade, ensuring that Portuguese ports were closed to British shipping. Portugal was divided into three territories; the Entre-Dour-e-Minho province in the northwest was granted to the king of Etruria in exchange for Tuscany.

TREATY OF FORT CLARK 1808
By the terms of this this treaty, agreed at Fort Clark (Fort Osage), the Osage nation ceded all the land

east of the fort in Missouri and in Arkansas north of the Arkansas River to the US. Fort Clark would be established as a federal trade factory, with a blacksmith stationed there to provide utensils for the Native Americans. New regulations were agreed on the fur trade. The Osage were to receive an annual payment: $800 to the Great Osage nation and $400 to the Little Osage nation.

CONVENTION OF ERFURT 1808
Reaffirming the provisions of the Treaty of Tilsit in the previous year, the Erfurt Convention also called upon Britain to cease its war with France, and recognized the Russian conquest of Finland and Sweden. In the eventuality of a French war with Austria, it was agreed that Russia would come to the aid of France.

1809–1813

TREATY OF AMRITSAR 1809

The Sikh leader, Ranjit Singh, had established the kingdom of Punjab. He had gradually expanded his territories, and by 1808 was threatening the Sikh chiefs in Malwa on the south side of the Sutlej River. The chiefs appealed to Britain for protection, and in 1809 the British attacked Singh's forces there. Singh was impressed by the efficiency and discipline of the British troops and realized his weakness. He was prepared to negotiate with the East India Company, and the Treaty of Amritsar fixed Punjab's frontier at the Sutlej, preventing any further southern expansion. The British agreed not to interfere with Singh within his own territory, and he was free to expand northwards, eventually gaining control of Peshawar and Kashmir.

TREATY OF THE DARDANELLES 1809

Signed between the Ottoman Turks and the British, this treaty (also known as the Treaty of Çanak) asserted the principle that no warships should be allowed to enter the Straits of the Dardanelles and the Bosporus. The specific target of the agreement was Russia, regarded as a threat to Britain since the Treaty of Tilsit (1807), and the treaty would ensure that Russia's Black Sea fleet could not enter the Mediterranean. In addition, Britain's trading and consular privileges in the Ottoman Empire were reasserted, while the British promised to aid the Ottomans if the French declared war against them.

TREATY OF HAMINA 1809

This treaty (also called the Treaty of Frederikshamn) ended the Finnish War fought between Sweden and Russia (1808–09), in which Sweden – an ally of Britain against Napoleon – had challenged the might of Napoleon's sometime ally, Russia, for control of the Baltic. Russian troops had overrun Swedish possessions in Finland and reached within 45 miles (70 km) of the Swedish capital. Sweden capitulated and ceded Lappland, Västerbotten, Aland, and all provinces to the east to Russia, about a third of Sweden's territory, which became the grand duchy of Finland. The new duchy was autonomous and self-governing, retaining its Protestant religion, while the laws passed under Swedish rule – the Swedish constitution of 1772, amended in 1789 – remained in force. The Swedes had fought against the loss of the Aland Islands, which were culturally and linguistically purely Swedish, and a strategic outpost in the Baltic, but were forced to surrender them to Russia.

TREATY OF SCHÖNBRUNN 1809

The 1809 campaign on the Danube against Napoleon had been disastrous for Austria, culminating in a decisive defeat at the Battle of Wagram in July 1809. Emperor Francis I was reluctant to go to the negotiating table until the French emperor had issued an ultimatum to Francis I, threatening to re-open hostilities. The treaty was harsh, imposing arduous conditions on Austria, which was forced to give up lands to Bavaria, the duchy of Warsaw, and Russia. Much of Austria's coastline was ceded to France, rendering Austria land-locked. A total of 3.5 million people were taken out of Austrian territory, and Austria owed France 75 million francs in war debts. Finally, Austria was forced to join the Continental System, banning trade with Britain, and was compelled to reduce the Austrian army to 150,000 men.

TREATY OF FORT WAYNE 1809

William Henry Harrison, the governor of the Indiana territory, negotiated the Treaty of Fort Wayne with the Delaware, Eel River, Miami and Potawatomi peoples, and later the Kickapoo and Wea, to acquire 3 million acres of land, mainly along the Wabash River. Harrison promised large payments to the tribes, and only the Miami resisted the deal; they were concerned that the Wea, who were not present at the negotiation, were the main inhabitants of the land and should therefore be consulted. They also insisted that they should be paid per acre, and not a global price for the entire tract. Harrison was prepared to address the Wea's absence, but would not concede a dollar-per-acre deal. Eventually the Potawatomi persuaded the Miami to accept the deal. The Wea were also persuaded to concede when they were offered a large subsidy.

TREATY OF PARIS 1810

This treaty formally ended the war between France and Sweden, following the Russian defeat of Sweden in 1809 and signature of the Treaty of Hamina. The most important result of the treaty was that Sweden closed its ports, joined the Continental System and declared war on Great Britain. One of Napoleon's marshals, Jean-Baptiste Bernadotte, was elected crown prince of Sweden in 1810 and the House of Bernadotte remains the Royal House of Sweden.

TREATY OF BUCHAREST 1812

The Russo-Turkish War had lasted from 1806–12, starting with Sultan Selim III's deposition of the pro-Russian rulers of Walachia and Moldavia, both Ottoman vassal states. When the French occupied Dalmatia, threatening to penetrate into the Danube, the Russians decided to mount an offensive, advancing into Moldavia and Walachia to protect the Russian border. The sultan promptly blocked the Dardanelles to Russian ships and declared war

Treaty of Paris
1810

under direct rule by
Napoleon

under rule by members
of Napoleon's family

dependent state

on Russia. Over the prolonged conflict, Russia won
several important victories. The Treaty of Bucharest,
which formally ended the war, ceded the eastern
half of Moldavia, known as Bessarabia, to Russia,
ensuring that Russia became a major player in the
Danube region. In Transcaucasia, where the conflict
had also been played out, the frontier remained
essentially unchanged, with the Russians returning
several places they had captured.

TREATY OF GULISTAN 1813
This peace treaty between Russia and Persia ended
the Russo-Persian War (1804–13). Both powers had
clashed over the Caucasian region; Persia claimed
Georgia and Azerbaijan, but Russia had formally
annexed Georgia. While Persian troops had the
numerical advantage over the Russians, they were
outclassed technologically. The Persians sought a
military alliance with France, but the French had
already made an alliance with Russia in 1807, and

were therefore unable to help Persia. At the Battle
of Aslanduz on 31 October 1812, Russian forces
completely obliterated the Persian army. The treaty
was a humiliation for the Persians, as they were
forced to concede most of their Caucasian territories,
including Georgia, Daghestan, Azerbaijan and parts
of northern Armenia, to the Russians. Russia was
granted exclusive rights to station its military fleet in
the Caspian, and both countries made a mutual free
trade agreement.

TREATY OF KALISZ 1813
The Convention of Kalisz, signed between Russia
and Prussia, committed Prussia to re-joining the
war against Napoleon, setting the stage for the final
chapter in the Napoleonic Wars. The Prussians, who
had agreed to a humiliating treaty with France at
Tilsit (1807), had been forced to fight on Napoleon's
side. However, during the retreat from Moscow
General Yorck, who led the Prussia corps, defected,

1813–1815

signed a separate agreement with the Russians and was allowed to retreat into East Prussia. His actions were very popular in Prussia, and negotiations began between Russia and Prussia. Russia and Prussia entered into an alliance and Prussia agreed to provision any Russian troops stationed in its territory. Both sides would provide troops for the war against Napoleon, and agreed not to enter into separate negotiations with him. Russia agreed that Prussia should regain all the German territory lost by the Treaty of Tilsit, and only retained the Polish territory agreed in the First Partition (1772).

TREATIES OF REICHENBACH 1813
With Napoleon in retreat, it was imperative for his opponents to consolidate and strengthen their alliance. Several treaties were negotiated and concluded at Reichenbach in June 1813. Britain and Russia signed an agreement in which Britain agreed to pay £1,333,334 to Russia towards the maintenance of both its army and fleet. The treaty between Britain and Prussia, agreed that Britain would pay £666,666 to maintain Prussian troops. A clause was inserted in both these treaties stipulating that British officers would accompany the operations of the army. Finally, in the Reichenbach Accord, signed between Austria, Prussia, and Russia, Austria agreed to declare war against Napoleon in the event that he rejected its peace conditions.

TREATY OF PETERSWALDAU 1813
Signed between Britain and Russia in July, Britain agreed to pay for a German legion of 10,000 soldiers to fight under the Russians against Napoleon.

TREATY OF TÖPILTZ 1813
A further step in the building of a Sixth Coalition against Napoleon, the Töplitz Treaty was signed by Russia, Prussia, and Austria in September 1813. They made a mutual support agreement, with each side committing to provide 60,000 troops. Further agreements were made at Töplitz between Great Britain and Austria.

TREATY OF RIED 1813
Bavaria was Napoleon's most important ally in the Confederation of the Rhine. However, Bavaria's substantial military support was met with diminishing rewards, and relations began to fray. Napoleon's plans to divorce his wife Josephine and marry the eldest daughter of the Habsburg Emperor, Marie-Louis, raised the specter of a French-Austrian *rapprochement*, perhaps bringing Habsburg retaliation for Bavaria's opposition over the preceding decade. On the eve of the Battle of Leipzig, 8 October 1813, King Maximilian-Joseph of Bavaria agreed to join the allies against Napoleon, on condition that he preserved the territorial integrity of his kingdom. Napoleon was decisively defeated.

TREATY OF FULDA 1813
The Battle of Leipzig, 16–19 October 1813, saw the Coalition armies of Russia, Prussia, Austria, and Sweden decisively defeating Napoleon. Napoleon's allies included Polish and Italian troops as well as Germans from the Confederation of the Rhine. Napoleon's defeat ended the French presence east of the Rhine, and meant that the German states defected to the Coalition. Signed by King Frederick I of Württemberg and the Austrian foreign minister Prince Metternich, the Treaty of Fulda agreed that Württemberg was no longer a member of the Confederation of the Rhine.

TREATY OF KIEL 1814
Anti-French allies Great Britain and Sweden signed this treaty with French allies Denmark and Norway in Kiel in 1814, ending the hostilities that had taken place in the Napoleonic Wars. Frederick of Denmark joined the Sixth Coalition, ceding Heligoland to Britain and the kingdom of Norway to Sweden, in exchange for Swedish Pomerania. The preceding year Sweden had joined the alliance of the Reichenbach; Prussia had accepted Sweden's claim to Norway, and had helped the allies clear Napoleon's troops from northern Germany. Denmark, an ally of Napoleon's, was left isolated and bankrupt, and was forced to accept the loss of Norway, although Denmark retained the Norwegian dependencies of Greenland, Iceland, and the Faroe Islands.

TREATY OF FONTAINEBLEAU 1814
Signed between the Austrian Empire, Russia, and Prussia – the victorious Sixth Coalition nations – and Napoleon Bonaparte in April 1814, this treaty stripped Napoleon of his powers as French Emperor, although he was allowed to retain his title. His family and successors were prohibited from taking power in France. Napoleon was exiled to the Mediterranean island of Elba. Great Britain, nervous of Napoleon's proposed proximity to both France and Italy, both of which had strong Jacobin factions, feared that Napoleon could initiate further conflicts, and refused to sign the treaty. Napoleon grandly acceded to the allies' demands, stating "there is no personal sacrifice, not even that of life itself, which he [Napoleon] is not willing to make for the interests of France."

TREATY OF PARIS 1814
The treaty ended the war between France and the Sixth Coalition, providing a draft of a final

settlement that would result in the Congress of Vienna. With the restoration of the Bourbon king, Louis XVIII, to the throne of France, the Allies agreed lenient terms in the Treaty of Paris, eager to assist the transition to a monarchy, while strengthening the states that bordered France. The Treaty of Paris was signed by France and the Allied powers: Great Britain and Ireland, Russia, Prussia, Austria, Portugal, Sweden, and Spain. France retained her boundaries of 1792 and most of her lost colonies were restored, except St Lucia, Mauritius, Tobago, and Malta. Various states gained independence: Switzerland; Holland and Belgium, united under the House of Orange; Germany was to become a federation of independent states; Italy, to consist of several states, apart from territory ceded to Austria. France would retain the art treasures plundered by Napoleon and the revolutionary armies, and agreed to abolish the slave trade. In secret, the Allies agreed that Austria would receive the territory of Venetia, and the Kingdom of Sardinia would receive Genoa.

ANGLO-DUTCH TREATY OF 1814

Also known as the Convention of London, this treaty restituted the Dutch colonies that were lost after 1803 during the Napoleonic Wars. The treaty dealt with colonies all over the world, including the Americas, Asia, and Africa, with the exception of the Cape of Good Hope and British Guiana. The British ceded the island of Branca off the coast of Sumatra in exchange for Cochin in India and its dependencies. Following a British initiative, the Dutch extended the ban on slave ships to their own ports.

CONVENTION OF MOSS 1814

Following the Treaty of Kiel in January 1814, Norway was declared independent of Denmark and ceded to Sweden. The Norwegians sought independence and immediately became embroiled in a short war with Sweden (26 July–7 August). At the Convention of Moss a more equitable solution was agreed, which would treat Norway as an equal partner rather than a conquered territory. The king of Sweden agreed to accept the Norwegian constitution, allowing Norway to retain its own government and institutions. Christian Frederick, the claimant to the Norwegian throne, relinquished all claims to the Norwegian crown and leave the country. Once the Norwegian parliament was convened, its first duty was to ratify the convention.

TREATY OF FORT JACKSON 1814

The Creek War of 1813–14 between the Red Stick faction of the Upper Creeks and the US culminated in General Andrew Jackson's decisive victory at the Battle of Horseshoe Bend on 27 March 1814. The subsequent treaty forced the Creeks to cede over 21 million acres of land in the Mississippi Territory (mainly in present-day Alabama and Georgia) to the US, opening up a vast and fertile territory for white settlement. The justification for this land grab was the argument that the Creeks had waged an "unprovoked" war, to be paid for in territorial concessions. The treaty also stipulated that the Creek should cease communicating with the British and Spanish, and should allow the government to build forts, trading houses, and roads in Creek territory.

THE LONDON PROTOCOL 1814

Signed by the Great Powers – Great Britain, Prussia, Austria, and Russia – this treaty awarded the territory of Belgium and the Netherlands to William I of the Netherlands, who became "sovereign prince." The ambition was to meld Belgium with the Netherlands completely, with the Belgian provinces represented in the States General, whose sittings would alternate between Belgian and Dutch towns. All inhabitants were to share the same fundamental constitutional rights. However, many Belgians feared that the Catholic Church would be undermined.

TREATY OF GHENT 1814

The US declared war on Great Britain in 1812, because of three main issues: the British economic blockade of France; the thousands of neutral American seamen who were impressed in the British navy against their will; British support of the tribes in the Great Lakes, who were hostile to the US government. The US also hoped to exploit the British preoccupation with their wars against France to make territorial gains in Canada and Florida. After an initial spate of American maritime victories and some success in the Great Lakes region, the British regained control of the high seas and blockaded the eastern seaboard. The downfall of Bonaparte in 1814 turned British attention to the US and Washington D.C. fell to them in August. But the US pushed back in Baltimore and Lake Champlain and the British forces retreated to Canada. The Treaty of Ghent, signed on 24 December, concluded the war. All conquered territory was returned and commissions were tasked with the agreement of a US-Canada border. The treaty effectively opened up the Great Lakes region to American expansion.

TREATY OF PARIS 1815

The "Hundred Days" was the period between 1 March and 18 June, during which Napoleon escaped from his exile on the island of Elba, and raised an army with the intent of liberating France from the Allies and resuming his conquest of Europe. On 16

Congress of Vienna 1815

The Final Act of the Congress of Vienna was signed on 9 June 1815, with remarkable *sang-froid* as Napoleon's still to be defeated army was then converging on Waterloo. Fortunately, Wellington prevailed, so the nine months of high diplomacy and intrigue did not go to waste, while the repercussions for France's recidivist delinquency would be meted out in a subsequent second Treaty of Paris, a few months later.

By the standards of such negotiations, the Congress, judged on results, was remarkably successful. The 18th century had been dominated by all-out European conflicts, and beset by many others. Nothing of this magnitude would occur for a century after Vienna. This derived in part from the strength of motivation in the participants. At Utrecht (1713) and Paris (1763), the balance of power was a theoretical construct. In 1815, Europe had experienced the military domination of one power, Napoleonic France, and was determined to avert its recurrence. Even more heinous than instigating two decades of war was the threat posed to the established order by the principles of Revolutionary France, and its exported version, Napoleon's imperialist iconoclasm.

The representatives of the Great Powers – Britain, Russia, Austria, Prussia – had begun to gather in Vienna at the end of the summer, 1814. Territorial settlements were the first order of business. Talleyrand, the Machiavellian French foreign minister had the guile to recognize opportunity in the negotiators' conflicting objectives. Originally exiled from the 'top table' of Britain, Russia, Austria and Prussia, Talleyrand managed to insinuate himself as spokesmen for second-tier attendees like Portugal, Sweden and Bavaria. There, he engineered a deterrent alliance with England and Austria against Russia which forced Tsar Alexander to the negotiating table over Poland. While the tsar received most of the Napoleonic duchy of Poland and became king of Poland, he was not allowed to unite the new territory with the part of Poland that had been incorporated into Russia in the 1790s; Prussia received the province of Posen, and most of Saxony. Austria made several acquisitions including Lombardy and Venetia. A United Kingdom of the Netherlands was created, and the number of German principalities streamlined from 360 to 38, forming the German Confederation under the presidency of the Austrian Empire. The papal lands were restored, as were the kingdoms of Sardinia and Naples. Other concerns were also addressed by the Congress: the rights of German Jews, navigation rights on European rivers, the abolition of the slave trade, the restoration of the Bourbon monarchy, the constitution of Switzerland.

The Congress also examined the very nature of diplomacy, creating the Vienna Regulations, which introduced new rules about diplomatic organization and precedence that overhauled the old systems of the *ancien régime*. Diplomats were organized into three tiers – ambassadors, envoys, chargés d'affaires – remaining the basis for diplomacy to this day.

In March 1815, in the middle of negotiations, the unthinkable happened and Napoleon escaped from captivity on the island of Elba, reoccupied the throne of France, mustered his forces and began the military adventure known as the "Hundred Days," which would eventually lead to his defeat at Waterloo. The allies banded together to defeat him but, alarm at his widespread popular support would lead to a further cherrypicking of French territories and the imposition of massive reparations.

The Congress also sought a new political system within Europe, rejecting the balance of power that had been the result of the Treaty of Utrecht a century earlier, with its opposing military alliances. Napoleon had shattered the delicate balance of power and created an empire. Instead the delegates developed a "System of Peace." This would be one multilateral power bloc in Europe, which would be maintained and upheld by a series of regular congresses (the Congress System), the first attempt to build a continent-wide order based on active cooperation between the states. The Congress system lasted until 1823 when the delegates stopped meeting regularly. Yet the power bloc philosophy survived for several decades; after the wave of revolutions in 1848, the monarchs of Russia, Austria and Prussia cooperated to crush the insurgents. But the Ottoman Empire had been excluded from the European peace and when, in 1853, Russia broke ranks and decided to move aganst the Ottoman Empire, the British and French formed an alliance and sent an expeditionary force leading to the Crimean War, and the end of consensus.

With the benefit of hindsight, the Congress showed scant regard for national self-determination, but in that it was of its time. The determination to bottle the revolutionary genie probably exacerbated the tensions which would boil over in the "Year of Revolutions," 1848. It produced no apparatus for the ongoing maintenance of international relations. However, when the League of Nations was formed a century later it kept the peace for a fraction of the time achieved by the Congress. What could not possibly have been foreseen at Vienna is that Prussia - bolstered there after near annihilation as a prop against Russia and France – would emerge to dominate Europe and ultimately shatter the Pax Britannica enforced by British naval, commercial, and industrial supremacy.

Europe in 1815 After the Congress of Vienna

— German Confederation

0 — 200 km
0 — 200 miles

Iceland
to Denmark

Norwegian Sea

Arctic Circle

N

Faeroe Islands to Denmark

Finland

St Petersburg

United until 1905

Christiania

Stockholm

Scotland

Edinburgh

North Sea

Baltic Sea

RUSSIAN EMPIRE

Copenhagen

DENMARK

Hamburg

IRELAND

Dublin

GREAT BRITAIN

Wales

England

Amsterdam

London

Brussels

NETHERLANDS

HANNOVER

P R U S S I A

Berlin

Warsaw

REPUBLIC OF CRACOW

PRUSSIA

SAXONY

Prague

Cracow

Paris

BAVARIA

BADEN

Stuttgart

WÜRTTEMBERG

Vienna

Buda ■ Pest

Hungary

AUSTRIAN EMPIRE

Moldavia

ATLANTIC OCEAN

F R A N C E

NEUCHATEL

SWITZERLAND

LOMBARDY VENETIA

Transylvania

Wallachia

Bucharest

SARDINIA

PARMA

Genoa

MODENA

Zara

Adriatic Sea

OTTOMAN EMPIRE

Montenegro

MASSA AND CARRARA

Florence

TUSCANY

PAPAL STATES

LUCCA

Corsica

Rome

Oporto

ANDORRA

Madrid

PORTUGAL

Lisbon

S P A I N

Balearic Is.

SARDINIA

Naples

KINGDOM OF THE TWO SICILIES

Sicily

Ionian Islands to Great Britain

Aegean Sea

Athens

Gibraltar
to Great Britain

Algiers

Tunis

M e d i t e r r a n e a n   S e a

Crete

MOROCCO

ALGERIA

TUNIS

129

1815–1822

June the Prussians were routed at the Battle of Ligny. Two days later Napoleon confronted Wellington at the Battle of Waterloo, where he was defeated and surrendered. The Allies felt that more onerous terms should be imposed on France, because Napoleon's adventure revealed that there was still widespread support for his cause. However, the Allied desire for the success of the Bourbon restoration meant that rigorous terms were inevitably modified. By the terms of the Treaty of Paris, signed 1 November 1815, France was reduced to its 1789 frontiers, which meant that territory was ceded to Sardinia and Switzerland. The war indemnity demanded was 700 million francs and the French had to accept an Allied army of occupation in 17 border fortresses, and pay for its maintenance. It was agreed that art treasures, plundered from all the conquered lands of Europe, were to be restored by France.

TREATY OF SPRINGWELLS 1815
Signed at Fort Wayne, this treaty ended the conflict between the US government and members of the Delaware, Seneca, Shawnee, Miami, Ottawa, Chippewa, Potawatomi, and Wyandot Indians. In order to secure the allegiance of the Indians as allies, the US government effectively forgave them for the support given to the British in the war of 1812.

SUGAULI TREATY 1816
The expansion of Nepal began under King Prithvi Narayan Shah, who had united a number of small states to form a powerful Nepal. Defeated at the battles of Nalapani, Jaithak and Makawanpur in the Anglo-Nepalese War (1815–16), the Nepalese signed the Sugauli Treaty with the East India Company, which pronounced perpetual peace and friendship, and renounced all claim to disputed territories. The East India Company agreed to grant pensions to dispossessed chiefs. The king of Nepal renounced all land west of the River Kali and also agreed not to challenge the king of Sikkim; any differences between the two monarchs were to be arbitrated by the East India Company. A British representative was appointed in Kathmandu, and the British agreed the right to recruit gurkhas into the British army.

TREATY OF ST LOUIS 1816
Signed between the Council of Three Fires (the Ottawa, Ojibwa, and Potawatomi tribes) and the US government, by the terms of this treaty the tribes ceded a 20-mile strip of land to the US, connecting Chicago and Lake Michigan with the Illinois River. It was destined to be the site of the Illinois and Michigan Canal, built in 1848. The tribes were paid compensation of $1,000 worth of merchandise over a twelve-year period.

RUSH-BAGOT TREATY 1817
Following the British-American War of 1812, this was an exchange of notes between Richard Rush, the US Secretary of State, and Charles Bagot, British minister to the US. It agreed that naval forces belonging to both countries on the Great Lakes would be limited to one military vessel belonging to each country on Lake Champlain and Lake Ontario and two belonging to each on the upper lakes. This effectively led to the demilitarization of the US–Canadian border.

TREATY OF FORT MEIGS 1817
Also known as the Treaty of the Maumee Rapids, this agreement ceded the remaining tribal lands of the Wyandot, Seneca, Shawnee, Delaware, Potawatomi, Chippewa, and Ottawa in northwestern Ohio to the US government. Newly released land in the Ohio Valley was auctioned to white settlers.

TREATY OF TITALIA 1817
Signed between the Chogyal (monarch) of Sikkim and the British East India Company, this treaty returned Sikkim territories that had been annexed during the Anglo-Nepalese War (1814–16). The Sikkimese granted the British trading rights that extended as far as the Tibetan frontiers, and agreed that EIC goods that passed through Sikkim would be free of duties. In the event of any territorial disputes with neighbors, it was agreed that the British would be called in to negotiate.

TREATY OF 1818
Also known as the "Convention respecting fisheries, boundary and the restoration of slaves" this treaty, signed between Britain and the US, established the boundary between the US and Canada at the 49th parallel. Under the terms of the treaty, US fisherman were allowed to operate along the coasts of Newfoundland and Labrador, while both nations agreed to joint control of Oregon territory. The treaty heralded a new, more positive, chapter in the relationship between Britain and the US.

TREATY OF ST MARY'S 1818
A supplement to the Treaty of Fort Meigs of 1817, it agreed that the US would grant the Shawnee, Ottawa, Wyandot, and Seneca additional sums of money for the lands that had been ceded in Ohio. In addition the US government agreed to set aside tracts of land that the American Indians would own, effectively creating reservations.

TREATY OF THE CREEK AGENCY 1818
Signed on the Flint River in Georgia, this treaty between the US and Creek nations agreed that the

Native Americans would cede two tracts of land to the US, in exchange for $120,000 to be paid over an eleven-year period. It was signed by 18 representatives of the Creek nations.

TREATY OF ST LOUIS 1818

Aso known as the Osage treaty, by this agreement the Osage ceded their territories between the Arkansas and Verdigris Rivers to the US. The treaty was a result of the Euro-American and eastern tribes' push into Osage lands. The Osage land cessions were used to push the Cherokee further west.

ADAMS–ONÍS TREATY 1819

Also known as the Transcontinental Treaty or Purchase of Florida, this agreement between the US and Spain divided their North American claims, with Spain formally ceding Florida and Oregon county in exchange for recognition of their claims of sovereignty over Texas. Effectively, the US and Spain had defined the western boundaries of the Louisiana Purchase and Spain had surrendered its claims over the Pacific Northwest.

TREATY OF DOAK'S STAND 1820

This treaty was signed between the US and Chocataw nation. The Chocataw agreed to give up one-half of their remaining territory, effectively ceding about 5.5 million acres to the US. In exchange the US ceded land to the Chocataw in present-day Arkansas, as well as paying them an annuity for 16 years.

TREATY OF CÓRDOBA 1821

Eleven years after the outbreak of the Mexican War of Independence the Spanish viceroy approved a plan to make Mexico into an independent monarchy. After ten bitter years of fighting a new, liberal government took power in Spain, prepared to make concessions to the Mexican revolutionaries, who were calling for redistribution of land and racial equality. Mexican Conservatives insisted on independence as a way of maintaining their advantage. Under the plan outlined in the treaty, Mexico would become an independent constitutional monarchy; the Catholic Church would still occupy a dominant position in Mexican society; Mexicans of Spanish descent would have greater rights than Mexicans of mixed ancestry or pure Indian blood. In 1822 Augustín de Iturbide, the royalist leader, was proclaimed emperor of Mexico – just a year later he was deposed and the Mexican Republic was founded.

TREATY OF CHICAGO 1821

Ottawa, Chippewa, and Potawatomi representatives ceded all their lands in Michigan Territory south of the Grand River to the US, with the exception of a handful of small reservations. They also gave the US permission to build a road from Detroit to Chicago, completed in 1835.

FIRST TREATY OF INDIAN SPRINGS 1821

By the terms of this treaty the Creeks ceded their remaining land east of the Flint River to the US. Georgian representatives were keen to acquire land in the northern part of the state that would drive a wedge between the Creek and the Cherokee, preventing them from becoming allies. Citizens of Georgia had also lodged claims, probably inflated, against the Creek for $350,000 for backdated trade transactions. The Creek refused to cede the land in the northern part of the state or to move west, but they did agree to cede a large tract of land that bordered the Flint River, of approximately 4.3 million acres. The US agreed to pay the Creek $10,000 on signing and $40,000 after the accord was ratified, as well as an annuity totalling $200,000 over the next 14 years, and an agreement to clear Creek debts of $250,000.

CAPITULATION OF QUITO 1822

This Capitulation followed the defeat of Spanish forces at the Battle of Pichincha, the last battle of the Ecuadorian War of Independence (1820–22). The war was fought between several South American armies and Spain over control of the lands of the Royal Audience of Quito, a Spanish colonial administrative jurisdiction. Following the battle, Ecuador joined Simón Bolívar's Republic of Gran Colombia. In 1830 Ecuador separated from Gran Colombia and became the independent Republic of Ecuador.

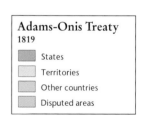

Adams-Onis Treaty
1819

- States
- Territories
- Other countries
- Disputed areas

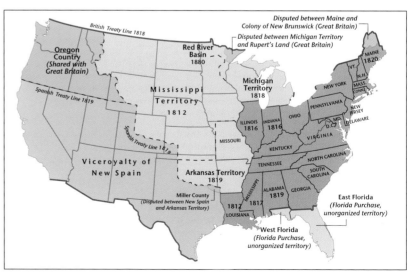

1823–1828

TREATY OF MOULTRIE CREEK 1823

Signed in Florida – which the US had purchased from Spain in 1819 – the treaty was an agreement between the US government and chiefs of the Seminole Indians. The Seminoles placed themselves under US protection and gave up all claim to lands in Florida in exchange for a reservation of some 4 million acres. The US government would give financial aid, farm implements, cattle, and hogs to the Seminoles who would allow roads to be built across the reservation and would apprehend any runaway slaves and return them to US jurisdiction.

SECOND ANGLO-DUTCH TREATY 1824

Also known as the Treaty of London, this treaty aimed to settle territorial and trade disputes arising from the Anglo-Dutch Treaty of 1814. Britain's establishment of Singapore on the Malay Peninsula in 1819 further exacerbated the tension between Britain and the Dutch. Under the terms of the 1824 treaty, the Netherlands ceded all its factories in India to Britain, withdrew all objections to the British occupation of Singapore, and ceded Malacca and all its dependencies to Britain. In return, Britain ceded Bencoolen and all its possessions in Sumatra to the Netherlands. Neither party could sign any treaty with any ruler or state in the other's sphere of influence. These clauses effectively brought Malaya and Singapore under British control while most of what is today Indonesia came under Dutch rule.

RUSSO-AMERICAN TREATY OF 1824

Signed in Saint Petersburg between Russia and the US, this treaty gave Russian claims on the Pacific Northwest coast of North America, south of parallel 54°40' north (the Oregon Country) to the US.

ANGLO-RUSSIAN TREATY 1825

Signed between Russia and Britain, the treaty fixed Russia's southernmost boundary of Alaska at the line of 54°40'. Russia, however, retained its rights to trade in the area south of this latitude.

ANDERSON-GUAL TREATY 1824

Formally, the General Convention of Peace, Amity, Navigation, and Commerce, this was the first bilateral treaty that the US concluded with another American country; in this case, Colombia. The treaty granted reciprocal most-favored nation status.

OSAGE TREATY 1825

This was the third treaty signed by the chiefs of the Osage nation with the US government in which they had been forced by encroaching white settlers and other tribes, especially the Cherokees, to cede tracts of their territories in Missouri and Arkansas.

Under the terms of the Osage Treaty, the Osage ceded all their remaining land and agreed to move to a reservation along the Kansas border. In all, the tribe had ceded a total of 96.8 million acres in the three treaties, for a total compensation of $166,000.

TREATY OF ST LOUIS 1825

Under the terms of this treaty, signed between the US government and delegates from the Shawnee nation, the Shawnee were forcibly relocated from Cape Geredeau in Missouri to southeastern Kansas, close to the Neosho River. In return for Cape Geredeau, the US gave the Shawnee a sum of $11,000 and leased to them a blacksmith shop for five years, providing all tools and 300 pounds of iron annually. Peace and friendship between the two nations were renewed and perpetuated.

SECOND TREATY OF INDIAN SPRINGS 1825

The Creek Confederacy, also known as the Muscogee, and the US had signed the First Treaty of Indian Springs in 1821. In 1824, an attempt to secure a treaty that would force the Creek to cede their territory east of the Mississippi River to the US had failed. The 1825 treaty was negotiated with six chiefs of the Lower Creek, and talks were led by William McIntosh. He agreed to cede all Creek lands east of the Chattahoochee River, including the sacred Ocmulgee National Monument, to Georgia and Alabama, and accepted relocation west of the Mississippi to an equivalent parcel of land along the Arkansas River. In compensation, the Creek nation would receive $200,000 and $200,000 was paid to McIntosh. The fraudlent treaty was nullified and replaced by the Treaty of Washington of 1826.

TREATY OF PRAIRIE DU CHIEN 1825

Due to the encroachment of white settlers and Native Americans into Sioux territory, the Sioux Nation came into conflict with other tribes. Inter-tribal warfare was disrupting the fur trade, and the influx of miners and squatters into Indian territories was increasing tensions between the tribes and settlers. To address these problems, the US government invited thousands of Indians, representing all the tribes in the Upper Mississippi, to gather at Prairie du Chien, Wisconsin. The resultant treaty called for peace among all the tribes and established boundaries between white settlers and the Sioux, Ojibwe, Sauk and Fox, Menominee, Iowa, Ho-chunk, Ottawa, and Potawatomi nations.

UNITED STATES-CENTRAL AMERICA TREATY 1825

Formally, the Treaty of Peace, Amity, Commerce, and Navigation between the United States of

America and the Federal Republic of Central America, this was the second bilateral US treaty concluded with a sovereign state in the Americas. The Federal Republic of Central America (1821–41) was a republican democracy, which comprised the present-day states of Honduras, Guatemala, Nicaragua, El Salvador, and Costa Rica. The treaty became the model for later treaties since it contained a complete catalogue of rules governing political and commercial relations, including full reciprocal treatment.

AKKERMAN CONVENTION 1826
Russo-Turkish relations had deteriorated rapidly in the two decades following the Treaty of Bucharest (1812). The Turks had violated the treaty by occupying the Danubian principalities of Moldavia and Walachia, and encroaching on Serbian territorial possessions and autonomy. In March 1826 Russia issued an ultimatum demanding Turkish adherence to the Bucharest agreement and the Turks entered into negotiations. Under the terms of the Convention, Turkey granted autonomy to Serbia and recognized the autonomy of Moldavia and Walachia, including a seven-year term of office for the *hospodars* (princes), who could thenceforth not be dismissed without consent of the Russian ambassador in Istanbul. Turkey also agreed to allow Russian ships freedom of the Black Sea and the Danube River and to open the Bosporus and the Dardanelles to merchant vessels of any nation sailing to or from Russia. Turkish repudiation of the Convention led to the Russo-Turkish War (1828–29).

TREATY OF MISSISSINWAS 1826
Under the terms of this treaty, the Miami people – one of the Great Lakes tribes – agreed to cede to the US the bulk of the reservation lands in Indiana granted to them by previous treaties. In compensation, the families of certain Miami notables were given estates in Indiana. The US government agreed to buy out some of the estates granted by the previous Treaty of St Mary's (1818), and small reservations were to be carved out along the Eel and Maumee rivers. The tribe was also to be compensated with $31,040.53 the first year; and $26,259.47 in goods the next. Promises were made of a $15,000 annuity thereafter.

TREATY OF YANDABOO 1826
The First Anglo-Burmese War (1824–26) arose from friction between Arakan in western Burma and British-held Chittagong to the north. Britain's superior firepower forced the Burmese to sue for peace. Under the Treaty of Yandaboo's terms, the Burmese agreed to cede to the British Assam, Manipur, Arakan, and the Tenasserim coast south of the Salween River. They also agreed to cease all interference in Cachar and the Jaintia Hills district; to pay an indemnity of £1 million in four installments; and to allow an exchange of diplomats between Burma and Calcutta.

BURNEY TREATY 1826
Signed between Thailand and the British, this treaty acknowledged Thai control over the four northern Malay states of Kedah, Kelantan, Perlis, and Terengganu. The treaty further guaranteed British ownership of Penang and their rights to trade in Kelantan and Terengganu without Thai interference. The four Malay states were not represented in the treaty negotiations.

TREATY OF LONDON 1827
The Greek War of Independence had begun in 1821 when the Greeks rebelled against Turkish rule. The Greek cause was saved by the intervention of the European powers – Britain, France, and Russia. Favoring the formation of an autonomous Greek state, they offered to mediate between the Turks and the Greeks. In the Treaty of London, the European powers declared that the Turks should recognize the independence of Greece, with the Turkish sultan as its supreme ruler. When the Turks refused, the European powers sent their fleets to Navarino where, in 1827, they destroyed the combined Turkish and Egyptian fleets. Despite the military and naval success of the European powers, Turkey refused to yield on Greek statehood. The treaty had also bound Russia to refrain from making any territorial or commercial gains from Turkey.

TREATY OF TURKMENCHAY 1828
The Treaty of Gulistan (1813) had failed to resolve the issues between Russia and Persia over the Caucasian region and, in 1826, the two nations clashed again in the Russo-Persian War. The Treaty of Turkmenchay was imposed by Russia following its victory over Persia in the conflict. Under the terms of the treaty, the border between Russia and Persia was established along the Aras River. Russia was given the khanates of Erivan and Nakhchivan. The fortress of Abbas-Abad, together with the adjacent territory, was also given to Russia. Furthermore, Russia obtained the right to navigate all of the Caspian Sea.

TREATY OF MONTEVIDEO 1828
By 1828 an armed conflict (known as the Cisplatine War) between Argentina and Brazil over an area known as Banda Oriental (roughly present-day Uruguay) had ended in stalemate. Britain, anxious

1828–1831

to create a buffer state between Argentina and Brazil to protect its trade interests in the region, proposed making the Banda Oriental an independent state. With British mediation, Argentina and Brazil signed the Treaty of Montevideo, whereby the two countries renounced their claims to the territories that would become integral parts of the newly independent state of Uruguay. However, they retained the right to intervene in the event of a civil war and to approve the constitution of the new nation.

TREATY OF LIMITS 1828
Signed by the United States and Mexico, this treaty confirmed the boundaries established in the Adams-Onis Treaty (1819). This was the start of the tension between Mexico and the United States over Texas in the years to come.

TREATY OF ADRIANOPLE 1829
In the Treaty of London (1827) Russia had promised not to make any territorial gains at the expense of Turkey, but when Russian forces crossed the Danube into the Ottoman-controlled province of Dobruja, it sparked the Russo-Turkish War (1828–29). Russian forces had advanced into Bulgaria, the Caucasus, and northeastern Anatolia before the Turks sued for peace. Signed between Russia and Turkey, the Treaty of Edirne (also known as the Treaty of Adrianople) gave Russia most of the eastern shore of the Black Sea and the mouth of the Danube. Turkey recognized Russia's title to Georgia and other Caucasian principalities and opened the Dardanelles and Bosporus to Russian shipping. The Turks acknowledged the independence of Greece and reaffirmed the Akkerman Convention (1826). The treaty strengthened the Russian position in eastern Europe and weakened that of the Ottoman Empire.

LONDON PROTOCOL 1829
This agreement between Russia, Britain, and France amended the first London Protocol of 1828 which had created an autonomous Greek state encompassing the Peloponnese, Morea, and the Cyclades only. According to the second London Protocol of 1829, Greece would become a separate state, enjoying complete autonomy under the rule of a hereditary Christian prince. The prince would be selected by the European powers, but would recognize the suzerainty of the Ottoman sultan and pay an annual tribute of 1.5 million Turkish piastres. The borders of the new state would run along the line of the Gulf of Actium in the west to the Pagasetic Gulf in the east, thereby including the Peloponnese and continental Greece, as well as the Cyclades.

TREATY OF PRAIRIE DU CHIEN 1829
In 1825 the first Treaty of Prairie du Chien had established peace and delineated boundaries between several tribes of Native Americans. Two further treaties were negotiated simultaneously at Prairie du Chien in 1829. In the first of the treaties, the Council of Three Fires (the Chippewa, Ottawa, and Potawatomi tribes) ceded to the US an area in northwestern Illinois and southwestern Wisconsin, as well as the areas now occupied by the cities of Wilmette and Evanston. In the second treaty the Ho-Chunk ceded territory to the US between the Fox River in Wisconsin and the Rock River in Illinois.

LONDON PROTOCOL 1830
This was a revision of the Protocol of 1829. Under its terms, Greece would be fully independent from the Ottoman Empire, but its borders were reduced to a line running from the Aspropotamos River to the Maliac Gulf. Leopold of Saxe-Coburg (the future king of Belgium) was selected as the first king of Greece, but he rejected the offer.

TREATY OF DANCING RABBIT CREEK 1830
Signed between the Choctaw tribe and the US government, this was the first removal treaty carried into effect under the Indian Removal Act (1830), which gave President Andrew Jackson the authority to exchange lands west of the Mississippi River for Indian lands in the East. Under the terms of the treaty, the Choctaws in Mississippi ceded 11 million acres of land east of the river in exchange for payment and about 15 million acres in Oklahoma.

TREATY OF THE EIGHTEEN ARTICLES 1831
Five European powers proposed a treaty designed to separate Belgium from Holland and to recognize the independence, territorial integrity, and permanent guaranteed neutrality of the new Belgian state. The Dutch king, William I, rejected the treaty and sent the Dutch army into Belgium. This invasion prompted the armed interference of France. To avert further conflict, the five powers drafted a new treaty, the Treaty of Twenty Four Articles, finalized in London in June 1832. Although it was accepted by Belgium, it failed due to the resistance of Holland, and the situation was not resolved until 1839.

FEDERAL PACT 1831
The Pact was first signed by the Argentine provinces of Buenos Aires, Entre Rios and Santa Fe (and later by Corrientes) with the intention of creating a federal military alliance to confront the Unitarian League (provinces of Argentina, established in 1830, which aimed to unite the country under unitarian

Essequiba, Demerara and Berbice
were united to form British Guiana
from 1831

Caribbean Sea

Cartagena
1939, 1956

Caracas
1954

VENEZUELA

Llanos

PANAMA
(Independent)
1903)
*1903-39 US
protectorate*

Bogata *1948*

COLOMBIA
*1858 Granadine Confederation
1861 United States of Colombia
1886 Republic of Colombia*

1907

BRITISH
GUIANA

1904

DUTCH
GUIANA

FRENCH
GUIANA

1900

*1905
to Brazil*

1929

Quito

*1880-1922
to Ecuador*

*1905
to Brazil*

Negro

ECUADOR

1942

*1880 to Ecuador
1942 to Peru*

1904 to Brazil

Manaus

Amazon

Belem

Fortaleza

Natal

B   R   A   Z   I   L

A m a z o n i a

Recife

PERU

*1903
to Brazil*

*Guaporé
formed
1943*

Xingu

Araguaia

San Francisco

Salvador

*1902
to Peru*

Lima
1938

A

1880

La Paz

BOLIVIA

Mato Grosso

1927 to Brazil

Arica
1879

1879

1870 to Brazil

Chaco
*1932-35
to Para.*

*1880
to Bol.*

Parana

1879

PARAGUAY

1870

Sao Paulo

Rio de Janeiro
1906, 1942, 1947

Tropic of Capricorn

*1874
to Arg.*

Asuncion

1927 to Brazil

PACIFIC

OCEAN

Gran Chaco

1874 to Arg.

CHILE

ARGENTINA

Porto Alegre

1909

Juan
Fernandez
(Chile)

Santiago *1923*

Valparaiso

Pampas

Buenos Aires
1910, 1936

Montevideo *1933*

URUGUAY

La Plata

ATLANTIC

OCEAN

Bahia Blaca

Patagonia

1881 to Argentina

Disputed between
Chile and
Arg. 1899-1902

Falkland
Islands
*1833 to Britain
(disputed between
Argentina and Britain)*

Tierra
del Fuego

South America
1830-1956

▬▬▬	Confederation of Peru and Bolivia 1839-39
✕	Battle of the War of the Pacific 1879-84
1927	Boundary with date of final agreement
● *1927*	Seat of Pan-American Congress with date

1832–1838

principles). The Federalists, united under the Pact, confronted the Unitarians, who were defeated. The Federal Pact embraced the principle of free trade and self-governing provinces but left the issue of control over customs revenues ambiguous.

TREATY OF CUSSETA 1832
This treaty, also known as the Third Treaty of Washington, was an agreement between the US government and the Creek Nation, which aimed to relieve tensions between the Creeks and white squatters who were encroaching on their land. Under the terms of the treaty, the Creeks were compelled to cede the remainder of their land in Alabama east of the Mississippi River. The US agreed to make payments to the Creeks of approximately $350,000. Effectively, the treaty aimed at gaining control over Native Americans and their land in the South, and removing them west of the Mississippi.

TREATY OF CONSTANTINOPLE 1832
Intense negotiations took place between Britain, France, Russia, and the Ottoman Empire to settle the future of Greece. It was eventually agreed that Greece would include the Peloponnese, the mainland up to a line between Actium and Vólos, and the Cyclades – but not the Ionian Islands or Crete. Turkey would relinquish all sovereignty over the area, but would be indemnified in the sum of 40,000,000 piastres for its loss. Prince Otto of Bavaria had been offered the crown of Greece, and had accepted.

LONDON PROTOCOL 1832
The Protocol, signed by Britain, France, and Russia, marked the end of the Greek War of Independence, created modern Greece as an independent state free of the Ottoman Empire, and reiterated the borders agreed in the Treaty of Constantinople.

TREATY OF HÜNKÂR İSKELESI 1833
In 1831 Egypt had invaded the Ottoman Empire, resulting in the Egyptian-Ottoman War (1831–33). By December 1832 the Egyptians were threatening Istanbul. Neither the British nor the French were in a position to provide the Turks with military assistance so the Turkish sultan, Mahmud II, appealed to Turkey's former enemy, Nicholas I of Russia, for help. Nicholas complied and sent Russian forces and ships to Istanbul. The Treaty of Hünkâr İskelesi formalized the Russo-Ottoman military alliance and agreed that, for a period of eight years, they would come to each other's defense in the event that either was attacked by a foreign power. In a secret article, it was also agreed that Turkey would

close the Dardanelles to any foreign warships should Russia request it.

CONVENTION OF KÜTAHYA 1833
The invasion of Turkey by Egypt (Egyptian-Ottoman War 1831–33), and the subsequent arrival of Russian forces close to Istanbul in response to an appeal for help by Turkey's Sultan Mahmud II, alarmed Britain and France. They pressurized the sultan to insist on a Russian withdrawal and negotiated the Convention of Kütahya. Under its terms, the Egyptians would withdraw their forces and the Ottomans would cede Syria, Adana, and Crete to Egypt. However, the Convention proved unsatisfactory, resulting in the Second Ottoman-Egyptian War in 1839–41.

TREATY OF CHICAGO 1833
This, the second treaty that the Ottawa, Chippewa and Potawatomi tribes had signed with the US government, granted the US all their land from the Rock River in Illinois to the Grand River in Michigan in exchange for a sum of $100,000.

TREATY OF DESMICHELS 1834
Algeria, although nominally controlled by the Ottoman Empire, was deeply divided between those who supported the *dey* (governor) and the mass of Algerians who opposed him and who had begun launching a series of revolts in the early 19th century. The country, weakened by these internal divisions, was unable to combat an invasion by French forces in 1830. Instead, opposition was organized by religious brotherhoods like that led by Muhi al-Din who, already aging, elected his son Abd al-Qadir in his place. An effective military leader, Abd al-Qadir's campaigns against the French forced them to sign the Treaty of Desmichels, which gave him control of the area around Oran, with the title of "Commander of the Believers."

TREATY OF NEW ECHOTA 1835
Despite the assimilation by the Cherokee of settler culture, and their formation of a government modeled on that of the US, nothing protected them against the land hunger of white settlers. When gold was discovered on Cherokee land in Georgia, agitation for their removal increased. The treaty, signed between a tiny minority of the Cherokee and the US government, ceded to the US all Cherokee land east of the Mississippi River in exchange for $5 million. The treaty was repudiated by an overwhelming majority of the tribe, who took their case to the US Supreme Court, which decided in their favor. Georgia officials ignored the court's decision and the tribe was removed. Their eviction

and the forced march during the fall and winter of 1838–39 became known as the Trail of Tears.

BATMAN'S TREATY 1835

This was an agreement between John Batman, an Australian businessman, and a group of Wurundjeri elders. For a purchase price including tomahawks, knives, scissors, flannel jackets, red shirts, and a yearly tribute of similar items, Batman obtained about 200,000 hectares (2,000 square km) around the Yarra River and Corio Bay. Batman's claim to the land was based on the European idea of land ownership and legal contracts whereas for the indigenous people land was not about possession but belonging. Governor Bourke of New South Wales almost immediately declared the treaty invalid, declaring the British crown owned the entire land of Australia; only it could sell or distribute land.

TREATIES OF VELASCO 1836

These two treaties were intended to conclude the Texas Revolution (1835–36) that began when colonists (primarily from the United States) in the Mexican province of Texas rebelled against the increasingly centralized Mexican government. They were signed following the defeat of Mexican forces, commanded by General Santa Anna, at the Battle of San Jacinto in May 1836. Under the terms of the public treaty, hostilities would cease and Santa Anna would withdraw his forces below the Rio Grande and not take up arms again against Texas. A second, secret, treaty agreed that the Texans would release Santa Anna in exchange for his pledge to use his influence to secure Mexican recognition of Texan independence. However, the treaties were violated by both governments and not legally recognized by either; Texan independence was not recognized by Mexico, nor was her boundary determined.

TREATY OF WASHINGTON 1836

With this treaty, signed between the US government and representatives of the Ottawa and Chippewa nations of Native Americans, the tribes ceded an area of approximately 13,837,207 acres in the northwest portion of the Lower Peninsula of Michigan, and the eastern portion of the Upper Peninsula of Michigan.

MUNICH COIN TREATY 1837

This treaty standardized the silver content of the gulden, which was the coin that circulated among the states south of the Main River, and gave the currency the status of legal tender. The treaty was initially agreed to by Bavaria, Baden, Württemberg, Nassau, Hesse-Darmstadt, and the Free City of Frankfurt. Later, Hesse-Kassel and Hamburg also agreed to the treaty.

TREATY OF TAFNA 1837

Following the signing of the Treaty of Desmichels, Abd al-Qadir had managed to expand the amount of territory under his control, had imposed his rule on all the tribes of the Chelif, and had occupied Miliana and Médéa. Furthermore he had mobilized Algerian support of his movement and defeated the French, forcing them to sign the Treaty of Tafna. Under the terms of the treaty, his territory was further increased, thus making him master of the whole interior of Oran and the Titteri.

TREATY OF BALTA LIMANI 1838

Also known as the Anglo-Ottoman Treaty, this was a formal trade agreement signed between the Ottoman Empire and Great Britain. The terms of the treaty stated that Turkey would allow British merchants and their collaborators to have full access to all Turkish markets and to be taxed the same as local merchants. Duties were set at 3 percent on imports; 3 percent on exports; 9 percent on transiting exported goods; and 2 percent on transiting imported goods. In a move designed to weaken the power of Muhammad Ali Pasha, governor of Egypt, the treaty also forbade the formation of commercial monopolies (of which opium was the most prominent outside Egypt) in the Ottoman domains. Although the treaty was technically binding on Egypt, Muhammad Ali Pasha succeeded in evading its application.

TREATY OF BUFFALO CREEK 1838

There were four treaties of Buffalo Creek. This, the second of the treaties, was signed between the Seneca, Mohawk, and Cayuga nations, the Oneida Indian Nation, the Onondaga and Tuscarora tribes and the United States. Under the terms of the treaty, the New York Indians agreed to cede to the US the 500,000 acres of land near Green Bay which they had received in the Menominee Treaty (1831), except for a tract eight by twelve miles, equivalent to 100 acres for each of the 654 Oneida that were living there. This established the boundaries of the Oneida Reservation of Wisconsin. The Seneca agreed that the US government would sell to the Ogden Land Company their five remaining reservations: Buffalo Creek, Tonawanda, Oil Springs, Cattaraugus, and Allegany. The Seneca would relocate to a tract of land in Kansas, west of Missouri.

DRESDEN COINAGE CONVENTION 1838

In part inspired by the Munich Coin Treaty, the Convention standardized the silver content of the *thaler*, which was the currency used in the Zollverein – the German Customs Union, which was a coalition of German states formed to manage tariffs

1839–1842

and economic policies within their territories. The treaty also established permanently fixed exchange rates between the two currencies.

EDICT OF TOLERATION (HAWAII) 1839
Decreed by King Kamehameha III of Hawaii, this edict allowed for the establishment of the Catholic Church in Hawaii and granted religious toleration throughout the islands. The king, who preferred the religious traditions of ancient Hawaii, had come under pressure both from American Protestant missionaries and the French government. The French had threatened to use force if the king failed to sign the edict as they were seeking to protect the work of the Congregation of the Sacred Hearts of

Jesus and Mary. Under this threat, Kamehameha paid the $20,000 in compensation for the deportation of the priests and the incarceration and torture of converts.

TREATY OF LONDON 1839
This treaty (also called the Convention of 1839, and the London Treaty of Separation), came into being because the Dutch would not sign either the Treaty of the Eighteen Articles or the Treaty of the Twenty-Four Articles in 1831. The Treaty of London provided international recognition for the new state of Belgium, formed from the southern provinces of the Netherlands. It also confirmed the independence of the German-speaking part of Luxembourg. The

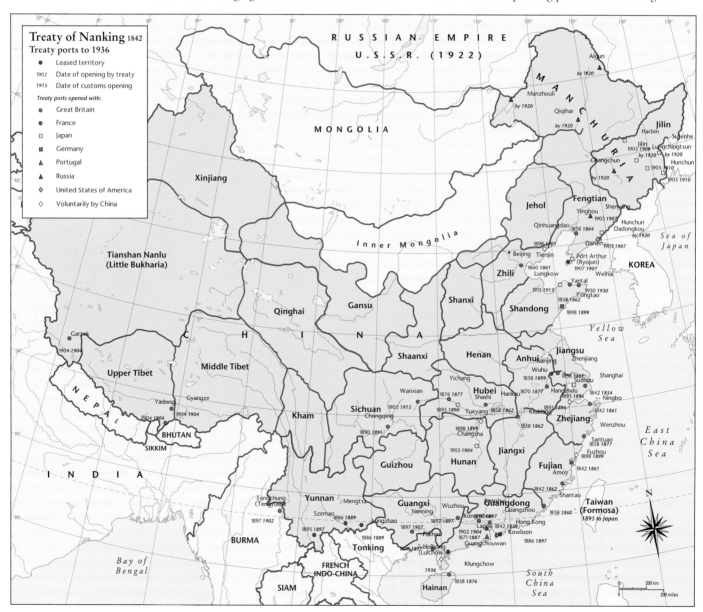

treaty bound the signatories – Britain, Austria, Prussia, France, Russia, and Holland – to protect Belgium if it was attacked.

TREATY OF WAITANGI 1840

In the late 1830s growing numbers of British migrants arrived in New Zealand. European speculators were buying up vast tracts of land, and some of the settlers were causing trouble. The British government, judging that annexing the country could protect the Maori, drew up this treaty. Signed by Britain and various Maori chiefs from the North Island of New Zealand, it established a British governor of New Zealand, recognized Maori ownership of their lands, forests, fisheries, and other possessions, and gave them the rights of British subjects. In return, the Maori people ceded New Zealand to Queen Victoria, giving her government the sole right to purchase land. Effectively, the treaty gave Britain sovereignty over New Zealand, and gave the governor the right to govern it. The Maori believed they had ceded to Britain a right of governance in return for protection, without giving up their authority to manage their own affairs. The English and Maori versions of the treaty differed significantly, the cause of much disagreement.

TREATY OF NANKING 1842

The First Opium War (1839–42), fought between Britain and Qing dynasty China, arose from China's attempts to stop foreign traders (primarily British) from illegally exporting opium (mainly from India) to China, a trade that had increased dramatically from about 1820. Following their defeat, the Chinese signed the Treaty of Nanking, which agreed that British merchants could now trade at five "treaty ports" and with whomever they pleased. The Qing government was obliged to pay Britain a total of $21 million, partly in war reparations, partly for opium they had destroyed in 1839, and partly to repay debts owed to British merchants. Britain agreed to withdraw all its troops and refrain from interfering with China's trade. In addition, the Qing agreed to make Hong Kong Island a crown colony, ceding it to the British Queen "in perpetuity." This was the first of what the Chinese later called the "unequal treaties" on the grounds that Britain had no obligations in return.

WEBSTER-ASHBURTON TREATY 1842

Signed between the US and Britain, this treaty settled issues over the boundary between the US and Canada. It also resolved the Aroostook War, a non-violent dispute over the location of the Maine–New Brunswick border. It established the border between Lake Superior and the Lake of the Woods, originally

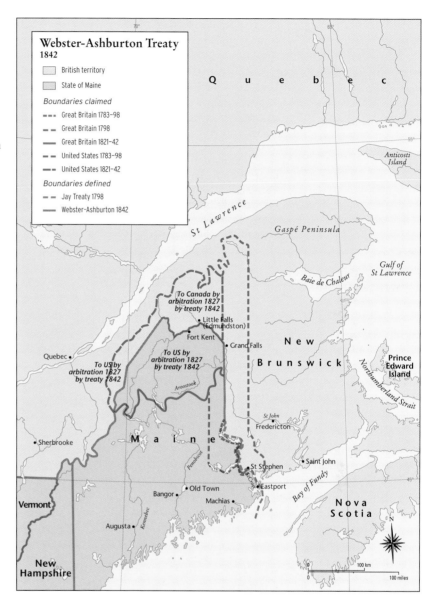

defined in the Treaty of Paris (1783); reaffirmed the location of the border (at the 49th parallel) in the westward frontier up to the Rocky Mountains as defined in the Treaty of 1818; defined seven crimes subject to extradition; agreed to suppress the slave trade, and to the shared use of the Great Lakes. In addition, the treaty retroactively confirmed the southern boundary of Quebec that had been marked out in 1771–73. As a result of the treaty, the US ceded 5,000 square miles (12,950 sq km) of disputed territory along the Maine border, including the Halifax–Quebec Route, but kept 7,000 square miles (18,130 sq km) of the disputed wilderness. In addition, the US received 6,500 square miles of land along the Minnesota–Canada border, which included the Mesabi Range.

1843–1850

TREATY OF MAASTRICHT 1843

With the split between Belgium and Holland finally settled in 1839, this Treaty established the border between Belgium and Holland. In the area around Baarle it proved impossible to come to a definitive agreement and, in place of a fixed border, each of 5,732 tiny parcels of land (known as the Baarle enclaves) had their nationality laid down separately. In addition, part of the left bank of the River Meuse, near Maastricht, was returned to Holland.

TREATY OF THE BOGUE 1843

During negotiations over the Treaty of Nanking (1842), China and Britain had agreed that a supplementary treaty would be needed. The Treaty of the Bogue laid down detailed regulations for Sino-British trade and specified terms under which Britons could reside in the newly-opened ports of Shanghai, Nigbo, Xiamen, Fuzhou, and Guangzhou. The treaty also granted British citizens in China extraterritorial rights, by which they were to be under the control of their own consuls and were not subject to Chinese law. It also included a most-favored-nation clause, guaranteeing to Britain all privileges that China might grant to any other foreign power.

TREATY OF TANGIERS 1844

At the Battle of Isly (1844) a French force pursuing the Algerian resistance leader Abd al-Qadir, who had frequently sought refuge in Moroccan territory, defeated the Moroccan army. Under the terms of the treaty, the Moroccan government agreed to arrest and outlaw Abd al-Qadir, reduce the size of its garrison at Oujda, and establish a commission to demarcate the border between it and Algeria.

TREATY OF TEHUACANA CREEK 1844

Sam Houston, president of Texas, had made it a priority to end hostilities between Native Americans and white settlers in Texas. In 1843 the Treaty of Bird's Fort was signed by representatives of tribes that included the Caddos, Delawares, Chickasaws, Cherokees, Wacos, and others. Houston also wanted to make peace with the Comanches. In 1844 Buffalo Hump and other Comanche leaders signed the Treaty of Tehuacana Creek in which they agreed to surrender white captives and cease raiding Texan settlements. In exchange, the Texans would cease military action against the tribe, establish more trading posts, and recognize the boundary between Texas and Comanchería.

TREATY OF WANGHIA 1844

Signed between the US and the Qing Empire, this treaty was negotiated to secure for the US the same rights that other European nations had received from the Chinese. Modeled after the Treaties of Nanking (1842) and the Bogue (1843), the treaty granted the US extraterritoriality, which meant that US citizens could only be tried by US consular officers; fixed tariffs on trade in the treaty ports; gave US citizens the right to buy land for churches and hospitals; and overturned a Chinese law that forbade foreigners from learning the Chinese language. In addition, the treaty gave the US "most favored nation" trading status with China, and gave its navy the right to enter Chinese ports of trade.

TREATY OF WHAMPOA 1844

This treaty granted to France and its citizens the same rights and privileges in China that Britain and the US had received by the Treaties of Nanking (1842), the Bogue (1843), and Wanghia (1844). The practice of Christianity was legalized in China.

OREGON TREATY 1846

Oregon Country was a disputed area that had been jointly occupied by both Britain and the US since the Treaty of 1818. Joint occupation had been confirmed by treaty in 1827. In 1842 the Webster-Ashburton Treaty partially delineated the northeastern US-Canada border, but left the border of the Oregon Country still unsettled. By 1843, increased American immigration into the area along the Oregon Trail became a burning issue. Under President James Polk, a supporter of Manifest Destiny (divine sanction for the territorial expansion of the US), a compromise was reached: the Oregon Treaty set the border in the Strait of Juan de Fuca through the major channel. The "major channel" was not clearly defined, giving rise to further disputes in the future. Britain retained full control of Vancouver Island.

TREATY OF LAHORE 1846

Following the Sikh Empire's defeat by the East India Company in the First Anglo-Sikh War (1845–46), the British East India Company signed this treaty with the Sikhs and the seven-year-old Maharaja Duleep Singh Bahadur. The Sikhs lost Jammu, Kashmir, Hazara, and the territory between the Sutlej and Beas Rivers to the British. In addition, the Sikh regular army was reduced to 20,000 infantry and 12,000 cavalry. The British agreed to respect the bona fide rights of *jagirdars* (a type of feudal land grant) in the Lahore territories. The Koh-i-Noor diamond also became British property.

TREATY OF AMRITSAR 1846

This treaty formalized the terms of the Treaty of Lahore. Under Article 1 of the treaty, the British

sold Kashmir to Gulab Singh Dogra, the Raja of
Jammu, for 7.5 million rupees (75 lakhs). Gulab
Singh thus became the founder and first maharaja
of the princely state of Kashmir and Jammu. The
British undertook to aid the maharaja in protecting
his territories from external enemies.

MALLARINO-BIDLACK TREATY 1846

This treaty (also known as the Treaty of New
Granada) represented an agreement of mutual
cooperation between New Granada (Panama and
Colombia) and the US. Under its terms, the US
was granted a right-of-way across the Panamanian
isthmus in exchange for its guarantee of neutrality
for the isthmus and the sovereignty of New Granada
thereafter. The treaty had been prompted by a threat
of British intrusion on the Central American coast.
After gold was discovered in California in 1848, the
US spent seven years constructing a trans-isthmian
Panama Railway, which was completed in 1855.

TREATY OF CAHUENGA 1847

The forces of the US and Mexico had been fighting
each other in Alta-California (a territory of Mexico)
in the Mexican-American War (1846–48). This
informal agreement demanded that the Californians
should surrender their artillery and that all prisoners
from both sides should be freed. Those Californians
who promised to remain at peace, and to obey
the laws and regulations of the US, were allowed
to return to their homes. In future, they would
be allowed the same rights and privileges as were
allowed to US citizens, and would not be compelled
to take an oath of allegiance until a treaty of peace
was signed between the US and Mexico.

TREATY OF CANTON 1847

This was another of the so-called "unequal treaties"
between Western powers and China that followed
the First Opium War (1839–42). The treaty's terms,
similar to the Treaty of Wanghia (1844), provided
that Sweden-Norway would have the same privileges
in China as other treaty powers. It was therefore
given commercial access to the five treaty ports of
Canton, Amoy, Fuzhou, Ningbo, and Shanghai, and
granted extraterritorial rights. Sweden-Norway was
allowed to send consuls to China and its trade was
subjected to fixed tariffs only.

TREATY OF GUADALUPE HIDALGO 1848

Following the defeat of its army and the fall of its
capital, Mexico signed this peace treaty with the US
which officially ended the Mexican-American War
(1846–48). It was officially entitled the Treaty of
Peace, Friendship, Limits and Settlement between
the United States of America and the Mexican

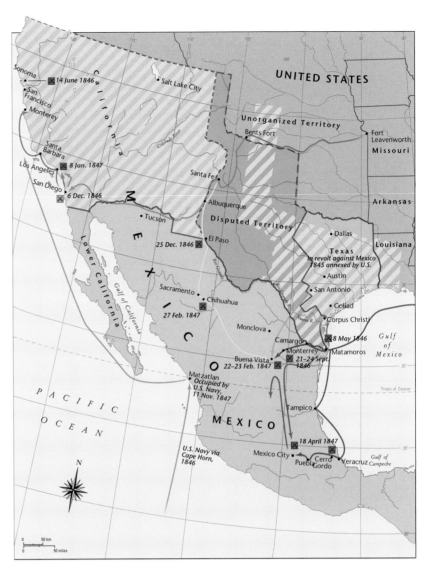

Republic. Under its terms, Mexico formally gave up
all claims to Texas and recognized the Rio Grande
as America's southern boundary. The treaty added
an additional 525,000 square miles to US territory,
including the land that makes up all, or parts of,
present-day Arizona, California, Colorado, Nevada,
New Mexico, Utah, and Wyoming. In return, the
US paid Mexico $15 million and agreed to settle all
claims of US citizens against Mexico.

ARANA-SOUTHERN TREATY 1850

In the late 1840s attempts by Argentina to regulate
traffic on the Paraná and Uruguay rivers had
interfered with Anglo-French trade with landlocked
Paraguay. In retaliation, Britain and France
blockaded the River Plate. Although their action was
militarily successful, it was costly in both men and
ships and the two countries decided to end hostilities
and lifted the blockade. The Arana-Southern Treaty,

US Expansion
in the West
1845-47

→ Movement of
Mexican forces

Movements of
U.S. forces

→ U.S. Navy

→ Kearny

→ Doniphan

→ Stockton

→ Wool

→ Taylor

→ Scott

☒ U.S. victory

☒ Mexican victory

▨ Territory lost to
United States

1850–1855

also known as the Convention of Settlement, re-established friendly relations between the three nations. It was viewed as a considerable triumph for the Argentine dictator General Rosas as it was the first time the emerging South American nations were able to impose their will on two European empires. The Convention also conceded Argentina's claim to the Falkland Islands.

CLAYTON-BULWER TREATY 1850
This treaty was negotiated between the US and Britain in response to plans to build a canal across the isthmus of Panama to connect the Pacific and Atlantic Oceans. Britain had large and ill-defined territorial claims in three affected regions: British Honduras, the Mosquito Coast, and the Bay Islands. The treaty agreed that neither Britain nor the US should have exclusive control over the projected canal nor colonize any part of Central America, but both countries would guarantee the protection and neutrality of the canal. However, the wording of the treaty proved so ambiguous that it became one of the most discussed and difficult treaties in the history of Anglo-US relations.

PUNCTATION OF OLMÜTZ 1850
Signed between Prussia and Austria, this agreement followed Prussia's unsuccessful attempt in 1849–50 to create a confederation of the majority of German states under its protection. The attempt had evoked strong opposition from Austria, as well as displeasure from Russia and France. According to the agreement – which was concluded through the mediation of Russia – Prussia was forced temporarily to renounce any unilateral steps toward eliminating the territorial and political fragmentation of Germany, which had been sanctioned by the Congress of Vienna (1814–15). Prussia also agreed to abandon its aim of creating a confederation of German states under its domination. The treaty is also known as the "humiliation of Olmütz" as it was seen by many as a capitulation by the Prussians to the Austrians.

TREATY OF TRAVERSE DES SIOUX 1851
With European-American settlers wanting yet more land, the US government negotiated this treaty with the Sisseton and Wahpeton bands of Dakota (Sioux) Indians, by which the Dakota ceded large tracts of their territory in southern and western Minnesota, and agreed to move to two reservations along the Minnesota River. In exchange, they would receive annuities of cash and goods. Treaty violations by the United States, and late or unfair annuity payments, caused increasing hunger and hardship among the Dakota. In 1862, tensions erupted, leading to the Dakota War.

TREATY OF MENDOTA 1851
This treaty, negotiated between the US and the Mdewakanton and Wahpekute bands of Dakota (Sioux) Indians, was signed within a fortnight of the Treaty of Traverse des Sioux. The treaty stipulated that the Indians were to receive $1,410,000 in return for relocating to the Lower Sioux Agency, a reservation on the Minnesota River. They also ceded a significant portion of southern Minnesota. This treaty and the Treaty of Traverse des Sioux are significant in Minnesota's history as together the Dakota opened up 24 million acres of their land to white colonization.

TREATY OF FORT LARAMIE 1851
Many white migrants to western North America had already passed through the Great Plains on the Oregon and Santa Fe Trails, but the California gold rush (1848–55) had greatly increased traffic. The US government assembled many of the Plains Indian tribes living between the Arkansas and Missouri Rivers with the aim of avoiding tribal rivalry by defining the territory for each tribal group. Under the terms of the treaty, the tribes agreed to guarantee safe passage for settlers and to allow roads and forts to be built in their territories in return for promises of an annuity of $50,000 for 50 years. The US Senate ratified the treaty, adding Article 5, which adjusted compensation from 50 to ten years, if the tribes accepted the changes.

TREATY OF KULJA 1851
Throughout the 18th century, Russia had gradually advanced into Kazakhstan. In the wake of the First Opium War (1839–42), and encouraged by the success of Britain, France, and other western powers in extracting concessions from China, Russia began to send merchants into Chinese Central Asia. The resulting Treaty of Kulja was negotiated on general terms of equality and reciprocity. It granted the Russians trading rights in the area, specifying the trade routes, the times of year trade was allowed, and warehousing facilities. It also established that the Russians were not subject to Chinese law while in the territory, but could be under the control of their own consul at Chuguchak (modern Tacheng) and Kulja. The treaty was followed by an accelerated Russian expansion into Central Asia.

LONDON PROTOCOL 1852
The First War of Schleswig (1848–52) – an uprising by Schleswig-Holstein's German majority in support of independence from Denmark and close association with Germany – ended with the signing of the Protocol by the five major European powers – Austria, France, Prussia, Russia, and Britain.

Under the terms of this peace agreement, Germany returned Schleswig-Holstein to Denmark. In return, Denmark undertook not to tie Schleswig more closely to Denmark than to its sister duchy of Holstein. The Protocol also resolved the question of the succession to the Danish throne, the powers agreeing to accept a third candidate, a cousin of King Frederick VII via a female line of succession.

SAND RIVER CONVENTION 1852

Signed between Britain and the Voortrekkers (Boers or Afrikaans), this convention was provoked by the Boers' invasion of the interior of southern Africa north of the Orange River as part of the Great Trek. Under its terms the independence of Boers living north of the Vaal River was recognized. This laid the foundation for the South African Republic, which was established later in 1852. In 1854, the similar Bloemfontein Convention was signed with the Boers who lived north of the Orange River. This then became the independent Orange Free State. The conventions guaranteed the right of the Boers to self-government without the interference of Britain, and contained clauses prohibiting slavery and permitting the Boers – but not the Africans – access to firearms.

CONVENTION OF KANAGAWA 1854

Since the beginning of the 17th century the Tokugawa Shogunate (the feudal Japanese military government) had pursued a policy of isolating the country from outside influences. This policy was prompted by a fear that the spread of Christianity and trade with western powers would serve as a pretext for the invasion of Japan by imperialist forces. By the early 19th century, this policy of isolation (*sakoku*) was increasingly under pressure. In 1852, a fleet of American warships, under the command of Commodore Matthew Perry, sailed into Edo Bay. Aware that they were unable to resist such a force, the Shogunate signed the Convention, which agreed to admit US ships to the ports of Shimoda and Hakodate, and to accept a US consul at Shimoda. The treaty opened Japan to trade with the US, and thus to the West.

ANGLO-JAPANESE FRIENDSHIP TREATY 1854

This treaty was the first to be signed between Britain and Japan. Under its terms, the ports of Nagasaki and Hakodate were opened to British vessels, and Britain was granted most favored nation status with other western powers. The British negotiator, Sir James Stirling, came under immediate criticism as the treaty made no provision for formal trade relations with Japan. The treaty was similar to the Convention of Kanagawa which had been signed between the US and Japan six months earlier.

TREATY OF MEDICINE CREEK 1854

This treaty was signed between the US and nine tribes and bands of Native Americans, including the Nisqually and Puyallup, who occupied the lands lying around the head of Puget Sound, Washington. Under the terms of the treaty, the tribes relinquished 2.24 million acres of tribal land to the US in exchange for three 1,280-acre reservations, cash payments over a period of 20 years, and recognition of traditional fishing and hunting rights. The original Nisqually reservation was in rocky terrain and unacceptable to the Nisqually, who were a riverside fishing people. In 1855 they went to war and their chief was hanged for murder.

CANADIAN-AMERICAN RECIPROCITY TREATY 1854

Britain's abrogation of protective tariffs (the Corn Laws) in 1846 led Canada to look for new export opportunities for its products. Its governor general, Lord Elgin, negotiated the treaty with the US in an attempt to stimulate the Canadian economy. The treaty's principal provisions were for the admission of US fishermen to Canada's Atlantic coastal fisheries and a similar privilege to enable Canadian fishermen to fish US coastal waters north of 36° N latitude. It also established free trade between the two states in a considerable list of natural products, especially timber and wheat. The treaty was to remain in force for ten years.

BOWRING TREATY 1855

Signed between Thailand and Britain, the treaty lifted many restrictions imposed by Thai kings on foreign trade. It set a 3 percent duty on all imports and permitted British subjects to trade in all Thailand's ports; to own land near Bangkok; and to move freely about the country. The treaty also allowed the establishment of a British consulate in Bangkok and guaranteed it full extraterritorial powers. Officially a Treaty of Friendship and Commerce, it is nonetheless claimed by Thailand to be an "unequal treaty" as Britain's demonstration of its military might during the First Opium War (1839–42) with China discouraged Thailand from any attempts to prevent Western trade. The treaty was followed by a succession of similar agreements between Thailand and many European powers, the United States, and Japan.

TREATY OF HELLGATE 1855

Signed between the US and the Native American tribes located in western Montana – the Bitterroot

1855–1858

Salish, Pend d'Oreilles, and the Kootenai. The negotiations were plagued by serious translation problems; one observer commented "not a tenth of what was said was understood by either side." Under the treaty's terms, the tribes were to relinquish their territories to the US in exchange for payment that totaled $120,000. The territories ceded were from the main ridge of the Rocky Mountains at the 49th parallel to the Kootenai River, and Clark Fort to the divide between the St Regis and Coeur d'Alene Rivers. From there the ceded territories extended to the southwestern fork of the Bitterroot River and up to Salmon and Snake Rivers.

TREATY OF SHIMODA 1855
A year after the Convention of Kanagawa (1854) was signed between Japan and the US, the Treaty of Shimoda was signed between Japan and Russia. Under its terms, the ports of Nagasaki, Shimoda, and Hakodate were opened to Russian vessels. In addition, the treaty declared that the border between Japan and Russia would be drawn between the two islands of Iturup and Urup, in the Kuril chain north of Hokkaidō. Iturup, Kunashir, the Habomai Islands, and Shikotan were defined as Japanese territory. The treaty also allowed for a Russian consul to be stationed at one of these ports, and for Russia to be given most favored nation status. This treaty effectively ended Japan's 220-year-old policy of national seclusion (*sakoku*).

TREATY WITH THE KALAPUYA etc., 1855
During the early 1840s, the increasing number of migrants using the Oregon Trail to settle in the largely unclaimed Oregon Territory had led to conflict between Native Americans and white settlers. The treaty was negotiated to bring peace to the region. Also known as the Treaty of Dayton, it was signed between the US and bands of the Kalapuya tribe, the Molala tribe, the Clackamas, and several others in the Oregon Territory. Under its terms, the tribes ceded almost all of the fertile Willamette Valley to the US. In exchange, they secured promises of a reservation and long-term support from the US government in the form of money, supplies, health care, and the promise of protection from further attacks by settlers. During the winter of 1855–56, the tribes were forcibly removed from the Willamette Valley to Grand Ronde Reservation.

POINT ELLIOTT TREATY 1855
Signed between the US and representatives of the Native American tribes of the greater Puget Sound region in the recently formed Washington Territory, this treaty was prompted by the increased occupation of tribal lands by European-American settlers from 1845 onwards. The treaty established a number of reservations and guaranteed fishing rights. In exchange, the US agreed to pay the tribes and bands $150,000. The treaty, convened by Isaac Stevens, governor of Washington Territory, was negotiated in Chinook Jargon, a simplified language of trade that meant that many of the legal complexities involved in the negotiations were lost in translation. Furthermore, Stevens assumed that the Native Americans were all one nation, rather than separate and distinct tribes.

POINT NO POINT TREATY 1855
This treaty, also convened and conducted by Governor Isaac Stevens, was signed between the US and the S'Klallam, the Chimakum, and the Skokomish tribes. Under its terms, the original inhabitants of northern Kitsap Peninsula and Olympic Peninsula were to cede ownership of 438,430 acres of their ancestral land and to move to a 3,840-acre reservation. In exchange, they would receive a payment of $60,000. The treaty also called for the tribes to stop trading at Vancouver Island (British held), to exclude alcohol from the reservation, and to free all of their slaves.

TREATY OF NEAH BAY 1855
While the Makah, an indigenous people living in Washington in the Pacific Northwest, had been successful fishing people for thousands of years, US negotiators wanted them to become farmers on land which was not suited for agriculture. The area they proposed as the Makah Reservation in Clallam County did not include any of the five main Makah villages (the Makah lived in permanent villages). Under the terms of the treaty, the majority of the Makah tribal lands were to be restricted to the designated reservation in exchange for $30,000. The Makah people's right to fish, hunt whales, and seals in the region were preserved.

QUINAULT TREATY 1855
Also known as the Quinault River Treaty and the Treaty of Olympia, this agreement was signed between the US and the Native American Quinault and Quileute tribes. These tribes were located in the western Olympic Peninsula, north of Gray's Harbor in the recently formed Washington Territory. With this treaty the Territory's governor, Isaac Stevens, continued his policy of consolidating tribes, often requiring them to move far from their homeland to a reservation that was to be occupied by several unrelated tribes. The treaty established the Quinault Indian Reservation in exchange for $25,000, which was to be paid over a number of years. It also

required the Quileute and the Hoh – considered a subset of the Quileute – to move to the reservation as well, although few did so. The negotiations were conducted in the little-understood Chinook Jargon, which resulted in confusion and legal problems which continue to the present day.

TREATY WITH THE NEZ PERCE 1855
By the mid-1800s, the vast mineral, timber, and agricultural wealth of the ancestral homeland of the Nez Perce Nation was under siege by miners and settlers. In 1855, Governor Stevens convened the Walla Walla Council where he met with representatives from the Umatilla, Yakama, Nez Perce, Cayuse, and Palouse tribes. At the Council the Nez Perce were coerced into giving up their lands and moving to the Umatilla Reservation in Oregon Territory, together with the Umatilla, Walla Walla, and Cayuse tribes. However, the tribes were so bitterly opposed to this plan that Stevens concluded this treaty with the Nez Perce. Under its terms, the Nez Perce relinquished almost 5.5 million of their some 13 million acres of tribal land in Idaho, Washington, and Oregon territories to the US, in exchange for a nominal sum. In addition, no white settlers were allowed on the reservation, and the Nez Perce were able to continue hunting and fishing.

TREATY WITH THE CONFEDERATED UMATILLA, CAYUSE, AND WALLA WALLA TRIBES 1855
At the Walla Walla Council, convened by Governor Stevens in 1855, the Walla Walla, Cayuse and Umatilla tribes ceded 6.4 million acres of their homeland in northeast Oregon. Then the tribes relocated to what was called the Confederated Tribes of the Umatilla American Indian Reservation (CTUIR). In exchange for ceding most of their territories they received supplies and annuities from the federal government, who then tried to encourage them to take up subsistence farming. The tribes reserved the right to fish, hunt, and gather traditional foods and medicines throughout the ceded lands. The Walla Walla Council was a watershed in Oregon's history, and it triggered a major war between many Oregon and Washington tribes and the US government.

TREATY WITH THE YAKAMA CONFEDERATED TRIBES AND BANDS 1855
Signed between Governor Stevens and representatives of the Yakama tribe, this treaty, agreed at the Walla Walla Council, created from the original 10.8 million acres of Yakama lands a reservation of 1.3 million acres. Several Native leaders believed that the representatives at the Council did not have the authority to cede communal land and had not properly gained consensus from the Council or tribe. A dispute over the treaty led to the Yakima War (1855–1858), waged against the US.

"BUFFALO TREATY" 1855
Flying in the face of much of the US government's reservation policy, this treaty (also called the Lame Bull Treaty) agreed the federal creation of common hunting grounds to be shared "in peace.". It was signed between the Blackfoot tribes and the "Western Indians" (Nez Perce, Walla Walla, Cayuse Spokane, Kootenai, Yakima, and Salish-speakers). The recognition of these hunting grounds meant that the hunters of the Columbia River drainage area would continue their traditional seasonal migrations.

TREATY OF PARIS 1856
The Crimean War (1853–56) had been caused by Russia insisting on its right to protect Orthodox Christians and their holy places in the Holy Land, which was then a part of the Ottoman Empire. The longer-term causes were the decline of the Ottoman Empire and the unwillingness of Britain and France to allow Russia to gain territory and power at Turkey's expense. This treaty followed Russia's defeat and formally concluded the war. It was signed between the combatants – Russia on one side and France, Britain, Sardinia, and Turkey on the other. Under its terms, the independence and territorial integrity of Turkey was guaranteed. In addition, Russia was required to surrender Bessarabia to Moldavia. Both Walachia and Moldavia were reorganized as autonomous states under Turkish suzerainty; the Black Sea was closed to all warships while the Danube was opened to shipping of all nations. The treaty severely limited Russia's influence in the region.

TREATY OF TIENTSIN 1858
The treaty is a collective name for several documents signed in June 1858 that ended the first phase of the Second Opium War, which had begun in 1856. Under the treaty's terms, eleven more Chinese ports were opened for foreign trade, including Newchwang, Taiwan, Hankou, and Nanjing. In addition, foreign vessels, including warships, could now navigate freely on the Yangtze River; foreign legations were now permitted in Beijing; all Christians in China were given religious liberty; and the import of opium was legalized.

TREATY OF AIGUN 1858
Russia's drive to expand eastwards as far as Manchuria, the homeland of the Qing dynasty (the

1858–1862

Manchu rulers of China) had been checked by the Treaty of Nerchinsk (1689) which had attempted to define a Sino-Russian boundary and thus avoid further conflict. However, with the Qing dynasty heavily involved in the Taiping Rebellion (1850–64) and the Second Opium War (1856–60), Russia saw its chance to gain new territory. The resulting Treaty of Aigun (one that China considers yet another of the "unequal treaties") was negotiated, pushing the Russian boundary to the Amur and Ussuri Rivers, but leaving territory east of the rivers in "joint possession" to be settled in future negotiations. Russia received over 231,660 square miles from China. In addition, Russia gained more control over regional trade and near exclusivity in the use of the Amur, Ussuri, and Sungari Rivers.

TREATY OF AMITY AND COMMERCE 1858
Also called the Harris Treaty after the US consul Townsend Harris, this treaty followed the Convention of Kanagawa (1854), which had opened up certain Japanese ports to US ships. Under the terms of this new treaty, two more ports, Kanagawa and Nagasaki, were opened to foreign trade, with two more to follow in 1860 and 1863. It also exempted US citizens living in the ports from the jurisdiction of Japanese law; guaranteed them religious freedom; arranged for diplomatic representation and for a tariff agreement between the US and Japan. The treaty served as a model for similar treaties signed by Japan with other foreign countries in the ensuing weeks. These "unequal treaties" curtailed Japanese sovereignty for the first time in its history.

TREATY OF ZURICH 1859
This treaty was a reaffirmation of the terms of the preliminary Peace of Villafranca, signed between Austria and France four months earlier, which had brought the Second Italian War of Independence (also called the Austro-Sardinian War, The Franco-Austrian War or Italian War of 1859) to an official close. It actually comprised three separate treaties. The agreement between France and Austria reaffirmed the terms of the preliminary peace; peace was re-established between the two emperors, Napoleon III and Franz Joseph I; and Lombardy was ceded to France. A second treaty between France and Sardinia saw France cede Lombardy to Sardinia. The third treaty, signed by all three powers, re-established a state of peace between Austria and Sardinia. While Austria had emerged triumphant after the suppression of liberal movements in 1849, its status as a great power in Europe was now seriously challenged, and its influence in Italy severely weakened.

COBDEN-CHEVALIER TREATY 1860
In the mid-19th century France and Britain, traditional competitors and often enemies, imposed heavy tariffs on one another's goods. The treaty, named after its two main originators, Richard Cobden and Michel Chevalier, was a triumph over domestic protectionist factions in both countries. All French products, except for wines and brandy, were allowed free entry into Britain, while France reduced its tariffs on a variety of British goods, imposing an average value of 15 percent, and no longer banned the import of British textiles. This trade agreement turned out to be a prudential investment. Franco-British trade doubled in less than 20 years, and an epidemic of copycat free trade agreements spread across the continent. An important component of the treaty was its "most favored nation" clause, which meant that any lower tariffs negotiated with a third country would automatically be matched. Erstwhile enemies became inveterate, if mistrustful, allies.

CONVENTION OF PEKING 1860
Beginning with the First Opium War (1839–42), China experienced its "century of humiliation" marked by the systematic prostration of the decaying Qing Dynasty by the major European powers. The process was afforded a legal veneer by the "unequal treaties," the Convention of Peking a prime example. Any transgression by the Chinese was seen as an opportunity for punitive sanction, and the Second Opium War was cynically confected by Britain (a local boat allegedly flying the British flag had been seized for piracy). Britain was soon distracted by the Indian Mutiny, but the French, Americans, and Russians were more than happy to join in the action, scenting further lucrative concessions. An initial peace was signed at Tianjin (1858), but perceived Chinese non-compliance led to the storming of Beijing (Peking) and burning of the Summer Palaces. The Peking Convention ceded Hong Kong to Britain, much of Manchuria to Russia, and initiated swingeing reparations and sweeping free trade concessions.

FRANCO-MONEGASQUE TREATY 1861
The Grimaldi dynasty originated in Genoa in the 13th century and seized the fortress at Monaco as its stronghold (1297). Enduring various vicissitudes, the dynasty gained independence from Spain (1633) and France (1641), was occupied by Revolutionary France (1793–1814), before being awarded to the Kingdom of Sardinia at the Congress of Vienna. The reunification of Italy saw Monaco's return to France (1860). The Grimaldis saw an opportunity, and gained their independence by the 1861 Treaty,

selling their neighboring domains of Menton and Roquebrune, receiving 4 million francs in recompense. They swiftly capitalized on their success, opening bathing facilities, casinos and opera houses. The rail-link to Paris (1868) cemented Monaco's popularity as an upmarket resort.

THE TREATY OF COMMERCE AND NAVIGATION 1862

In 1858, the Senator for South Carolina James Henry Hammond envisaged the impact if the southern states withheld their cotton crop: "England would topple headlong and carry the whole civilized world with her, save the South. No, you dare not make war on cotton. No power on earth dare make war on it. Cotton is King." The southern determination to secede, and provoke Civil War, was driven by this analysis. In fact, King Cotton proved less indispensable than imagined; the British and other European powers quickly found alternative sources of supply. But its denial was a potential concern for the northern war effort. Early Union campaigns aimed to occupy and corral southern cotton-producing areas. The Union's Treaty of Commerce and Navigation with the Ottoman Empire opened another source of supply: Egyptian cotton prices would rise by 1,200 per cent through the increased demand. Meanwhile the South was starved of vital cotton export revenue by the Union naval blockade.

CONVENTION OF SCUTARI 1862

The Petrović-Njegoš dynasty of Prince-Bishops of Montenegro were technically vassals of the Ottomans, but in their lawless mountain fastness they enjoyed a high degree of autonomy, indulging their passion for blood-feuds, cattle-rustling, and poetry. Early rebellions were eventually crushed, but a famous victory at Grahovac (1858) left them clutching a precarious independence. In 1861, the Ottomans decided to act. Their general Omar Pasha marched on the Montenegrin capital Cetinje, forcing Nikola I to sue for peace at the Convention of Scutari, once more recognizing Ottoman suzerainty. But the Montenegrins were too boisterous to be cowed for long. In 1876, they joined in rebellion with Serbia and Hercegovina, winning the decisive battle at Vucji Do in July. When the Russians also joined in, the Ottomans were forced to seek peace, recognizing Montenegrin independence.

FIRST TREATY OF SAIGON 1862

The French began to establish a colonial presence in Vietnam at the end of the 18th century, which they gradually expanded, often using the protection of Catholic missionaries as a pretext. Tu Duc, the Nguyen emperor of Vietnam (r. 1847–83) was an

unworldly isolationist, who suffered a battery of rebellions led by, *inter alia*, Confucian scholars and Christian converts. His resultant suppression of Christians, including the execution of Christian missionaries, was all the excuse the French needed. In the Cochinchina campaign (1858–62) a military expedition with Spanish support captured both Tourane and Saigon. The Vietnamese fought back fiercely, but were eventually defeated at the decisive Battle of Ky Hoa. The resultant Treaty of Saigon established the French colony of Cochinchina in South Vietnam. The French were also granted free trade and travel on the Mekong River, plus the Vietnamese were required to pay a phased indemnity of a $4 million.

1863–1868

TREATY OF HUÉ 1863

After the First Treaty of Saigon was signed on 5 June 1862, establishing the French colonial province of Cochinchina, the French decided that a "belt and braces" instrument of ratification for their acquisitions would be appropriate: this was accomplished through the Treaty of Hué on 14 April 1863. The terms of the Saigon Treaty were confirmed; there were also embellishments favoring the colonial power. Three Vietnamese ports were declared open to French trade, the untrammeled promotion of Catholic missionary activity was guaranteed, and the French were granted control over the conduct of the Vietnamese foreign affairs. In addition, Saigon was confirmed as capital of the French colony. A Vietnamese legation travelled to Paris to complete the negotiations; one of these ambassadors committed suicide on returning home when the French breached the terms of the Treaty.

TREATY OF RUBY VALLEY 1863

The Shoshone, with tribal lands in eastern Nevada, had taken to attacking settlers crossing the land via the Overland Trail. The Treaty stipulates the cessation of all hostilities, and specifies that the Shoshone should "permit" a range of activities: mining for minerals, the construction of a railway, the establishment of military posts and settlements. In return, they were to receive 20 annual payments of $5,000. The treaty has been the subject of protracted legal disputes since the 1940s. The Shoshone have refused offers reaching $145 million dollars to settle their claims, and have tried to exercise their ownership by blocking construction of a nuclear waste landfill.

TREATY OF LONDON 1864

By the Treaty of Paris concluding the Napoleonic Wars, the United States of the Ionian Islands (which included Corfu, Kephalonia, Ithaca, Zakynthos and Kythera) had been placed in a British protectorate. Once mainland Greece won its independence from Ottoman rule in 1832, the inhabitants of the islands were in favor of joining the new state. With the accession of the Anglophile Prince George of Denmark to the Greek throne, the British saw little advantage in maintaining the protectorate (their Maltese protectorate already provided a Mediterranean naval base). By the Treaty of London, Britain ceded the islands to Greece, although it retained use of the port on Corfu.

TREATY OF VIENNA 1864

The Second Schleswig War of 1864 ended in crushing defeat for the kingdom of Denmark at the hands of Prussia and Austria. By the Treaty of Vienna, Schleswig was placed in Prussian administration, while Holstein was administered by Austria. The duchy of Saxe-Lauenburg was ceded to their joint control, but Prussia gained sole control the following year at the Convention of Gastein in return for financial compensation to Austria. The Danish king Christian IX was so distraught at the loss of territory that he secretly attempted to negotiate the wholesale entry of Denmark into the German Federation in return for the maintenance of its territorial integrity. The German Chancellor Bismarck rejected the offer, anticipating a Danish revolt would result. A dispute over the handling of Schleswig-Holstein would be the pretext for the subsequent Prussian War with Austria (1866).

TREATY OF TARBAGATAI 1864

Tarbagatai, in terms of sheer territorial volume, was the most unequal of the "unequal treaties" that were forced upon the Chinese Qing Dynasty during the "century of humiliation." By the Treaty, China ceded some 350,000 square miles (900,000 sq. km) to Russia along its lawless western frontiers. After the Treaty of Peking (1860), China and Russia had established a border commission to determine the disputed boundary, but its work had been disrupted by the Dungan rebellion (1862–77). By moving military forces into the disputed area, Russia was able to control the outcome of the survey. However, the rebellion of the Tajik warlord, Yakub Beg, would delay its occupation of the newly annexed territory, necessitating further border protocols at Khovd (1869) and again at Tarbagatai (1870).

PEACE OF PRAGUE 1866

The "Misery of Austria" began with its crushing defeat by Prussia in the war of 1866. The master of *realpolitik*, Otto von Bismarck, was careful not to impose humiliating peace terms (he threatened to throw himself from the battlements of Nikolsburg Castle rather than accept Prussian King Wilhelm's demands for the annexation of Vienna). Instead, he realized that securing Austria's place in Europe would benefit Prussia and controlled Austria more subtly through his now unchallenged domination of the German states, from which, under the terms of the Peace, the Habsburgs were formally excluded. The southern German states were obliged to pay substantial indemnities to Prussia for their support of Austria during the war, while Austria was forced to cede Venetia to France (who promptly handed it to Italy). Prussia annexed Hesse, Schleswig-Holstein, Hanover, Frankfurt, and Nassau. The effect of the Peace was to render Austria a reliable, but strictly subordinate, ally of Prussia, affording Bismarck a powerful strategic axis in Central Europe.

MEDICINE LODGE TREATY 1867

The Indian Peace Commission (1866–68) was convened to establish the causes of the wars with the Plains Indians, and found that dishonest dealings by the United States were a major contributory factor: it also proposed the separation of "friendly" and "hostile" tribes, and adopting more equitable and conciliatory policies towards the former category. The coterminous Medicine Lodge Treaty did not vary significantly from the pattern. Constituted of three separate agreements with various Southern Plains Indian tribes – the Kiowa, Cheyenne, Comanche, Arapaho, and Plains Apache – it secured their vacation of their traditional homelands for (smaller) reservations in Oklahoma. The treaties were never formally validated by the tribespeople, and would be later violated, repeatedly, by the government, allocating reservation land deemed to be "surplus" to settlers without Indian consent.

TREATY OF LONDON 1867

Prussia's dramatic and sudden victory over Austria in the summer of 1866 provoked the "Luxembourg crisis" when, to counter Prussia's new dominance, the grand duke of Luxembourg agreed to sell his principality to Emperor Napoleon III to avoid French entry into the conflict. Placing the mighty fortress of Luxembourg in French hands infuriated Prussia: the Treaty of London was the thrashed-out compromise. The personal union between the House of Luxembourg and the Dutch royal family of Orange-Nassau was reaffirmed, and the neutrality of both the grand duchy of Luxembourg and the kingdom of Belgium guaranteed by the signatories, which included all the main central European powers and Britain. In addition, the Prussian garrison was directed to withdraw from the Luxembourg fortress, which was then to be dismantled.

BURLINGAME TREATY 1868

In the era of the "unequal treaties" the Burlingame Treaty of 1868 was – temporarily – a rare exception. Anson Burlingame was US Minister to China from 1861, but he quit his post to assist a Chinese legation to Washington in the negotiation of a more equitable follow-up to the Treaty of Tianjin (1858). The treaty bearing his name, offered China most-favored nation status in commerce with the United States, reciprocal religious and educational freedoms, the right to appoint Chinese consuls in American ports, freedom of immigration for its citizens to the United States, and recognition of Chinese rights of "eminent domain." The treaty was initially respected, as it stimulated US-Chinese commerce, and the flow of cheap Chinese labor fueled American construction (especially of its transcontinental railroads). However, growing tensions would lead to the abrogation of the immigration provision in the Chinese Exclusion Act (1882).

TREATY OF FORT LARAMIE 1868

The Treaty of Laramie concluded Red Cloud's War, and effectively rewarded the Lakota Sioux and their allies for their aggression, awarding them lands previously allocated to the Crow who had supported the government. The Lakota were guaranteed ownership of the Black Hills of Dakota, forming part of a vast Sioux reservation that stretched west to Montana. The treaty banned white settlement, or passage, without prior Indian consent. An element of tacit subversion was included, with financial incentives for adopting a farming lifestyle, and stipulations for the provision of an "English education" to Indian children. Teachers and artisans were designated to take up residence within the reservation. In the 1870s, gold would be discovered in the Black Hills, leading to repeated violations of the treaty by prospectors. After war broke out, the government seized the Black Hills in 1877, and the rest of the Great Reservation was broken up and divided into much smaller lots.

BANCROFT TREATIES FROM 1868

George Bancroft was an eminent US statesman and academic, who studied as a post-graduate at a number of German universities. As a result of this experience, he turned his attention to the subject of naturalization, which at the time was frequently used by expatriates as a means of evading military service and other legal obligations in their native countries. He arranged the first Bancroft Treaty with Prussia in 1868 (subsequently, a total of 25 would be arranged involving 34 foreign counterparties). Their key features were: a specified term of residence, by which both countries would recognize naturalization to have occurred (typically five years); provision for naturalized citizens to be prosecuted on their return to their country of origin for crimes committed before their departure; stipulation that naturalized citizens would resume their former nationality if they returned for two continuous years to their native country. The last Bancroft Treaty was introduced in 1937.

TREATY OF WASHINGTON 1868

Without great enthusiasm, Chief Ross of the Cherokee nation signed a treaty in 1861, transferring its loyalty from the United States to the Confederate government. Captured in 1862, he reaffirmed his and his people's loyalty to the Union, although a number of Cherokee companies continued to

Treaty of Bern 1874

In 1840, Rowland Hill's proposals for the reform of the British postal system were introduced. The innovations of uniform rates and prepayment attested by an adhesive stamp – encapsulated in the iconic "Penny Black" – revolutionized the nation's postal service, massively escalating demand. At the same time, the steam revolution in transport through ships and rail networks was rapidly increasing the speed, range, and potential volume of postal deliveries. However, fundamental obstacles remained. International mail delivery was still subject to bilateral treaties between nations (by 1874, Germany had collected 17 such agreements, France 16), then subject to complex transit calculations involving different currencies and units of weight and measurement. US Postmaster-General Montgomery Blair described the European system as "almost beyond belief" and suggested an

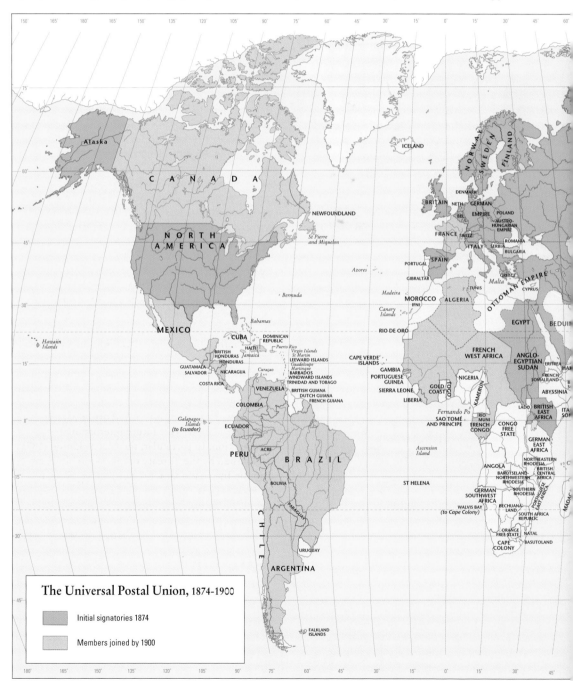

The Universal Postal Union, 1874-1900

Initial signatories 1874

Members joined by 1900

international conference to discuss rationalization.

The conference took place in Paris in 1863, with 15 nations represented, and while establishing certain basic principles, the outbreak of war between France and Germany postponed further action. In the meantime, postal authorities were leapfrogged by a further conference in Paris, where a group of European nations established the International Telegraph Union (ITU) in 1865. At this point the

impetus for postal integration passed to Germany. There, an aristocratic dynasty, the Thurn-und-Taxis, had run postal services as a hereditary concession since the days of the Holy Roman Empire. Following the establishment of the German Empire in the immediate aftermath of the Franco-Prussian War (1870–71), Bismarck commissioned his Postmaster-General Heinrich von Stephan to modernize the service.

Stephan went further, and reconvened an International Postal Union Congress with 22 countries represented, including all the major European powers, the United States, Egypt and Turkey, this time in Bern in 1874. The Congress agreed "a single postal territory for the reciprocal exchange of correspondence between their post-offices." Standard postal rates were specified, but member-countries were allowed a degree of latitude. The Congress also established the Universal Postal Union (UPU), as its international governing body. Article 10 of the Treaty stated: "The right of transit is guaranteed throughout the entire territory of the Union. Consequently, there shall be full and entire liberty of exchange, the several Postal Administrations of the Union being able to send reciprocally, in transit through intermediate countries, closed mails as well as correspondence in open mails, according to the requirements of trade and the exigencies of the postal service."

Since 1948, the UPU has become a specialist agency of the United Nations in common with the International Telecommunication Union (successor to the earlier ITU). The UPU coordinates postal policies amongst member nations. Still with its headquarters at Bern, French is the official language of the UPU, with English introduced as a working language in 1994.

These early intergovernmental organizations became the models for future international cooperation. In particular, the Metric Union (1875) established by the "Treaty of the Metre" in Paris, and the International Union of Railway Freight Transportation (1890) owed a debt to the preceding work of the postal services. International offices dealing with industrial and literary copyright (1883, 1886), and the International Office of Public Health (1907) also owed a debt to the UPU precedent. Such organizations were concomitants, reflections, and intensifiers of the second Industrial Revolution, which bracketed the turn of the 20th century. The standardization they implemented combined with transformations in technology, transport, and communication to pave the way to globalization.

1871–1875

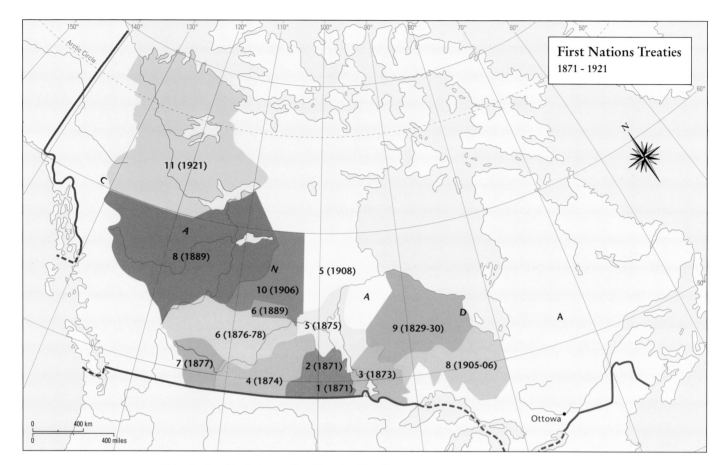

First Nations Treaties
1871 - 1921

fight for the Confederacy. In 1866, the Chief's "pretended treaty" with the Confederacy was annulled, granting an amnesty to Cherokees who had allied to the Confederate cause. The Treaty of Washington regularized relations with the Cherokee nation: it prevented the US trading and taxing its peoples without their consent. At the same time, it established the government's right to forge rights of way, including rail links, through their territory. It also seized parts of their Kansas reservation for settlement, including the "Cherokee Outlet," which had previously afforded the tribe access to their traditional hunting grounds.

TREATIES 1 AND 2 1871
During the Red River Rebellion (1869–70) Louis Riel, the local leader of the Métis in Manitoba (mixed French/First Nation extraction) had resisted the imposition of an English-speaking (and Francophobic) lieutenant-governor. The unrest had been swiftly quelled by a military expedition, but the Canadian government decided that there was an urgent need to regularize relations with the Native American populations of the region. Representatives first approached the Chippewa and Swampy Cree of Southeast Manitoba at Stone Fort

in 1871. In return for the cession of 16,700 square miles (42,750 sq. km) of land, the Indians were allotted 160 acres per family of five, and a present of $3, plus a $3 annuity. Chiefs received $25, Headmen $15. In addition, schools, farm animals, and basic agricultural tools were promised. After completing Treaty 1, the government commissioners moved to Manitoba Post, an ex–Hudson's Bay Company fort on the north shore of Lake Manitoba, where they contracted an agreement on similar terms with the Ojibwa and Cree peoples of the region. Both Treaties, which involved verbal promises "outside'" the written agreements, would prove controversial, and Treaties 1 & 2 were subsequently amended in 1875, to include a record of the verbal commitments.

NORTH-WEST ANGLE TREATY (TREATY 3) 1873
Following the negotiations of Treaties 1 and 2, the Saulteaux tribe of Ojibwa First Nations were well aware that the government was intent on taking their land, and were able to secure significantly better terms than their predecessors. Their terms included a prepayment of $12, an annuity of $5, and a land allocation of 640 acres per family of five. They also secured a guarantee of reserved hunting and

fishing rights. The treaty is significant as the basis for a number of subsequent court cases concerning the relative responsibilities of the Canadian central and provincial governments in respect of their aboriginal peoples.

PANGKOR TREATY 1874
British colonialism could be supple in its application, as evidenced by the appointment of a British resident to "advise" the Sultan of Perak by the Pangkor Engagement of 1874. The appointment arose through disputes between local Malay rulers and also unrest within a large immigrant population of Chinese, attracted by the booming tin industry. The disturbances had reached the point where they were beginning to threaten the powerful commercial interest of Britain's Straits Settlements (Singapore, Malacca, and Penang). The new governor, Andrew Clarke, was requested to resolve the matter. A succession struggle in Perak afforded a fortuitous opening and Clarke was able to secure the ascent of Raja Abdullah; the new resident James Birch controlled his administration and revenue collection. Soon thereafter similar arrangements were negotiated with Selangor and Negeri Sembilan, painlessly safeguarding and promoting British interests in the peninsula.

SECOND TREATY OF SAIGON 1874
The First Treaty of Saigon (1862) opened the way to the creation of the French colony of Cochinchina (1864) comprising the three southernmost provinces of Vietnam. Three years later, French Admiral de la Grandiere seized three further provinces, provoking outrage amongst the Vietnamese, intensified in 1873 when a French arms dealer, Jean Dupuis, was captured on the Red River. The Governor of Cochinchina sent the Inspector of Indigenous Affairs, Francis Garnier, to mediate. Garnier promptly stormed the capital of Tonkin, Hanoi, and claimed it for France. The Vietnamese emperor called upon local Chinese mercenaries, the Black Flag Army, for help, and during the ensuing siege of Hanoi, Garnier was killed. At this point, the French decided matters had gone far enough, and drew up the Second Treaty of Saigon, by which their annexation of the six southern provinces was formally recognized, but they renounced further claims on Tonkin.

TREATY 4 1874
After the completion of indigenous Treaties 1, 2 and 3, the Canadian government was on a roll, and in a hurry, with a transcontinental railroad to rival its southern neighbour's efforts waiting to be built. The area covered by the treaty was vast, the whole of southern Saskatchewan plus segments of neighboring territories. Negotiations took pace at Fort Qu'Appelle in September 1874, and were attended by chiefs of the region's Cree, Assiniboine and Saulteaux Ojibwa tribes. After initial dissension, the tribes were rallied by the Plains Cree Chief, Loud Voice, and eventually agreed to identical terms to those offered in Treaty 3 the previous year. Fear of starvation through the destruction of the buffalo herds, combined with pressure from encroaching settlement, influenced their decision.

TREATY OF ST PETERSBURG 1875
Chekhov visited the Russian penal colony of Sakhalin in 1891 and described the "lying, cunning, cowardice, meanness, informing, robbery, every kind of secret vice (which formed) the arsenal (of this) slave-like people." The indigenous Giliak people received 3 roubles for each severed head of an escaped convict they presented to the authorities. Yet Russia valued the island as a strategic fortress opposite the Amur River, for its coalmines to supply its growing Pacific fleet, and as the most forbiddingly remote repository for its convicts. Following the Treaty of St Petersburg with the Empire of Japan, it happily ceded the Kurile Island chain in the Bering Sea to convert its occupation of Sakhalin from partial to total. In addition, it granted compensation to Japanese residents of Sakhalin, access for the Japanese fishing fleet to the Sea of Okhotsk, and ten years free use of the region's ports to Japanese ships.

CONVENTION DU METRE 1875
The enlightenment fervor of Revolutionary France led to the adoption of the world's first metric system, with its anchoring measure the metre, set at 1/10,000,000 of a quadrant of the Great Circle of the Earth. In 1875, the growing movement for international standards, which had witnessed the Geneva Convention (1864) and Universal Postal Union (1874), led to a Convention in Paris to establish an International Bureau of Weights and Measures. The Convention was attended by 17 nations, including most of the European major powers (although Britain was a prominent absentee) and the United States. It established three international bodies: the General Conference, International Committee, and International Bureau of Weights and Measures. A stubborn Britain discreetly joined up in 1884.

RECIPROCITY TREATY 1875
In the 1870s, the Hawaiian economy was overwhelmingly based on exports of sugar (and, to a much lesser extent, rice) from the island group's plantations. A pressure group of powerful

1875–1879

businessmen urged the king, Kalakua, to form a Reciprocity Commission to enable the passage of a free-trade agreement with the United States, Hawaii's core market. The move provoked opposition from native Hawaiians, who saw it as a potential "nation snatching treaty," and in the US, from southern planters and from sugar refiners, who saw it as a threat to their interests. Nevertheless, the treaty was signed in 1875, leading to a huge increase in Hawaiian sugar exports. A San Franciscan sugar refinery magnate Claus Spreckels (who had succeeded in getting a protective clause built into the treaty) soon dominated the Hawaiian sugar industry. By an 1884 extension to the treaty, the US gained the use of Pearl Harbour as a naval facility.

TREATY 5 1875–76
Much of the initiative for Treaty 5, between the Dominion of Canada and the Saulteaux and Swampy Cree tribes, came from the indigenous peoples themselves, who, having become apprised of the terms of the previous four treaties, were keen to avail themselves of the financial and other inducements on offer, as well as the protections afforded against encroachment. The federal government was lukewarm, the territory in question, a vast area of central Manitoba girdling Lake Winnipeg, was of doubtful agricultural potential. However, the tribes found a champion in Alexander Morris, the lieutenant-governor of Manitoba and North-West Territories. The negotiations lasted a year, hampered by the harsh terrain and vast distances to be covered. There was also dissatisfaction that the terms offered were less favorable than previous treaties, reflecting the lower value the government placed on the land.

JAPAN–KOREA TREATY 1876
From 1868, the Meiji government of Japan embarked upon a headlong modernization and industrialization program in emulation of the western powers. It also decided to emulate western gunboat diplomacy, mirroring US Commodore Matthew Perry's armed enforcement of trade upon Japan in its tactics with Korea, then a closed society ruled by a Queen Regent. In 1875, a Japanese gunboat was sent to Korean waters, where it landed at Ganghwa Island. When the nearby Korean forts opened fire, the gunboat silenced them with a bombardment. The following year, a Japanese fleet arrived, demanding an apology and the signature of a treaty between the two countries. The Treaty of Ganghwa was "unequal," granting Japan access to the Korean ports of Incheon, Busan, and Wonsan without reciprocation. It also granted Japanese citizens privileges and protections on Korean soil. A rash of further unequal treaties would follow for Korea.

TREATY 6 1876
The Plains and Woods Cree and Assiniboine of central Saskatchewan and Alberta were in a parlous state by the mid-1870s. The slaughter of the buffalo threatened starvation, while a wave of smallpox epidemics threatened extinction. Nevertheless, the treaty negotiations, which took place at Forts Carlton and Pitt, were contentious; the Indians, used to ranging over vast territories, were resistant to the allotted (comparatively) tiny plots of land. In the end, they settled for substantially larger plots (2,880 acres per family of five) than were granted in the previous numbered treaties. In addition, Leiutenant-Governor Morris, mindful of the Indians recent travails, inserted two further new provisions: protection against "plague and pestilence," and the offer of a "medicine chest" to be kept by the Indian agent, for the treatment of the reservation population. The Indians took this to mean the provision of full healthcare, an expectation that would be sorely disappointed.

LONDON PROTOCOL 1877
The slow-motion disintegration of the "Sick Man of Europe," the Ottoman Empire, became a preoccupation of the Great Powers in the 19th century. From 1875, rebellion swept the Balkans, and widespread outrage was caused by the brutality of Turkish suppression. As Russia armed to support its fellow Slavs, the Great Powers held a conference in Constantinople (without inviting the Turks in their own capital). They produced a joint communiqué demanding Turkish reforms, and proposing joint protectorates for Bulgaria, Bosnia, and Herzegovina: the Turks remained obdurate. In London in March, the Protocol, signed by six powers, repeated the demands for reform: still the Ottomans refused. Britain then tried, vainly, to fetter any Russian attempt to use the impending war to create client states. Lord Salisbury commented: "English policy is to float lazily downstream, occasionally putting out a diplomatic boat-hook to avoid collision."

TREATY 7 1877
The last of the numbered Treaties effected the cession of 51,000 square miles (130,000 sq. km) of southern Alberta. The tribes involved included Blackfoot, Kanai, Sarcee and Stoney Nakoda. There had been no great urgency on the government part to transact a further treaty until, following the Battle of the Little Bighorn, the arrival of large numbers of refugee Lakota Sioux. To stabilize the situation, David Laird, the regional lieutenant-governor, and James Macleod, commissioner of the North-West Mounted Police, opened negotiations

in 1877. The allotted plots (1,658 acres) per family of five, were modest given the nature of the territory. Softened up by "sweeteners" of Winchester rifles and commemorative medals, the chiefs acquiesced. Subsequently, it became apparent they were unaware that they were sacrificing their land rights: great hardship resulted.

CYPRUS CONVENTION 1878

The "Cyprus Tribute" was fixed at £92,799 11 shillings and three pence, with all the "scrupulous exactitude characteristic of faked accounts," according to a British governor. The Tribute was meant to represent the excess of the island's revenues over its expenditures, and was payable annually to the Ottoman Empire via the secret Cyprus Convention, in return for Britain being awarded control of the island. The Tribute was never actually paid; Britain retained the money to pay off debts owed by the Ottomans in respect of the Crimean War. The arrangement further disgruntled the Cypriots who would have preferred *enosis*: union with Greece. Britain, with misgivings, had entered the agreement to procure a base against Russia's threatened "warm water" expansionism into the Mediterranean. In 1914, when the Ottomans allied with the Central Powers, Britain annexed Cyprus as a crown colony.

PACT OF ZANJÓN 1878

The Guerra Grande (1868–78) was the first and most protracted of three rebellions that culminated, with US intervention, in Cuban liberation from Spanish rule. The rebellion was led by wealthy sugar planters in the east of the island, fighting for tariff reform, representation in the Spanish parliament and an effective ban on the slave trade. The conflict was distinguished by its brutality, with ethnic cleansing and machete charges. The Pact, agreed from "mutual exhaustion," promised an amnesty for the rebels, representation for Cubans in the Spanish parliament, and greater freedom of assembly and of the press. It provided for the manumission of slaves involved in the war, leading to the abolition of slavery on the island in 1888. The Pact was little more than a truce: rebel leaders released under the amnesty resumed the struggle in 1879.

TREATY OF SAN STEFANO 1878

In 1877, Russia responded to a wave of Slavic revolts in the Balkans by declaring war on the Ottoman Empire. Soon, they had swept through the Caucasus in the east, while their main armies closed on Constantinople. Under intense pressure from the other European Great Powers (who feared Russian dominance in the eastern Mediterranean) the Russians agreed to peace talks, signing the Treaty of San Stefano on 13 January 1878. Its terms caused alarm; Russian gains in the Caucasus, and the confirmation of the independence of Serbia, Montenegro, and Romania were considered unexceptionable, but not a purported Russian involvement in the government of newly liberated Bosnia Herzegovina. Worst of all was the creation of a "Greater Bulgaria" under Russian control, giving it effective command of both the Black Sea and the Dardanelles. Intensive Great Power pressure, led by Britain, resulted in the terms being substantially revised at Berlin later in the year.

TREATY OF BERLIN 1878

Alarmed by sweeping Russian gains at the treaty of San Stefano with the Ottoman Empire earlier in the year, the Great Powers hastily convened a congress in Berlin. Here, the independence of Serbia, Montenegro, and Romania was confirmed but in Bosnia, Russia's envisaged role per San Stefano was replaced with occupation, solely, by Austria-Hungary. In the east, parts of Armenia were returned to the Ottomans, but the new Romania's loss of Bessarabia to Russia was confirmed, to their annoyance: they were compensated by the acquisition of Dobruja. The main focus was Bulgaria. Britain was fundamentally opposed to making a Russian client state of Greater Bulgaria. With Prussian Chancellor Bismarck orchestrating, Bulgaria was divided into three: a much-truncated autonomous Principality of Bulgaria; an autonomous, but separate East Rumelia; while Macedonia was returned to the Ottomans. Russia's ambitions were checked, but the treaty's imperfect recognition of the intraregional aspirations for independence left the Balkans a powder keg.

TREATY OF GANDAMAK 1879

Lord Lytton, Viceroy of India, described Afghanistan contemptuously as "an earthen pipkin between two metal pots." But concerns about the infiltration of the other "metal pot," Russia, repeatedly drew the British into its forbidding terrain. After the Afghan ruler, Sher Ali, refused entry to Lord Lytton's diplomatic mission in 1878 (while a Russian mission was cordially entertained), a furious Lytton resolved to smash the "pipkin." Sher Ali fled before the invading British, dying soon after in exile, and the British recognized his son, Mohammed Yakub as Amir by the Treaty of Gandamak. Its terms effectively rendered him a British vassal, specifying his foreign relations would be conducted in accordance with British "wishes and advice." Shortly after British troops left Kabul, their envoy, Sir Louis Cavagnari, was assassinated, and the war resumed.

1881–1883

BOUNDARY TREATY BETWEEN CHILE AND ARGENTINA 1881

Chile was embroiled in the War of the Pacific (1879–83) with Bolivia and Peru and, though winning, desperately wanted to avoid a war with Argentina as well. So President Pinto instructed his negotiator, Diego Barras Arana, to be flexible in boundary negotiations and to secure a deal. The eventual agreement defined a border following the watershed of the Andes to 52 degrees south, where it dog-legged first east (giving Chile Atlantic access), then south again, bisecting Tierra del Fuego. Most of the border area was wilderness (at the time, both Argentina and Chile were engaged in frontier wars with the native Tehuelche and Mapuche) and deemed of little value. But in 1899 and 1902, legal cases arose over boundary demarcation in the Atacama Desert, in the far north, and Straits of Magellan, in the far south.

TREATY OF AKHAL 1881

Shah Naser al-Din of Persia (r. 1848–96) was an effete autocrat and Anglophile under the thumb of European commercial interests, and dependent on regional warlords for his military. In two wars (1804–13, 1826–28), the Russians had ejected Persia from the Caucasus: from the 1830s, they began an inexorable, although far from invincible expansion in Central Asia. Having annexed the khanates of Khiva, Khokand and Bukhara they moved west, into Turkmenistan, which was territory traditionally, but tenuously, claimed by Persia. Shah Naser was in no position to argue. By the Treaty of Akhal, he ceded Merv, Salakhs and Eshgh Abad in the province of Khwarazm to Russia. The treaty intensified British concerns at the height of the "Great Game," about Russia's increasing domination of Central Asia.

TREATY OF BARDO 1881

Humiliated by the defeat by Prussia in 1871, the French were ripe for a piece of low-risk military adventurism to restore national morale. Tunisia offered the pretext by sheltering rebels from the French colony of Algiers: an added incentive was trumping Italian attempts to establish a colony there. In April 1881, two French armies landed and converged on Tunis. There, the generals marched into the Bardo palace of the local ruler Sadok Bey, and presented him with the treaty to sign, which, after some prevarication he did. Tunisia thus became a French protectorate: their resident being appointed, simultaneously, prime minister, head of the Treasury, and commander of the Armed Forces. Not all Tunisians were enamored with the turn of events, but rebellions later in the year in Sfax and Kairouan were swiftly suppressed.

TREATY OF ST PETERSBURG 1881

The Dungan Revolt (1862–77) reportedly arose from an argument over bamboo between a Han merchant and a local Uighur. By its end, the population of western China had been reduced by over 20 million through war deaths and emigration. Russia exploited the unrest to occupy the River Ili valley, purportedly for the protection of its citizens. Once the revolt was crushed, the Chinese sent an envoy to recover the lands. The resulting Ttreaty of Livadia (1879) allowed Russia to keep the bulk of the occupied territory, and required China to pay an indemnity of 5 million roubles. The outraged Qing Government sentenced the envoy to death, and sent Zeng Jize to renegotiate. At St Petersburg, he accomplished a rare reverse of an "unequal treaty." The bulk of the contested land was returned; in compensation, the indemnity was increased to 9 million roubles, and Russia gained an expanded consular network, and duty-free trade deals in western China.

TRIPLE ALLIANCE 1882

The Three Emperors League between Germany, Austria-Hungary, and Russia was formally announced in 1872, but was undermined by the Russo-Turkish War and the subsequent Treaty of San Stefano (1878), which alienated Austria-Hungary, and the Congress of Berlin which alienated Russia by correcting its earlier Balkan gains at Ottoman expense. German Chancellor Bismarck needed a new military alliance to avoid war on two fronts, and in 1882 secretly organized the Triple Alliance, again with Austria-Hungary, but with Italy as the third partner. Italy, despite tensions with Austria-Hungary, a former occupier of their territory prior to Risorgimento (1871), was persuaded to enter the Alliance by German promises of support in the acquisition of a colonial empire. Italy was receptive to Bismarck's overtures: their designs on Tunisia had just been thwarted by the French Treaty of Bardo (1881). Subsequently, Romania and Serbia joined the original Triple Alliance partners, creating a powerful central European bloc.

KILMAINHAM TREATY 1882

"The uncrowned king of Ireland," Charles Parnell was in Kilmainham Jail for organizing opposition to the Second Lands Act (1881), when he negotiated an accommodation with British Prime Minister Gladstone. The Act had introduced certain key reforms in respect of Irish tenant farmers, the so-called "Three Fs" of Free Sale, Fixity of tenure, and Fair rent. However, Parnell and the Irish Land League wanted the ability to reduce rents, and prevent eviction for rent arrears in the event of poor

harvests. To this end, he had organized widespread
rent boycotts, the cause of his imprisonment. The
"treaty" (Gladstone did not recognize it as such)
secured the passage by Gladstone of the Arrears
of Rent (Ireland) Act (1882), which cancelled
£2 million of tenant rent arrears. Parnell and
his supporters were released, to national acclaim.
But relations with the British government were
immediately soured by the Phoenix Park murders of
the senior British officials in Ireland.

CHINA-KOREA TREATY 1882
In July 1882, the "Imo Incident" witnessed a mutiny
of Korean troops, swelled by a disaffected civilian
population. They murdered bureaucrats, and even
attacked members of the royal family. Particular fury
was vented against Japanese merchants and officials,
newly arrived in Korea after the enforced trade
treaty imposed by Japanese gunboat diplomacy in
1876. The Chinese sent in their own troops to quell
the rebellion, and, while restoring order, arrested

the Daewongun, the father and regent of the Korean
Emperor, who was accused of encouraging the
rebellion. China exploited the authority conferred
by its intervention to conclude a treaty requiring
Chinese intercession in future Korean diplomatic
negotiations. For example, in the US-Korea Treaty
of 1882, China requested the clause "Korea is
a dependency of China, but autonomic in both
domestic and foreign relations" – to US chagrin.
With this leverage, China encouraged further
Korean treaties with Western powers to undermine
Japanese influence.

PARIS CONVENTION FOR THE
PROTECTION OF INDUSTRIAL
PROPERTY 1883
When an International Exhibition of Inventions
was held in Vienna in 1873, it was boycotted by
many potential foreign exhibitors, fearing their ideas
would be copied or stolen. The Paris Convention
was organized to tackle this problem. It established

The Berlin Conference 1885

The Berlin Conference of 1884–85 was the high watermark in the so-called "Scramble for Africa," when countries in Europe began to turn to Africa for its rich and exploitable natural resources as well as its growing markets and labor supplies. Countrees such as France, Britain, Portugal, and Spain began to investigate the opportunities that were available in Africa, and to lay claim to certain territories, which inevitably led to conflict amongst the European powers. By the 1880s Stanley's charting of the Congo Basin (1874–77) had removed the last fragment of *terra incognita* from the map of Africa, and areas of British, French, Portuguese, and Belgian control. Germany, hitherto uninterested in colonial ventures, felt compelled to act, especially as rivalries between France and Britain were escalating. Chancellor Bismarck decided to intervene and the European powers were invited to a conference in Berlin.

The Berlin Conference has been widely debunked; its resolutions "as empty as Pandora's Box", its safeguards "as hollow as the pillars of the great saloon." Its façade of a civilizing mission, resolved to end African and Islamic slavery, was lampooned in Conrad's "International Society for the Suppression of Savage Customs." Nevertheless, if one accepts that the colonization of Africa by this stage was an inevitability, the Conference at least had the merit of attempting to enunciate some ground rules. Perhaps its most influential provision, Article 34, set out the Principle of Effective Occupation. To claim possession of territory, the relevant European power could not simply plant a flag, they had (in theory, at least) to demonstrate a degree of administrative control sufficient to allow safe transit and commerce in the territory, without which the claim might not be recognized by other signatory powers. The principle excited vigorous debate; Germany was keen on strict compliance as a means of prising laxly controlled claims from established colonial powers like France and Britain, who combined to water down its implementation. A number of conflicting land claims were resolved, between France and Italy in the Horn of Africa, for example. Portugal's claim to the vast linking hinterland of its colonies in Angola and Mozambique was vetoed by Britain, who subsequently occupied the contested territory.

The provision that became most notorious was the allocation of vast tract of central Africa to the International Congo Society, a philanthropic front for King Leopold of Belgium. In the years that followed the Congo Free State became notorious for the brutalization of its native peoples and the plundering of its natural resources.

The Conference undoubtedly acted as an accelerant to the colonization process: the Scramble for Africa had begun before the Conference, but the "principle of effectivity" encouraged the conversion of trading posts into formal occupation or annexation. Sometimes traditional rulers were coerced into signing treaties, using force and local wars broke out, for example between the French and the Berbers and Bedouin. Meanwhile the British, who had conquered the Zulu state in 1879, set about dismantling the independent Boer Republics of Transvaal and the Orange Free State. By 1902 90 percent of all African land was under European control. By 1914, the only remaining independent states on the continent were Ethiopia and Liberia.

While the Conference represented the climactic point of the colonial era, it also carried the seeds of its destruction. Further provisions of the Conference guaranteed free trade in both the Congo and Niger River basins, at odds with the mercantilist-protectionist traditions of colonization. For all his legendary rapacity, King Leopold could not make a tariff-free Congo profitable. Also, there was a significant ghost at the feast in 1885, the frequently dissenting voice of the American delegation. One such, John Kasson, averred that modern international law implied the requirement of "voluntary consent of the natives whose country is taken possession of, in all cases, where they had not provoked the aggression." Britain's subsequent predilection for protectorates revealed their increasing sensitivity to this issue, valuing the fig leaves of consent or invitation, however coercive. Within a few years of the completion of the Scramble, the colonial powers had battled themselves to exhaustion in a hugely destructive world war, and the one remaining dynamic world power would be projecting – far more forcibly and comprehensively – the anti-colonial Wilson doctrine of national self-determination.

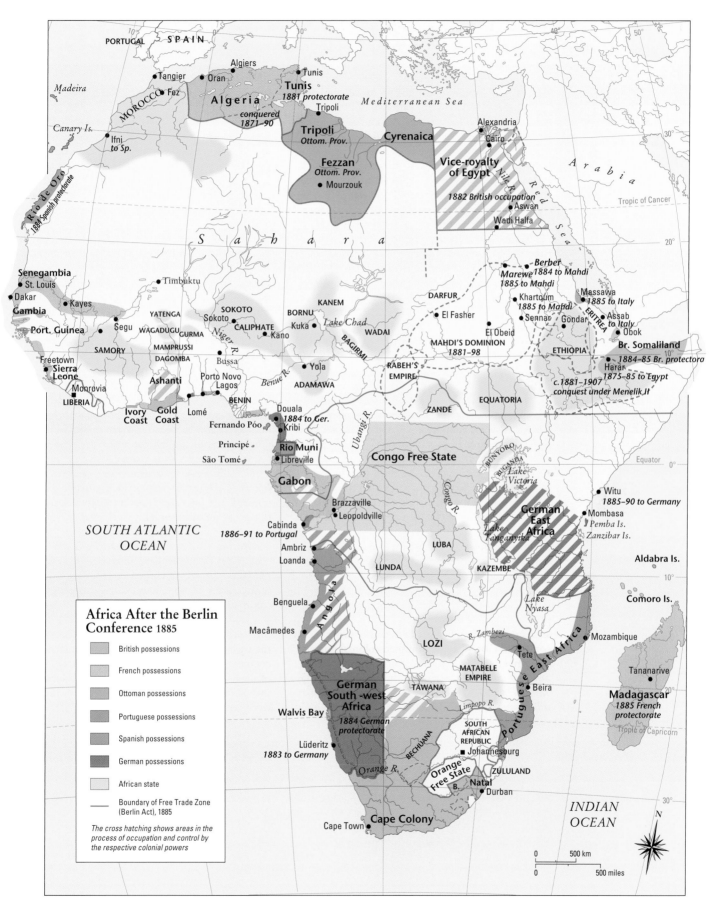

Africa After the Berlin Conference 1885

British possessions

French possessions

Ottoman possessions

Portuguese possessions

Spanish possessions

German possessions

African state

Boundary of Free Trade Zone (Berlin Act), 1885

The cross hatching shows areas in the process of occupation and control by the respective colonial powers

PORTUGAL

SPAIN

Madeira

• Tangier

Algiers •

Oran •

• Tunis

MOROCCO

Fez •

Algeria

Tunis
1881 protectorate

Mediterranean Sea

Tripoli •

Canary Is.

Ifni
to Sp.

conquered 1871–90

Tripoli
Ottom. Prov.

Cyrenaica

Alexandria •

Cairo •

Fezzan
Ottom. Prov.

• Mourzouk

Vice-royalty of Egypt

Arabia

Nile R.

Red Sea

Tropic of Cancer

1882 British occupation

• Aswan

Rio de Oro
1884 Spanish protectorate

S   a   h   a   r   a

• Wadi Halfa

Senegambia

• Timbuktu

• St. Louis

• Dakar   • Kayes

Gambia

Port. Guinea

YATENGA

SOKOTO

• Segu   Sokoto •

WAGADUGU   GURMA

SAMORY

MAMPRUSSI

DAGOMBA

KANEM

BORNU

• Kuka

Lake Chad

CALIPHATE

• Kano

Niger R.

DARFUR

• El Fasher

Berber
1884 to Mahdi
Marewe 1885 to Mahdi

• Khartoum
1885 to Mahdi

Sennar •

Massawa
1885 to Italy

ERITREA

Gondar •

Assab to Italy

• Obok

Br. Somaliland

MAHDI'S DOMINION
1881–98

• El Obeid

BAGIRMI

WADAI

Benue R.

• Yola

ADAMAWA

RABEH'S EMPIRE

ZANDE

• Harar
1884–85 Br. protectora

ETHIOPIA

1875–85 to Egypt

Freetown •

Sierra Leone

• Monrovia

LIBERIA

Ashanti

Ivory Coast   **Gold Coast**

Porto Novo •

Lagos •

Lomé •

BENIN

Douala •
1884 to Ger.

Kribi •

Fernando Póo

c.1881–1907 conquest under Menelik II

EQUATORIA

Príncipe •

São Tomé •

Rio Muni

Libreville •

Gabon

Ubangi R.

Congo Free State

BUNYORO

BUGANDA

Lake Victoria

Equator

• Witu
1885–90 to Germany

SOUTH ATLANTIC OCEAN

Brazzaville •

• Leopoldville

Cabinda •
1886–91 to Portugal

Congo R.

LUBA

Lake Tanganyika

German East Africa

• Mombasa
Pemba Is.
Zanzibar Is.

Aldabra Is.

Ambriz •

Loanda •

LUNDA

KAZEMBE

Lake Nyasa

Comoro Is.

Benguela •

Angola

LOZI

R. Zambezi

Tete •

Portuguese East Africa

• Mozambique

Macâmedes •

Limpopo R.

MATABELE EMPIRE

Beira •

Madagascar
1885 French protectorate

Tananarive •

German South-west Africa

Walvis Bay

1884 German protectorate

TAWANA

BECHUANA

SOUTH AFRICAN REPUBLIC

■ Johannesburg

Tropic of Capricorn

Lüderitz •
1883 to Germany

Orange R.

Orange Free State

B.

ZULULAND

• Natal

• Durban

INDIAN OCEAN

Cape Town •

Cape Colony

N

0   500 km

0   500 miles

1883–1890

a basic framework for the treatment of patents, trademarks, and industrial designs, introducing three governing precepts. First, member countries had to confer the same protection for industrial property to foreign nationals afforded to their own nationals. Second, member country rules governing industrial property were to be standardized. Third, rights of priority, for the first applicant for a patent, trademark, or industrial design, were agreed among member countries. Copyright would be addressed at a subsequent convention in Berne (1886). There were notable absentees from the initial Paris Convention, including the United States and United Kingdom, but membership grew rapidly and remains in force in 2017 with 177 members.

TREATY OF ANCÓN 1883
The War of the Pacific was a conflict ranging from the Andean mountains and Atacama Desert to the eponymous Ocean. Chile first conquered the province of Antofogasta, denying Bolivia access to the sea; then invaded its main adversary, Peru, occupying Lima in January 1881. The Peruvians continued to fight a guerrilla war for almost three years, before suing for peace. The Treaty of Ancón formally ceded the coastal province of Tarapaca to Chile. To the north, the provinces of Tacna and Arica remained in Chilean hands, but a plebiscite within ten years of the treaty was agreed to determine their future. In fact, the plebiscite was never held, the counterparties unable to agree on the protocols under which it would be conducted, and they remain Chilean territory to this day. The annexed provinces were rich in saltpeter, rendering them valuable acquisitions.

TREATY OF HUÉ 1883
After victory at the Battle of Thuân An, French commissioner-general Harmand sent an ultimatum to the Vietnamese Emperor, threatening to "destroy your dynasty root and branch" if his terms were not immediately accepted. "If we wanted to...we could seize for ourselves the entire kingdom, as we have done in Cochinchina." The terms included the creation of French protectorates in Annam and Tonkin, and French garrisons in the forts in remaining Vietnamese territory. The southern provinces of what remained of Vietnam were annexed by the French colony of Cochinchina, and a French resident-general with sweeping powers was installed in the imperial court. As a "good-will gesture," Vietnamese imperial debts to France were written off. The French committed to both drive Black Flag mercenaries from Tonkin and keep the Red River open to trade – measures that were consonant with their own commercial interests.

TREATY OF HUÉ 1884
The draconian Treaty of Hué concluded, effectively at gunboat point, in 1883, was never formally ratified by the French Assembly and was considered brutal even by the bombastic standards of the imperialism of the day. In 1884 via the Tientsin Accord, France had secured the vacation of Chinese claims to suzerainty over Vietnam, and thus felt disposed to be (slightly) more magnanimous. The new treaty annulled the annexation by French Cochinchina of the rump Vietnam's southern provinces. In addition, to appease China, a clause in the prior treaty placing Vietnamese-Chinese diplomatic relations under French control was deleted. Nevertheless, Annam and Tonkin remained French protectorates, with garrisons and French residents placed in the main towns and forts. The transfer of real power was symbolized at the signing ceremony, when a massive silver and gold seal bestowed previously by the Chinese Emperor to Vietnam was melted down.

ANGLO-PORTUGUESE TREATY RE CONGO RIVER 1884
For most of the 19th century, Britain was unquestionably the main colonial power in sub-Saharan Africa, but generally coexisted comfortably with its main competitor, Portugal, whose minimalist governance barely interfered with British commercial activities. In 1884, the impending Congress of Berlin threatened to disrupt this cosy alignment of interests with the arrival of dynamic new colonial players on the scene. Britain and Portugal attempted a pre-emptive strike by their treaty of 26 February 1884, by which Britain recognized Portuguese sovereignty over both sides of the mouth of the Congo River, gaining privileged commercial access in return. German Chancellor Bismarck was too astute to be stymied in this way. The Berlin Conference's "Principle of Effective Occupation" effectively negated Portugal's claim in the Congo, and threatened much of its other African colonies as well. Nevertheless, the existence of the treaty enabled Portugal to gain an enclave on the Congo coast at Cabinda in recompense.

TREATY OF SIMULAMBUCO 1885
The Ngoyo kingdom of Cabinda had become wealthy in the 18th century through its participation in the trans-Atlantic slave trade. Abolition led to a downturn in its fortunes, and with kingship no longer commanding an assured revenue base, central rule effectively dissolved in the 1830s. As a result of the Congress of Berlin (1884–85), Portugal was awarded the enclave of Cabinda in return for renouncing its claims to the mouth of the Congo River. No-one consulted the Ngoyo. As it

turned out, they were rather pleased, a rare case of amicable colonization. Hastening to comply with the Congress's Principle of Effective Occupation, Portugal signed the Treaty of Simulambuco with the "princes and governors" of Cabinda, dividing the new territory into three provinces: Cacongo, Loango, and Ngoio.

BERNE CONVENTION 1886
The Berne Convention was sweeping in its ambition, defining literary, artistic, and scientific domains of conception. In keeping with the preceding Paris Convention (1883) governing industrial property, it sought to equalize and standardize treatment of authors amongst its member countries, and laid down principles of national Interest, Automatic Protection and Independence of Protection. It also defined rights *inter alia* to translate, adapt, perform, and reproduce protected works. "Moral rights" protected works from mutilation, deformation, modification, and derogatory treatment. Duration of protection was also specified: in general, 50 years from the death of the author, but reduced for applied arts (e.g. photography). The concept of fixing copyright at the moment of creation, rather than requiring some form of registration was introduced. Ten countries were the first ratifiers of the Convention in 1887, with the United States a significant absentee.

TREATY OF BUCHAREST 1886
Once the Ottoman yoke had been cast off, the liberated Balkan states wasted no time in redirecting their martial impulses against one another. One such outbreak of sibling rivalry was the Serbo-Bulgarian War (1885). Serbia objected to the incorporation of Eastern Rumelia into a unified state of Bulgaria, and, with tacit Austro-Hungarian support, declared war, only to be decisively defeated within a fortnight. Concerned that Serbia would be overrun, Austria-Hungary threatened Bulgaria with their own intervention unless a peace was concluded. The Treaty of Bucharest (1886) was the result, with absolutely no territorial adjustments. However, success in the war cemented Bulgarian unification. Correspondingly, defeat undermined the ruling dynasty in Serbia (King Milan I abdicated in 1889), and led to a realignment towards Russia rather than Austria-Hungary.

REINSURANCE TREATY 1887
In 1887, the League of the Three Emperors fell apart when two emperors – Tsar Alexander and Franz Joseph – fell out over the Balkans. German Chancellor Bismarck responded with one of his trademark fine-tunings of the balance of power in the secret Reinsurance Treaty with Russia. A cunning contrivance, the treaty stipulated reciprocal neutrality in the event of either going to war with another Great Power, excepting a Russian attack on Austria or a German attack on France. However, benevolent neutrality would be maintained if Germany or Russia were not the aggressor. In addition, Bismarck recognized Bulgaria and the Black Sea as Russian spheres of influence, promising neutrality if Russia intervened in the Bosphorus. Bismarck left office in 1890, and his successor refused Tsar Alexander's request for a renewal of the treaty, driving Russia towards an alliance with France.

TREATY OF BERLIN 1889
The period 1881–89 witnessed a bitter civil war in Samoa, a conflict exacerbated by the proxy meddling and arms peddling of the United States, Britain, and Germany, all of whom had designs on the islands. Samoa's value lay as a strategic naval staging post in the Pacific, and the cash crop cultivation of cacao and copra. In March 1889, the three powers had each gathered a fleet of warships in Apia harbor while a massive cyclone approached. No nation would show fear by heading for the relative safety of the open sea. Carnage was the result. The loss of warships seems to have brought the belligerents (temporarily) to their senses. The following month, representatives agreed a three-way condominium in Samoa, plus the restoration of the Samoan monarch, with his kingdom's neutrality and independence guaranteed. Civil war broke out again in 1898.

TREATY OF WUCHALE 1889
The "Theft of Tunis" by France in 1881 outraged Italian public opinion. Thereafter, Italian foreign policy had two cardinal aims: to establish a colonial presence; and to obstruct France wherever possible. The Italian occupation of Massawa (1885), a French target on the Red Sea coast, served both purposes admirably. Having gained a colonial toehold, the Italians attempted to expand it by sleight of hand. The ancient kingdom of Ethiopia, a neighbor of Massawa, was in the grip of civil war, and a protracted famine caused by a rinderpest epidemic in its cattle. When Menelik II seized power, the Italians presented him with a treaty at Wuchale, written in Amharic, which ceded Eritrea to Italy and otherwise professed cordial relations. The Italian version rendered Menelik's whole kingdom an Italian protectorate. When he learned of the subterfuge, an enraged Menelik tore up the treaty, and the Italians prepared to invade to enforce their claims.

HELIGOLAND-ZANZIBAR TREATY 1890
After the fall of Bismarck, his successor as German

Convention of Calcutta 1890

The First Opium War (1839–42) ushered in China's "century of humiliation," during which a succession of unequal treaties were imposed during the unravelling of the Qing Dynasty and the civil wars that followed. The unequal treaties forced China to open up its ports to trade, lease territories to foreign powers, and make concessions of sovereignty to foreign "spheres" of influence following military defeats, Large reparations were demanded from China. Foreign residents and Christian missionaries were to be allowed to live in Chinese cities, and were subject to their own consular authorities rather than China's own legal system.

In this context, the Convention of Calcutta seems remarkably innocuous. Signed in 1890, it was meant to define the border between Sikkim, then a British Protectorate, and Tibet, then under the loose control of China. In territorial terms, it was not aggrandizing on Britain's part, but a commercial motive obtained, to open cross-border markets for the goods of the British Raj in India. At the time, British attention in the region was absorbed by the "Great Game" with Russia, and its perceived designs on India: Sikkim-Tibet was not considered a flash-point frontier.

When, little more than a decade later, Britain briefly occupied Tibet, it was to deter Russian, not Chinese, expansionism. A century later, Sikkim and Tibet are now border provinces of the Asia's two emerging superpowers. China is motivated to undo the perceived injustice of the unequal treaties: Hong Kong has been returned to the fold after the expiry of the British 99-year lease (1997); uninhabited islands are being occupied and fortified in the South China Sea; the Senkaku Islands are contested with Japan; and Taiwanese independence is threatened. India, for its part, is in perpetual dispute with Pakistan over Kashmir, and has had arguments with Bangladesh, Myanmar, and Sri Lanka over border issues. In 1962 China and India were briefly, unofficially, at war over the Aksai Chin region, which is well to the west of the area covered by the Calcutta Convention. There were skirmishes in Sikkim in 1967.

In early 2017, the Chinese cited the Convention to support claims to the Doklam plateau region on their border with Bhutan. The Sino-Indian border – the Line of Actual Control – runs for 2,100 miles (3,500 kilometres), much of it over the "roof of the world" through forbidding, inaccessible, and barren territory, but these are the world's "growth stock" nuclear powers, so apparently trivial disputes may have grave consequences.

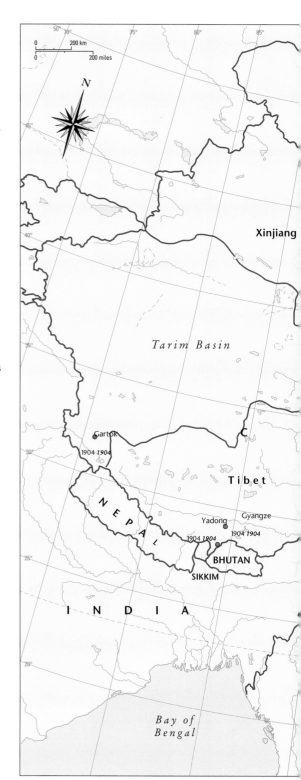

RUSSIAN EMPIRE
U.S.S.R. (1922)

Outer Mongolia

M O N G O L I A

Inner Mongolia

Algun
by 1920

Manzhouli
by 1920

Qiqihar
by 1920

M A N C H U R I A

Harbin

Jilin
Sufenhe
Jilin *by 1920*
1905 1909 Longjing
Changchun *by 1920*
Hunchun
by 1920 1905 1910
1905 1910

Fengtian
Yinghou Shenyang
1903 1907 Hunchun
Qinhuangdao 1858 1864 Dadongkou
Beijing 1898 1901 Dalian *by 1920*
Tianjin 1907 1907 1903 1907
Lushunkou
(Port Arthur) **KOREA**

Sea of Japan

Tokyo

JAPAN

Pacific Ocean

Zhili
1860 1861 Longkow Weihaiwei
Yantai
Shandong 1915 1915 1930 1930
1858 1862 Qingdao
1898 1899

Yellow Sea

Gansu

I N A

Shanxi

Shaanxi

Henan

Anhui **Jiangsu**
Nanjing Zhenjiang
Wuhu 1858 1861 Shanghai
1858 1899 Suzhou
1870 1877 Hangzhou 1842 1854
1895 1894 Ningbo
1896

Hubei
Yichang Shashi Hankou
1876 1877
Sichuan 1895 1896 1858 1862
1902 1915 Yueyang Jiujiang **Zhejiang**
Wanxian 1895 1896
1858 1862 Wenzhou

Chongqing **Hunan** 1858 1862
1890 1891 1898 1899
Changsha *East China Sea*
Jiangxi Sand'uao
1903 1904 1858 1877

Guizhou Fuzhou
Fujian 1898 1899
1842 1861
Yunnan Xiamen (Amoy)
Mengzi 1842 1862
Simao 1886 1889 Shantou
Guangxi Longzhao **Guangdong** Taiwan
Nanning Sanshui 1858 1860 *1895 to Japan*
1895 1897 1897 1897 Wuzhow Guangzhou
1886 1889 Jiangmen
1897 1907 Lappa (Wanzai Island) 1842 1859 Hong Kong
Beihai 1902 1904 Kowloon
1876 1877 1871 1887 1886 1897
Leizhou Quangzhouwan
1936 Qiongshan
FRENCH INDO-CHINA
Hainan *South China Sea*
1858 1876

SIAM

Treaty of Calcutta
1890
(and Treaty Ports)

○   Leased territory

1902   Date of opening by treaty

1915   Date of customs opening

Treaty ports opened with:

●   Great Britain

●   France

○   Japan

●   Germany

●   Portugal

○   Russia

○   United States of America

○   Voluntarily by China

Note: Internal borders during the period of this map are subject to change. The borders shown represent the period early 1900s

163

British Gulf Treaties 1900

Britain's engagement with the Arabian/ Persian Gulf started in the 1790s when the region was known as the "Pirate Coast" from the frequent raids on British shipping by Arab buccaneers. British strategic concerns had also been raised by Bonaparte's 1798 invasion of Egypt and France's military alliance with Persia (1807–09), both of which revived the specter of France's designs on India following the defeat of the French and their Indian allies at the Battle of Plassey in 1757. In 1820 Britain signed a treaty for the suppression of piracy with the sheikhs of the Gulf Coast. It was not a conspicuous success; skirmishes, conflicts and raids continued intermittently until the 1830s, when various sheikhdoms began to make short treaties banning hostilities during the pearling season. These culminated in the Perpetual Treaty of Maritime Peace in 1853, the first of a series of treaties that would transform the "Pirate Coast" into the "Trucial Coast," which was signed by the rulers of Abu Dhabi, Dubai, 'Ajman and the Qawasim families of Sharjah and Ras al-Khaimah. These were at first renewed annually, followed by a ten-year truce in 1843 and clinched with a perpetual maritime truce in 1853. The original signatories, which became known as the Trucial States, are now the United Arab Emirates (UAE).

In the course of time 47 other rulers were invited to join the system, including Kuwait (1841), Bahrain (1861), and Qatar (1916). Under the terms of these various truces rulers gave up the right to wage war at sea in return for British protection against piracy and other forms of maritime aggression. A number of rulers also signed exclusive agreements with Britain, including those of Bahrain (1880 and 1892), the Trucial States (1888 and 1892), Kuwait (1899), Najd and Hasa (1915, annulled in 1927 after the Saudi conquests), and Qatar in 1916. The sheikhs agreed not to dispose of any territory, except to the United Kingdom and not to enter into relationships with any other states. Despite the protectorate status of this coast, the British did not choose to interfere with administrative matters, leaving the sheikhs to control domestic and commercial affairs. This version of Pax Britannica cast Britain in the role of protector, mediator, and arbiter between competing sheikhdoms, as well as guarantor of the settlements. In arrangements similar on those between the British Raj and the rulers of Indian states, the sheikhs and emirs of the Gulf bound themselves to exclusive political relations with Britain and ceded control over their external affairs to the Government of India, with authority transferred to London after India gained independence in 1947.

With the discovery of oil in the 1930s the region is now one of the world's wealthiest and most technologically advanced, with cities such as Kuwait City, Doha (Qatar) Abu Dhabi and Dubai (UAE) creating science-fiction fantasy worlds with unmanned airborne taxis, indoor ski-slopes, artificial islands and skyscrapers that dwarf Manhattan's tallest. Yet formerly this was one of the world's poorest and least hospitable regions. The debilitating climate, disease-ridden conditions and high death toll justified the Gulf's reputation as a "white man's grave." With the climate claiming the lives of many Britons it was difficult to find men who would accept postings there, with the Viceroy of India, Lord Curzon, complaining that "the best men will not go to so disagreeable a station, and such as go clamor till they are taken away." As historian James Onley observed in *The Arabian Frontier of the British Raj* (2008) every political officer of the Indian Government sent to the region "suffered seriously from ill health at some point during his assignment."

These adverse conditions, however, had an important if unintended benefit. As in India, the system of Pax Britannica was actually administered by a complex network of hundreds, if not thousands of agents charged with advising rulers, gathering intelligence, and even, in some cases, defending the interests of local people. The vast majority of the personnel who ran the system were Arabs, Persians or Asians (i.e. non-Europeans), when even the gunboats that enforced the truces largely manned by Indian sepoys, so Britain's informal empire in the Gulf had a high level of de facto autonomy and administrative sophistication, features that would enable the region to navigate the rapids of sudden wealth and full independence with a degree of élan rarely found in other post-colonial situations.

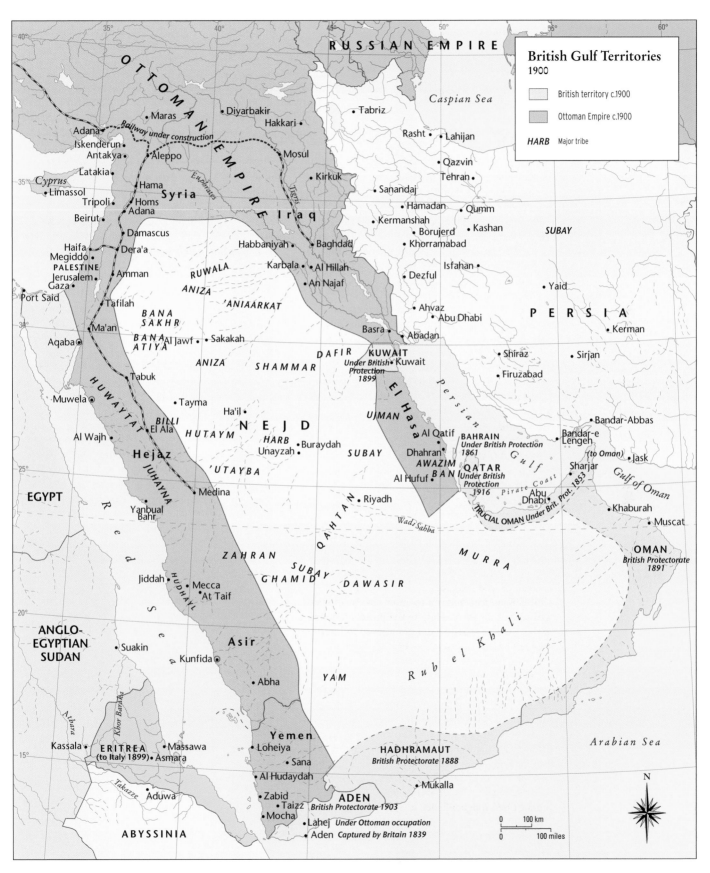

1891–1898

chancellor, Leo von Caprivi, performed a foreign policy pivot, electing not to renew the secret Reinsurance Treaty (1887) with Russia, and instead attempting more cordial relations with Britain. The Heligoland-Zanzibar Treaty was an early fruit of this strategy. The agreement defined the respective spheres of influence of the two powers, and enacted mutually advantageous exchanges of territory. Germany surrendered its Zanzibar protectorate (plus a strip of adjacent mainland necessary for Britain to build its Lake Victoria railway) in return for British recognition of its claims in Tanganyika and South West Africa. Britain additionally donated the "Caprivi Strip" providing German South West Africa with access to the Zambezi. In West Africa, the borders between respective colonies in Nigeria and Cameroon were agreed. As a final sweetener Britain handed over the North Sea island of Heligoland, which it had held since 1814.

TREATY OF MADRID 1891
The Madrid Agreement Concerning the International Registration of Marks formed a logical successor to the Paris Convention (1883), which addressed Industrial Property Rights. The Agreement established a methodology for uniform systems of application for trademarks within member countries, but fell short of achieving international registration. Nationally registered trademarks are communicated to other member countries, rather than automatically entered on all member registers. These shortcomings have meant that major countries, including the United States, United Kingdom, Japan, Canada as well as the bulk of Asia and South America have not enrolled in the system, and registration as a whole has continued to lag well behind signatories to the Paris Convention, or the Berne Convention on Copyright (1886).

TREATY OF THE HAGUE 1895
Despite visits from Portuguese and Spanish explorers from the 1520s onwards, New Guinea was largely ignored by would-be colonizers until the Dutch claimed the island west of the 141-degree line of longitude in 1828; they abandoned their settlement shortly afterwards, administering their theoretical colony from their Residency on the spice island of Ternate. In 1883, the Australian state of Queensland attempted to incorporate part of the island, followed closely by the Germans taking possession of the Northeast in 1884. This spurred the Dutch to return, and in 1895, they met with the British at The Hague to delineate respective claims. It was agreed to divide the island east/west along the 141-degree parallel, with the western sector allotted to the British. At the northern end of the line the boundary abutted the

German claim, at the southern end it veered from the parallel to follow the Bensbach River.

TREATY OF SHIMONOSOKEI 1895
The First Sino-Japanese War (1894–95) began as a contest for dominance in Korea, but ended with Japan the dominant Asiatic power, so comprehensive was their victory over the Qing Dynasty. By the Treaty of Shimonoseki, China recognized the independence of Korea, and ceded the strategic Liaodong Peninsula to Japan. Japan also received Taiwan and its offshore Pescadores island chain. China was additionally forced to pay a large financial indemnity. Shocked by the sudden shift in the balance of power, and zealous to protect their own interests in the region, Russia, Britain, and France quickly enacted the Triple Intervention, forcing Japan to renounce Liaodong in return for an increased indemnity. Meanwhile, the population of Taiwan bitterly resisted Japanese occupation, resulting in a brutal campaign of suppression.

TREATY OF FRIENDSHIP, COMMERCE AND NAVIGATION BETWEEN BRAZIL AND JAPAN 1895
After the Brazil-Japan Treaty was signed to promote commercial contacts in 1895, a legation was established in Tokyo, and a consulate in Yokohama, with the Brazilian ambassador Henrique Lisboa, an unqualified devotee, swooning "when I think of the delicious fatherland of 'Madame Chrysanthemum' my imagination can only see it covered with colored and sweet flowers and inundated with happy rays of sunshine." He was equally impressed with Japanese industry, efficiency, and modernity. But his efforts to promote Japanese emigration were thwarted at both ends. Japanese travelers, who made exploratory visits to Brazilian plantations, were shocked at their squalor and indiscipline. Meanwhile, Brazilian functionaries warned of "mixture with inferior races." However, a US ban on Japanese immigration in 1907, and an Italian prohibition on subsidized transportation of its citizens to Brazil (1902), encouraged both governments to overcome their reservations.

TREATY OF ADDIS ABABA 1896
The Italian attempt to dupe the Ethiopian Emperor Menelik II through the Treaty of Wuchale (1895) backfired: when he learned the Italian version made him their vassal, he repudiated the agreement entirely. The Italians resolved to enforce their authority by military means, invading Ethiopia in 1895, banking on support from tribes hostile to Menelik. However, when presented with a common enemy, the Ethiopians formed a united front,

enabling Menelik to assemble a massive army, which – thanks to the Emperor's modernization program – was surprisingly well-equipped. A legation to fellow Orthodox Christians in St Petersburg had even obtained a corps of Russian military advisers. The Italians were crushingly defeated at Adawa (1896) and forced to sue for peace. At Addis Ababa, Ethiopian independence was recognized and, in 1897, the United Kingdom and France both accorded Ethiopia the same recognition: it would be the only African kingdom to be accorded this respect by the European powers.

TREATY OF LI-LOBANOV 1896

After the humiliation of the Sino-Japanese War (1894-95), Qing Dynasty China requested Russian aid in meeting the huge indemnity payments due to Japan. Naturally, Russian Finance Minister Sergei Witte scented the chance for another unequal treaty. The "sting" came in three parts. First, the Russo-Chinese Bank was established to handle the loans. Second, Russia made a secret guarantee to protect Chinese territorial integrity. Third, to ensure that protection, Russia requested the building of railroads through northeastern China and access to Chinese ports for Russian warships. Naturally these railroads and docking facilities would have to be protected by Russian troops, who received extraterritorial jurisdiction. Finally, to ensure other Great Powers did not become aware of Russia's de facto annexation of most of northeastern China, the arrangements were routed through the Russo-Chinese Bank, so the Russian occupation was, to outward appearances, a joint commercial venture.

TREATY OF CONSTANTINOPLE 1897

The Treaty of Constantinople (1832) established Greek independence, and an influential political faction within the new state became wedded to the irredentist notion of recreating the Greek-speaking dominion of the old Byzantine Empire, an idea that was motivated by *enosis*, the desire for reunification with Greece of the still subjugated Greek populations. The Cretan rebellion of 1897 offered a test case for the project, but after an initial victory at Livadeia on the island, Greek forces were rapidly defeated by the Ottomans on the mainland and forced to sue for peace. Under the new Treaty of Constantinople, signed in December, Crete became an autonomous state under Ottoman suzerainty. The Ottomans achieved minor territorial gains in Thessaly, but insisted on maintaining an army of occupation until substantial reparations were paid. However, the European Great Powers intervened to alleviate the terms of the treaty. Crete would accomplish *enosis* in 1908.

FRANCO-ETHIOPIAN TREATY 1898

The enclave of French Somaliland was established (1883-87) at a time of competing colonial projects in the Horn of Africa. At this time, Léon Chefneux, a French merchant, had managed to inveigle the position of "Ethiopian consul to all Europe" in the court of Emperor Menelik II and, in 1894, secured authorization for the construction of a railroad from Djibouti to Addis Ababa. At the Fashoda incident (1898), Lord Kitchener's British forces in Sudan repulsed (bloodlessly) a French attempt to establish an east/west axis across the continent, simultaneously reinforcing Britain's north/south Cairo to the Cape axis of dominance. This reverse, together with Menelik II's routing of an invading Italian army at Adawa (1896), promoted a more conciliatory French approach in the Horn of Africa. Under the terms of the 1898 treaty, France treated Ethiopia as an equal counterparty, and amicably agreed the borders between their dominions. The railway would be completed in 1917.

FRENCH AND BRITISH TREATY RE NIGERIA-DAHOMEY 1898

By the closing years of the 19th century, the scramble was turning to a jostle in Africa, as the colonizing powers frequently clashed in their voracious pursuit of the remaining territorial tidbits. France and Britain were particularly captious, coming close to conflict in the Fashoda incident on the White Nile and at Busa in Nigeria. The Benin Massacre in West Africa, when a British trading mission was hacked down by local warriors, led, by way of reprisal, to the complete destruction of the king's court and capital, and its unexpectedly sudden annexation. This made issues of demarcation between Nigeria and the neighboring French colony of Dahomey a matter of urgency. The French themselves had only recently established control in Dahomey (1894), after two fierce wars with the local Fon tribe and their units of Dahomey Amazons. The 1898 treaty established a border that proved durable.

THE TREATY OF PARIS 1898

For future United States president (and combatant) Theodore Roosevelt, the Spanish-American War of 1898 constituted a "splendid little war." By the terms of the Treaty of Paris, Spain ceded to the United States both Puerto Rico and Guam, and was required to evacuate Cuba, which became a US protectorate. In return for the Philippine Archipelago, Spain was given a pay-off of $20 million. The United States had acquired, virtually overnight, an overseas empire. Public opinion was broadly favorable to this, having been stirred to support the war by a jingoistic press, especially

1899–1900

after the mysterious sinking of the USS *Maine* (allegedly by Spanish sabotage) in Havana Harbor during the lead-up to the war. But an influential body of opinion was firmly opposed. In the case of Cuba, this found executive expression in the Teller Amendment to the Congressional resolution backing the war, effectively debarring annexation.

The treaty acquisitions were denounced as a "vulgar, commonplace empire" in the US Senate. This strand of opinion was intensified by the ensuing war in which the Filipinos sought independence. In Puerto Rico, the Creole planter class welcomed American occupation, but the failure to offer statehood belatedly fuelled an independence

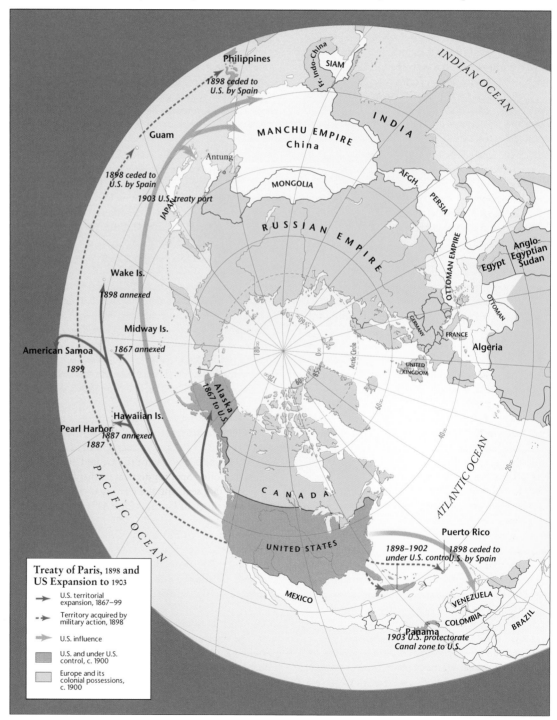

Philippines
1898 ceded to U.S. by Spain

Fr. Indo-China

SIAM

INDIAN OCEAN

Guam

MANCHU EMPIRE
China

INDIA

1898 ceded to U.S. by Spain

Antung

MONGOLIA

AFGH.

PERSIA

1903 U.S treaty port

JAPAN

R U S S I A N   E M P I R E

OTTOMAN EMPIRE

Anglo-Egyptian Sudan

Egypt

Wake Is.
1898 annexed

GERMANY

FRANCE

OTTOMAN

Midway Is.
1867 annexed

Arctic Circle

Algeria

American Samoa
1899

UNITED KINGDOM

Alaska
1867 to U.S

Hawaiian Is.

Pearl Harbor
1887 annexed
1887

C A N A D A

ATLANTIC OCEAN

PACIFIC OCEAN

Puerto Rico

UNITED STATES

1898–1902 under U.S. control *1898 ceded to U.S. by Spain*

MEXICO

VENEZUELA

Treaty of Paris, 1898 and US Expansion to 1903

→ U.S. territorial expansion, 1867–99

⇢ Territory acquired by military action, 1898

→ U.S. influence

▮ U.S. and under U.S. control, c. 1900

▯ Europe and its colonial possessions, c. 1900

COLOMBIA

BRAZIL

Panama
1903 U.S. protectorate Canal zone to U.S.

movement in the 1920s. Meanwhile Cuba was handed over to a civilian government in 1902, but was reduced to puppetry by the successor to Teller, the Platt Amendment, reserving America the right to intervene militarily in its affairs, a right which would be exercised repeatedly.

The so-called Disaster of 1898 polarized Spanish politics. The country was be torn apart by labor unrest and the separatist movements of the Catalans and Basques. Within the armed forces a "never again" resolve crystallized into a growing Fascist faction which, under General Francisco Franco, would ultimately prevail over Socialist Revolutionaries in the Spanish Civil War (1936–39).

FRENCH AND BRITISH TREATY RE NILE AND CONGO 1899

Major Jean Baptiste Marchand's expedition from Brazzaville hardly smacked of imperial might: just twelve French officers and a hundred or so Senegalese irregulars on a borrowed Belgian steamer. But in reaching Fashoda (1898) on the White Nile, they hoped to complete a French east/West axis across Africa – and confound a coveted British north/south axis into the bargain. Unfortunately for Marchand, the British, supposedly overrun by Mahdist rebels, had achieved a stunning victory at Omdurman weeks earlier. The British commander, Lord Kitchener, duly arrived at Fashoda with a small army. A diplomatic imbroglio ensued; national pride was at stake and communications between Paris and London were tortuous from such a remote location. Marchand's position according to Kitchener, was "as impossible as it is absurd." The French, reluctantly, climbed down: by the Treaty of March 1899, the demarcation of respective spheres of influence ran along the Nile/Congo. England, not France, had their axis.

TRIPARTITE CONVENTION OF 1899

From the 1880s, the Samoan islands were ravaged by a succession of civil wars arising from a disputed royal succession. The situation was exacerbated by the proxy manipulation of Germany, on the one hand, and the United States and Britain on the other, who supported rival contenders for the throne, armed the combatants, and often became involved in the battles. The Tripartite Convention was a recognition that the crisis demanded resolution. By its provisions, the British withdrew from Samoa, but gained significant compensation, including the acquisition of German possessions in Tonga and the Solomon Islands, and some commercial concessions in Africa. With Britain mollified, Samoa was partitioned between Germany (who formed a protectorate of the eastern islands, known as German

Samoa) and the United States, who would establish a naval station on the western islands.

TREATY 8 1899

Skookum Jim Mason, a First Nation native of the Yukon, reputedly made the discovery that sparked the Klondike Gold Rush (1896–99). Until then, the Canadian government had shown little interest in extending its sequence of numbered treaties to the sparse and far-flung Indian population of the country's northwest. But the prospect of mineral wealth focussed attention, and a traveling commission signed up Indian communities in 1899. The land offer was spartan: (640 acres per family of five). Initial payments were $32 for chiefs, $22 for headmen, $12 for the rest, the comparable annuities were $25, $15, and $5. As before, the tribes were offered agricultural implements and some livestock; promises were made about healthcare and the provision of teachers. The subsequent record was the usual litany of delayed payments and broken promises, particularly regarding hunting and fishing rights, later hamstrung by the Game Act (1917).

TREATY OF PARIS 1900

By the Treaty of El Pardo (1778) with Portugal, Spain obtained the island of Fernando Po in the Bight of Biafra plus a large stretch of the adjacent coastal hinterland, christening it Spanish Guinea. Their intention was to develop slaving there to support their then vast American Empire. However, attempts at colonization were devastated by yellow fever, and the colony was soon abandoned. Fernando Po was occupied by the British after 1807, and used for policing of the abolition of slavery. In 1844, the Spanish returned and began to explore the continental interior. However, in 1898 Spain was convulsed by the sudden loss of most of its empire, after its calamitous war with the United States. France exploited Spanish disarray at the Treaty of Paris (1900), securing the reduction of Spain's claimed territory in Guinea, from 117,000 square miles (300,000 sq. km) to 10,150 square miles (26,000 sq. km) to the benefit of French Congo.

TREATY OF WASHINGTON 1900

The Sulu Sultanate ruled over the southwestern extreme of the Philippines archipelago from the beginning of the 15th century. The Sultanate fought resolutely against Spanish colonization for centuries, but finally ceded sovereignty in 1878, only to rebel again in 1895. Then the Americans arrived. Having expelled the Spanish, they faced stiff resistance from native Filipinos to their occupation. To avoid fighting on too many fronts, the Americans concluded the Bates Treaty (1899) with the Sultan

The World in 1900

The world map in 1900 was dominated by a handful of nations, whose wealth, material and technological resources, and expansionist drive had secured them huge empires, sometimes through wars, but most frequently through treaties, many of which ruthlessly exploited or bamboozled subject peoples into signing away their birthright. European colonization peaked by 1900, with the exception of the fragmentation of the Spanish Empire. France took possessions in Madagascar and French West Africa, Indochina and the South Pacific. Portugal lost territories in South America and Asia, but expanded into Africa. The Dutch exerted dominance over the East Indies. The Russian Empire spread from the Black Sea to the Pacific Ocean and Germany had acquired Togo, German East Africa, German Southwest Africa and Kamerun. Italy controlled Eritrea and Italian Somaliland. The US now included Alaska and Puerto Rico. The foremost global power was the British Empire, which now controlled nearly a quarter of the earth's land area, with colonies and trade networks in Africa, India, the West Indies, the East Indies, Australia and New Zealand. The colonizers not only took away their territories' sovereignty, but also repressed indigenous cultures and beliefs, generating tension.

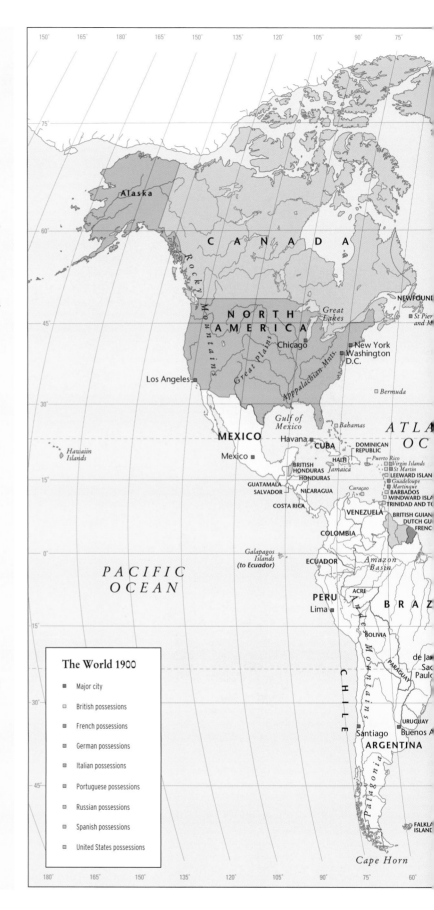

The World 1900

- ■ Major city
- ▫ British possessions
- ▪ French possessions
- ▪ German possessions
- ▫ Italian possessions
- ▫ Portuguese possessions
- ▪ Russian possessions
- ▫ Spanish possessions
- ▫ United States possessions

ARCTIC OCEAN

ICELAND

NORWAY

SWEDEN

FINLAND

Siberia

St Petersburg

R U S S I A N

E M P I R E

DENMARK

Moscow

A s i a

BRITAIN

NETH.

GERMAN

Berlin

EMPIRE

POLAND

London

BEL.

AUSTRO-

HUNGARIAN

EMPIRE

Paris

Vienna

SWITZ.

Budapest

FRANCE

ROMANIA

Gobi Desert

ITALY

SERBIA

Black Sea

Beijing

Port Arthur

JAPAN

PORTUGAL

SPAIN

Rome

BULGARIA

KHIVA

QING

Weihaiwei

KOREA

Azores

Istanbul

Caspian

EMPIRE

Jiaozhou

Tokyo

Lisbon

Madrid

Athens

Sea

BUKHARA

Nanjing

GREECE

GIBRALTAR

Ceuta

Malta

OTTOMAN EMPIRE

PERSIA

Tehran

Shanghai

Melilla

CYPRUS

AFGHANISTAN

Himalayas

Madeira

TUNIS

Cairo

KUWAIT

Delhi

NEPAL

BHUTAN

Taiwan

MOROCCO

ALGERIA

BAHRAIN

Canary

IFNI

EGYPT

BEDUINS

TRUCIAL

Gwadar

Chandemagore

Macao

Hong Kong

Islands

Sahara Desert

OMAN

(to Oman)

INDIA

Burma

Guangzhouwan

C

Arabian

Diu

Dam

PACIFIC

RIO DE ORO

ANGLO-

OMAN

Peninsula

Bombay

Yanaon

OCEAN

EGYPTIAN

HADHRAMAUT

Arabian

Goa

VERDE

FRENCH

SUDAN

ERITREA

Aden

Socotra

Sea

Madras

SIAM

FRENCH

ISLANDS

WEST AFRICA

FRENCH

Pondicherry

INDO-CHINA

Manila

GAMBIA

SOMALILAND

Mah

Karikal

Bangkok

PHILIPPINE

Guam

PORTUGUESE

NIGERIA

BRITISH

Saigon

ISLANDS

GUINEA

SOMALILAND

BRITISH

SIERRA LEONE

GOLD

Addis Ababa

ABYSSINIA

CEYLON

NORTH

COAST

KAMERUN

BORNEO

LIBERIA

ITALIAN

MALAYA

BRUNEI

Fernando Po

LADO

BRITISH

SOMALILAND

Singapore

SARAWAK

SAO TOME

RIO

EAST

MALDIVE

AND PRINCIPE

MUNI

AFRICA

ISLANDS

Borneo

KAISER

FRENCH

CONGO

Lake

Batavia

New

WILHELM'S

Ascension

CONGO

FREE

Victoria

DUTCH EAST INDIES

Guinea

LAND

Island

STATE

GERMAN

Zanzibar

Seychelles

Sumatra

Java

PAPUA

EAST

Solomon

ANGOLA

AFRICA

Amirante

Chagos

PORTUGUESE

Islands

Islands

Islands

TIMOR

NORTHEASTERN

Comoro Islands

Cocos

Christmas

RHODESIA

BRITISH

Islands

Island

ST HELENA

CENTRAL

AFRICA

Santa Cruz

BAROTSELAND-

Islands

NORTHWESTERN

MADAGASCAR

RHODESIA

GERMAN

SOUTHERN

INDIAN

New

SOUTHWEST

RHODESIA

PORTUGUESE

Caledonia

AFRICA

EAST AFRICA

Mauritius

OCEAN

WALVIS BAY

BECHUANA-

Réunion

(to Cape Colony)

LAND

AUSTRALIAN

SOUTH AFRICA

REPUBLIC

NATAL

COLONIES

ORANGE

FREE STATE

CAPE

BASUTOLAND

COLONY

Cape Town

Sydney

Cape of

Good Hope

NEW

ZEALAND

SOUTHERN OCEAN

1900–1903

of Sulu, guaranteeing its autonomy plus financial inducements. Owing to Sulu's anomalous status, the US concluded the Treaty of Washington (1900) with Spain confirming the cession of "Cagayan Sulú and Sibutú" and their dependencies (the Sulu Chain). Once they had gained effective control in the Philippines, the US unilaterally abrogated the Bates Treaty (1904). The natives of Sulu joined with fellow Moro Muslims in Mindanao in a protracted rebellion against American occupation (1899–1913).

UGANDA AGREEMENT 1900
In the 1880s, competition between Catholic and Protestant missionaries in the kingdom of Buganda on the shores of Lake Victoria spilled over into civil war between rival factions. Buganda's conquest of regional rival Bunyoro was achieved with British military backing, until their king, Mwanga, rebelled. The British quickly deposed Mwanga and exiled him to the Seychelles, then in 1899, sent in Sir Henry Hamilton Johnston as consul-general to sort out the governance and disposition of the Uganda protectorate. With only a token colonial presence, the 1900 Agreement delegated administration to a cabinet of loyal Protestant chiefs, with the child-king as nominal ruler. The British however held the reins of power, introducing strict weapons quotas, taking over the collection of tribute and imposing new "gun" and "hut" taxes.

HAY-PAUNCEFOTE TREATY 1901
The long gestation period of the Panama Canal provoked tensions between the British and Americans in respect of their rival spheres of influence. This was complicated by the nebulous status of the potential route for the Canal. In the Clayton-Bulwer Treaty (1850) both countries agreed the prospective Canal's neutrality and "equality of use." Additionally, each country forswore any attempt at a monopoly of the project, or to "fortify, occupy, or colonize" its hinterland. By 1901, with receding influence in Central America, Britain took a more relaxed view, while the Americans were annoyed by the constraints imposed by the existing Treaty. Under Hay-Pauncefote, they acquired the right to build and manage the Canal, and to fortify it, provided the Canal was open for the use of all nations, and never taken by force. A subsequent dispute arose when the Americans attempted to exempt their own ships from canal tolls, which Britain argued contravened the principle of equality.

BOXER PROTOCOL 1901
The Righteous and Harmonious Fists (Anglicized as Boxers) comprised a plethora of millenarian cults that sprung up in northern China in the late 19th century. They practiced martial arts, were strongly xenophobic, and believed themselves invulnerable to bullets. In 1899, the privation caused by severe drought and anger over foreign interference, especially missionary activity, spiraled into open rebellion. They began burning churches, killing Chinese Christians, then attacking foreigners, singling out missionaries. The uprising had first tacit, then open, support from the Empress Dowager. An eight-nation expeditionary force was dispatched to crush the rebellion, defeating the Imperial Army in the process and occupying Beijing. Peace was concluded by the Boxer Protocol of 7 September 1901. No further territorial concessions were forced upon the Chinese, but reparations amounting to $333 million at the time were imposed. Subsequently, some of the beneficiaries waived their reparation payments, directing their use for Chinese education.

ANGLO-JAPANESE ALLIANCE 1902
Whether to forge a diplomatic alliance with Russia or Britain was a question that taxed Japanese diplomatic circles at the turn of the 20th century. Russia's 1900 occupation of Manchuria threatened Japan's zealously guarded hold on Korea as well as Britain's huge vested commercial interest in China. An alliance with Russia could secure a free hand in Korea, but an alliance with Britain would deter Russian expansionism. Both routes were discreetly explored, and the British proved more enthusiastic. The alliance of 1902, the first between a European Great Power and an Asiatic state against a western rival, specified each would remain neutral in the event of war between the other and one rival power. If the war involved more than one rival power, the ally would offer active support. The agreement was renewed in 1905 and 1911; Japan complied by entering World War I on the British side.

TREATY OF VEREENIGING 1902
By the end of the Second Boer War (1899–1902), Lord Kitchener's use of concentration camps to corral the Boer civilian population was arousing political and public opposition. Deaths by disease (mostly women and children) in the camps vastly exceeded battle casualties. But the systematic hunting down of Boer guerrillas eventually left them no quarter, and by the Treaty of Vereeniging, the Boer Republics of Orange Free State and Transvaal became colonies of the British Empire. All Boer fighters had to surrender, disarm, and swear allegiance to the crown. In return self-government was promised in due course (and honored in 1906–07), and a general amnesty applied. The Dutch language would be allowed in schools and

courts, and Boer property rights upheld. In addition, £3 million was vouchsafed to aid in post-war reconstruction. In a harbinger of future discord, discussion about black suffrage was left pending.

MACKAY TREATY 1902

The Boxer Protocol (1901) included provision for the western signatories to enter into renewed commercial agreement with China. The Mackay Treaty represented the British exercise of this provision, although its terms confirmed that China was belatedly learning how to fight its corner in such negotiations. Uniquely, it required Great Britain "give every assistance" to reform of the Chinese judicial system, and be prepared to "relinquish her extraterritorial rights" when such reform was achieved: China was tiring of overweening foreigners acting with impunity and immunity. A key success for the British was abolition of the unpopular – and notoriously corrupt – *likin* internal tariff. In return, the Chinese insisted on increases in import and export duties (although Indian opium was pointedly exempted from the increase in the former). The Chinese showed similarly increased resilience in concurrent negotiations with the Japanese and Americans. By 1905 British merchants in China were complaining that the Chinese authorities were violating aspects of the Mackay agreement.

CUBAN-AMERICAN TREATY 1903

In 1901, the Platt Amendment had laid down a set of preconditions for the withdrawal of American troops from Cuba. Troops were withdrawn the following year, but the 1903 treaty was concluded in compliance with Platt, confirming its provisions. These included the right of the United States to intervene in Cuban affairs, as it did, emphatically, by renewing its occupation of the island (1906–09). A further provision was the American leasing of a "naval and coaling facility" at a place "of its choosing." It chose Guantánamo Bay, at the annual lease of $2,000. Interestingly, Article II permits "all things necessary to fit the premises for use as coaling or naval stations only, and for no other purpose," which would seem to preclude its later adoption as a prison facility.

HAY-HERRÁN TREATY 1903

Hay-Herrán, between the US and Colombia, was stillborn, as the Colombians maintained that Tomás Herrán, the diplomat who signed it, was acting without their authority. The American intention was to obtain control, through a 100-year lease, of the six-mile (10 km)-wide strip of land across the Isthmus of Panama through which they planned to

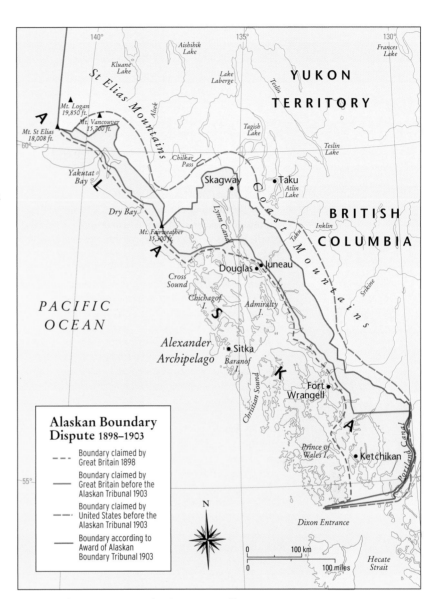

excavate the Panama Canal. They were willing to pay $10 million upfront, plus $250,000 annually, in gold. The Colombians, learning that the American investment in the new Panama Canal Company topped $40 million, thought they had been shortchanged and repudiated the Agreement. This proved unwise. America simply fomented a coup in Panama and then blocked any attempt at suppression by Colombia by posting a warship nearby and closing the railroad. It then concluded a treaty with the new Republic of Panama, with the same financial terms previously offered to Colombia, but with more latitude in terms of territorial occupation.

HAY-HERBERT TREATY 1903

The British had nursed a dispute since 1821 over the border between colonial Canada and the panhandle

1903–1907

of (at that time) Russian Alaska. America purchased Alaska in 1867, thus inheriting the dispute. Neither party was motivated to seek a definitive resolution until the Klondike Gold Rush suddenly made this remote region and, specifically, control of and access to its coast, a burning issue. An old treaty between the Hudson's Bay Company and a Russian competitor, set the border "10 leagues from the sea." The Canadians sent their North West Mounted Police to occupy part of the Lynn Canal (a long fjord with sea access) which appeared to comply with this stipulation: they were driven off by armed American prospectors. A joint panel of politicians (three American, two Canadian and one British) was convened to adjudicate, and the Hay-Herbert compromise was reached, which deprived the Canadians of direct access to the sea through Canadian territory. The Canadian public was outraged at the outcome, blaming British appeasement.

TREATY OF PETRÓPOLIS 1903
In the early 1900s, Brazil's western frontiers were ill-defined and hotly contested as a rich source of rubber, for which demand was booming. In the Amazonian province of Acre, a Bolivian syndicate, financed by Wall Street speculators, was making inroads, which the Brazilian government was determined to block. By the Treaty of Petrópolis, José Paranhos (who would earn the sobriquet 'Father of Brazilian diplomacy') purchased 74,610 square miles (191,000 sq. km) of Acre from Bolivia for £2 million. In return, a strip of Brazilian land was ceded to Bolivia together with a pledge to build a rail-link between Riberalta in Bolivia and Porto Velho in Brazil, by-passing the Madeira River rapids. The railway would bankrupt American entrepreneur Percy Farquhar: its completion was closely followed by the collapse of the rubber boom.

SOUTHERN AFRICAN CUSTOMS UNION 1903
Prior to the Second Boer War (1899–1902) early impetus for some form of Customs Union in southern Africa came from the then independent Transvaal and Orange Free State trying to mitigate the prohibitively high rail-freight and import duties charged by the British colonies in the Cape and Natal. After the discovery of gold in its territory (1886), Transvaal's interest waned, but Cape Colony and Orange Free State established a Custom Union Convention (1889) joined shortly afterward by the British protectorates of Bechuanaland and Basutoland. The situation was transformed by Boer incorporation into the British Empire through the Treaty of Vereeniging (1903). Southern Africa high

commissioner Lord Milner, now had the power to push the deal through and his "kindergarten," a team of stellar graduates dedicated to realizing his pipedreams, expedited the details. To the earlier roster, Swaziland, Natal and Sothern Rhodesia were signed up within the year.

TREATY OF BJÖRKÖ 1905
In a departure from gunboat diplomacy, cousins Kaiser Wilhelm II and Tsar Nicholas II rendezvoused in their yachts off the coast of Finland in July 1905. There they agreed a secret mutual defense pact, the Treaty of Björkö, between their two empires. In its final clause, Russia undertook to advise its ally, France, once the treaty became effective. The two rulers had not advised any of their senior ministers before concluding this agreement. The tsar's foreign minister, Vladimir Lamsdorf, observed that it was "inadmissible to promise at the same time the same thing to two governments whose interests were mutually antagonistic." Wilhelm's Chancellor von Bülow also disowned the arrangement. Although it flew in the face of diplomatic protocol, the idea had its merits: France had hardly been a sterling ally during Russia's recent humiliation at the hands of Japan. The British had allied with Japan; Russia and Germany allied would effectively block Britain in both Europe and the Far East.

TAFT-KATSURA AGREEMENT 1905
There was no formal treaty concluded between American Secretary for War William H. Taft and Japanese Prime Minister Count Katsura when they met in Tokyo in July 1905. However, there was a memorandum of understanding, and the degree of mutual understanding appeared considerable. Count Katsura indicated that Japan's sole aspiration with regard to the Philippines was to see "those islands governed by a strong and friendly" nation. But, the question of Korea intervened. What strong and friendly power could provide the guidance Korea so sorely needed? Mr Taft and the Count were of one mind: Japan. President Roosevelt concurred and the Korea-Japan Treaty followed in November.

CONVENTION OF KARLSTAD 1905
In the early 19th century Sweden was awarded Norway in return for briefly joining the coalition against Napoleon. The Norwegians rebelled, but were overcome through the intervention of the adopted Crown Prince Carl John (aka Jean Baptiste Bernadotte, Napoleon's general), who became king in 1844. The Union became more amicable, but economic priorities differed, and this was increasingly reflected in Norwegian politics. In June 1905, the Norwegian parliament unanimously

called for dissolution of the Union; in a national plebiscite, two months later, only 184 votes in the whole of Norway were cast for retaining the Union. Dissolution talks were held at Karlstad in September; although armies were readied at the borders, all issues were ultimately resolved, with Norwegian independence recognized by Sweden on 26 October.

JAPAN-KOREA TREATY 1905

Japan had a busy summer season in 1905. At the end of May, they destroyed the Russian fleet at Tsushima. In July, they reached an understanding with the United States over Korea. In August, their renewed treaty with Britain recognized Japan's right "to take such measures of guidance, control and protection in Korea as she may deem proper and necessary." In September, at the Treaty of Portsmouth, Russia's humiliation was completed, with their enforced evacuation of Manchuria and recognition of Japan's claims to Korea. By November the nights were drawing in for Korea; Japanese troops occupied the Imperial Palace in Seoul, and the Japanese Prime Minister ordered the Korean emperor and cabinet to sign the treaty presented to them. The Korean chief minister protested, and was dragged away, screaming. The cabinet signed, and Korea became a Japanese protectorate. The emperor wrote to eight European heads of state, protesting, but to no avail.

TREATY 9 1905

As Canada's numbered treaties progressed, some of the Indian communities had been able to negotiate enhanced terms, having learnt from their predecessors (either directly or through those advising them). However, with Treaty 9, the Dominion and Ontario governments allowed no leeway and the First Nations had to take the reservations allotted to them: these would be 640 acres per family of five; annuity payments were fixed at $4 (lower than any previous treaty). Given the disputes that had arisen around previous treaties, its provisions were extremely explicit: signatories would "cede, release, surrender, yield up… their rights" and the territory would be opened up to "settlement, immigration, trade, travel, mining, lumbering." The indigenous peoples were already suffering from encroachment and the increasing scarcity of game, particularly beaver. The communities signed up: 131,640 square miles (337,000 sq. km) of northern Ontario and adjacent provinces were surrendered.

TREATY 10 1906

Treaty 10, which was implemented in 1906–07, covered 85,940 square miles (220,000 sq. km) of northern Saskatchewan and Alberta. The terms offered, both in terms of reservation size and initial/annuity payments essentially replicated Treaty 8, which had been applied in the lower sectors of these provinces. The first requests for a treaty in this region had been made in 1879, at the time of the first numbered treaties, and one tribal leader asked if the monetary awards might be backdated: unsurprisingly, this request was declined.

TREATY OF LIMITS (BRAZIL-NETHERLANDS) 1906

The three colonies of the Guianas – British, Dutch, and French – had vaguely determined southernmost boundaries, enveloped by dense rainforest. Nobody seemed unduly concerned until the discovery of gold in the interior of Suriname, the Dutch colony, in 1885. The jungle suddenly acquired value and justified a border dispute. Tsar Alexander III of Russia, no less, arbitrated in 1888 between French and Dutch Suriname. In 1899 an arbitration panel, convened in Paris, adjudicated on the boundaries of British Guiana with Venezuela. The focus of contention then moved south, where Suriname and its colonial neighbors abutted Brazil. The Treaty of Limits (1906) decreed the boundary between Suriname and Brazil as the watershed falling between Suriname's coastward flowing rivers and Brazil's Amazon tributaries. Despite the frontier being virtually inaccessible, an expedition was mounted to lay 60 boundary markers in the jungle.

HAGUE CONVENTION 1907

Francis Lieber was wounded at Waterloo and fought in the Greek War of Independence, before emigrating to the United States. During the American Civil War, he established a code of legal conduct in warfare at the request of Abraham Lincoln. The two Hague Conventions (1899 and 1907) borrowed liberally from the Lieber Code. The latter gathering established some major conventions regarding proper conduct in war relating *inter alia* to: the pacific settlement of international disputes; the opening of hostilities; the law and customs of war on land. Provisions were also made regarding the rights and duties of neutral states, the conduct of naval warfare, and appropriate use of munitions including the rather *outré* "prohibition of the discharge of projectiles and explosives from balloons." The Conventions established at the Hague, as subsequently amended, are still in force.

TRIPLE ENTENTE 1907

After the signing of the Anglo-Russian Entente on 31 August 1907, the Triple Entente refers to the "understanding" that linked Russia, France, and Britain, supplemented by additional agreements with

1909–1915

European Alliances
July 1914

- Austro-German Alliance, 1879–1918
- ▷ Triple Alliance, 1882–1915
- ▷ Franco-Russian Alliance, 1894–1917
- Triple Entente, 1907–1917
- Neutral

Japan and Portugal. The Entente acted as a powerful counterweight to the Triple Alliance of Germany, Austria-Hungary, and Italy. The Triple Entente was not an alliance of mutual defense and all three countries were free to make their own foreign policy decisions. The alliance of France and Britain with the autocratic Russian Empire was controversial. and mistrust between the allies persisted even after the inception of World War I.

ANGLO-SIAMESE TREATY 1909
From 1893 to 1907, the French manufactured a succession of wars and crises to annex large areas of the kingdom of Siam (Thailand) into their

Indochinese colony. Chulangkorn, the King of Siam (r. 1868–1910) had modernized his state, abolishing slavery and prostration before dignitaries, while introducing railways, electric lighting, a national education system, and effective central and local government. The treaty with Britain regularized their border with Burma to the south, and offered a counterbalance against French expansionism. However, by crudely carving up the states, its provisions would form the catalyst for later insurgency. Kelantan, Perlis, Kedah, and Tringganu were awarded to Britain, while Yala, Pattani, Narathiwat, Songhkla, and Satun were confirmed to Siam. In a mark of respect for the quality of

Chulangkorn's reforms, the British agreed to the removal of extraterritoriality for its subjects in Siam.

JAPAN-KOREA TREATY 1910

In 1907, a Korean delegation to the Hague Convention on the rules of war was denied entry, an eloquent demonstration that any protections established would not be extended to them in their fight to avoid Japanese rule. Japan had already imposed protectorate status on Korea, but an insurrection continued, culminating in the assassination of the Japanese resident-general Itō Hirobumi. On "National Humiliation Day," 29 August 1910, the Emperor of Korea was compelled to make "the complete and permanent cession to His Majesty the Emperor of Japan of all rights of sovereignty over the whole of Korea." He refused to sign, but his prime minister did so in his stead, ushering in 35 years of Japanese rule. This period witnessed extensive modernization in Korea, but very much at the service of Japanese imperialism.

TREATY OF ATHENS 1913

The First Balkan War (1912–13) would result in the virtual elimination of the Ottoman Empire in Europe at the subsequent Treaty of London. Dissatisfied with its share of the spoils, Bulgaria promptly declared war on its recent allies, Serbia and Greece. The Ottomans and Romania exploited the situation to seize chunks of Bulgaria's recently won territory. Bulgaria was forced to sue for peace. When the dust had settled, Greece and the Ottomans gathered in Athens to conclude their treaty in November 1913. Thessaloniki, Ioannina and their hinterland were ceded to Greece, as was Crete (which had effectively divorced itself from Ottoman control five years earlier). Turkish citizens in Greek territory were granted minority rights. The disposition of the North Aegean islands was put to Great Power arbitration. Greece was still left with a sizeable diaspora in Turkish territory, but contention would be suspended by the advent of World War I.

TREATY OF CONSTANTINOPLE 1913

Bulgaria had started the Second Balkan War (16 June–18 July 1913) and ended up fighting alone against five enemies. Its position became untenable when both Romania and the Turks invaded Bulgarian territory, forcing it to sue for peace with its Balkan combatants at Bucharest in August 1913. The following month, Bulgarian envoys moved on to Constantinople to reach terms with the Ottomans. After the pulverizing losses of the First Balkan War, the Ottomans gained a short-lived territorial recovery, with Bulgaria acknowledging their recapture of Adrianople and the surrounding

portion of eastern Thrace. In return, the Ottomans ceded the port of Dedeağaç to Bulgaria, and political/commercial relations were restored. The Ottomans and Bulgaria would fight on the same (losing) side, allied to the Central Powers in the forthcoming World War I.

BRYAN-CHAMORRO TREATY 1914

The Nicaraguan Canal route predated the Panamanian option: it was first proposed to Congress by Henry Clay in 1826. When the United States finally chose Panama, the Nicaraguan president José Zelaya opened negotiations with Germany and Japan to mount a competing project. But Zelaya was ousted (1909) with the aid of US marines, and the coup leader, Emiliano Chamorro, was installed (with American connivance) as Minister to the United States. Chamorro used his new position to negotiate the 1914 treaty, by which Nicaragua received $3 million in return for rights to any canal built in Nicaragua in perpetuity, a renewable 99-year option to establish a naval base in the Gulf of Fonseca and a renewable 99-year lease to the Great and Little Corn Islands in the Caribbean. The treaty outraged Nicaragua's neighbors: Colombia maintained the Corn Islands were their territory, while El Salvador and Costa Rica considered the naval base violated their sovereignty.

TREATY OF LONDON (LONDON PACT) 1915

At the outbreak of World War I, Italy formed part of the Triple Alliance with Germany and Austria-Hungary. Ill-prepared for war, Italy strove for neutrality but, when this proved impossible, shopped around for the best deal. By the London Pact, the Triple Entente of the United Kingdom, Russia and France secured an alliance with Italy in return for the promise of territorial gains from Austria-Hungary, in particular, Tyrol and Trieste, and a stake in German East Africa. In the event of victory, the pact also assigned territorial acquisitions to Serbia and Montenegro, neither of whom was present at its negotiation. When news of the secret pact leaked out, Italian Prime Minister Salandra was forced to resign. Italy complied with the terms agreed by promptly declaring war on Austria-Hungary, but did not declare war on Germany until 1916. Post-war, the pact was not honored, the "mutilated victory" arousing outrage in Italy.

TREATY OF KYAKHTA 1915

In its dying days, the Chinese Qing Dynasty attempted to impose control in Mongolia through a program of colonization and economic exploitation. The Mongolians responded with the Revolution of 1911, which succeeded with informal Russian

The Sykes-Picot Agreement 1916

The Sykes-Picot agreement – named after the British and French diplomats who signed it – was made in secret, with Russia's assent, in May 1916. With the Ottoman Empire entering the war on the side of Germany, the allies of the Triple Entente decided that in the event of victory over Germany, Austria, and their Ottoman ally they would divide the Ottoman Empire's Arab provinces into British and French "spheres of influence." Britain was allocated the coastal strip between the Mediterranean and the River Jordan, Transjordan and southern Iraq, with enclaves including the ports of Haifa and Acre, while France was allocated southeastern Turkey, northern Iraq, all of Syria, and Lebanon. Russia was to get Istanbul, the Dardanelles, and the Ottoman Empire's Armenian districts.

Kept hidden for more than a year, the Anglo-French pact caused a furore when it was first revealed by the Bolsheviks after the 1917 Russian Revolution, with the Syrian Congress, convened in July 1919, demanding "the full freedom and independence that had been promised to us." Not only did the agreement map out – unbeknownst to the Arab leaders of the time – a new system of western control of local populations, it also directly contradicted the promise that Britain's man in Cairo, Sir Henry MacMahon, had made to the ruler of Mecca, the Sharif Hussein, that he would have an Arab kingdom in the event of Ottoman defeat. In fact, that promise itself, which had been conveyed in MacMahon's correspondence with the Sharif between July 1915 and January 1916, left ambiguous the borders of the future Arab state, and was later used to deny Arab control of Palestine. MacMahon had excluded from the proposed Arab kingdom "portions of Syria lying to the west of the districts of Damascus, Homs, Hama and Aleppo [that] cannot be said to be purely Arab." This clause led to lengthy and bitter debates as to whether Palestine – which Britain meanwhile promised as a homeland for Jews under the terms of the November 1917 Balfour Declaration – could be defined as lying "west" of the *vilaye*t, or district, of Damascus.

Sir Mark Sykes, the Middle East advisor to the secretary of state for war, Lord Kitchener, who signed the Sykes-Picot agreement with the French diplomat Francois-Georges Picot, was somewhat Francophile in comparison with the Cairo-based "Arabists," led by T.E. Lawrence ("Lawrence of Arabia"). The latter had supported the Sharif Hussein's son Faisal in the Arab revolt, by blowing up Ottoman trains and other acts of daring-do. Sykes thought the "Arabists" were in danger of alienating the French. In view of the devastation the French were suffering on the Western Front (with the loss of a million men more than the British), compounded by the failure of the Gallipoli campaign, Britain, he felt, had a compelling need to humor its French ally. France could claim historical interests in Greater Syria stretching back to the 16th century and point to the protection that it had granted Lebanon's Christian Maronites in 1649. This protection was called upon in 1860, when the French sent 6,000 troops to defend the Maronites when large numbers of them were being slaughtered in a civil war with the Druzes.

In the event, the hope of the "Arabists" for an independent Arab kingdom under British tutelage was trumped by French ambitions. In the course of the murderous and costly Mesopotamian campaign against the Ottoman army (1915–18) the British had installed themselves in Iraq, and on a visit to London the French leader George Clemenceau conceded that the British should have Mosul, and a free hand in Palestine (which was supposed to be international under the Sykes-Picot terms), with the French acquiring the German stake in what became the Iraqi Petroleum Company.

Though Lawrence took Faisal to the Paris peace conference, and arranged for him to meet British Prime Minister David Lloyd George, his plan for an Arab kingdom based in Damascus was doomed. In 1920 the French took over Damascus, expelled King Faisal, and imposed a form of direct rule that lasted till the British army (with token Free French forces) removed the colonial Vichy government in 1941. British claims that French control in Syria violated the Sykes-Picot concept of "spheres of influence" in the Arab areas were undermined by the degree of control the British were exercising in Palestine, Transjordan, and Iraq.

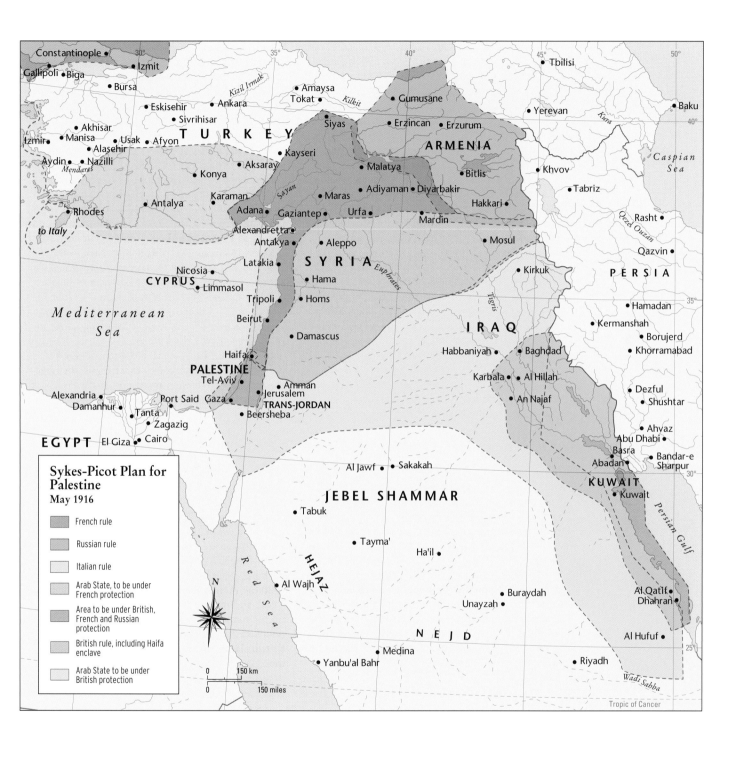

Sykes-Picot Plan for Palestine
May 1916

French rule

Russian rule

Italian rule

Arab State, to be under French protection

Area to be under British, French and Russian protection

British rule, including Haifa enclave

Arab State to be under British protection

1916–1918

backing. The subsequent Bogd Khanate (1911–24) estranged the Russians by embarking on a campaign of reunification, occupying much of Inner Mongolia while China was torn apart by civil war. With the outbreak of World War I, Russia was motivated to regularize the situation on its eastern frontiers. At Kyakhta, Russia, Mongolia, and the Republic of China met to formalize Mongolia's status, recognizing a (very high) degree of autonomy within the Chinese Republic, but not full independence. When the Russian Empire fell in 1917, Mongolia was occupied by a pro-Japanese Chinese warlord (1919). In 1921, the Russian Red Army supported a successful Communist revolution in Mongolia.

TREATY OF BUCHAREST 1916

The Entente powers in World War I were fond of the ruse of offering chunks of Austria-Hungary to tempt putative allies. It worked with Italy in the London Pact, and it worked with Romania at the Treaty of Bucharest. Romania's shopping list included Transylvania, Crisana and Maramures. In addition, it was promised parts of Bukovina, which held a Romanian population, and the Banat in Hungary, which did not. The treaty was signed on 17 August, and on 27 August, Romania duly declared war on Austria-Hungary, and immediately invaded with a huge army. By Christmas, a German and Bulgarian counterattack had overwhelmed the Romanians and occupied Bucharest. However, Romania retained a rump government in the provincial city of Iasi, re-entering the war on the day before armistice. In the aftermath of the Treaty of Versailles, it would wage war with the other nascent Balkan states to enforce its territorial claims.

THE BALFOUR DECLARATION 1917

On 2 November 1917 the British Government issued a statement, known as the Balfour Declaration, named after Foreign Secretary Arthur James Balfour, that announced its support for a "national home for the Jewish people" in Palestine in the event of a victory over the Ottoman Empire, which had ruled the country, with intermissions, for more than four centuries. The wording, which had been through numerous drafts during months of lobbying and counter-lobbying by Jewish nationalist leaders (Zionists), and their opponents, was deliberately vague. The term "national home" had no precedent in international law and left open the question of Jewish statehood as sought by the Zionists, while allowing for an interpretation that was primarily cultural and spiritual for non-Zionist Jews. While stating that the homeland should be "in" Palestine (a region administered by the Ottomans as part of Greater Syria), the boundaries were not specified. The British government later confirmed that by using the word "in" they meant that the proposed national home was not intended to cover the whole of Palestine. While the Declaration was immediately welcomed by Jewish communities in Palestine, who from 1918 would celebrate 2 November as Balfour Day, it was strongly opposed by leaders of the Christian and Muslim communities (as well as by some long-resident Jews) who comprised around 90 percent of the Arab-speaking population at that time.

Both Balfour and his Prime Minister David Lloyd George were evangelical Christians who regarded the return of Jews to their ancient homeland as the fulfillment of biblical prophecy. But *realpolitik* also played its part. The British hoped that a formal declaration in favor of Zionism would gain Jewish support for the allied cause in the US (which had just entered the war) as well as in Russia, where the anti-Semitic tsarist government had been overthrown with the help of the empire's Jewish population. Lloyd George, moreover, regarded a friendly Jewish presence in Palestine as a desirable counterweight to the Maronite Christians in Greater Syria (now Lebanon) with their long-standing links with France, and to Eastern Orthodox communities in the Levant with their traditional ties to Russia. Lloyd George saw British-dominated Palestine as an essential post-war goal, an important land bridge between British-ruled territories of Egypt and the Indian Raj. In due course the mandate Britain received from the newly-formed League of Nations for the governance of Palestine after the Ottoman defeat made explicit reference to the Balfour Declaration, a remit that made for constant friction between Jewish and Arab communities.

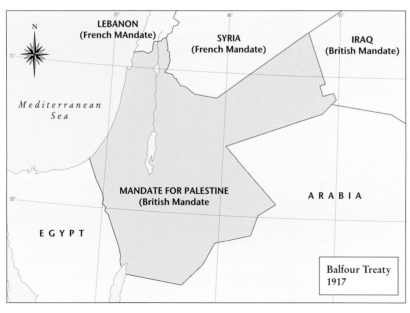

LEBANON (French MAndate)

SYRIA (French Mandate)

IRAQ (British Mandate)

Mediterranean Sea

MANDATE FOR PALESTINE (British Mandate

ARABIA

EGYPT

Balfour Treaty 1917

LANSING-ISHII AGREEMENT 1917

President Wilson espoused the Open-Door policy under which the Great Powers would have equal access to Chinese commerce. In January 1915, Japan presented a secret ultimatum to China, the 21 Demands, effectively asserting her hegemony in the region. Involved in World War I, the European powers were in no position to force Japan to stand down, but Britain, their closest ally, combined with the US to reverse the most harsh demands, which would have placed Japanese "advisers" in control of China's economy and finances. The Lansing-Ishii Agreement, which was never became a formal treaty, was an attempt by the US to revive the Open-Door, with vague American and Japanese pledges to abide by the Open-Door policy. In practice, its attendant reference to Japan's "special interests" in China, gave them the excuse to continue to circumvent the Open-Door.

CORFU DECLARATION 1917

In December 1914, Nikolai Pašić, the Serbian premier, declared the military objective of the liberation of the south Slavs from Habsburg rule, to be unified with Serbia in a single state. Serbia was subsequently overrun and occupied for the duration of the war, rather undermining Pašić's negotiating position. In the summer of 1917, he met with representatives of the Croat-led Yugoslav Committee in Corfu, which had been formed in Paris. Impetus to secure agreement had been provided by the leakage of the terms of the secret Treaty of London (1915), which made manifest the Allied Powers' intention of keeping the Slav states separate, with Italy replacing Austria-Hungary as regional suzerain. The six-week negotiation proposed the creation of the unified Kingdom of Serbs, Croats, and Slovenes, under the Serbian ruling dynasty. Universal male suffrage, religious freedom, judicial equality, and territorial integrity were also propounded, but Croat demands for a federal framework were not endorsed.

TREATY OF BREST-LITOVSK 1918

In the turbulent aftermath of the Russian October Revolution, the Ukraine People's Republic declared independence. It was immediately at the mercy of the Bolsheviks, who had substantial forces stationed in Ukrainian territory. Recognition by the Allied Powers was impossible: they considered Ukraine a part of their (now defunct) ally, the Russian Empire. Ukraine turned to the Central Powers; in the "Peace for Bread" Treaty at Brest-Litovsk (9 February 1918) Ukraine offered access to its grain basket in return for assistance expelling the Bolsheviks. The treaty defined Ukraine's boundaries, including some territorial concessions from Austria-Hungary: a German army recaptured Kiev from the Bolsheviks on 2 March. The following day, the Bolsheviks recognized the Ukrainian Republic in their own Treaty of Brest-Litovsk with the Central Powers. Ukraine's treaty provoked outrage and unrest in Poland, and in April, the Republic was overthrown by a coup before restoration later in the year.

TREATY OF BUCHAREST 1918

After the abrupt collapse of the Russian Empire, and Russia's exit from World War I, Romania was a captive of the Central Powers in eastern Europe. In the circumstances, the treaty's territorial provisions were surprisingly lenient. They were required to cede Dobruja to Bulgaria and the Central Powers, but Bessarabia was recognized as part of Romania: in aggregate, the country's post-war borders were more extensive than at the war's outset. Austria-Hungary was handed control of the strategic Carpathian mountain passes. In addition, no formal annexation or suzerainty was imposed, although German bureaucrats were placed in charge of the country's administration, finances, and economy. Most crucially, Romania's oil industry was leased to Germany for 90 years. The treaty's shelf-life was short. Signed in May (but not by Romania's king), ratified in July, it was denounced in October and nullified at the Armistice in November. Its territorial transfers were formally reversed in the Treaties of Neuilly, St Germain and Trianon in 1919.

TREATY OF BATUM 1918

In 1918, the Armenian army fought a last-ditch battle for survival against Ottoman invaders, with successive victories at Sardarapat, Abaran, and Karakilsa. Their determination is unsurprising, since the Ottomans had systematically committed genocide against their Armenian citizens since 1915; the Ottoman general and representative at Batum described the "Special Organization" which conducted the massacres as "butchers of the human species." With Ottoman armies still occupying its territory, the Treaty of Batum, in which two new Transcaucasian republics, Azerbaijan and Georgia, joined Armenia, reinstated the Ottoman border of 1878, then with the Russian Empire. The treaty was short-lived. After armistice, Armenia seized Kars and Androupol, then the three new republics fell to fighting one another. Future Turkish leader Kemal Atatürk reversed Armenian gains (with Bolshevik support), before the republics were incorporated into the Soviet Union (1922).

ARMISTICE OF MUDROS 1918

The initiative veered dramatically in the closing

Treaty of Versailles 1919

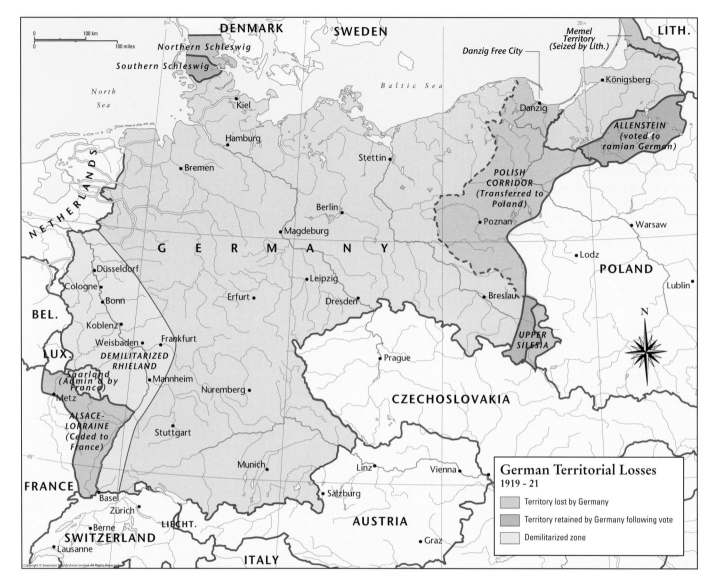

German Territorial Losses
1919 - 21

Territory lost by Germany

Territory retained by Germany following vote

Demilitarized zone

Versailles was the most important of the post–World War I treaties, which ended the state of war between the Allies and Germany. The other Central Powers signed a series of separate treaties in 1920: at St Gemain-en-Laye, Trianon, and Neuilly. The treaty with the Ottomans was made at Sevres. The Armistice was signed on 11 November 1918, but it took six months of allied negotiations at the Paris Peace Conference to conclude the treaty negotiations.

In a speech delivered in Westminster in January 1918, American President Woodrow Wilson attempted to pave the way to peace with good intentions. His recipe for a "peace without victory" comprised Fourteen Points (French Foreign Minister Clemenceau observed drily "the Good Lord only managed ten") including free trade, mutual disarmament, national self-determination, decolonization, and the formation of a League of Nations dedicated to the maintenance of peace.

His European allies, particularly Clemenceau, were less inclined to clemency. The actual terms imposed at Versailles were far more punitive, and the contrast between the reality and Wilson's idealistic prefiguration nurtured a powerful sense of victimization in the defeated nations, particularly within Germany, which the Nazis would later exploit to the full.

In reality, the terms were less swingeing than those Germany itself had imposed ten months earlier on a similarly prostrate Russia at Brest-Litovsk. And France, which had suffered the greatest losses and devastation amongst the Western Allies, had powerful motives for feeling vindictive.

Nevertheless, under Versailles, Germany lost Alsace-Lorraine to France; Sudetenland to Czechoslovakia; West Prussia and Silesia to Poland; and Eupen-Malmédy to Belgium. The Rhineland was demilitarized and occupied, and Saarland, with its coal mines, placed under French control. Schleswig's future allocation was made subject to plebiscites (the north would opt for Denmark, the south reverted to Germany). In eastern Europe Germany was ato recognize the independence of Czechoslovakia and cede parts of Upper Silesia to Poland, as well as recognizing Polish independence. All Germany's colonies were parcelled out between the victorious allies. Germany's navy and air force were slashed, its army capped at 100,000 and decapitated of its leadership, and its heavy industry hobbled. The final ignominy was Article 231, the "war-guilt" clause, which held Germany to be solely responsible for the war and imposed massive reparation payments.

British Prime Minister Lloyd George foresaw that allocating territory "containing large masses of Germans clamoring for reunion with their native

German Losses in Africa 1920

German Territories redistributed by the League of Nations in 1920

- British Mandate
- French Mandate
- Belgian Mandate
- Union of South Africa Mandate

German Losses in the Pacific 1920

German Territories redistributed by the League of Nations in 1920

- Japan or under Japanese control 1914
- Japanese Mandate
- British Mandate
- Australian Mandate
- New Zealand Mandate

land" to neighboring states would precipitate future conflict. A clear precedent occurred in post-war events in eastern Europe, where accompanying treaties to Versailles witnessed the dismantling of the Austro-Hungarian and Ottoman Empires, and a series of wars between the successors bent on national or ethnic *revanchement*. The sense of injustice in Germany was intensified by the *Dolchstosslegende*: the myth that Germany's army could have won the war but were "stabbed in the back" by defeatist Socialist politicians. Its prevalence undermined the legitimacy of Germany's fragile democracy under the Weimar Republic. When its economy also spiraled into hyperinflation under the burden of reparations, the stage was set for an authoritarian takeover, with the promise of restoring German might, and righting the injustices of Versailles. Once Hitler had seized power, and embarked upon a program of rectifying Versailles by force, the major powers were in the grip of the Great Depression, absorbed by domestic crises, and there was no appetite for determined collective deterrence: another world war became inevitable.

1918–1919

months of World War I. On the Western Front, the early successes of the German spring offensive were dramatically reversed. In the east, the Ottomans were gaining ground in the Caucasus when the Macedonian Front abruptly collapsed, leading Bulgaria to sue for peace at Salonika (29 September), and leaving Constantinople at the mercy of the Allied armies. Urgent diplomatic representations to the Central Powers made clear to the Ottomans that the war was lost; their war cabinet then resigned, and the new Grand Vizier Ahmed Izzet Pasha approached the British seeking peace terms. The Armistice of Mudros (30 October) was harsh but not draconian. Immediate Turkish demobilization and the surrender of its fleet and naval facilities were demanded. Allied garrisons occupied the Dardanelles and Bosporus forts (the cause of so much Allied bloodshed). Remaining Turkish forces from Tripolitania to Persia were required to surrender forthwith.

ARMISTICE OF VILLA GIUSTI 1918

After Bulgaria's withdrawal from the war through the Armistice of Salonika on 29 September, Austria-Hungary (in common with Germany and the Ottomans) appealed first to the United States, seeing Woodrow Wilson's Fourteen Points manifesto as their best hope of leniency. Rebuffed, with their armies in headlong retreat in the wake of the rout at Vittorio Veneto, they had no choice but to accept unconditionally the terms offered at the Armistice of Villa Giusti. Its provisions stripped Austria-Hungary of all of its navy and all but a token residual army. The Allies occupied their whole Adriatic coastline, and demanded their withdrawal from a broad swathe of hinterland from the Tyrol to Dalmatia. When the Emperor Charles I signed the terms on 3 November 1918, he knew it was the death-knell of the Empire; within ten days he stood down.

ARMISTICE WITH GERMANY 1918

By the second week of November, Germany was swept by rebellion, and her allies had sued for peace, one after another. On 9 November, the Social Democrats assumed power, just in time to become the scapegoats for the stab-in-the-back myth, which would later be so effectively propagated by various right-wing diehards, and ultimately the Nazis. The Allies disagreed over their approach: US President Wilson, after forcing the Kaiser's abdication, advocated relative leniency; France, which had suffered by far the greatest losses, wanted a punitive settlement. The eventual terms were harsh enough: withdrawal of German forces forthwith from all occupied territories; Allied occupation of the Rhineland; internment of the German fleet;

and virtual disarmament of its army. In addition, the treaties Germany had enforced in the east at Brest-Litovsk and Bucharest were renounced. No negotiation was permitted, the resumption of hostilities was promised in the event of non-compliance.

TREATY OF RONGBATSA 1918

From 1720, the Chinese Qing Dynasty governed Tibet for two centuries in a fairly laid-back manner through a local resident (Amban) and small standing army. This was until British Colonel Younghusband mounted a "trading mission" that turned into an invasion, with massacres of the locals and an imposed treaty (1904) meant to exclude Russian intervention. This galvanized the Chinese to assert their sovereignty with a military expedition, which led to the exile of the Dalai Lama. Then the Qing Dynasty fell, the Tibetans rebelled, and the Chinese occupying army mutinied; the Lama returned and observed the relationship of China and Tibet was "one of patron and priest not based on subordinacy of one to the other." However, at the Simla Convention (1914), Tibetan representatives agreed borders with envoys from China and India, acknowledging Chinese suzerainty. When China sought to enforce this, their invasion was repulsed and at Rongbatsa (1918), de facto Tibetan independence was recognized.

TREATY OF SAINT GERMAIN-EN-LAYE 1919

Following the defeat of the Central Powers in 1918, the Allies set about drafting a series of treaties that would impose harsh sanctions upon Germany and its allies, which were considered to have caused and perpetuated the war. Signed by representatives of Austria on one side and the victorious allies on the other, this was the treaty that dissolved the Austro-Hungarian Empire. The new Republic of Austria was to accept the independence of Hungary, Czechoslovakia, Poland, and the Kingdom of the Serbs, Croats and Slovenes. Many of the Central European territories ceded by the Austrians to these newly independent nations contained significant German-speaking majorities, and the Allies simply assumed that minority peoples would be content to leave Austria. Austria was forbidden from entering into any alliance with Germany without the agreement of the League of Nations. The vast reduction in territory, population and resources left Austria weak and economically debilitated.

TREATY OF NEUILLY 1919

Signed on 27 November 1919, this was the treaty that required Bulgaria to cede various territories post-World War I. Thrace was ceded to the Allies,

1919–1920

Faisal-Weizmann Agreement 1919

Proposed new Jewish State

and eventually awarded to Greece. A substantial area on its western border was ceded to the Kingdom of the Serbs, Croats and Slovenes. The region of Dobruja was returned to Romania. In addition Bulgaria was rerquired to reduce its army to just 20,000 men, pay reparations of £100 million and recognize the newly founded Kingdom of the Serbs, Croats and Slovenes. In Bulgaria this treaty is referred to as the Second National Catastrophe.

FAISAL-WEIZMANN AGREEMENT 1919

Chaim Weizmann was head of the British Zionist federation. The future first President of Israel, he was instrumental in the momentous Balfour Declaration (1917) which averred that the British government would "favor the establishment in Palestine of a national home for the Jewish people." The key remaining obstacle to Zionist ambitions was potential opposition to the Jewish state from Arab nationalist movements in the region. The Faizal-Weizmann Agreement, transcribed by the illustrious Lawrence of Arabia before the Paris Peace Conference (1919), had the purported agreement of Emir Faisal of Hejaz. It states that "all necessary measures to encourage and stimulate immigration of Jews into Palestine on a large scale" should be taken, and endorses the Balfour Declaration. The document proved controversial, as Faisal could not read English. His appended note in Arabic made his support conditional on the British honoring their promises to the Arabs: given their subsequent record, the Agreement was nullified.

ANGLO–AFGHAN TREATY OF 1919

The Third Anglo–Afghan War, from 6 May–3 June, had broken out following an attempted invasion of British India by the new Emir Amanullah Khan who was keen to curry favor amongst his political rivals. He also aimed to take advantage of Britain and Russia's vulnerability following World War I and the ongoing Russian civil war, and hoped to gain some form of political concession. Britain did not want to risk instability within India and therefore recognized Afghanistan's full independence. The treaty (also called the Treaty of Rawalpindi) ended Britain's political control of Afghanistan but also ceased British arms imports from India and the subsidy that was previously paid to the Emir.

TREATY OF TRIANON 1920

The Treaty of Trianon, signed 4 June 1920, detailed the terms of Hungary's post-war punishment, which included large territorial losses and severe restrictions to military capabilities, with the Hungarian army being limited to just 35,000 troops. The signature of the treaty was initially delayed by political instability within Hungary, which experienced a brief Soviet revolution throughout 1919. The historical Kingdom of Hungary lost over 70 percent of the territory it had held back in 1914 to the newly established states of Czechoslovakia and the Kingdom of Serbs, Croats and Slovenes, as well as the Kingdom of Romania and Austria. These border alterations left 30 percent of the total ethnic Hungarian population outside Hungary and greatly reduced the country's economy as it was now completely landlocked.

SEVENTH TREATY OF PARIS 1920

Having been a territory of the Russian Empire since 1818, the majority of Bessarabia's inhabitants were ethnically Romanian, or Moldavian, and had been moving increasingly towards nationalist sentiments. Following a vote by the recently elected Bessarabian council, the Sfatul Țării, independence from Russia was announced on 6 February 1918 and the Moldavian Democratic Republic was formed. But the Moldavian Democratic Republic found itself in a treacherous position between Bolshevik Russia, Ukraine, and the Austrians in the west, so the Sfatul Țării voted to join the Kingdom of Romania on 9 April 1918. The Seventh Treaty of Paris, signed 28 October 1920, officially recognized the unification of Bessarabia with Romania. It contained the signatures of the principal Allied powers and Romania, although Japan did not ratify the treaty, and the Soviet Union did not recognize the union.

TREATY OF BRNO 1920

On 7 June 1920 Austria and Czechoslovakia signed the Treaty of Brno, which guaranteed the rights of the respective ethno-linguistic groups found in each country. The border between Austria and Czechoslovakia, which had recently been established following the disintegration of the Austro-Hungarian Empire in 1918, had divided ethnic groupings, so that large populations, such as the Sudeten Germans, were now resident as diasporas outside their country of ethnic origin. The treaty confirmed the rights of these minority groups as citizens of the country in which they lived and guaranteed both Austria and Czechoslovakia would naturalize them accordingly, allowing minority languages to be used in the educational system.

TREATY OF RAPALLO 1920

This treaty ceded a number of small territories on the northeast edge of the Italian peninsula, which had formerly been the Austrian littoral, and small areas of territory in northern Dalmatia with its Adriatic islands, to the Kingdom of Italy. These concessions were agreed between Italy and the newly formed Kingdom of Serbs, Croats, and Slovenes as amelioration for Italy's anger over the abandonment of the terms agreed in secret in the 1915 Treaty of London, which promised Italy some territories that contained Slavic majority populationsm in direct contravention of the post–war aspiration that regional populations would not forcibly be placed under foreign rule. The secret agreement of the Treaty of London was given as justification for its later nullification.

FIRST TREATY OF TARTU 1920

This was the official recognition of Estonian independence from Russia following the Estonian War of Independence, which had broken out in November 1918. It marked the important step of international recognition of the Soviet government as signatory of a treaty, although the governments of the western nations did not initially recognize Estonia's independence. The treaty confirmed Estonian sovereignty over Narva, which was an important regional center of industry. Estonia also received 15 million gold rubles for its prior input to the Russian economy and was granted use of one million hectares of Russian forest for logging. In return Russia was granted rights to build port facilities in Tallinn.

SECOND TREATY OF TARTU 1920

On 14 October Soviet Russia signed a second Treaty of Tartu with Finland, demarcating the new Finland–Russia border and detailing a land swap in which Finland ceded a small area of the Karelian Isthmus near St Petersburg in exchange for the territory of Petsamo at the far north of the Finland–Russia border on the Barents Sea. As this territorial exchange separated Russia from Norway, Finland agreed to allow border access via the territory of Petsamo. Finland also agreed to withdraw its troops from the Russian territories of Reboly and Porosozero, which it had occupied after the local population opted to join Finland following a vote.

TREATY OF MOSCOW 1920

Russian forces had failed in attempts to secure their military presence in Georgia and had not succeeded in imposing political authority through a Bolshevik coup in early May 1920, following Georgia's declaration of independence on 26 May 1918. The Treaty of Moscow, signed 7 May 1920, was the official *de jure* recognition of the independence of the Georgian Democratic Republic and its Menshevik government from Bolshevik Russia. A seemingly tactical relinquishment of Russian sovereignty over Georgia held a secret stipulation that the Bolshevik party be allowed to continue its operations within the country. Georgia also agreed to refuse entry

across its borders to any troops or political groups that were considered enemies of Soviet Russia. The Bolshevik party within Georgia continued to pressurize the Georgian government and a subsequent crackdown on Bolshevik activity led to a Russian invasion in February 1921.

TREATY OF SÈVRES 1920

As one of the belligerents of World War I, the Ottoman Empire was subjected to harsh punishments by the Allies. The initial severity of the terms imposed on the Ottoman Empire under the Treaty of Sèvres, signed 10 August 1920, was even greater than those imposed upon Germany and former Austro-Hungary. The majority of the Ottoman Empire's territory, besides the Turkish heartland around Ankara, was split between the European Allies, whilst Armenia gained its independence. The Ottoman colonial lands of the Middle East were allocated as League of Nations mandates; the British mandates of Iraq and Palestine and the French mandate of Syria and Lebanon were established until sufficient local governance capacity could be established to grant independence. In addition to enormous territorial losses, the Ottoman Empire lost its financial independence. Complete control of the national bank and budget was surrendered to the Allies and duties on any goods passing through Ottoman territory were abolished. Finally, all three branches of the Ottoman military were heavily restricted. The success of the fledgling Turkish national movement led to the nullification of the Treaty of Sevres with the signing of the Treaty of Lausanne in 1923.

LATVIAN–SOVIET PEACE TREATY 1920

In the aftermath of World War I, fighting continued in eastern Europe as Soviet Russia attempted to extend its political influence towards the newly

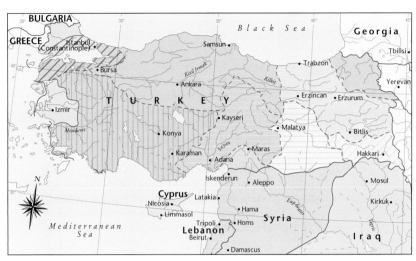

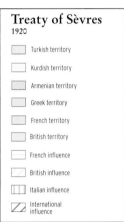

Treaty of Sèvres
1920

- Turkish territory
- Kurdish territory
- Armenian territory
- Greek territory
- French territory
- British territory
- French influence
- British influence
- Italian influence
- International influence

1920–1921

independent countries on its western border. The Red Army had been involved in a number of concurrent conflicts including the Russian Civil War, fighting in various occupied eastern European territories and the Polish–Soviet War. A brief period of Soviet government was established with the declaration of the Latvian Socialist Soviet Republic on 17 December 1918. Pressure from the independence movements in the Baltic states, White Russian forces, and the threat of Poland establishing political influence in the region led Russia to agree peace terms with the Baltic states and Finland. The Latvian–Soviet Peace Treaty was signed on 11 August 1920, officially recognizing Latvian independence from Soviet Russia and the right of citizens within the territory to determine their own Russian or Estonian nationality.

TREATY OF ALEXANDROPOL 1920
The Turkish–Armenian War of 1920 quickly deteriorated into catastrophe for the First Armenian Republic as Turkish Nationalist forces edged closer to the Armenian capital Yerevan. After less than two months of fighting, Armenia was at the point of capitulation and was forced into negotiations with the Turkish nationalists who drew up a series of severe territorial demands under the Treaty of Alexandropol. Armenia had recently expanded its borders to include former Ottoman territory under the agreements made within the Treaty of Sèvres, but was now forced to renounce those claims and sign away territory in the Armenian heartland. With the signature of the Treaty of Alexandropol on 3 December 1920 Armenia ceded over half its territory and agreed to strict limitations of its military strength. Although the treaty was signed by the First Armenian Republic's Foreign Minister, Alexander Khatisian, a Bolshevik invasion had in fact established Soviet rule in Armenia the previous day. Armenia was now a Soviet Socialist Republic, invalidating the Treaty of Alexandropol.

SVALBARD TREATY 1920
The Svalbard archipelago, which sits between the Barents Sea and Arctic Ocean, was first discovered by the Dutch just before the turn of the 17th century. The archipelago went on to be considered a free territory, used as an outpost for whaling and later mining operations by a number of different nations. Norway, Sweden, and Russia entered into talks to discuss joint administration of the islands before World War I broke out and derailed the process. The Svalbard Treaty was signed as part of the wider peace negotiations of Versailles and, whilst establishing Norwegian jurisdiction over the territory, it also allowed citizens and companies of any nationality to reside and operate there, provided they respect rule of Norwegian law. It also ensured that the archipelago would remain demilitarized whilst the Norwegian government pledged to protect its environment and could only collect taxes that would be used to maintain the Svalbard territory itself.

FRANCO–POLISH ALLIANCE 1921
In the aftermath of the Polish–Soviet War, both France and Poland were keen to establish a defensive alliance against their common enemy Germany and the growing threat of expansionist Soviet Russia. The political alliance signed on 19 February outlined an agreement to pursue common diplomatic and foreign policy goals in Europe and to increase economic activity between the two countries. On 21 February a military pact was also signed in secret in Paris. This second pact outlined military actions to be taken in the event of an attack against either of the two signatories by Germany or Soviet Russia. France was obliged to provide assistance to Poland but not necessarily military personnel. The Franco–Polish alliance would be built upon later in the 1920s with League of Nations recognition and an additional alliance with Czechoslovakia.

ANGLO–IRISH TREATY 1921
The Irish War of Independence had erupted in January 1919; the Anglo-Irish Treaty, signed on 6 December, established the sovereignty of the Irish Free State. The island was partitioned and six counties separated to form the region known as Northern Ireland, which was given the choice of joining the Irish Free State or remaining within the United Kingdom, which its parliament elected to do. The Irish Free State did not gain full sovereignty but became a dominion of the British Empire with self-governing status like former colonies such as Australia and Canada. It came into existence on 6 December 1922. Many were enraged that the full Republic had not been realized, which led to the Irish Civil War between June 1922–May 1923. Britain withdrew its armed forces from the Irish Free State following the treaty agreement, although it maintained use of three deepwater ports.

PEACE OF RIGA 1921
In the aftermath of World War I, war broke out between the Second Polish Republic, looking to regain lands that had been taken from it by Imperialist Russia, and Soviet Russia, seeking to spread communism to its neighboring states. After initial Russian success, Poland managed to achieve a crucial victory in the Battle of Warsaw and the young Soviet state, which was concurrently

fighting against the Baltic countries and its own counter-revolutionaries, decided to enter peace negotiations with Poland in August 1920. The full Peace of Riga was not signed until 18 March 1921, after a lengthy negotiation process in which the Soviets relinquished large areas of Belarusian and Ukrainian territory. The Polish delegation rejected control of areas of Belarusian and Ukrainian territory, including Minsk, as the Polish National Democrats did not want territory containing a large non-Polish population. Additionally, Russia agreed to allow Poland to carry out its territorial dispute with Lithuania unimpeded, whilst Poland agreed to recognize Soviet rule in Belarus and Ukraine.

THOMSON–URRUTIA TREATY 1921
US motives behind its support for the Panamanian revolt, which led to independence from Colombia in 1903, lay in its interests in securing rights to the construction and operation of the Panama Canal. After repeated failed attempts to pass a treaty between the US and Colombia, the reconciliatory Thomson–Urrutia Treaty was drawn up and signed by representatives of both countries on 6 April 1914. However, the treaty was rejected by the US Senate due to anger over wording, which confessed to America's "sincere regrets" over its interference in Panama. World War I further delayed ratification and there were ongoing disputes over concessions made by both countries in redrafted versions of the treaty. Colombia finally ratified the treaty on 13 October, receiving $25 million in instalments, in exchange for Colombian recognition of Panamanian independence, and cessation of US aspirations for further use of certain Colombian territories.

TREATY OF BERLIN 1921
Although US President Woodrow Wilson played a key role in the negotiation and vision behind the Treaty of Versailles, strong domestic opposition to the treaty and what it might entail for future US interests meant that the US Senate failed to ratify the treaty and a series of proposed amendments in March 1920. Many US politicians viewed the League of Nations as an overarching power, which would have jurisdiction over US foreign policy and may well force America to become involved in another costly, distant war. Nevertheless, the US was not opposed to the general post-war peace process, agreeing to a separate bilateral treaty with Germany. The Treaty of Berlin was signed on 25 August 1921; it contained much of the same content as the Treaty of Versailles regarding the terms of Germany's post-war reparations and rights, but did not include the contentious articles surrounding League of Nations jurisdiction and membership.

TREATY OF MOSCOW 1921
Around the end of World War I revolutionary governments in both Russia and Turkey moved closer towards diplomatic alignment as they aimed to combat what they saw as western imperialism. Both governments agreed to commence friendly relations under the Treaty of Moscow, also known as the Treaty of Brotherhood. The treaty agreed a territorial boundary between the two countries and the Georgian, Armenian and Azerbaijan Soviet Socialist Republics, which included the transfer of Batumi to Georgia and Kars to Turkey. Soviet Russia also agreed to recognize the Grand National Assembly of Turkey as the legitimate government of Turkey, and promised it would supply it with funding and arms.

TREATY OF KARS 1921
The Treaty of Kars was signed on 13 October 1921 by representatives of the Georgian, Armenian and Azerbaijan Soviet Socialist Republics, Soviet Russia, and Turkey. The borders agreed to in the Treaty of Kars were the same as those agreed to in the Treaty of Moscow, earlier that year. The Turkish–Armenian border was established allowing Turkey to retain large areas of the preceding First Armenian Republic, which it had occupied during the Turkish–Armenian War in 1920. The Nakhchivan area was established as an Azerbaijani exclave between Armenia and Iran, with a small border with Turkey at the northwestern corner. Additionally, territory along the Black Sea, which had once been the Batum Oblast within Imperial Russia, was split between Turkey and Georgia. The Georgian territory, Adjar, would become its own Autonomous Soviet Socialist Republic within Georgia, and Turkey was given free use of the port of Batumi.

TREATY OF ANKARA 1921
Under the secret Sykes–Picot Agreement of 1916, the Triple Entente powers had agreed on separate spheres of influence in the Middle East should they emerge victorious from World War I. France was allocated control over territory in Syria and southeastern Turkey, but experienced tough resistance from Turkish forces who were angered by French intervention in Turkish territory. They were also displeased by French support of Armenia, which was currently being persecuted by Turkey. The Treaty of Ankara established a new border between French-controlled Syria and Turkey, returning most of the Turkish territorial concessions agreed to in the Treaty of Sèvres. France recognized the legitimacy of the Grand National Assembly as the government of Turkey, whilst receiving Turkish recognition of Syria's position under French protection.

1921–1927

RUSSO–PERSIAN TREATY OF FRIENDSHIP 1921

Following a concerted effort by the Soviet administration to build friendly relations with Persia in order to combat British influence in the region, the Treaty of Russo–Persian Friendship was signed on 26 February 1921. Russia agreed to respect Persia's borders, whilst both sides agreed to combat activity by groups that were hostile to the government of the other nation. In the case of Soviet Russia this meant the White Russian army and other anti-Bolshevik forces, although it reserved the right to invade Persia if it was deemed to be acting against Soviet interests. The treaty also guaranteed Persia and Soviet Russia equal shipping rights on the Caspian Sea.

TREATY 11 1921

Treaty 11 was the last of the sequence of treaties through which the government of Canada secured use of the lands of the indigenous peoples of North America. It secured rights for the Canadian government to settle and utilize more than 360,000 square miles (932,395 sq. km) of land in the modern-day Northwest Territories and Yukon. Specifically the government was keen to secure access to areas in which significant oil reserves had been discovered. Signatures were gathered from elected representatives of over 20 different First Nations between 1921–22. For use of their lands the indigenous populations were allocated small plots for each family, along with hunting and fishing tools, a lump sum followed by yearly payments, and access to education. The treaty has since been disputed, as it has been argued that the indigenous signatories were not made fully aware of the terms to which they were agreeing.

ANGLO–AFGHAN TREATY OF 1921

Following on from the Anglo–Afghan Treaty of 1919, relations between Britain and Afghanistan deteriorated. Britain was angered by Afghan interference in tribal disputes along the turbulent India–Afghanistan border. The ratification of the Treaty of Friendship Between Afghanistan and the Soviet Union on 20 April 1921 increased the urgency with which Britain sought to establish its right to political influence over Afghanistan, as it was an important buffer zone between India and Soviet Russia. Over the course of 1921, both the Afghan and British negotiators held by their key demands, with Afghanistan refusing to cease negotiations with other states and Britain refusing to commit to a defensive pact with Afghanistan. The eventual terms agreed in the treaty were mostly small extensions of the 1919 agreement. The

border was confirmed along with Afghanistan's independence. Both sides agreed to inform each other of military operations along the border and arms imports through India were permitted again.

WASHINGTON NAVAL TREATY 1922

The world's major naval powers gathered at the Washington Naval Conference between November 1921 and February 1922 to discuss measures to curb naval expansion following World War I. The countries with the three most powerful navies, Britain, the US, and Japan, all had different priorities and had conflicting interests, especially in the Pacific. Three separate treaties were agreed: the main Five-Power Treaty, signed 6 February 1922; and two secondary agreements known as the Four and Nine Power Treaties. A tonnage limit between the US, Britain, Japan, France, and Italy was set for both capital ships and aircraft carriers. Additional limits to the tonnage and armament of new ships of each class were set, with aircraft carriers being limited to 27,000 tons, capital ships to 35,000 tons, and smaller warships to 10,000 tons.

TREATY OF RAPALLO 1922

Following World War I, Germany had been subjected to harsh punishment under the Treaty of Versailles and Soviet Russia had become isolated due to international distrust of its new Communist government. Both countries turned to each other in pursuit of economic ties, signing an initial agreement in 1921. The Treaty of Rapallo formalized their relationship as they agreed to renew diplomatic relations free of existing debts and territorial claims against each other. Both sides agred to "cooperate in a spirit of mutual goodwill in meeting the economic needs of both countries". Germany extended friendly diplomatic relations to the rest of the existing Soviet Socialist Republics in a secondary agreement. More crucially, a secret agreement was finalized on 29 July 1922 in which Germany agreed to provide training for Soviet air forces and military officers in Russia in return for the use of Russian territory for German military exercises.

TREATY ON THE CREATION OF THE USSR 1922

Signed by representatives of the Russian and Transcaucasian Soviet Federative Socialist Republics, and the Ukrainian and Byelorussian Soviet Socialist Republics, this treaty united all four under a single centralized Soviet federal government. The treaty outlined the structure of a common foreign policy, armed forces, economic plan, legal framework, and education system for all of the constituent republics of the Union of Soviet Socialist Republics. Russia's political domination of the other Soviet republics continued as the treaty firmly established the seat of the central government in Moscow. Each Soviet republic would vote for representatives who would be posted to the Congress of Soviets of the Soviet Union In addition to the treaty, a Declaration of the Creation of the USSR, which outlined the ideals and motivation behind the formation of the Soviet Union, was also signed.

TREATY OF LAUSANNE 1923
Following the rejection of the highly contentious Treaty of Sèvres by Mustafa Kemal Atatürk, negotiations between Britain, France, Italy, and the Grand National Assembly of Turkey began at the Conference of Lausanne on 20 November 1922. Discussions proved contentious, as the Turks refused to accept many of the propositions made by the Europeans. The final treaty, signed by Britain, France, Italy, Greece, Romania, Japan, and Turkey, contained compromises by both sides. Turkey's full independence was recognized and it was granted full control of its military and economic affairs. It was allowed to keep former territories it had taken from Armenia in 1920 but renounced claims to former Ottoman territories including Syria, Iraq, Cyprus, Libya, Sudan, and the Dodecanese Islands, which went to Italy. Additionally, the treaty protected the rights of Christian and Muslim minorities living within Turkey and Greece and allowed all shipping to pass through the Turkish Straits.

BRUSSELS AGREEMENT 1924
Under the Brussels Agreement signatory states agreed to partake in a new international scheme through which merchant seamen could receive free treatment for sexually transmitted diseases. The groundbreaking initiative would provide treatment for seamen, regardless of nationality, at ports of participating nations, overseen and monitored by the Office International d'Hygiène Publique, in an effort to combat the problem of venereal diseases, which were especially prevalent in mariners. Many nations from all over the world would sign up to the agreement over the following decades but the US and USSR were two notable non-signatories.

TREATY OF ROME 1924
Following the 1920 Treaty of Rapallo, which detailed territorial exchanges between Italy and the Kingdom of Serbs, Croats and Slovenes, the Free State of Fiume was established as a small independent state between the two signatories. Over the next four years Fiume experienced constant political turbulence as different parties vied for control. The ethnic mix of Italians and Slavs within the small state led to increasing unrest. By 27 January 1924 Italy and the Kingdom of Serbs, Croats and Slovenes had reached an agreement whereby the Fiume would be split and annexed between them. Italy gained sovereignty over the city of Fiume along with land that connected it to the Italy in the west, whilst the Kingdom of Serbs, Croats and Slovenes took control of the rest of the state, which included the port of Sušak. These two towns agreed to share the administrative duties of both ports.

LOCARNO TREATIES 1925
The Locarno Conference of October 1925 was convened at the behest of German Foreign Minister Gustav Stresemann in an attempt to re-establish Germany's diplomatic standing in Europe. The finalized treaties, signed on 1 December 1925, determined the manner in which Germany's borders and territorial claims would be regulated in the future. The main agreement, signed by Germany, France, Britain, Belgium, and Italy, was a treaty of mutual guarantee in which all signatories agreed to recognize Germany's existing borders with France and Belgium. In the event of conflict between any of Germany, France, and Belgium, the remaining signatories were obliged to provide military assistance to the country under attack. Additionally Germany signed treaties with France, Belgium, Czechoslovakia, and Poland in which both parties agreed to settle border disputes through an arbitration tribunal. France agreed mutual assistance treaties with Poland and Czechoslovakia in the event of attack by Germany. While western Europe was protected from German attack through defensive pacts, Poland and Czechoslovakia were vulnerable as they could only rely on jurisdiction to settle disputes.

TREATY OF BERLIN 1926
The Treaty of Berlin was signed by representatives of Germany and the Soviet Union on 24 April 1926 in order to strengthen the friendly diplomatic relations that had been established under the 1922 Treaty of Rapallo, and was extremely popular with the German people. The Treaty of Berlin committed both countries to a position of neutrality in the event of an attack against the other by a foreign power. In addition, both countries agreed to abstain from entering any alliance that would involve a financial boycott against the other. Despite committing both countries to neutrality with regards to the other, the Treaty of Berlin was only valid for five years, after which it would be revisited and could be extended.

TREATY OF JEDDAH 1927
Following Ibn Saud's conquest of the Kingdom of Hejaz and the subsequent formation of the Kingdom

1928–1935

of Hejaz and Nejd in January 1926, Britain began negotiations to ensure that the newly founded kingdom would not expand further north into the British mandate of Transjordan and the British-administered Kingdom of Iraq. With the signature of the Treaty of Jeddah, Britain recognized the sovereignty of the Kingdom of Hejaz and Nejd, with Ibn Saud as its ruler. Ibn Saud consequently agreed to respect the borders laid out in the treaty and ensure that his forces would not engage in any activity against Britain's protectorates in the region, which were important centers of oil production.

KELLOGG–BRIAND PACT 1928

The Kellogg–Briand Pact emerged after an initial proposal for a bilateral peace treaty between the US and France was made by the French Minister of Foreign Affairs, Aristide Briand. Briand's aim to secure a non-aggression pact between the two countries in April 1927 was viewed by US policymakers as a legal commitment that could potentially drag America into providing defensive assistance to France if it came under attack. In response to the proposal, which at its core held an important desire for peace, US Secretary of State Frank B. Kellogg envisaged a multilateral peace treaty that would be open to all countries. Kellogg and Briand subsequently drew up a proposal for a treaty that would outlaw wars of aggression, only permitting military action in self-defense, and instead proposing the settlement of disputes via peaceful action. The pact would allow countries to commit to existing defensive alliances signed since World War I. The first signatories, France, the US, and Germany, committed themselves to the pact on 27 August 1928, with many others doing so within the following year.

ITALO–ETHIOPIAN TREATY OF 1928

The Italo–Ethiopian Treaty of 1928, signed 2 August, established an official state of friendship between Italy and Ethiopia, known as Abyssinia at the time. Italy and Ethiopia agreed to take any future disputes to the League of Nations, whilst Ethiopia was granted access to the port of Asseb in Italian-controlled Eritrea, where it could access maritime trading opportunities via the Red Sea. A road from the coast into Ethiopia would be constructed in a joint effort by both countries. Superficially, this was a treaty of friendship, but in reality Ethiopia hoped to limit the possibility of Italian interference in its territory, whilst Mussolini saw economic access to Ethiopia as a way of strengthening Italian-controlled Somalia and Eritrea. Both would regard their own commitments within the treaty as of secondary importance in the years to come.

LATERAN TREATY 1929

The dispute between Italy and the Catholic Church had reached new levels of severity following Italy's occupation and full annexation of the Papal States by 1871. The unification of Italy left the papacy and the Catholic Church with no sovereign territory of its own and the state and Church locked in an ongoing power struggle. The Lateran Treaty, which actually comprised three individual agreements, formally recognized Vatican City as an independent sovereign state with the pope as its head of state. In return, the pope recognized the Kingdom of Italy and its jurisdiction over the former papal territories and agreed to revoke the prior excommunication of the king of Italy. Italy also agreed to pay Vatican City 1 million lire and Italian state bonds amounting to 1,000 million lire. A final arrangement was made to establish Catholicism as the official state religion of Italy and grant priests of the Church special rights, although they were prohibited from engaging in political activism.

GENEVA CONVENTION 1929

The Geneva Convention of 1929 outlined a set of standards to which signatories must abide with regards to the captivity and treatment of prisoners of war. Key principles of the agreement state that all prisoners of war must be treated in a humane manner, provided with adequate shelter and food that is of a similar standard to that of the soldiers of the nation holding them captive. The prisoners must be provided healthcare, a sufficient standard of hygiene, facilities to practice their religion, and the opportunity to engage in sporting and other basic leisure activities. Additionally they must not be forced into hard labor or labor that is directly related to war and their country must be informed of their capture as soon as possible. The treaty was signed by 46 countries on 27 July 1929, although nine did not complete its ratification and a number of other countries went on to ratify the treaty but were not initial signatories.

INTERNATIONAL CONVENTION FOR THE SUPPRESSION OF COUNTERFEITING CURRENCY 1929

In an effort to tackle the almost universal issue of counterfeit currencies, the League of Nations drafted a treaty that would enforce a coordinated international response to the problem. Efforts to combat counterfeiting had thus far been hampered by the scale of the practice, which involved criminal operations working across international borders, and against which cooperation offered the best chance of success. States that adopted the convention in April 1929 agreed to recognize acts of currency counterfeiting as an extraditable international criminal offense and to establish their own administrative bodies to communicate with other countries and maintain up to date records of valid international currencies in use.

NILE ACCORD 1929
Water rights within the Nile basin became an increasing source of disagreement as agricultural and industrial processes led to rising demand for water. The lucrative cotton industry required large scale redirection of water for irrigation, eventually leading to clashes between the two major interests in the region, Egypt and Sudan. Sudan was a condominium of Britain and Egypt, which nominally shared joint administration over the territory, although Britain effectively controlled it. Egypt had gained independence from Britain in 1922, but Britain retained significant influence over the country. The Nile Accord, otherwise known as the Nile Waters Agreement, was signed by Egypt and Britain on behalf of Sudan, and agreed allocations of water for both countries based upon figures for the Nile's yearly output. Egypt was given exclusive rights to the river during the 20 January–15 July dry season and was allowed to veto any upstream construction that might affect its water share.

LONDON NAVAL TREATY 1930
The London Naval Treaty followed the naval armament restrictions agreed to in the Washington Naval Conference of 1921–22, and an attempt to reconcile the disagreements that had resulted in the failure of the Geneva Naval Conference of 1927. The treaty outlined further restrictions to the individual tonnage limits of certain types of naval vessel for each country and split cruisers into two categories, light and heavy, based upon whether their guns were greater than 6.1 in caliber.

STATUTE OF WESTMINSTER 1931
The Statue of Westminster was a British Act of Parliament that officially recognized the full legislative independence of the self-governing Dominions of the British Empire, establishing them as equal sovereign entities. Dominions were given the right to enact the statute, which would grant them full legal freedom, but were able to choose to keep certain areas of British law if they wished. The details of the treaty's implementation varied between each Dominion in which it was enacted. The treaty became effective in Canada, South Africa, and the Irish Free State immediately but was subject to ratification by the governments of Australia and New Zealand, whilst Newfoundland chose not to pass the statute.

POLISH–SOVIET NON-AGGRESSION PACT 1932
Poland was eager to strengthen its position in the event of future aggression by either Germany or the USSR, and had been left somewhat vulnerable following the Locarno Treaties of 1925. By agreeing to pursue a policy of non-aggression with the USSR, Poland hoped to reinforce the general commitment to settlement of disputes via peaceful means that had been laid out in the 1928 Kellogg–Briand Pact. The Polish–Soviet Non-Aggression Pact also bound both parties to neutrality if either was attacked by another country, although its initial term was only three years, after which it could be renewed.

GERMAN–POLISH NON-AGGRESSION PACT 1934
Although both Germany and Poland maintained their mutual distrust, the geopolitical climate pushed them towards a bilateral non-aggression pact. Following the rise to power of the Nazi party in 1933, Germany became increasingly isolated on the international stage. Seeking to buy time for remilitarization, Nazi Germany was keen to agree a policy of non-aggression on its eastern border with Poland. Meanwhile, Poland wanted further insurance against the possibility of invasion by the two historically aggressive powers, Germany and the USSR, between which it sat. Poland signed many similar treaties during the inter-war period in an attempt to secure allegiances in the event of a future invasion. The non-aggression pact, which was signed for a term of ten years, recognized the current German–Polish border, whilst easing economic sanctions between the two countries. Against pressure from Germany, Poland defended its right to maintain its previous alliances.

BALKAN PACT 1934
On 9 February 1934 Yugoslavia, Turkey, Romania, and Greece entered into a mutual-defense treaty. Collectively the parties to this pact became known as the Balkan Entente. They agreed to uphold their current borders and retract any territorial claims against each other and the countries surrounding them. Although the pact only secured four signatories, it was initially also open to Bulgaria, which decided to abstain because of disagreements over Bulgarian minority rights in Greek Macedonia. Albania, on the other hand, was excluded from the agreement due to Italian interests in the country. The aim of the pact was to ensure stability in the Balkans by protecting the signatories' borders, promoting mutual assistance and non-aggression, and maintaining the status quo, but it proved ineffective against growing German influence.

1935–1939

FRANCO–SOVIET TREATY OF MUTUAL ASSISTANCE 1935

After the final ratification of a Franco–Soviet non-aggression pact in 1933, France was keen to pursue a more comprehensive alliance with the USSR as a counter to growing German aggression. Initial propositions were made to establish an "eastern Locarno" that would safeguard Germany's eastern borders through a multilateral defense treaty, but Poland objected to granting Russian troops access to its territory in the event of a German attack. Signs of Germany's rearmament hastened the general desire for a rapprochement between France and the USSR and convinced Britain to support the alliance. Although the Franco–Soviet treaty temporarily bridged the ideological divide between capitalist France and the communist USSR, its main purpose was to restrict Germany. The treaty that was eventually agreed was significantly watered down by France's Locarno obligations, which meant that any action against Germany required the consent of Britain, Italy, and Belgium.

TREATY OF ESTABLISHMENT, COMMERCE AND NAVIGATION 1935

The USSR and Persia reconfirmed the details of their joint shipping rights in the Caspian Sea with the signature of the Treaty of Establishment, Commerce and Navigation ini August 1935. In 1921 they had previously agreed terms under which they both held the right to sail commercial and military vessels bearing their own country's flags on the Caspian Sea, and the 1935 treaty reiterated this agreement and effectively restricted any other nations from using the Caspian Sea for any type of shipping. Additionally, the agreement granted joint fishing rights outside a ten-nautical-mile coastal zone, inside which each country's fishing rights were exclusive. Even though the treaty of 1935 supposedly granted Persia equal maritime rights, the Soviet Union's military and commercial shipping strength in the Caspian Sea remained vastly superior.

ANGLO–EGYPTIAN TREATY 1936

Increasing civil unrest led by the Egyptian Wafd Party was gradually pushing Britain towards granting Egypt's full independence. By the mid-1930s Britain's most pressing concern was the threat posed by Italy's nearby colonial expansion into Africa. Egypt held the British Empire's most vital strategic possession in the Middle East, the Suez Canal, along with the port of Alexandria, which was an important naval staging post for the eastern Mediterranean. The treaty laid out the terms for Britain's withdrawal from Egypt, which was now recognized as a fully sovereign nation. British troops were withdrawn from their positions across the country; a total of 10,000 soldiers, 400 pilots, and support personnel were permitted to defend the immediate area around the Suez Canal, which Britain recognized as Egyptian territory. Britain would supply and defend the Egyptyian army, the port of Alexandria was to remain an active base for British troops and the Royal Navy for a further eight years and Britain reserved the right to occupy Egyptian territory in case of war.

FRANCO–SYRIAN TREATY OF INDEPENDENCE 1936

Syrian calls for independence were temporarily placated by a number of legislative freedoms granted by the French government in the early 1930s. The National Bloc party rejected draft treaties of independence, because they left areas of Syria, including the Alawite State and the Jabal al-Druze region, under French control. After widespread protests and a general strike, the French agreed to recognize the National Bloc as Syria's rightful political leadership. After over six months of negotiations the Franco–Syrian Treaty of Independence was signed on 9 September 1936. This treaty included the areas that had been left under French control in earlier proposals as part of the new Syrian Republic. It also promised the removal of French forces and political influence over a 25-year period. Despite passing the Syrian legislature, the French government did not ratify the treaty because of increasing fears of German aggression and Syrian independence was not fully realized until 1945.

TREATY OF SAADABAD 1937

Signed by delegates of Turkey, Iran (Persia), Iraq, and Afghanistan at the Iranian Shah's Saadabad Palace, this treaty constituted a multilateral non-aggression pact, sometimes referred to as the Oriental Entente. They recognized each other's established borders and agreed to encourage diplomatic cooperation in regional matters, especially the ever-present interference by the European powers. Turkey, Iran, and Iraq were all keen to combat the threat of Kurdish separatism within their borders, whilst Afghanistan and Iran needed political alliances to help stave off interference by the USSR and Britain, between which they both sat as a contested buffer zone. Mustafa Kemal Atatürk sought stability on Turkey's eastern border and was key to the formulation of the alliance alongside Afghanistan's King Mohammed Zahir Shah.

MUNICH AGREEMENT 1938

Hitler's expansionist rhetoric began to edge Europe closer towards full-blown war following the remilitarization of the Rhineland in March 1936 and the Anschluss that annexed Austria to Nazi Germany in March 1938. Hitler used the large German population living in Czechoslovakia to justify demands for annexation of the outer Czechoslovakian territory known as the Sudetenland. By 1938 over 40 percent of the ethnic German population of Czechoslovakia were members of the pro-annexation Sudeten German Party. The Czechoslovakian President Edvard Beneš repeatedly rejected German demands for territory whilst Hitler accused him of persecuting the Sudeten Germans. Hitler used the threat of war to bring France, Britain, and Italy to the negotiating table. After a conference between Germany and the three other major European powers the Munich Agreement ruled that the Sudetenland and other areas of German majority population were to be annexed by Germany by 10 October.

MOLOTOV–RIBBENTROP PACT 1939

The Molotov–Ribbentrop Pact, named after its signatories, the German and Soviet foreign ministers, was signed on 23 August 1939 and committed Germany and the USSR to mutual neutrality in the event of conflict with another state; it was concluded at a time when the USSR's separate negotiations with Britain and France were breaking down. The USSR and Germany pledged to maintain a stance of non-aggression towards one another and, in a separate economic agreement signed four days earlier, committed the USSR to supply Germany with raw materials in exchange for arms and other vital equipment. In addition, a secret agreement was made to determine spheres of influence in eastern Europe. The eastern and western regions of Poland were to be annexed by Germany and the USSR, with a central area becoming a German protectorate. Most of the rest of eastern Europe was assigned to the Soviet sphere, whilst Lithuania and the Free City of Danzig went to Germany, which began its invasion of Poland just days later on 1 September.

PACT OF STEEL 1939

The Rome–Berlin Axis was solidified with the signing of the Pact of Steel in Berlin, which joined Nazi Germany and Fascist Italy in an alliance of economic cooperation and military assistance in the event of war. The pact had initially been open to Japan, which had chosen not to become embroiled in a war against European nations. Aside from the ideological similarities between Nazi Germany and Fascist Italy, an alliance between the two countries offered Italy assistance for its colonial expansion, which was opposed by Britain and France, and secured Germany's southern front so that troops

Frontiers Post-Molotov-Ribbentrop Pact
by the end of 1940

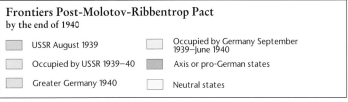

USSR August 1939

Occupied by USSR 1939–40

Greater Germany 1940

Occupied by Germany September 1939–June 1940

Axis or pro-German states

Neutral states

D-Day landings in June
...t of Allied victory fueled
... on the approach to be
*...*rmany. The most influential
*...*orgenthau, American Chief
*...*ry who advocated German
*...*n-threatening statelets,
*...*auldron of wars," the Ruhr, and
...o a purely agricultural economy.
*...*ces, like US Secretary of State,
... British Foreign Secretary, Anthony
*...*ch a program would diminish
*...*y to make reparations and drive its
popular *...* ommunism.

When the London Protocol was agreed on
12 September 1944, defining Allied Zones of
Occupation in post-war Germany, the debate still
raged. On 21 September, the Morgenthau Plan was
published, achieving the rare feat of uniting the
German and American press in its denunciation.
Josef Goebbels used the "Jew Morgenthau's" plan
to turn Germany into a "giant potato patch" to
steel German resolve to fight on. On 14 November,
American and British Occupation Zones were
formally designated in an addendum to the Protocol,
and at Yalta (February 1945) it was agreed that a
French Occupation Zone would also be designated.
The final boundaries were established at Potsdam
(July 1945); the east-west boundary established
initially in London was retained, despite the fact that
American forces had advanced up to 200 miles (320
km), beyond the pre-agreed line. In return, Soviet
forces permitted the Western allies access to their
pre-agreed zones of occupation in Berlin.

In the US Zone Joint Chiefs of Staff (JCS)
Directive 1067 decreed that the military government
should "take no steps towards the economic
rehabilitation of Germany." This was overturned by
the new Secretary of State, General George Marshall
via JCS 1779, proclaiming an "orderly, prosperous
Europe requires the contribution of a stable and
productive Germany." The zones defined by the
London Protocol were about to become the test-
tubes of radically different and competing social,
economic, and political philosophies: Churchill had
already dubbed the border with Soviet-controlled
Europe an "Iron Curtain."

The culmination of the experiment would be the
events of 1989–91, which would witness the collapse
of communism in eastern Europe, the destruction
of the Berlin Wall, then of the DDR (under the
Western model) and the dismantling of the Soviet
Empire. It is questionable whether such an outcome
could have occurred if Morgenthau's policy had
prevailed; it would surely have forestalled the
German "economic miracle."

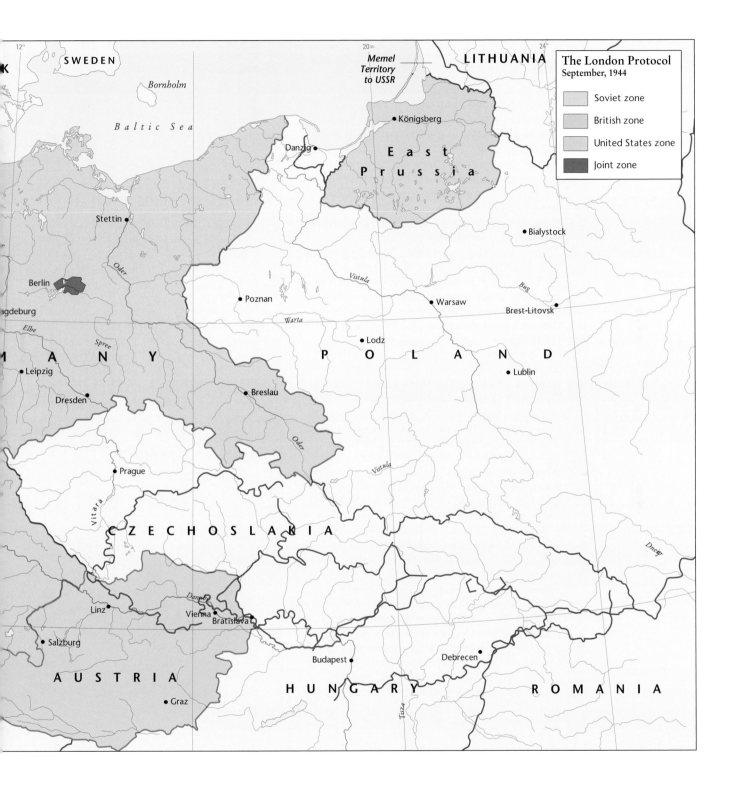

SWEDEN

Bornholm

Baltic Sea

Danzig

Memel
Territory
to USSR

LITHUANIA

Königsberg

**E a s t
P r u s s i a**

Stettin

Bialystock

Oder

Vistula

Poznan

Bug

Warsaw

Brest-Litovsk

Berlin

agdeburg

Warta

Lodz

P   O   L   A   N   D

Elbe

Leipzig

Spree

Dresden

Breslau

Lublin

Oder

M A N Y

Vistula

Prague

Vltara

C Z E C H O S L A K I A

Dnestr

Linz

Danube

Vienna
Bratislava

AUSTRIA

Salzburg

Budapest

Debrecen

H   U   N   G   A   R   Y

R   O   M   A   N   I   A

Graz

Tisza

The London Protocol
September, 1944

Soviet zone

British zone

United States zone

Joint zone

International Civil Aviation 1944–1947

The fierce crucible of technological innovation afforded by two global wars acted on each occasion as a catalyst for the development of framework aviation legislation. The Paris Convention of 1919, organized under the auspices of the International Commission for Air Navigation (ICAN), established the initial General Principles: each nation's absolute sovereignty over the airspace above its territory (and waters); the requirement of aircraft to be registered to a state, and to be assigned the nationality of that state; equity of application of airspace rules to all aircraft (registered to Convention signatories) operating within that airspace, subject to reasonable protections in respect of sovereignty and national security; and equity of treatment under national laws for the aircraft (registered to Convention Signatories). Over 30 nations signed or subsequently ratified the Treaty, but not the US, which objected to the Convention's association with the League of Nations. Nevertheless, ICAN was inaugurated at a time when commercial air traffic was overwhelmingly dedicated to airmail services. In 1925, a Committee was charged with codifying Private Air Law, and in 1929, a subsequent Convention in Warsaw established rules for liability in international carriage by air transport.

Building upon Paris and intervening additions, the Chicago Convention of 1944 performed two functions: to flesh out a framework for International Air Law, and to establish the Constitution for a revamped International Organization responsible for governance and compliance. In attendance were 52 states (Saudi Arabia and the Soviet Union declined).

An International Air Service Transit Agreement, defined and enshrined the "Two Freedoms" of travel over member airspace, and non-traffic related stops in member states; an International Air Transport Agreement detailed supplementary freedoms in relation to commercial transport and 12 Technical Annexes detailed regulation and operational procedure in areas such as air traffic control, airworthiness, staff training and qualification.

The ICAO operated on a provisional basis until its formal ratification in March 1947, when it was established as a specialized, autonomous agency of the United Nations, headquartered in Montreal. At the time of its inception, commercial passenger traffic stood at 9 million passengers per year: by 2014, that had increased to 3 billion. Air travel demands uniquely stringent standards of safety and relentlessness of investigation when those standards fail, and indeed to balance commercial viability with the maintenance of effective security. The fact that, in the Age of Terror, the ICAO is not the object of widespread opprobrium reflects widespread appreciation of its ethical and technical standards.

International Civil Aviation Organization, 1947

Initial Council Members

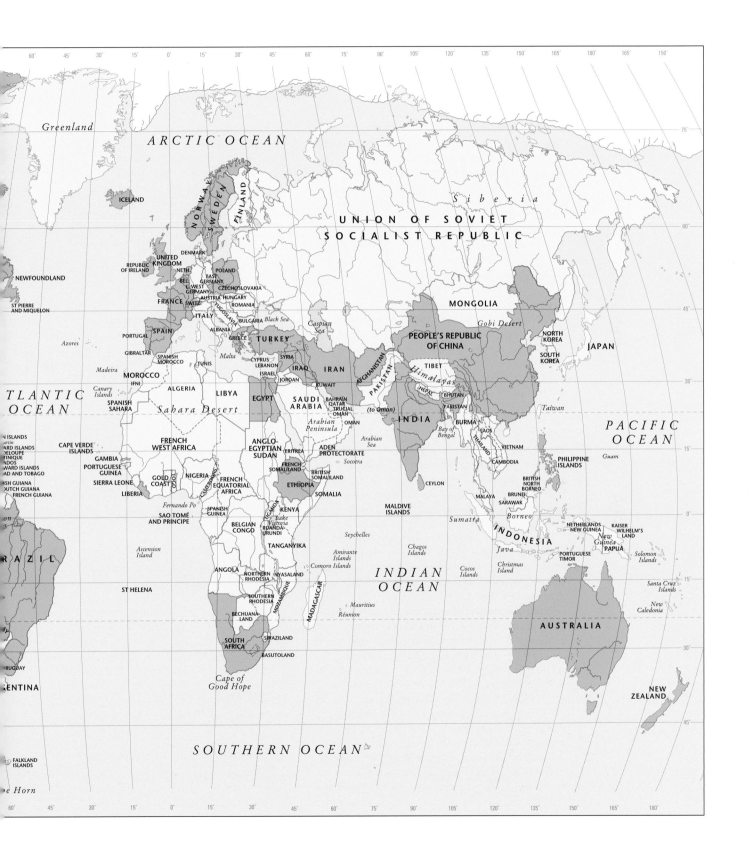

1940–1945

could be utilized elsewhere when war broke out. The treaty obliged both parties to provide extensive military assistance; neither could agree peace without the other's approval.

MOSCOW PEACE TREATY 1940
The Winter War (1939–40) between the Soviet Union and Finland began with the Russian invasion of Finland on 30 November 1939. Although massively outnumbered, Finnish forces were remarkably effective at holding off Soviet offensives, but Soviet pressure became too much and the Finnish government reluctantly began peace negotiations on 29 February. The Moscow Peace Treaty contained a number of harsh concessions that forced Finland to give up large areas of territory. Almost all of the important cultural region of Finnish Karelia was transferred to Russia, along with its vital industry and a number of large cities. The Salla region further north was also ceded to Russia whilst the Hanko Peninsula was leased for a term of 30 years to be used a Soviet naval base. In all, Finland lost 10 percent of its territory and 422,000 Karelians lost their home.

TREATY OF COMMERCE AND NAVIGATION 1940
On 25 March 1940 the USSR and Iran signed the Treaty of Commerce and Navigation, which reinforced the 1935 Treaty of Establishment, Commerce and Navigation. The Caspian Sea was declared as a joint Soviet/Iranian sea, effectively barring all other states from its waters. Both countries retained fishing rights across the sea, other than a 10-nautical-mile zone along each country's coast, within which they held exclusive rights. The treaty also made ambiguous references to commercial rights within the coastal zone that could be interpreted to mean oil drilling or mining. Subsequent treaties would be needed to clarify these ambiguities.

TREATY OF CRAIOVA 1940
With the signature of this treaty, Romania ceded the territory of Southern Dobruja, which it had originally taken as part of the 1913 Treaty of Bucharest, to Bulgaria. Alongside the territorial transfer, both countries agreed to swap their populations of ethnic Hungarians and Romanians, left as diasporas following earlier border changes. A total of 110,000 ethnic Romanians and 65,000 ethnic Bulgarians were relocated to their countries of ethnic origin. The transfer of territory was supported by the main Allied and Axis nations alike, as Southern Dobruja was recognized as having been a historically Bulgarian territory.

TOKYO CONVENTION 1941
Following the Nazi occupation of France, its colonial territories around the world were left in a perilous position, as they were susceptible to attack from various states that saw an opportunity to capitalize on France's weakness. In the Franco–Thai War (October 1940–May 1941) Thailand attempted to reclaim territory from French Indochina. Japan intervened and pushed for a resolution to the conflict as it wanted to minimize European power in Asia whilst maintaining its relations with the Vichy French German client state. The Franco–Thai Convention, signed in Tokyo, agreed that France would ceded its border territories in Laos and Cambodia to Thailand but retain the majority of the territory it had originally taken from Thailand under treaties in 1893, 1904, and 1907. In return for the territory, Thailand was required to pay the French 6 million French Indochinese piastres.

ANGLO–SOVIET TREATY OF 1942
The 1941 Anglo–Soviet Agreement had formalized a British–Soviet military alliance in the wake of Nazi Germany's invasion of the USSR; the following year a 20-year political and military alliance was established. Both countries pledged additional support for each other's war efforts and also agreed to cooperate on matters regarding the post-war landscape of Europe. Although the British rejected Stalin's proposals for well-defined spheres of influence, the 1942 treaty confirmed that both parties would commit to long-term consultation with each other in the event of a Nazi defeat.

THE BRETTON WOODS AGREEMENT 1944
A new global exchange rate system was needed to combat the political and financial turbulence caused by uncoordinated exchange rates in the post-World War I era. Policymakers realized that the rigidity of the gold standard as a currency exchange regulator could have disastrous effects upon the global economy in the post-World War II era, just as it had done post-World War I. The Bretton Woods Conference was convened in New Hampshire between 1–22 July 1944 to discuss the creation of a new international currency exchange rate arrangement. All 44 allied nations were represented at the conference, which established the new structure known as the Bretton Woods System. Under the new system, US dollars became the international reserve currency and all signatories to the agreement would be able to exchange their currency for US dollars. The International Monetary Fund was also established to act as a regulator and central reserve to which countries would commit a certain amount of their own currency and gold.

TITO–ŠUBAŠIĆ AGREEMENT 1944

The Axis occupation of Yugoslavia during World War II resulted in a complex conflict during which Yugoslavian rebels fought against occupying troops and the pro-Nazi puppet administrations. Meanwhile, separate guerrilla groups were engaged in a concurrent civil conflict which pitted Communist partisans, led by Josip Broz Tito, against the royalist Chetniks, led by Draža Mihailović, for control of the country's legitimate government. Under the guidance of western leaders, dialogue was established between Tito and the new leader of the Yugoslav Royal Government in exile, Ivan Šubašić, with the goal of easing the post-war political transition. Under the first Tito–Šubašić agreement (June 1944) the Communists and royalists agreed to share power in a joint government until democratic elections could be held. In the second Tito–Šubašić Agreement (November 1944) Šubašić relinquished a significant amount of the royalist government's power, paving the way for Tito's Socialist Yugoslavia.

TREATY OF VARKIZA 1945

The Axis occupation of Greece was opposed by a number of separate Greek partisan groups from across the political spectrum, who were also engaged in a power struggle to determine Greece's post-war political orientation. A power vacuum followed the German withdrawal in October 1944 and clashes continued between the various Greek political factions. The Treaty of Varkiza, signed on 12 February 1945 by representatives of the royalist Greek government-in-exile and the main resistance movements, was overseen by Britain, whose troops had led the Allied liberation of Greece. The Greek government agreed to enact a number of reforms of government institutions and to hold new elections. They also extended an amnesty regarding any politically motivated crimes that had been committed during the war and to allow members of the Greek People's Liberation Army to join a new national army. In return the Greek People's Liberation Army agreed to lay down its arms and release prisoners it had taken during the conflict.

UNITED NATIONS CHARTER 1945

The United Nations Charter, signed by 50 nations on 26 June 1945, established the United Nations and laid out its fundamental mission, ideals, and tenets of membership. The 1942 Declaration of The United Nations was a 26-party agreement, which formed the basis of the United Nation's constitution and its commitment to upholding world peace in a similar

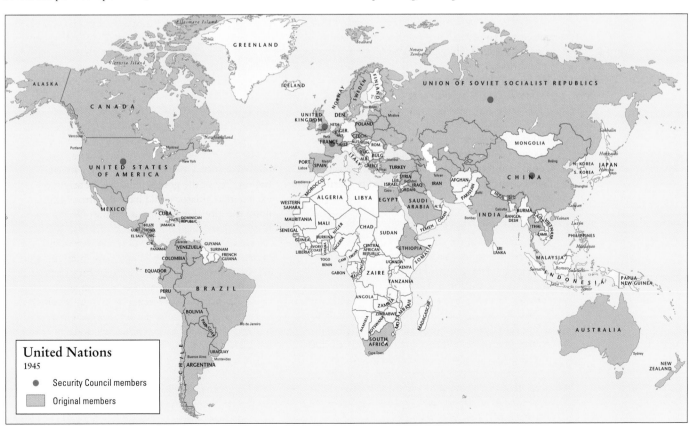

United Nations

1945

● Security Council members

▢ Original members

1945–1949

vein to the failed League of Nations. Within the United Nations Charter were 19 chapters containing 111 articles. The articles covered the United Nations' powers of jurisdiction, its membership structure, and the purposes of its various departments and organs. All member states would be part of the General Assembly and the International Court of Justice was established as the United Nations' judiciary power. A Security Council was established to preside over the United Nations as a ruling body. The US, USSR, Britain, China, and France were given permanent positions on the Security Council, while other nations are elected to fill a further ten temporary positions.

WANFRIED AGREEMENT 1945
Following the establishment of the Allied post-war occupation zones in Germany, American supplies were transported south from the US-controlled North Sea port of Bremerhaven, through the British occupation zone, to the main US occupation zone via the Bebra–Göttingen railway line. Near the village of Werleshausen, a 2.7-mile (4.3-km) stretch of the railway line crossed into the Soviet zone. Soviet soldiers had been repeatedly harassing trains carrying US supplies and causing major disruption to the American logistical operation since the start of the post-war Allied occupation. Under the Wanfried Agreement, a territorial exchange was agreed, securing the border-crossing stretch of railway within the American occupation zone in exchange for a comparable area of territory, which was transferred to the Soviet zone. Due to the exchange of whisky and vodka after the signature of the treaty, the railway line became known colloquially as the Whisky–Vodka line.

BERMUDA AGREEMENT 1946
This bilateral air transport agreement established a precedent for over 3,000 similar bilateral agreements. Signed by the US and Britain, it resolved issues surrounding the rights of British and American trans-Atlantic civil air carriers over allocations of the share of route capacity. As the American air fleet was significantly larger, comprising Pan American, Trans World Airlines, and American Export Airlines, the British authorities wanted to guarantee a proportional share of the market for the British Overseas Airways Corporation. Britain had resorted to restricting the number of American flights permitted to land in the UK. The Bermuda Agreement outlined permitted routes on which British and American carriers could run services and set a pricing structure. This secured the fifth freedom of the Chicago Convention between the two countries, which had hitherto been disputed.

GRUBER–DE GASPERI AGREEMENT 1946
As a former constituent of the Austro–Hungarian Empire, the Italian province of South Tyrol has a large German-speaking population of Austrian heritage. Upon the dissolution of the Austro–Hungarian Empire the territory was annexed to Italy and subjected to a campaign of Italianization under Mussolini's fascist regime, after which it was briefly occupied by Germany following Italy's exit from the Rome–Berlin Axis. During the post-World War II territorial reshaping of Europe, Italy was allowed to retain sovereignty over South Tyrol, but the province's majority German-speaking/Austrian ethnic population was a contentious issue in Austria. The Gruber–De Gasperi agreement was negotiated and signed on 5 September 1946, beginning the process of granting autonomy to the Italian province of South Tyrol/Alto Adige whilst also granting Austria consultative input. The German-speaking population was also granted cultural freedom and German was established as an official language.

LAKE SUCCESS PROTOCOL 1946
As part of the wider transfer of the functions of the now defunct League of Nations to the United Nations, the Lake Success Protocol formalized the handover of the responsibilities of the League of Nations' Advisory Committee on Traffic in Opium and Other Dangerous Drugs. The complex transfer of power to a fundamentally new system of authoritative bodies was enacted through the Lake Success Protocol of December 1946. The treaty made amendments to number of previous international agreements and entered into effect upon signature by each United Nations member state's representative.

TREATY OF MANILA 1946
Under the Treaty of Manila the US government relinquished sovereignty over the Philippines. The Republic of the Philippines gained full independence, ending the period of American colonial rule that began with the Spanish cession of the Philippines to the US under the 1898 Treaty of Paris. Under the Treaty of Manila the Republic of the Philippines assumed responsibility for any prior debt it owed and the two countries agreed to conduct friendly relations. The US also retained the right to station significant numbers of troops in the Philippines. The independence process was ratified on 22 October 1946.

TREATY OF LONDON 1946
The Treaty of London granted full independence to the British protectorate of the Emirate of Transjordan. The treaty completed the independence

process that had begun with the signing of the Organic Law of 1928. Although the Organic Law introduced a new Transjordanian constitution, control over the protectorate was still firmly in British hands. Following the 1946 Treaty of London, another new constitution was implemented, the Hashemite Kingdom of Transjordan was established, and longtime Emir Abdullah I became king. Despite Transjordan's independence, Britain retained the use of military bases across its territory.

GENERAL AGREEMENT ON TARIFFS AND TRADE 1947

Representatives of 23 nations signed the General Agreement on Tariffs and Trade in Geneva on 30 October 1947. Under the initial GATT, signatories became party to a multilateral trade pact that promoted the reduction of barriers to trade and established an equal reduction of trade tariffs between all signatories. The GATT was expanded over many consecutive rounds of negotiation throughout the 20th century. In total, the 1947 agreement formalized 45,000 tariff concessions which were applicable to 10 billion dollars worth of international trade. Subsequent GATT negotiations greatly expanded on the groundwork of the Geneva Round and were instrumental in the establishment of the World Trade Organization, which would succeed the GATT in 1995.

PARIS PEACE TREATIES 1947

During the Paris Peace Conference of July–October 1946, representatives of the Allied nations met to discuss the imposition of various measures upon the defeated European allies of Nazi Germany. The Paris Peace Treaties were signed by Italy, Hungary, Romania, Bulgaria, and Finland on 10 February 1947. The Paris Peace Treaties were more progressive in their provisions than the punitive post-World War I treaties, which sowed the seeds of future conflict. Although all of the signatory nations were required to pay reparations, mostly to the Soviet Union and other countries the Axis forces had occupied, they retained their political sovereignty. Italy lost the vast majority of its colonial possessions acquired both before and after its fascist regime, Finland also lost territory to the Soviet Union, against which it had fought the Winter War, whilst the borders of Hungary, Romania, and Bulgaria were restored to their pre-war positions. Political requirements championing the equal rights of all peoples were also imposed upon the signatories.

INTER-AMERICAN TREATY OF RECIPROCAL ASSISTANCE 1947

Also known as the Rio Pact, this multilateral defense treaty was signed by countries of North, Central, and South America. The US had aimed to secure what it saw as its back yard from European colonialism since the early 19th century. As the 20th century progressed, communism became the biggest threat to America's sphere of influence, and the announcement of the Truman Doctrine ushered in a new era of counter-Soviet foreign policy. The original 19 signatories of the treaty became party to a mutual security agreement that bound them to defend each other in the event of an attack against a member state by either a foreign power or another member state. The treaty came into effect on 12 March 1948 but was gradually shown to be largely ineffective as various international incidents occurred and aspects of the treaty were overlooked.

NORTH ATLANTIC TREATY 1949

As a counter to the growing power of the USSR in eastern Europe following World War II, American diplomats set about creating a treaty that would establish a defensive alliance in the event of Soviet aggression. The North Atlantic Treaty was signed on 4 April 1949 by the US, Canada, and ten European nations, together encompassing the North Atlantic region. These nations subsequently formed the North Atlantic Treaty Organization (NATO). The treaty laid out a number of terms that bound the signatories to defend each other if any one of them came under attack. It also promoted the settlement of disputes via peaceful means and negotiation but required NATO members to maintain their military capabilities to defend against outside aggression. Any attack against a NATO member state within the Europe/North America region was considered an attack against all member states and would be met by collective armed response. A further 17 states have joined NATO up to the present day.

FOURTH GENEVA CONVENTION 1949

The First, Second, and Third Geneva Conventions of 1949 implemented a number of revisions to prior conventions regarding the fair and humane treatment of wounded military personnel, shipwrecked military personnel at sea, and prisoners of war. The Fourth Geneva Convention of 1949 laid out comprehensive terms across 159 articles for the humane treatment of civilians in times of war, as opposed to members of the armed forces. It is strictly forbidden for occupying forces to carry out acts of violence, torture, and humiliation against civilians and acts of destruction against their property. Civilians accused of crimes must be dealt with under the normal framework of the law, free from discrimination, whilst executions and collective punishment are strictly forbidden. Occupying forces

1949–1952

are held responsible for provision of medical and food aid to civilians where possible. Any military or commanding personnel who commit a grave breach of the terms of the convention can be prosecuted for war crimes.

TREATY OF THE HAGUE 1949

The final stage of the Indonesian independence process from Holland ended in December 1949 with passing of the Treaty of The Hague. Negotiations had been hampered by Dutch demands for Western New Guinea to remain a colonial territory and their insistence that the new Republic of Indonesia should acquire debts accrued under the Dutch East Indies colonial administration. Indonesian and Dutch representatives were able to agree terms of Indonesian independence, including a new constitution and the withdrawal of Dutch military forces. A Dutch–Indonesian Union was also set up to act as a consultative body during the formation of the federal Republic of the United States of Indonesia. The Indonesian delegation eventually agreed to take on 4.3 billion Dutch guilders of debt and the issue of Western New Guinea was postponed for future negotiation.

TREATY OF LONDON 1949

The Treaty of London, formally known as the Statute of the Council of Europe, was signed on 5 May 1949. The statute was originally signed by ten European nations, officially founding the Council of Europe, an international organization that aims to promote adherence to the fundamental principles of human rights and democracy. This aspiration emerged after World War II when many politicians recognized that unity was required to avoid conflict in the future. The Council of Europe has no legal jurisdiction over member states but it promotes unity by coordinating common policy goals through treaties and assessment of member states' progress in the fields of human rights and equality. Although the Council of Europe has none of the legislative powers possessed by the European Union, it nevertheless founded the European Court of Human Rights, which legislates against member states accused of violating human rights laws.

LIAQUAT–NEHRU PACT 1950

In the aftermath of the partition of India and the formation of Pakistan as a separate dominion of the British Empire, ethnic tensions between Muslims and other religious groups in both India and Pakistan erupted into violence. Modern-day Bangladesh, which was at the time an exclave and province of Pakistan, was the site of much of this violence as large numbers of people fled across the border with

West Bengal to escape religious persecution. The Liaquat–Nehru Pact, also known as the Delhi Pact, was signed by Indian Prime Minister Jawahar Lal Nehru and Pakistani Prime Minister Liaquat Ali Khan. Both leaders agreed to protect minority rights within their own countries and to grant equal rights to any religious minorities. The more immediate terms of the pact ensured that refugees would be able to return to their homes to gather property and that abducted women would be released.

TREATY OF ZGORZELEC 1950

Both the German Democratic Republic and the Polish People's Republic had come under Soviet influence since the end of World War II but their border delimitation along the Oder–Neisse line, which had been agreed at the 1945 Potsdam Conference, left a number of formerly German towns in Poland. Some towns along the border were even split in two by the East German–Polish border and declarations of intent to return the divided towns to Germany by East German President Wilhelm Pieck raised fears amongst the Poles. Under Soviet pressure the Treaty of Zgorzelec was negotiated and the Oder–Neisse line was confirmed as the legitimate border between the two countries. The treaty was not recognized by the United Nations and thus the border had to be reconfirmed officially in later treaties.

MUTUAL DEFENSE TREATY (US–PHILIPPINES) 1951

This treaty committed the US and the Philippines to the usual terms of mutual defense and required that they seek resolution to any international disputes through peaceful means. Both countries were obliged to come to the aid of the other if either came under attack by a third party, specifically in the Pacific area. This was subject to consultation to ensure that any action accorded with each country's constitution. The US and Philippines were required to maintain their individual and shared capabilities to defend against an attack. The US–Philippines Mutual Defense Treaty is by far the most comprehensive and significant military alliance treaty the Philippines has concluded.

GENOCIDE CONVENTION 1951
The term "Genocide" was first coined by Jewish lawyer Raphael Lemkin who had experienced firsthand the atrocities in eastern Europe in both world wars and had subsequently played a crucial role in pushing international recognition of the crime. The United Nations General Assembly passed the Genocide Convention on 9 December 1948, defining genocide as a number of acts ranging from killing to prevention of births, which are aimed at a specific ethnic, religious, or national group. Since its implementation, many countries have voiced opposition to specific clauses within the convention but remain parties to it due to their ratification of, or accession to, the agreement.

TREATY OF SAN FRANCISCO 1951
Although Japan's military resistance to the Allies had ceased in 1945, the terms of Japanese compensation, relinquishment of territory, and the political footing on which the country would progress were not finalized until the Treaty of San Francisco. Japanese claims to overseas territories, including Korea, Taiwan, and Hong Kong, were voided and all Japanese foreign assets in formerly occupied countries were repossessed. Additionally, Japan was made to commit to a repayment scheme that allocated damages to occupied territories and Allied prisoners of war. A total of 48 nations were signatories to the treaty, although there were three abstentions, most notably the USSR which saw the treaty as a threat to Soviet interests in the Far East. Neither of the Chinese governments engaged in the Chinese Civil War were invited to the negotiations and thus the People's Republic of China later denounced the treaty. Following the 1951 signature, the treaty came into force on 28 April 1952 and Japan regained its sovereignty. Japan later signed a number of bilateral peace treaties with nations that were not party to the Treaty of San Francisco.

SECURITY TREATY 1951
Signed between the US and Japan on 8 September 1951 as a separate agreement alongside the wider international Japanese peace treaty, the Treaty of San Francisco, the Security Treaty dealt with the issue of a continued American military presence in demilitarized Japan. America was granted sole use of Japanese territory for military projection capabilities

in the Far East, although this did not constitute an American occupation. Japan was thus forbidden from allowing any other state to use its territory for deployment of military forces. The Security Treaty would later be revised in 1960.

US AND JAPAN MUTUAL DEFENSE ASSISTANCE AGREEMENT 1954
US policymakers wanted Japan to be able to develop its own defense capabilities, which had previously been forbidden under the post-World War II peace treaties. Efforts had been made during negotiation of the 1951 Security Treaty to persuade the Japanese to form their own small defense force, however the suggestion was met with disapproval. By 1954 both the sides were willing to commit to partial Japanese rearmament for solely defensive purposes. US forces would still be posted in Japan but the Japanese agreed to begin a program of defensive rearmament for the purposes of regional security.

ANZUS TREATY 1952
The US was keen to tighten security in the Pacific due to the Cold War Communist threat. The US agreed to the ANZUS Treaty as reassurance for Australia and New Zealand that the Pacific alliances had shifted to include Japan as part of the new anti-Communist alliance. The ANZUS Treaty came into force on 29 April 1952. Australian and New Zealand troops consequently took part in America's Vietnam

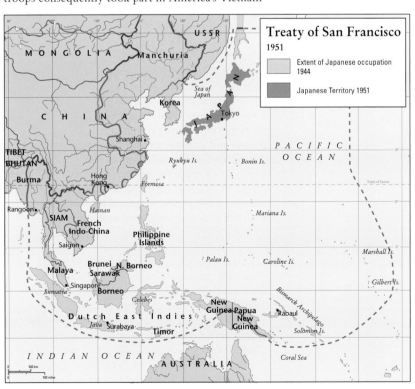

1952–1955

Korean War Demilitarized Zone
1953

NORTH KOREA

DEMILITARIZED ZONE (DMZ)

Military Demarcation Line

38th Parallel

Tunnel 2

Tunnel 4

Tunnel 1

Tunnel 3

N

SOUTH KOREA

War in the 1960s and 70s. Following New Zealand's ban on nuclear-powered/armed vessels in its waters in 1984, the American warship USS *Buchanan* was denied permission to make landfall in New Zealand. Diplomatic tensions mounted and the US suspended its ANZUS Treaty agreement with New Zealand in 1985, although military relations have been re-established since.

TREATY OF TAIPEI 1952

In a bilateral agreement with the Republic of China (modern day Taiwan), Japan concluded the Second Sino–Japanese War and renounced its territorial claim to Taiwan. Both the government of the Republic of China and the government of the Communist People's Republic of China had been left out of the Treaty of San Francisco negotiations due to US and British disagreement over which should be considered the legitimate representative of the Chinese people following the Chinese Civil War. Japan recognized the government of the Republic of China as the legitimate government of China and the Treaty of Taipei relinquished its claim to the territory of Taiwan.

GENERAL TREATY (FEDERAL REPUBLIC OF GERMANY AND WESTERN ALLIES) 1952

As part of the Bonn–Paris Conventions, the General Treaty was signed signed by representatives of the US, Britain, France, and the Federal Republic of Germany. It was agreed that West Germany would be granted independence as a sovereign state and

the occupation by the Western Allies would end. Sovereignty allowed West Germany to begin a program of defensive rearmament to counter the threat posed by growing Soviet power in Eastern Europe. Concerns about German rearmament, especially from France, derailed the negotiations. and West Germany's independence was postponed until the General Treaty had been rewritten with a clause committing it to a new military alliance, the Western European Union. West Germany was also accepted into NATO and the General Treaty came into effect on 5 May 1955.

INTERNATIONAL CONVENTION RELATING TO ARREST OF SEA-GOING SHIPS 1952

Initially signed by representatives of eight different states, this multilateral treaty commits parties to rules of arrest regarding ships flying the flag of any nation that is party to the agreement. The convention stipulates that parties agree to accept arrest of any ship flying their flag when stationed in the port of another signatory. Arrests can only be made upon approval of an arrest warrant in the local jurisdiction of the port in question. The treaty has 71 parties to date.

KOREAN WAR ARMISTICE AGREEMENT 1953

The Korean War (1950–53) between North and South Korea was ended by an armistice agreement signed by military leaders of the three main forces involved in the conflict, the Korean People's Army, the Chinese People's Volunteer Army, and the United Nations Command, representing the Republic of Korea. Discussions began in 1951 but were stalled by North Korean allegations of a United Nations Command aircraft bombing the site of negotiations in Kaesŏng. There was also disagreement about the process for transferring prisoners of war, as many Chinese and North Korean soldiers had refused repatriation. The eventual agreement, signed on 27 July 1953, solved this issue through the establishment of a Neutral Nations Repatriation Committee, which would repatriate soldiers within 60 days. A 2.5-mile (4-km) demilitarized zone would be constructed between North and South Korea. The two nations only agreed to cease military actions against one another and as such technically remain at war to this day as no official peace treaty has been signed.

CENTRAL TREATY ORGANIZATION 1954

Following a number of consecutive security agreements between 1954–55, a mutual defensive alliance, consisting of Turkey, Pakistan, Iraq, Iran, and the United Kingdom, was formed. The first agreement that formed the basis of the Central Treaty Organization, also known as CENTO, was a treaty of friendship and cooperation between Turkey and Pakistan on 2 April 1954. Turkey and Pakistan were keen to strengthen their regional defensive capabilities against the threat of attack from the USSR. Further discussions led to the signature of a defensive alliance between Turkey and Iraq (1955), with the UK, Pakistan, and Iran joining in the course of that year. The initiative behind the CENTO defensive pact was the formation of a strong boundary to hamper the USSR's efforts to expand its influence further southwest.

SOUTHEAST ASIA COLLECTIVE DEFENSE TREATY 1954

China and the USSR had recognized Communist leader Ho Chi Minh and his forces as the legitimate authority in Vietnam in 1950 and were supporting Communist activity throughout the region. This treaty, envisaged as a counter to the growing Communist influence in Southeast Asia, was signed on 8 September 1954, securing eight member states from across the world. Besides the Philippines and Thailand, all other signatory states were outside the immediate Southeast Asian region. Nearby Australia and New Zealand had vested interests in the security of the region, as did the US, UK, and France. Pakistan joined the alliance in hopes of securing additional support for its dispute with India. SEATO members were required to make a portion of their armed forces available for joint military exercises but active military cooperation did not extend much further than this. The SEATO mutual defensive policy was called into action for America's war in Vietnam but by the 1970s the alliance was largely defunct.

THE GENEVA ACCORDS 1954

When the French announced their intention to withdraw from Indochina, they relinquished power in Laos and Cambodia. However, in Vietnam war broke out between French troops and Vietnamese nationalists led by Ho Chi Minh. The French defeat at the Battle of Dien Bien Phu in 1954 was decisive, leading to the withdrawal of their troops from Vietnam. It was the task of the delegates at Geneva – including representatives from the US, UK, Soviet Union, China, the Viet Minh, and France – to arrange for Vietnam's eventual reunification and self government. In the short term, until 1956, Vietnam was divided into north and south along the 17th parallel, with plans in place for elections in 1956, self-government, reunification, and independence. All parties involved agreed to these provisions,

with the exception of the US, which was nervous about the spread of communism in Southeast Asia. For many Vietnamese nationalists the ideologies of commuism and nationalism were closely linked, and they viewed South Vietnam as a remnant of the French colonial regime.

ASIAN–AFRICAN CONFERENCE 1955

The conference was an attempt to promote cooperation between Asian and African countries in the face of the conflict and division thath was being fueled by the Cold War power struggle between the US and the USSR/China. Besides Indonesia, a core group of other Asian nations, India, Pakistan, Burma, and Ceylon, played active roles in the organization of the conference. Representatives from a total of 29 countries were present at the conference, by the end of which a 10-point declaration of shared goals for peace, cooperation and anti-colonialism had been agreed. The Asian–African Conference was an important first step for diplomatic cooperation between of countries of Asia, Africa, and the Third World, which had long been exploited at the hands of European colonialism and the more recent ambitions of the Cold War powers. It would give rise to the idea behind the Non-Aligned Movement, which promotes solidarity between developing countries which do not belong to any global power bloc.

AUSTRIAN STATE TREATY 1955

With the signature of the Austrian State Treaty by the World War II Allied occupying powers, the US, USSR, UK, and France, Austria was granted sovereignty as an independent country. Like Germany, Austria was divided into four separate occupied zones by the Allies at the end of World War II. Negotiations surrounding the terms of an Austrian independence treaty began in 1947 but were repeatedly stalled by developing east–west Europe tensions. Following Stalin's death in March 1953, Soviet attitudes towards a settlement with Austria improved. With the West German commitment to NATO agreed in 1954, the US was willing to accept Austrian proposals for neutrality upon independence. They had feared that if West Germany and Austria both became neutral, the Soviet Union would be able to exert an even tighter grip on Europe. The Austrian State Treaty came into force on 27 July 1955, and neutrality was declared by the Austrian government soon after.

SIMONSTOWN AGREEMENT 1955

The Royal Navy base at Simonstown had long been an important staging post for British naval power and used to protect maritime trade passing the Cape

Geneva Conference
1954
— Demarcation line

1955–1958

of Good Hope. Since South African independence in 1910, the Royal Navy had been allowed continued use of the base. The new Nationalist Party government of 1948 pushed for expansion of South Africa's naval capabilities, including use of the Simonstown naval base. Under the Simonstown Agreement of 1955 the Royal Navy handed the base over to the South African Navy and in return was granted use of the naval base, including during any war in which South Africa was not engaged. In return the Royal Navy agreed to assist the South African Navy's expansion plans by supplying six frigates, ten minesweepers, and four seaward defense boats at a cost of £18 million. The agreement was cancelled in 1975 in protest at the South African government's domestic apartheid policy.

WARSAW PACT 1955
The Warsaw Pact was forged with the signature of the Treaty of Friendship, Cooperation and Mutual Assistance on 14 May 1955. Alongside the USSR, seven other Eastern European countries, Albania, Bulgaria, Czechoslovakia, East Germany, Hungary, Poland, and Romania, all members of the existing Soviet economic union, the Council for Mutual Economic Assistance, became party to the Warsaw Pact collective defense treaty. Although the USSR's influence over these countries was already extensive and unquestionable, the Warsaw Pact was partly established as a reaction to the strengthening of NATO in Europe with the acceptance of West Germany into the alliance on 9 May 1955. Requests by the USSR to join NATO in March 1954 had also been declined and as such the USSR recognized a turn in the tide of power in Europe against its ambitions. The Warsaw Pact not only committed its members to a military defensive alliance under which a multinational force was established, it also established a joint Political Consultative Committee to encourage political cooperation.

SOVIET-JAPANESE JOINT DECLARATION 1956
The Treaty of San Francisco (1951) concluded peace between Japan and the Western Allied Powers over vociferous objections raised by the Soviet Union. In particular, they protested cession of Japanese islands to the United States, where US military bases were established. The Joint Declaration aimed to normalize relations between Japan and the Soviet Union, without constituting a formal peace treaty. By its provisions, the counterparties ended their state of war, and restored diplomatic relations: the Soviet Union also pledged to support Japan's application for United Nations membership. In addition, the Soviet Union waived any claims for war reparations

and, via a trade protocol, the counterparties awarded each other 'most favored nation' status. A territorial dispute over possession of the Kurile Islands was shelved, pending conclusion of a formal peace treaty, although the Soviet Union agreed the handover of the island of Shikotan and the Habomai chain of islets in the event of such a treaty.

ANGLO-MALAYAN DEFENSE AGREEMENT 1957
After Japanese occupation during World War II, the Federation of Malaya was established as a British protectorate in 1948. However, in the face of a Communist insurgency (the Malayan Emergency), the British planned for independence: national elections were held in 1955, and won in a landslide by the United Malay National Organization (UMNO). The independent Federation of Malaya (renamed Malaysia in 1963) came into being in 1957 with UMNO leader, Tunku Abdul Rahman, its first prime minister. Rahman fostered cordial relations with the former colonial power, claiming on inauguration that Malaya had been "blessed with good administration forced and tempered to perfection by generations of British administrators." The Defense Agreement cemented this goodwill, committing the United Kingdom (and Australia and New Zealand) to the defense of the new state. It was invoked during the confrontation between the enlarged Malaysia and Indonesia (1963–66).

THE TREATY OF ROME 1957
This was a logical successor to the Treaty of Paris (1951), which established the European Coal and Steel Community (ECSC). The post-war nations of Europe realilzed that appealing to mutual economic interest was the best way of bringing harmony and cooperation to a shattered continent. The success of ECSC led to a meeting in Messina, Sicily, in 1956, between the leaders of six European nations: France, Germany, Belgium, the Netherlands, Luxembourg, and Italy. They discussed the proposal to do away with all barriers to trade between the six nations, and establish a customs union. Further talks were held in Brussels and it was proposed that two new communities should be established: the European Economic Commission (EEC) and the European Atomic Energy Community (EURATOM). The new "common market" was predicated on four freedoms: of goods, peoples, services, and capital. The final treaty, signed in Rome in 1957, brought together four institutions: the European Commission, the Council of Ministers, the European Parliament, and the European Court of Justice. It laid the foundation for greater economic and political integration between the community of

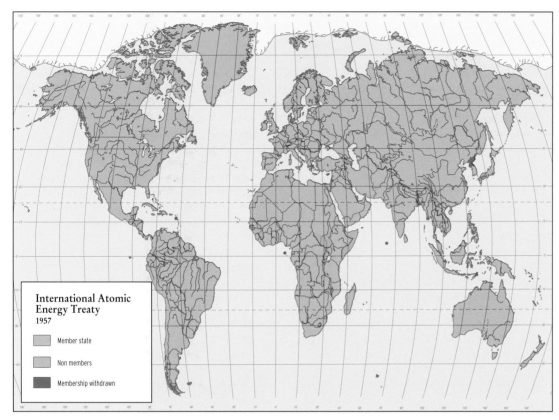

International Atomic
Energy Treaty
1957

Member state

Non members

Membership withdrawn

European nations, which eventually boasted, as the European Union (EU), 28 member nations.

INTERNATIONAL ATOMIC ENERGY TREATY 1957

President Eisenhower's "Atoms for Peace" address to the United Nations General Assembly proposed the creation of an international body to enable and regulate peaceful applications for nuclear power. Subsequent negotiations led to the approval of the Statute for the foundation of the International Atomic Energy Agency (IAEA), which came into force in July 1957. The IAEA's mission is founded on three pillars: Science and Technology; Safety and Security; Safeguards and Verification. It comprises, administratively, a Board of Governors, Secretariat and General Conference. Since the Nuclear Non-Proliferation Treaty came into force (1970), the IAEA has ensured compliance amongst its member states. At the same time, the Agency promotes and disseminates safe uses of nuclear power, for instance, through supervision programs for the construction of nuclear power stations in developing countries.

US-UK MUTUAL DEFENSE AGREEMENT 1958

During World War II, the United Kingdom's nuclear weapons development project merged with the Unites States Manhattan Project by the Quebec Agreement (1943). After the war, Britain determined it needed its own independent nuclear deterrent; work commenced in 1947, and the Atomic Weapons Establishment (AWE) was established at RAF Aldermaston in 1950. The first successful British atomic weapon test took place off Western Australia in 1952. Britain then developed the more powerful hydrogen bomb, conducting successful testing through Operation Grapple in the Pacific (1957–58). Following these tests, the UK and US entered into the Mutual Defense Agreement, which provided for a high degree of military nuclear cooperation between the two countries. It enabled the reciprocal exchange of classified information on nuclear weapons research, and of their component materials: enriched uranium, plutonium, and tritium. It also permitted the transfer of weapons parts and equipment, and UK use of the US Nevada test site.

CONVENTION ON THE TERRITORIAL SEA AND THE CONTIGUOUS ZONES 1958

The oceans of the world contain a number of "choke-points." Examples include the Bab-el-Mandeb at the mouth of the Red Sea, Straits of Hormuz controlling access to the Persian Gulf and the Straits of Gibraltar between the Atlantic and Mediterranean. Historically, perhaps the most

1960–1961

contentious have been the Turkish Straits between the Mediterranean and Black Sea. The United Nations attempted to tackle this frequently vexed question as part of the 1958 Convention of Law of the Sea; states cannot suspend the innocent passage of foreign ships through straits that are used for international navigation between one part of the high seas and another part of the high seas or the territorial sea of a foreign state. "Innocent" was defined as "not prejudicial to the peace, good order or security of the coastal state."

TREATY OF MUTUAL COOPERATION AND SECURITY 1960

The post-World War II Allied occupation of Japan (1945–52) oversaw the creation of a new constitution and the establishment of parliamentary democracy. Against a backdrop of economic reconstruction, Japanese disarmament and the disbanding of its armed forces occurred. The mass deployment of American occupying forces to Korea during the Korean War (1950–53) rendered Japan dangerously vulnerable. Japan was therefore allowed to establish a limited self-defense force by militarization of its police force. A more comprehensive remedy was essayed in a treaty providing for Mutual Security, first signed in San Francisco in 1952, and amplified in 1960. The treaty designated any attack against Japan or the United States perpetrated within Japanese territorial administration as dangerous to the respective countries' own peace and safety, and required both countries to act to meet the common danger. To support that requirement, it provided for the continued presence of US military bases in Japan.

INDUS WATERS TREATY 1960

The Partition that accompanied independence from Britain in 1947 divided the massive Indus River basin between India and West Pakistan. At the time of independence, a series of major irrigation projects were underway, and partition threatened to disrupt their completion. The treaty created the Permanent Indus Commission for the resolution of disagreements according to a scale of magnitude: questions were to be handled exclusively by the Commission; "differences" were to be referred to a Neutral Expert; and disputes referred to a seven-member panel, the Court of Arbitration. The World Bank, a co-signatory of the treaty, would appoint impartial arbitrators when requested to do so by either or both parties. The treaty also provided for the cross-border development of irrigation capacity, and mutual pre-notifications of construction activity and inspections. The regime has proved robust enough to survive frequent tensions, even conflicts, between its state counterparties.

TREATY OF MONTEVIDEO 1960

The Latin American Free Trade Association came into effect in 1962, through the 1960 Treaty of Montevideo. The original signatories were Argentina, Brazil, Mexico, Chile, Paraguay, Uruguay and Peru, with Colombia, Ecuador, Venezuela, and Bolivia joining soon thereafter. The treaty stipulated a 12-year transitional period to full free trade, while interstate tariff reductions were to be achieved by "effective reciprocity." Protections for less-developed members included relaxed implementation schedules, and financial/technical assistance for industrialization and agricultural mechanization. The treaty was limited to goods (not services), and incorporated no arbitration mechanism. The relapse of several of its members into dictatorship hampered implementation, as did the dramatic imbalances between levels of development: it would be superseded by the Latin American Integration Association in 1980.

LONDON AND ZURICH AGREEMENTS 1960

Post-World War II, a movement gained momentum amongst Greek Cypriots for union with Greece (*enosis*). The Orthodox Church of Cyprus, led by Archbishop Makarios, spearheaded the movement, alongside the guerrilla warfare of EOKA. It was countered in the late 1950s by Turkish Cypriot demands for *Taksim* – partition. Talks in London and Zurich produced a compromise. Cyprus was to become independent, remaining unified but separate from Greece. Greek and Turkish military forces would be permitted (in a 3:2 ratio) to monitor and uphold the agreements. Power-sharing would be instituted, with a president of Greek Cypriot and vice president of Turkish Cypriot extraction. The cabinet would be similarly divided (ratio 7:3). The British would retain two sovereign military bases on the island and a number of "reserved sites." Relations remained fraught, ultimately leading to the Turkish invasion and enforced partition of the island (1974).

ARMS COUNCIL AND DISARMAMENT AGENCY 1961

In the mid-1950s, the Russell-Einstein Manifesto (signed by eleven leading scientists and theoreticians including Bertrand Russell and Albert Einstein) protested against the existential threat posed by nuclear weapons and called upon world leaders to develop peaceful conflict resolution. Opposition to "Mutually Assured Destruction" through overwhelming nuclear arsenals gained mounting public and political support. In the United States, the Arms Control and Disarmaments Act (1961) was a response to these concerns, establishing the Disarmament Agency to act as a mechanism

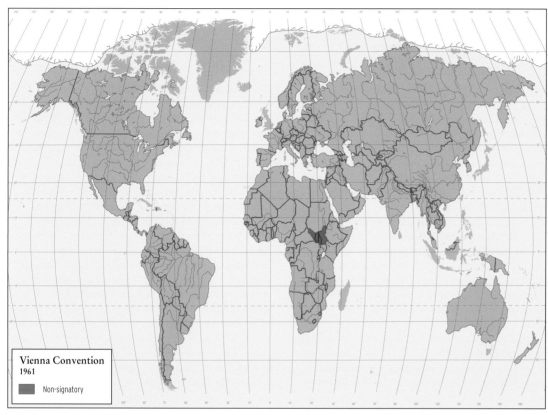

Vienna Convention
1961

   Non-signatory

for the "control and reduction of apocalyptic armaments" (including nuclear, chemical and biological weapons). Its purpose was to integrate arms control into American national security policy; its representatives managed US participation in international disarmament negotiations, but it also undertook reconnaissance of rival powers' weapons capabilities. The ACDA was one (of a plethora) of Agencies advising on the Strategic Arms Limitation Talks (SALT), initiated with the USSR (1969).

HAGUE CONVENTION 1961
The Apostille Convention was created by the Hague Conference on Private International Law. It streamlines the process of authentication of legal documents required in cross-border situations. Common examples are international marriages or relocations, applications for foreign study or citizenship, and business or investment transactions. Its objective is to facilitate use of public documents abroad between countries party to the Convention by replacing the pre-existing (and often cumbersome) chains of certification required with a single stamp of authentication, or apostille, issued by a recognized "Competent Authority."

COLUMBIA RIVER TREATY 1961
The Columbia River has the fourth highest water

volume of North American rivers. Much of its course is through high-walled rocky canyons, a combination ideal for the production of hydro-power. Joint Canadian and American exploration of potential dam sites began in World War II, deriving added impetus from catastrophic floods in 1948. Complementary interests were at play, the US needed the storage capacity of the British Columbian section of the river basin, while the government of that state needed American finance to compete its Two River hydroelectric strategy (the other river being the Peace). Four huge dams were built (three in Canada) and cross-payments agreed for power generation and flood control benefits. More recently, concerns have been raised about the treaty's adverse impacts on the environment and fisheries, plus depletion of irrigation resources.

VIENNA CONVENTION ON DIPLOMATIC RELATIONS 1961
The first attempt to codify the status of diplomatic immunity occurred at the Congress of Vienna (1815). At the same venue (1961), a thorough protocol for diplomatic relations was established. Amongst its provisions, the inviolability of the premises of a diplomatic mission, diplomatic bags, documents, archives and couriers was established. Diplomats were granted immunity from civil or

1961–1963

criminal prosecution (although this right may be waived by their home country). Diplomatic staff can be declared *persona non grata* by the host country: in these circumstances, the home country must recall the personnel concerned or jeopardize their immunity. A diplomatic mission can only be entered by the host country with the permission of the head of that mission, and its property protected from intrusion or damage. The Convention also reduces the categories of diplomatic representative to three: ambassadors and ministers-plenipotentiary (accredited to the host head of state), and chargés d'affaires (accredited to the host foreign minister).

ALLIANCE FOR PROGRESS 1961
President John F. Kennedy announced his ten-year plan to "build a hemisphere where all men can hope for a suitable standard of living and…. live out their lives in dignity and in freedom" and "once again transform the American continent into a vast crucible of revolutionary ideas." The goals were laudable: a 2.5 percent annual increase in per capita income; price stability; reduced income inequality; social housing; and land reform. The last, and most vital, ingredient – stable democracies – proved the most elusive, thwarted by the resistance of traditional elites. US matched loan assistance made limited inroads into Latin American debt repayments. Yet the income increase target was surpassed, and educational reforms produced substantial progress. Vitiated by the competing costs of Vietnam, the Alliance would be wound up in 1973.

SINGLE CONVENTION ON NARCOTIC DRUGS 1961
From the International Opium Convention of 1912 onwards, repeated attempts were made to control the manufacture, distribution, and use of narcotic drugs. The Paris Convention (1931) had, by the 1960s, become weighted down with supplementary protocols struggling to keep pace with the synthesis of new narcotics. The Single Convention attempted to both update and consolidate pre-existing protocols, and broaden their scope to encompass cannabis derivatives. It also merged pre-existing bodies to form the International Narcotics Control Board to monitor the enforcement of its restrictions, and the control of narcotic precursors. The Convention called for international cooperation to deter drug trafficking. The manufacture, distribution, and use of a compendium of drugs (and their precursors classified by type in four schedules) were proscribed, with the exception of production for medical and scientific purposes. Some manufacturing states, often poor, where narcotics production was often the main livelihood for a

sizable proportion of the population resisted stronger regulation and favored national control policies.

CONVENTION ON REDUCTION OF STATELESSNESS 1961
The Universal Declaration of Human Rights (1948) affirms "everyone has the right to a nationality." Without nationality, people are generally excluded from political participation, and access to health care, education, and rewarding employment. The Convention sets out rules to govern situations where the conferral or withdrawal of nationality would leave the person affected stateless. It covers four principal areas where the risk of statelessness obtains. States shall grant their nationality to children who would otherwise be stateless and have ties with them through birth in the territory or descent. The loss or renunciation of nationality in later life requires prior possession of another nationality. Deprivation of nationality on racial, ethnic, religious or political grounds is prohibited: such deprivation is permissible only where a person "conducts himself in a manner seriously prejudicial to the vital interests of the state." The treaty provisions for acquisition of territory must grant nationality to anyone affected who would otherwise become stateless.

NASSAU AGREEMENT 1962
By the advent of the Kennedy presidency, America increasingly viewed Britain's independent nuclear deterrent as a strategic liability: creating a tempting target it was bound to defend, but did not control. In the 1950s, the Soviet Union's installation of advanced surface-to-air missile systems rendered manned bombers near obsolete as a means of delivering a nuclear attack. The American air-launched ballistic missile, Skybolt, offered an apparent solution. But, with the British committed to its adoption, the US threatened cancellation to force Britain's induction into their planned Multilateral Force with dual-key control (both parties needing to authorize launch). A political crisis ensued in Britain, with its government threatening to go it alone. Nassau was the compromise hammered out with British Prime Minister Macmillan by which he obtained delivery of the most advanced US Polaris missiles in return for joining the Multilateral Force and supplying the US with a submarine base at Holy Loch.

NEW YORK AGREEMENT 1962
In 1949 the Netherlands surrendered sovereignty of the Dutch East Indies – bar West New Guinea (WNG). Indonesia campaigned diplomatically to acquire this remaining territory, despite its racially distinct indigenous population. In the late 1950s, positions hardened with the Dutch

incorporating WNG into the Kingdom of the Netherlands, while Indonesia abandoned United Nations (UN) mediation and fomented attacks against Dutch businesses. Under President Kennedy, the Americans sought an agreement that averted Indonesia falling under Soviet influence, and brokered the New York Agreement. WNG was placed in UN administration, to be replaced over time by Indonesian administration. Then, before 1969, a popular consultation held by local elders, would determine whether WNG would remain with Indonesia or separate. The eventual consultation, somewhat dubiously, overwhelmingly backed staying Indonesian.

VIENNA CONVENTION ON CONSULAR RELATIONS 1963

The Vienna Convention of 1961 codified the status and protections obtaining for diplomats, its 1963 successor extended this to consular staff. It defines the consul's legitimate remit, foremost being the protection of their home state's interests and nationals in the host country, but including promotion of commercial, cultural, economic, and scientific relations between their home and host countries. Immunities afforded consular staff mirror those laid down in the preceding Convention for diplomats: freedom of communication between consular staff and their home country must be preserved, consular bags and couriers must be inviolable, and consular premises are not to be entered without permission, and must be protected from intrusion or damage. The host state may (as with diplomats) declare consular staff *persona non grata*, requiring their departure in a "reasonable period of time" or else their immunity may be withdrawn. Arrested or detained foreign nationals must be notified without delay of their right to have their consulate notified.

VIENNA CONVENTION ON CIVIL LIABILITY FOR NUCLEAR DAMAGE 1963

Governing liability in the case of nuclear incidents at nuclear installations, the Convention renders the operator of the installation exclusively and absolutely (i.e. irrespective of fault) responsible for incident-related damages. The only potential exonerations relate to armed conflict or gross negligence by the victim. It further decrees the operator's mandatory possession of insurance to cover its liability. The Convention fixes minimum liabilities, which are time-bound (normally ten years from the incident date). The Convention does not cover nuclear materials in transit, or disposal sites (although storage facilities are addressed). The status of decommissioned sites is unclear, and exclusions

are offered to low-risk installations (e.g. research laboratories, uranium refineries).

PARTIAL NUCLEAR TEST BAN TREATY (PTBT) 1963

In the 1950s public concern mounted as the dangers of radioactive fall-out became apparent and the number of atmospheric and underwater tests escalated. Negative sentiment spiked following the Cuban missile crisis in October 1962 when, briefly, nuclear war seemed imminent. Within weeks of the confrontation, Anglo-American and Soviet draft proposals for a nuclear test ban had been exchanged. Concluded in August 1963 between the United States, Soviet Union, and the United Kingdom, the treaty banned nuclear tests in the atmosphere, underwater and in outer space. It did not ban underground tests, and did not constitute any supervisory body to monitor compliance, or specify any system of inspection or verification. Over 100 signatories had been added by the year end, the notable absentees being France and China, who continued to conduct atmospheric tests into the 1970s. Both the US and Soviet Union complied – although American testing (wholly underground) actually increased in the following decade.

ELYSÉE TREATY 1963

President de Gaulle's greeting on the Franco-German accord was effusive: "It not only turns the page on a long and bloody era of fighting and war, but also opens the door to a new future for Germany, for France, for Europe and therefore for the world!" German Chancellor Adenauer was more circumspect, and the lower house of his parliament, the Bundestag, even more so, insisting the Elysée treaty be prefaced with commitments to close links with the US, NATO, and eventual British membership of the European Economic Community – much to De Gaulle's chagrin. The treaty was short on substance, championing closer cooperation in foreign, cultural, and language exchanges, and founding a Franco-German Office, but it symbolically cemented an alliance that would drive future European integration.

STRASBOURG CONVENTION 1963

The progression of European patent law, as befits the subject matter, has been grinding and tortuous. The early Council of Europe designated a Committee of Experts to deliberate on the matter, leading to two Conventions dealing respectively with patent applications (1953), and patent classification (1954). The Strasbourg Convention was a further step, establishing the criteria for patentability – "inventions which are new, susceptible of industrial

1965–1970

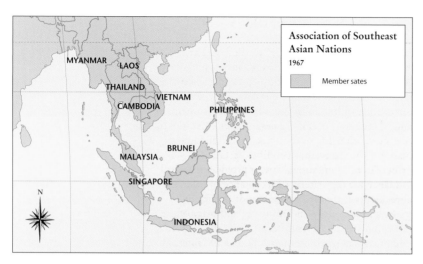

Association of Southeast Asian Nations
1967

Member sates

Cuban Missile crisis the following year triggered a movement to acquire similar status for Latin America, and the creation of a Commission, COPREDAL, to negotiate its implementation. The process was fraught; Brazil and Argentina harbored ambitions to acquire nuclear capacity for peaceful purposes and endemic political instability impeded progress. The eventual treaty was signed in Mexico by all Latin American states (bar Cuba, but with the addition of Jamaica and Trinidad & Tobago). Protocol I invited signatures of colonial powers on the continent (France, UK, Netherlands) to respect the agreement, by neither using or storing nuclear weapons in the region. Protocol II called for like assurances from the nuclear powers (all the official holders of nuclear weapons had signed by 1978). Cuba eventually signed in 2002, bringing the treaty into force throughout the region.

ASSOCIATION OF SOUTH EAST ASIAN NATIONS (ASEAN) DECLARATION 1967

The ASEAN Declaration was brokered by Thailand, which, at the time, was mediating territorial disputes between the Philippines, Indonesia, and Malaysia. With the Vietnamese conflict reaching its height, a mutual recognition dawned that collective economic progress and the preservation of territorial integrity in the region was best served by cooperation. With the inclusion of Singapore, the parties to the Declaration affirmed their mutual "primary responsibility for strengthening economic and social stability in the region" and, pointedly, "all foreign bases are temporary and remain only with the express concurrence of the countries concerned and are not intended to be used… to subvert the national independence… of states in the area." The bureaucratic machinery was initially modest with annual meetings of foreign ministers proposed, a Standing Committee and dedicated National Secretariats. The Association declared it was open to all states in the Southeast Asian region that subscribed to its "principles and purposes."

WORLD INTELLECTUAL PROPERTY ORGANIZATION CONVENTION 1967

WIPO's genesis can be traced to the Paris and Berne Conventions of 1883 and 1886, which established protections for intellectual property in relation to industrial applications, and literary/artistic works, respectively. Their bureaus were unified in 1893, before replacement by WIPO in 1970 through the 1967 Convention. WIPO has three main organs: the General Assembly, the Conference (the competent body for adopting changes to the Convention) and the Coordination Committee. WIPO's remit comprises the classification and standardization of

application and which involve an inventive step." Inventions that would prove deleterious to public order and morality are excluded, as are plant and animal varieties, with the exception of micro-biological processes and products.

MERGER TREATY 1965

Since the Treaty of Rome came into force in 1958, three European Communities ran in parallel: the original European Coal and Steel Community (ECSC), the European Economic Community (EEC), and the European Atomic Community (EURATOM). The process of unification had already begun, with the three communities sharing the Parliamentary Assembly and the Court of Justice. The effect of the Merger Treaty was to roll EURATOM and the ECSC into the EEC. Each Community remained legally independent but, henceforth, would have just one governing Commission and Council.

TREATY OF BASIC RELATIONS BETWEEN JAPAN AND THE REPUBLIC OF KOREA 1965

The strained relations between Japan and its previous colony Korea were gradually addressed over a series of conferences after the Treaty of San Francisco (1951), with normalization finally achieved by the 1965 treaty. By its provisions, the parties confirmed "the problem concerning properties, rights and interests of the two contracting parties and their nationals… is settled completely and finally." The price-tag for Japan was $800 million in grants and loans, by which, it understood, it would obtain exemption from further claims in respect of the excesses of the period of its occupation (1910–45).

TREATY OF TLATELOLCO 1967

The Antarctic Treaty (1961) established Antarctica as the world's first nuclear-weapon-free zone. The

intellectual property rights; the setting of standards for protection and enforcement of those rights; legal and technical assistance in the field to its member states; registration and filing activities.

OUTER SPACE TREATY 1967

The Committee on Peaceful Uses of Outer Space was established by the United Nations in 1959 in the preliminary stages of the US-Soviet Space Race. Its deliberations eventually produced the Outer Space treaty, which came into force in October 1967. The treaty exclusively limits use of the Moon and other celestial bodies to peaceful purposes, barring their use for weapons testing or military installations. Weapons of mass destruction are further barred from being placed in orbit round the Earth, Moon or any other celestial body. It further asserts that the exploration and exploitation of the resources of outer space are the "common heritage of mankind" and should not be subject to national appropriation. The one exception to this rule was space objects for which jurisdiction and control would be retained by the launching state – together with liability for any damage the object might cause.

TREATY ON THE NON-PROLIFERATION OF NUCLEAR WEAPONS (NPT) 1968

The Partial Nuclear Test Ban Treaty (1963) did not address the issue of proliferation, nor was it signed by two of the already extant nuclear-weapons-states (NWS): France and China. Central to NPT is the implicit bargain that its NWS parties will both pursue disarmament and share peaceful nuclear technology with its non-NWS parties, in return for the commitment by the latter never to acquire such weapons from any source. It also calls for all parties to pursue negotiations for the cessation of the nuclear arms race. Significant non-signatories were India, Pakistan, and Israel.

INTERNATIONAL CONVENTION ON THE ELIMINATION OF ALL FORMS OF RACIAL DISCRIMINATION (ICERD) 1969

Prior to ICERD's adoption in 1965, the United Nations General Assembly passed two resolutions condemning racial discrimination; its eventual scope omitted reference to religious discrimination, largely through pressure from Arab states. Its core provisions define racial discrimination (including by caste) – distinctions made by citizenship and positive discrimination are excluded. All races are to have equality before the law and effective protections and remedies for discrimination. Apartheid, discriminatory employment practices, propaganda based on racial supremacism, hate speech, and hate crime are all condemned.

VIENNA CONVENTION ON LAW OF TREATIES (VCLT) 1969

The "treaty on treaties" helpfully defines a treaty in Article I as "an international agreement concluded between states in written form and governed by international law, whether embodied in a single instrument or in two or more related instruments and whatever its particular designation." Created by the International Law Commission of the United Nations, the Convention codifies certain key principles of international law. It provides practical guidance for the criteria of acceptance of informal agreements as treaties – memoranda, letters of understanding etc. – including the authority of the respective parties, the substance of the undertaking, circumstances surrounding adoption and "internal acceptance as a treaty." Even countries that have not ratified the Convention have recognized its force as customary law.

ARUSHA AGREEMENT 1969

The Yaoundé Convention (1963) was an association agreement between the European Economic Community (EEC) and the Associated African States and Madagascar (AASM), mainly comprising ex-French and Belgian colonies, based on the principles of free trade and with measures of financial and technical assistance for the African counterparties. After the British applied for EEC accession in 1961, African Commonwealth countries began to seek agreements with the EEC; the former British East African colonies, Kenya, Uganda and Tanzania, concluded the Arusha Agreement. The Agreement, which was subject to Franco-Belgian pressure to avoid disadvantaging their ex-colonies, led to tariff quotas on commodities such as coffee, cloves, and tinned pineapples. In addition, minimum price guarantees and other defense mechanisms continued to protect East African agriculture against EEC competition. The Arusha Agreement would be linked up with Yaoundé association by the Lomé Convention (1975).

HAGUE 'HIJACKING' CONVENTION 1970

The hijacking of aircraft began to escalate in the late 1960s, and its association with political terrorism alarmed authorities. The Convention prohibited "unlawful acts of seizure or exercise of control of aircraft." Only civilian aircraft and offenses committed in-flight were covered. Furthermore, to qualify, either the place of take-off or place of landing had to be outside the territory of the state to which the aircraft was registered. Both international and domestic flights were otherwise covered. The Convention demands severe penalties for the crime of hijacking and the greatest measure of

1970–1972

assistance between party states in the apprehension, extradition, and prosecution of offenders. Where no other state requests extradition, a party state commits to conduct their prosecution though their own courts.

PATENT CO-OPERATION TREATY (PCT) 1970

The PCT represents a culmination of the often tortuous history of efforts to streamline the patenting process, making it feasible to seek simultaneous patent protection for an invention in many countries with a single international patent application rather than making a multitude of national filings. The PCT procedure commences with filing of an international application (either nationally or with the World Intellectual Property Organization (WIPO). An International Searching Authority (IAS) then provides a written assessment of the invention's patentability. This is followed by International Publication and, optionally, supplementary searches and examinations. Unfortunately, there is still no international patent so, after this process has been satisfactorily completed, the applicant must then pursue the grant of their patent with their national or regional offices, armed with the documentation of their international application and a pre-established, internationally recognized filing date.

BOUNDARY TREATY 1970

The eastern Mexican-American border is formed by the Rio Grande, a river whose channel is in constant flux. This created a rich store of potential boundary disputes, which led to the formation of the joint International Boundary and Water Commission (1889) to preserve the river course and demarcate the land boundary where natural and human activity resulted in its alteration. A key principle decreed accretion (gradual change) of the river course would alter the boundary, while avulsion (sudden change) would not: inevitably this led to definitional disputes, notably over the El Chamizal tract eventually resolved in 1963. The solution adopted by the Boundary Treaty was a joint US-Mexican construction project to replace the river back to its approximate course of 1907, with appropriate exchanges of tracts of land between Presidio, Texas and Ojinaga in Chihuahua. Costs were shared and the channel reinforced to deter future riverine misbehavior.

TREATY OF WARSAW 1970

The Treaty of Zgorzelec (1950) agreed the Oder-Neisse border between East Germany and Poland, which had been determined by the post-World

War II Potsdam Agreement. This represented a loss of German territory compared with its pre-war borders, and West Germany refused to recognize this agreement hatched between two Soviet bloc countries. In 1969, the new West German Chancellor, Willy Brandt, embarked on a radical new policy of rapprochement with the Soviet bloc, termed his Ostpolitik. The Treaty of Moscow (1970) with the Soviet Union includes the commitment by both parties that "they regard today and shall in future regard the frontiers of all states in Europe as inviolable such as they are on the date of signature of the present treaty, including the Oder-Neisse line." The subsequent Warsaw Treaty with the Polish government, which restated German acceptance of Oder-Neisse, was thus a formality, but of high symbolic significance.

CONVENTION ON PSYCHOTROPIC SUBSTANCES 1971

Pharmaceutical ingenuity continually bedeviled conventions controlling narcotics. The 1961 Single Convention had extended regulation to cannabis derivatives, but the signature drugs of the ensuing decade would be psychoactive, including LSD and Mescaline, as well as amphetamines and barbiturates. In 1968 the United Nations Economic and Social Council (ECOSOC) passed a resolution calling for the limitation of their use to medical and scientific purposes and the imposition of import/export restrictions. Meanwhile, ECOSOC's Commission on Narcotics argued over whether the Single Convention could be interpreted to apply to psychoactive drugs. Annoyed by this tardiness, the US and Canada enacted their own legislation before the 1971 Convention, which placed restrictions on four schedules of psychoactive drugs. The United Kingdom Misuse of Drugs Act (1971) and US Psychotropic Substances Act (1978) were national implementations of the Convention's provisions.

FIVE POWER DEFENSE ARRANGEMENTS (FPDA) 1971

In 1967, the United Kingdom decided to withdraw its military presence east of Suez, necessitating some successor arrangement to the Anglo-Malayan Defense Agreement upon its expiry in 1971. The FPDA, concluded between the United Kingdom, Malaysia, Singapore, Australia, and New Zealand, was effectively toothless: it merely provided that the Five Powers should consult immediately in the event of an armed attack on Malaysia and Singapore. There is no commitment to military intervention. However, the establishment of an Integrated Air Defense System under Australian control at RMAF Butterworth in Malaysia, and the holding of annual joint military and naval exercises by the Five Powers reinforced its deterrent value and the Arrangements have proved durable.

RAMSAR CONVENTION 1971

The Convention covers the conservation and sustainable use of wetlands of international importance and has been extended to over 2,000 sites worldwide. The largest single protected site is around the Pastraza River in Peru. Bolivia has the largest total protected area of any single country (greater in size than England), while the United Kingdom has the most individual protected sites (170). A triennial Conference of representatives of the Contracting Parties is a forum for policy formulation, and the Convention is upheld with cooperation between a number of international conservation agencies, including the World Wildlife Fund, the International Water Management Institute, Birdlife International and the Wildfowl and Wetlands Trust.

INTERNATIONAL PATENT CLASSIFICATION (IPC) AGREEMENT 1971

The Strasbourg IPC Agreement sets out the International Patent Classification system, with eight main sections comprising: Physics; Electricity; Human Necessities; Textiles, Paper; Chemistry, Metallurgy; Fixed Constructions; Performing Operations; Transporting; and Mechanical Engineering, Lighting, Heating, Weapons. The hierarchical system descends to 129 classes, 639 subclasses and close to 70,000 groups and subgroups. Each patent publication is assigned a symbol, of which the first letter (A-H) relates to the overall section, with the succeeding alphanumeric characters supplying its precise ascription; some patent publications with broader application are assigned more than one symbol. The IPC is under continuous review, and new editions are published annually.

SEABED ARMS CONTROL TREATY 1971

The Seabed Treaty made a Nuclear-Weapon-Free-Zones (NWFZ) of the ocean floor, at least outside coastal waters, forbidding the emplacement there of both nuclear weapons and other weapons of mass destruction. It also asserted that the exploration and exploitation of the seabed should be for solely peaceful purposes. The Soviet Union presented a draft of the treaty that called for complete demilitarization of the seabed beyond 12 miles (19 km). The United States countered with a proposal to ban placement of nuclear weapons and weapons of mass destruction on the seabed more than 3 miles (5 km) from the coast: the resultant ban of nuclear wepaons beyond 12 miles was the compromise.

CONVENTION FOR THE SUPPRESSION OF UNLAWFUL ACTS AGAINST THE SAFETY OF CIVIL AVIATION ("SABOTAGE" CONVENTION) 1971

The Hague "Hijacking Convention" (1970) defined the crime, but its major deficiency was that it only covered in-flight offenses. In Montreal, the Sabotage Convention addressed these omissions, criminalizing a list of offenses, including destroying or damaging air navigation facilities, or placing a device or substance on an aircraft that was likely to cause its damage or destruction, as was sabotage of an aircraft being serviced. In-flight sabotage or violence against persons, and "communicating information which is known to be false," which might jeopardize in-flight safety, were also addressed. More thorough than the Hijacking Convention, it still concentrated on acts against, or on, the aircraft itself: a 1988 Protocol added acts of airport sabotage.

INDO-SOVIET TREATY OF FRIENDSHIP AND CO-OPERATION 1971

India enjoyed cordial relations with the Soviet Union, fanned by Soviet premier Khrushchev in his 1955 visit, when he supported Indian sovereignty in both Kashmir (disputed with Pakistan) and Goa (then a Portuguese enclave). Growing Pakistani linkage with the United States, including arms sales, encouraged India to seek closer ties with the Soviets. Then, in 1971, East Pakistan's attempted secession led to brutal suppression and Indian intervention on the side of the rebels. India most feared China's entry into the war on the side of the Pakistani government. The treaty was aimed at averting this threat. Concluded in August, India entered the war against Pakistan on 3 December, and had achieved a crushing victory in weeks, leading to the creation of the independent state of Bangladesh.

ADDIS ABABA AGREEMENT 1972

In 1946, the colonial government in the Anglo-Egyptian condominium of Sudan, unilaterally united the region, previously administered separately as North and South Sudan. This led to a 17-year insurgency in the Christian/animist sub-Saharan South against the rule of the Muslim Arab North, beginning shortly before independence in 1956. At Addis Ababa, representatives of the Sudanese government and the South Sudan Liberation Movement met to negotiate an end to the war with ecumenical mediation. The South Sudan Autonomous Region was established, with a separate legislature and executive body. The Anya Nya ("Snake Venom") rebel fighters were to be integrated into the Sudanese military and police. A decade of relative peace ensued, with substantial

1972–1973

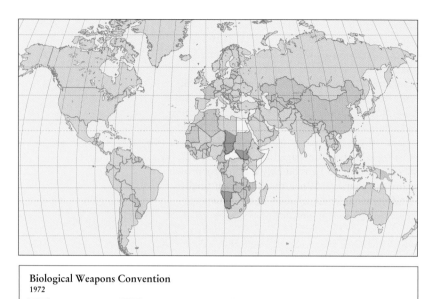

the German Democratic Republic (East Germany). Relations reached their nadir with the Soviet blockade of West Berlin (1959–62) during which the Berlin Wall was erected. Brandt's Ostpolitik began with the Moscow Treaty (1970) and Four Powers Agreement (1971), whereby the post-war status quo was mutually recognized for the first time. It bore fruit with the Transit Agreement (May 1972) guaranteeing access to West Berlin through East Germany. The Basic Treaty (December 1972) was a logical culmination, with East and West Germany recognizing one another as sovereign states for the first time.

BIOLOGICAL WEAPONS CONVENTION 1972
Herodotus describes Scythian archers dipping their arrows in rotting corpses in the 5th century BCE, perhaps the first recorded use of biological warfare. The Germans pioneered the industrialization of techniques in World War I, experimenting with anthrax, cholera, wheat fungus and, allegedly, plague. The 1925 Geneva Protocol banned chemical and biological weapons, with 108 signatory states but no apparatus for inspection or verification. In World War II, both Britain and the United States developed biological warfare research facilities, while the Japanese experimented on prisoners of war in Manchuria. The Biological Weapons Convention obliges signatories to "never in any circumstances to develop, produce, stockpile or otherwise acquire or retain microbial or other biological agents, or toxins." By 2015, 22 original members had expanded to 178, with frequent conferences tackling compliance and verification issues.

CONVENTION FOR THE CONSERVATION OF SINO-JAPANESE JOINT COMMUNIQUÉ 1972
After its formation in 1949, the People's Republic of China (PRC) established quite cordial relations with Japan, signing a treaty of cooperation in 1950. Relations chilled with Japanese recognition of Taiwan, but were renewed after the breakdown of Sino-Soviet relations in the early 1960s. After another reverse during the Cultural Revolution, President Richard Nixon's visit to Beijing in China (1972) produced a thaw, accentuated by the Japanese prime minister's coterminous promotion of better links between the two nations. By the Communiqué, and confirmatory Convention, Japan recognized the PRC as the legitimate government of China, and affirmed the ban on expansionism set out in Article 8 of the 1945 Potsdam Convention. Thereafter, diplomacy stalled somewhat until Chinese commercial liberalization from 1978 under the leadership of Deng Xiaoping. The 1980s

Arab petrodollar investment in Sudanese wheat, cotton, and sugar production. Then President Nimeiri of Sudan reneged on the treaty, imposing Sharia law, and abolishing the Autonomous Region. This time the civil war would last 22 years, one of the longest on record.

ANTI-BALLISTIC MISSILE TREATY 1972
The potential catastrophic consequence of the nuclear arms race drew the United States and the Soviet Union to the negotiating table in the 1970s. It became clear that the most effective way to curb the race was to limit each nation's capacity to mount defenses against such attack, introducing the ultimate deterrent of mutually assured destruction. The Anti-Ballistic Missile (ABM) Treaty confined each country to two fixed, ground-based defense sites of 100 missile interceptors each. One site was dedicated to the protection of the national capital, while the second could guard an intercontinental ballistic missile (ICBM) launch site. The treaty cleared the way to strategic arms limitation talks (SALT) from the 1980s, which led to dramatic reciprocal reductions in nuclear armories. President George W. Bush unilaterally withdrew from the treaty in 2001, post 9/11, arguing that it had become obsolescent in the face of international terrorism.

BASIC TREATY 1972
Willy Brandt, the West German Chancellor (1969–74) forged a new policy of détente towards the Soviet Bloc, abandoning the post-war Hallstein Doctrine, which deemed it an unfriendly act for any nation to recognize or engage in diplomatic relations with

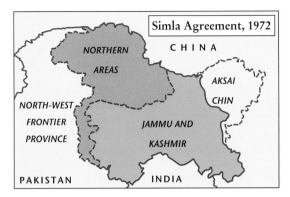

would prove a Golden Age of rapidly expanding commercial and diplomatic links between two of the world's fastest growing economies.

SIMLA AGREEMENT 1972
After independence in 1947, relations were often fraught between India and Pakistan, stoked by an estimated one million deaths associated with the process of partition. Kashmir, a predominantly Muslim area under disputed Indian control, deteriorated into open conflict in 1947 and 1965. The War of Independence (1971), which led to the formation of Bangladesh, was only successful because of Indian naval and military support, which included the bombardment of Bangladesh. The Simla Agreement was an attempt to normalize relations through bilateral negotiations. The Agreement defined the ceasefire line of the 1971 as the Line of Control, which India insists is the new border: Pakistan, which would thereby sacrifice territory, strenuously disagrees. The succeeding decades have witnessed sporadic, frequently futile, encroachments by both sides.

EUROPEAN PATENT CONVENTION 1973
The Patent Cooperation Treaty (1970) introduced an international system of application, registration, and search for patents. The European Patent Convention established an autonomous legal system for the granting of patents within its membership. The Convention built on preliminary work by the Council for Europe, which led to the Strasbourg Patent Convention (1963). The European Convention established a unified apparatus for the grant, validation, and extension of patents, as well as common procedures for enforcement, considering opposition and determining infringement.

VIENTIANE TREATY 1973
The Kingdom of Laos gained independence (1953) during the disintegration of French Indochina, but promptly dissolved into factional fighting led by three princely contenders for power. As the war in

neighboring Vietnam grew in magnitude during the 1960s, this crystallized into a struggle between the Royal Lao Army and the Communist Pathet Lao. The Pathet Lao received military support from the Viet Cong insurgents, in return they kept the Ho Chi Minh supply route open for their allies. This drew the ire of the Viet Cong's American enemies, leading to a massive bombing campaign directed at Laos. When the Paris Peace Accords (January 1973) signaled US disengagement from Vietnam, the warring factions in Laos quickly reached their own accord at Vientiane. When the Americans finally withdrew from Vietnam in 1975, the Pathet Lao capitalized by seizing power in Laos.

AGREEMENT ON THE TRANSFER OF CORPSES 1973
In 1937, 18 countries signed a convention regarding the transnational conveyance of corpses. The Strasbourg Agreement (1973) updated that Convention, setting out to lay down a uniform "mortuary *laissez-passer*," defining the conditions that could be required by a country for the "dispatch, transit, admission of corpses on its territory." Bodies of victims of infectious disease could now be transported, without the earlier requirement of one year's quarantine. Transport documentation was streamlined and standardized, and quality standards specified for coffins (thickness of wood, zinc or lead-lining etc.). Further conditions related to embalming and cremation, personal effects, and coffins containing multiple remains.

JAPAN-AUSTRALIA MIGRATORY BIRD AGREEMENT 1973
In 1900, one enlightened by-product of the Scramble for Africa was an international convention for the conservation of its wildlife. Nevertheless, most early initiatives were prompted by commercial interests. The United States concluded bilateral agreements with its neighbors for the protection of migratory birds during World War I, serving as models for future agreements. The American ornithologist T. Gilbert Pearson was instrumental in the creation of the International Committee for Bird Protection (1922), a non-governmental body that coordinated the activities of national associations for avian conservation. Australia entered bilateral agreements with Japan (1974) and China (1986), which established protocols for conservation of migratory bird species, their habitats and routes, together with research and enforcement initiatives.

THRESHOLD TEST BAN TREATY 1974
The 1974 treaty between the United States and the Soviet Union limited underground testing to 150

1973–1979

kilotons (approximately the power of the bomb dropped on Hiroshima in 1945). It also put in place complex systems of verification based on measures of seismic velocity and the geology of the test site. These were amplified in 1988, when the two powers agreed reciprocal onsite verification by the counterparties at testing events. Limitations were extended to so-called peaceful nuclear explosions (e.g. blasting tunnels through rock) in 1976.

TREATY OF OSIMO 1975
When Italy signed a peace treaty with the victorious Allied powers in 1947, the vexed question of the treatment of Trieste was left pending. The Treaty of Osimo with the then Republic of Yugoslavia was designed to achieve a definitive settlement. Trieste was divided into two zones. Zone A, including the city center and port of Trieste, remained in Italian hands. Zone B, comprising the southern suburbs and hinterland of the city, was allocated to Yugoslavia. In addition, Yugoslavia was granted free access to the port. Confusingly, Yugoslavia retained control of several villages in Zone A with predominantly Slav populations. The treaty excited controversy in Italy, both because of the secrecy with which the negotiations were conducted, and because sections of Istria with a long tradition of Italian (or Venetian) occupation were ceded. In the wake of the dissolution of Yugoslavia in the 1990s, the affected successor states, Croatia and Slovenia quickly endorsed the treaty.

TREATY OF LAGOS 1975
The Economic Community of West African States (ECOWAS), created through the Treaty of Lagos, was the first such organization formed in the wake of widespread independence and colonization. The Community has developed a broad remit, with projects for monetary union between, respectively, its Francophone and Anglophone members, and ambitions to harmonize fiscal policies and introduce a common market. Members have also cooperated in regional infrastructure projects and mobilizing peacekeeping forces to defuse conflicts in the region, for example Liberia (2003) and Gambia (2017). The Community has a Parliament, Court of Justice, Commission, and a non-aggression protocol between members.

ENVIRONMENTAL MODIFICATION CONVENTION 1976
During the Vietnam war, American forces made extensive use of the defoliant Agent Orange to remove forest cover for insurgents. Operation Popeye was an attempt to extend the monsoon by seeding clouds with iodide salts, to render the Ho Chi Minh Trail, the main insurgent supply route, impassable. Concern about the deployment of such techniques – first expressed in the US Senate – led to bilateral discussions with the Soviet Union, then the 1976 Convention. Since its 1977 ratification, the Convention has been criticized for the vagueness of its provisions, which refer to "widespread, long-lasting and severe" effects. In response, these terms were more tightly defined (1984). The Convention only tackles environmental modification for military or hostile purposes and has not been employed to address subsequent intra-state use, for instance herbicides deployed against Colombian insurgents, and deliberate deforestation in Indonesia and Brazil.

TREATY OF AMITY AND COOPERATION IN SOUTHEAST ASIA 1976
In 1976, the original founding members of ASEAN (Indonesia, Thailand, the Philippines, Malaysia, and Singapore) cemented and extended the ASEAN remit through the Treaty of Amity and Cooperation. By the turn of the century, all Southeast Asian countries (bar East Timor) had signed up to the treaty. Its principles include reciprocal respect of national sovereignty, peaceful dispute resolution, promotion of cooperation, and renunciation of the use of force. Thereafter, its enrolment was dramatically expanded, with participation by states as diverse as Russia, India, Pakistan, Japan, and Australia. In 1992 an ASEAN free trade zone was created, its importance magnified by the rapid growth and dynamism of the constituent economies.

CONVENTION ON LIMITATION OF LIABILITY FOR MARITIME CLAIMS (LLMC) 1976
Ships engaged in international trade commonly pass through the territorial waters, and visit the ports, of multiple states during a single voyage. Recognizing the difficulty and prohibitive expense if they had to comply with a patchwork of different national rules and standards, the International Maritime Organization (IMO) was founded (1948) as a specialized agency of the United Nation with a remit to standardize regulations. In 1957, a Convention limited the liability of the owners of sea-going ships, but its provisions were superseded by escalating potential costs, particularly from oil pollution. The LLMC was introduced to bring liability limits up to date, with a scale of compensation related to vessel tonnage and magnified for loss of life.

TORRIJOS-CARTER TREATIES 1977
Prior to the building of the Panama Canal, the United States acquired "perpetual" control of the Canal Zone, in questionable circumstances,

first by abetting Panamanian independence then concluding the self-serving Hay-Bunau-Varilla Treaty with a diplomat of dubious standing and authority. In 1964, Panamanians tried to hoist their national flag in the Zone, leading to clashes with US citizens. Early attempts to negotiate a settlement were confounded by political instability in Panama, eventually resulting in Omar Torrijos seizing power in a coup (1968). By 1975, US Secretary of State Henry Kissinger was warning that, if an agreement was not finalized, "there will be riots all over South America." In 1977, President Carter concluded three treaties that collectively transferred the Zone to Panama, but sanctioned US military intervention if its free passage or neutrality were threatened.

TREATY OF PEACE AND FRIENDSHIP BETWEEN JAPAN AND THE PEOPLE'S REPUBLIC OF CHINA 1977

By 1977, Deng Xiaoping was emerging as China's paramount leader, and promoting his program of the Four Modernizations of the economy, agriculture, technology, and national defense. Relations with Japan had already ameliorated through the Joint Communiqué of 1973, and subsequent Convention; Japan's economic miracle now rendered it an ideal beneficiary for Deng's move away from Mao's focus on the Soviet Union. Three issues remained: Taiwan, which Deng agreed to shelve; an anti-hegemony clause, by which both parties agreed neither to seek or support attempts to gain ascendancy in the Asia-Pacific region; and a third party clause, intended to avoid casting the Soviet Union as "gooseberry" of the rapprochement. Deng, who had proclaimed "poverty is not socialism, to be rich is glorious," capitalized on the treaty by visiting the tiger economies of Southeast Asia, and most momentously, a US state visit in 1979, ushering in an era of *détente*.

MOON TREATY 1977

The Outer Space Treaty (1967) established a basic legal framework governing state actions in space. Sponsored by the United Nations Legal Committee, the Moon Treaty aimed to build on the earlier treaty, by decreeing that jurisdiction of all celestial bodies belongs to the international community. Of its eleven signatories, none is a significant player in the space race and, to date, the treaty has had little impact. The critical event was its defeat in the US Senate in 1980, largely through lobbying against its proposed bans of private property or sovereignty in Space and alteration of the environment, held to impede potential space colonization and terraforming (modifying the space environment to make it Earth-like).

THE ACCESSION TREATY (GREECE) 1979

There was a large dollop of sentimentality in Greece's relatively rapid accession into the European Union. Jean-Claude Juncker, later Head of the European Commission, recalled "we did not want to see Plato playing in the second division." While Greek status as the birthplace of democracy lubricated the move, hard-headed political calculation also factored. Greece only emerged in 1974 from military dictatorship, and cementing political stability in the eastern Mediterranean was vital; the subsequent accessions of Portugal and Spain in their post-dictatorship decade derived from similar considerations. At the time, reservations were noted in respect of Greece: its large agricultural sector, lax administration, ineffectual tax collection, and high corruption. Post-membership, Greece boomed, but did not address its structural problems. Entry to the Eurozone (2001) justified by "cooked" government accounts in the heady days following the collapse of the Soviet bloc, would, in retrospect, leave it fatally exposed to any economic downturn.

TREATY OF MONTEVIDEO 1980

The Latin American Free Trade Association (LAFTA), formed in 1960, was hamstrung in its aim to create a continental tariff-free zone by the vast disparities between component states in economic development. Montevideo replaced LAFTA with a new model. The LAIA (Latin American Integration Association) dropped the all-out pursuit of free trade for a network of bilateral preference agreements, which could be more easily attuned to take out account of developmental variance. Cuba joined the Association as an observer before becoming a full member in 1999. Later, the membership was divided into three tiers according to development levels (with scope for adjustment over time), with Argentina, Brazil, and Mexico initially classified at the highest level.

AUSTRALIA NEW ZEALAND CLOSER ECONOMIC RELATIONS (CER) 1983

The entry of the United Kingdom, a major export market for both Australia and New Zealand, into the European Economic Community (1973) involved a major trade reorientation. The two countries had signed a Free Trade Agreement in 1965, but its implementation became clogged by bureaucracy, requiring a remedy: CER was the result. It proved effective, achieving the removal of all tariffs by 1990. It promulgated some radical simplifications: any goods that can be legally sold in one country can be legally sold in the other; with a few specified exclusions, the same latitude is extended to both services and occupations. Nevertheless, there are

1980–1985

major differences between the size and focus of the economies. Australia is New Zealand's major trading partner, while New Zealand ranks sixth for Australia behind China, Japan, the US, Korea, and Singapore.

SINO-BRITISH JOINT DECLARATION 1984
In 1898, when the British negotiated a 99-year lease for Hong Kong with the Qing Dynasty, they claimed it was "as good as forever." The Chinese, however, had long memories, and by the 1980s made it clear they intended to assume control on expiry of the lease. This created uncertainty in Hong Kong and threatened to undermine its dynamism as a financial and commercial powerhouse. By the Joint Declaration, the United Kingdom agreed to hand over Hong Kong on 1 July 1997. In return, China committed to preserving Hong Kong's territorial integrity, and agreed it would form a Special Administrative Region with a high degree of economic and political autonomy. It would retain its status as a free port, remain an international financial center with its own currency, be governed by its own inhabitants, and its Basic Laws would be preserved.

NIKOMATI ACCORD 1984
Following a long guerrilla war, the Marxist FRELIMO liberation movement achieved independence for Mozambique from Portugal under their leader, Samora Machel (1975). FRELIMO then faced an equally long insurgency from the right-wing RENAMO faction, which received support from the white-minority governments in neighboring South Africa and Rhodesia. FRELIMO returned the favor by offering aid and sanctuary to the African National Congress (ANC), who were resisting South Africa's apartheid regime. RENAMO's campaign of terror and economic sabotage forced FRELIMO to the negotiating table with South Africa. By the Nkomati Accord they agreed to desist from assisting the ANC in return for South Africa's promise to withdraw support for RENAMO. Neither party subsequently observed the Accord. Mozambique's civil war concluded in 1992, with a transition to (questionable) democracy.

OUJDA TREATY 1984
The idea of a Greater Maghreb – a political union of the neighboring North African states from Morocco to Libya – has a cultural and historical logic. For a thousand years, much of the area has been under common rule, from the Moroccan Almoravid dynasty to the Ottomans and French. There was a degree of cooperation between respective liberation movements against French and Italian colonialism but, with independence, this quickly disappeared.

In 1983, Tunisia, Algeria, and Mauretania signed the Maghreb Fraternity and Cooperation Treaty, leaving Morocco isolated. This was exacerbated by Mauretania's recognition of the Sahrawi Arab Democratic Republic, the secessionist state in territory claimed by Morocco in the Western Sahara. On the rebound, Morocco signed the Oujda Treaty with the grandiose Colonel Gaddafi of Libya, proclaiming a union of states, which looked to the creation of a Greater Arab Maghreb. But the egos involved were large, the political attention spans small: Gaddafi was soon plotting pan-African domination.

TREATY OF PEACE AND FRIENDSHIP BETWEEN CHILE AND ARGENTINA 1984
In 1978, the Beagle Conflict erupted between Chile and Argentina over three small islands at the eastern mouth of the Beagle Channel between the Atlantic and Pacific Ocean. At the time both countries were ruled by military dictatorships that had overthrown democratic governments and maintained power through ruthless suppression of dissent. With both sides threatening war, Pope John Paul II consented to mediate: a tortuous five-year negotiation ensued before agreement was reached. By the 1984 treaty, a complex disposition of protected navigation rights and exclusive economic zones managed to save face on both sides. Nueva, Picton and Lennox, the three islands whose ownership sparked the long dispute, are nowhere mentioned in the treaty.

PLAZA ACCORD 1985
The cornerstone of international monetary and exchange rate management was the Bretton Woods System agreed in 1944, which pegged currencies to the price of gold, and established the US dollar, also tied to the price of gold, as the global reserve currency. The system was abandoned in 1973 due to chronic dollar overvaluation as the US economy, and its global dominance, weakened. In the early 1980s, the US economy and the valuation of the dollar rebounded. As a consequence, US manufacturing struggled to export, while the other major developed economies were experiencing negative growth and massive trade surpluses. In 1985 at the Plaza Hotel, New York, the G5 (US, Japan, West Germany, France, and United Kingdom) agreed collective intervention in the foreign exchange markets to weaken the US dollar. Judged by this objective, the Accord was an undoubted success with the yen/dollar exchange rate halving in three years.

SCHENGEN AGREEMENT 1985
The Treaty of Rome (1957) was the foundation document of the future European Union and

enshrined the core principle of a single market in labor, goods, services and capital, with free movement of people an axiomatic consequence. The constituent Benelux countries (Belgium, Netherlands, Luxembourg) introduced freedom of movement as early as 1960. In 1985, they agreed at Schengen with France and West Germany to collectively move toward the abolition of border controls, including the harmonization of visa controls, and sight-only vehicle checks. In 1990 the Schengen Convention broadened the original agreement; all members of the Union subscribed by 1997, bar England and Ireland, who gained opt-outs. The Schengen Convention is now embedded in the *acquis communautaire*, the "acquired" common law of the European Union, and three non-Union members have joined the Schengen Area: Norway, Iceland, and Switzerland.

HELSINKI AGREEMENT ON REDUCTION OF SULFUR EMISSIONS 1985

Perhaps the first attempt to tackle trans-boundary pollution, whereby pollutants emitted in one country are deposited in another, was the 1909 Boundary Waters Treaty between the United States and the United Kingdom (in respect of

Canada). Concerns about growing marine pollution, particularly by oil, led to the London Ocean Dumping Convention (1972). Focus then turned to atmospheric pollution, and the growing damage to vegetation, especially trees, by the phenomenon of acid rain. This was adjudged to result from sulfur emissions, which were addressed in the Helsinki Agreement by the United Nations Economic Committee for Europe (UNECE). The Convention called for 30 percent reduction in national annual sulfur emissions or their trans-boundary fluxes by 1993. Overall the Convention obtained 25 (European) signatories. The Agreement was supplemented at Oslo (1994) and served as a model for a string of similar protocols.

TREATY OF RAROTONGA 1985

As developed nations increasingly became aware of the risks of radioactive contamination, the remote South Pacific became the nuclear weaponry test location of choice for the US, France, and the UK. The idea of a South Pacific nuclear-free zone was first mooted at a regional forum in Canberra (1983), and adopted at Rarotonga two years later. Most of the major South Pacific nations ratified the treaty, including Australia, New Zealand, Fiji, and Papua

Schengen Agreement
1985

☐ EU member states participating
▨ EU member states not participating/Obliged to join
☐ EU member states with an opt-out
▨ non-EU member states participating

1985–1989

New Guinea. It prohibits testing, usage, stationing, and possession of nuclear weapons in the waters surrounding the Pacific States, and has since been ratified by all the declared nuclear powers.

CHINA-AUSTRALIA MIGRATORY BIRD AGREEMENT (CAMBA) 1986

Australia has been especially proactive in its efforts to protect its migratory bird species, entering into bilateral agreements with Japan (1974), China (1986), and Korea (2007). The route from East Asia to Australia is of major importance to migratory birds, and given its size, China is a key link, both as a point of origin, destination, and refueling stop for birds in passage. CAMBA provided for the conservation of important habitats, including the establishment of sanctuaries, the regulation of hunting (particularly, timing of hunting seasons), and the commissioning of joint research programs to monitor bird population levels. Nevertheless, China's meteoric economic growth remains a challenge. In 2015 treaty-derived research revealed the near collapse of the tidal flats ecosystem on the shoreline of the Yellow Sea. The research also reveals various breeds of sandpiper suffering heavy impact, while populations of whimbrels, stints, and turnstones proved somewhat more resilient.

CONVENTION ON EARLY NOTIFICATION OF A NUCLEAR ACCIDENT 1986

The International Atomic Energy Agency (IAEA) was established in 1957. It is autonomous but reports through the United Nations (UN) General Assembly and Security Council. Two months after its creation, the Kyshtym nuclear accident occurred in the Urals, but was hushed up by the former Soviet Union. Other incidents took place in the following decades, including Three Mile Island in the United States (1979). However, it was the Chernobyl reactor explosion in Ukraine in the former Soviet Union (April 1986) that triggered the Notification Convention. Radioactive contamination from the explosion affected the Soviet Republic of Belarus and neighboring states in Scandinavia, it also dispersed through rivers and precipitation. The Convention established an early warning system for any accident with the potential for international trans-boundary release through the IAEA. All declared nuclear states have ratified the treaty, plus UN Agencies like the World Health Organization and World Meteorological Organization.

INTERMEDIATE-RANGE NUCLEAR MISSILES (IRNM) TREATY 1987

The Cold War became chillier in 1977, when the Soviet Union deployed its new class of IRNM,

the SS20. Rattled, NATO responded with its Double-Track Option. Either the Soviet Union agreed to mutual arms limitation or a massive counter-deployment would be initiated. Complex negotiations followed; an agreement was reached when Mikhail Gorbachev came to power in the Soviet Union. His new policy of *glasnost* (openness) produced the 1987 treaty with Reagan's United States. It required the counterparties to eliminate and permanently forswear all their intercontinental nuclear and conventional ballistic missiles with a range of between 313–3,440 miles (500–5,500 km). The treaty did not include sea-launched missiles. Rigorous inspection and verification protocols were appended. By 1 June 1991 a total of 2,692 missiles had been destroyed as a consequence of the treaty, followed by ten years of on-site verifications.

JOINT DECLARATION ON THE QUESTION OF MACAU 1987

The Portuguese colony of Macau, established in 1557, enjoyed a 20th-century renaissance as a gambling center before the Carnation Revolution (1974) ended dictatorship in Portugal and decolonization became the order of the day. Negotiations progressed sedately; in 1979, Beijing termed Macau Chinese territory under Portuguese administration. The Joint Declaration set out terms and a schedule for Macau's return to Chinese sovereignty as a Special Administrative System, effective 19 December 1999. As with Hong Kong, China maintains control over defense and foreign affairs, otherwise the one country, two systems dictum has been applied, with Basic Law and freedoms preserved. After the transition, Macau's economy boomed through tourism and rocketing gambling revenues.

NITROGEN OXIDE PROTOCOL 1988

The 1985 Helsinki Sulfur Emissions Protocol was effective – its targets were met, and many countries outside the Protocol voluntarily complied with its regime. However, it met with criticism for not taking into account the absolute and comparative emission levels of subscribing states at the point the target was fixed. The Sofia Protocol of 1988 in respect of Nitrogen Oxide Emissions attempted to address these concerns, introducing the concept of a national emission standard to ensure that countries with very high initial rates of emissions did not get a relatively easy ride. The Protocol also aimed to create a scientific coordinating apparatus, for the sharing of efficient control technologies. A further refinement it disseminated was "critical loads": pollutant volumes that can be demonstrated scientifically to trigger harmful effects.

UN CONVENTION AGAINST ILLICIT
TRAFFIC IN NARCOTIC DRUGS AND
PSYCHOTROPIC SUBSTANCES 1988
International narcotic regulation effectively
began with the 1909 Shanghai Conference from
which sprang the first international drug control
treaty (1912) dealing with opium and Indian
hemp. A number of supplements ensued before
the milestone Single Convention (1961), which
designated four schedules of controlled drugs, the
apparatus of control through the United Nations
Commission on Narcotic Drugs, and penal
provisions. The International Court of Justice was
designated as the arbiter of disputes concerning the
interpretation and application of the Convention,
and an International Narcotics Board was created to
monitor compliance. A 1971 Convention extended
regulation to psychotropic drugs, such as LSD.
Despite such provision, traffic in and use of illicit
narcotics continued to expand exponentially. The
1988 Convention attempted to stem the tide in
two ways: first, by targeting the organized crime
networks fueling the epidemic; second, by increasing
regulation of precursor chemicals used in the
manufacture of narcotics.

CONVENTION FOR THE SUPPRESSION OF
UNLAWFUL ACTS AGAINST THE SAFETY OF
MARITIME NAVIGATION (SUA) 1988
Attacks against sea-going vessels escalated from
the 1960s, motivated by piracy and terrorism.
Hotspots for piracy were oil tankers in the Gulf
of Guinea, commercial shipping, Vietnamese
boat people refugees in Southeast Asia, and yacht
hijackings associated with the drugs trade in the
Caribbean. Palestinian terrorists hijacked the cruise
ship *Achille Lauro* for ransom (1985), while both
the Irish Republican Army and Polisario in the
Western Sahara commissioned multiple maritime
attacks. SUA, prepared by the International
Maritime Organization (founded 1958), built upon
preceding conventions aimed at the hijacking of
aircraft. It outlaws seizure of ships by force, acts of
violence against those on board, and the planting
of destructive devices on ships. It also obliges
contracting states to extradite or prosecute offenders.

MONTREAL PROTOCOL 1989
In the 1970s, scientists detected a steady decline in
the amount of ozone in the Earth's stratosphere,
an effect which was especially pronounced over
polar regions, producing the infamous Ozone Hole
over Antarctica. The cause was determined to be
man-made agents: (hydro)chlorofluorocarbons
((H)CFCs), and halocarbons commonly used in
refrigerants, propellants and foam-blowing agents.

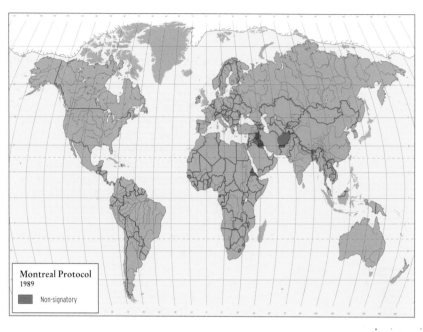

Montreal Protocol
1989
Non-signatory

Ozone insulates against ultraviolet radiation, linked
to a number of human health risks including cancer
and cataracts, and in sufficient concentrations is
deleterious to wildlife and crops. The Montreal
Protocol addressed the issue, and contained some
innovative features: an adjustment provision to
enable rapid adaptation to new scientific data;
and a trade provision, by which signatories could
only trade ozone-depleting substances with other
signatories, thus promoting enrolment to access
supplies. It became the first universally ratified (and
perhaps the most effective environmental) treaty in
United Nations history.

TREATY ON CONVENTIONAL ARMED
FORCES IN EUROPE (CFE) 1989
The Helsinki Accords (1975) were an attempt to
defuse Cold War tensions between the NATO and
Warsaw Pact nations. They brought into being
the Commission on Security Cooperation in
Europe, which, in the thaw following Soviet leader
Mikhail Gorbachev's accession, embarked on a
long consultation designed to achieve positive steps
towards demilitarization, which resulted in CFE.
The treaty sought both to reduce and balance levels
of major weapons/equipment systems between the
blocs, with individual ceilings for each component
state. Apart from national quotas, sub-regions were
defined with attendant weapons deployment limits.
Finally, no single country in either bloc was allowed
to hold more than a third of their respective total
allotment: the "sufficiency" rule. A 40-month time
limit for destroying excess weaponry was set with
thorough verification protocols.

1989–1991

TIMOR GAP TREATY 1989

The Dutch and Portuguese struggled for control of the island of Timor, a rich source of sandalwood, in the colonial era, eventually splitting the island until the Dutch west became part of Indonesia (1949). After their domestic Carnation Revolution, the Portuguese were already withdrawing from East Timor when Indonesia invaded (1975). The East Timorese then mounted a guerrilla war against Indonesian occupation, which was still raging when the Gap Treaty was concluded between Indonesia and Australia. Its purpose was to allot exploitation rights for petroleum reserves in the Timor Sea, between the island and the Australian mainland. As soon as the treaty was signed, Portugal, still recognized as the administering power in East Timor by the United Nations, instituted proceedings against Australia in the International Court of Justice. East Timor seceded from Indonesia in 1998, and replaced the Gap Treaty with the Timor Sea Treaty with Australia (2003).

WELLINGTON CONVENTION 1989

Drift nets – hung in weighted curtains from floats – were traditionally made of hemp, with large meshes, and relatively benign. In the 1950s, synthetic fibers were introduced, culminating in the Japanese monofilament deep-sea version (1976). These nets were indiscriminate, with extremely fine mesh, causing massive "by-catch" (catch not targeted by the fishermen, and usually dumped). The nets are particularly destructive of air-breathing birds and mammals, which will drown if unable to disentangle themselves rapidly. Non-biodegradable, "ghost-nets" continued to cause destruction, long after being discarded. The Wellington Convention called for a ban in the South Pacific on drift nets exceeding 1.6 miles (2.5 km) in length. In the same year, the United Nations General Assembly placed a moratorium on drift net fishing, following with a ban equivalent to the Wellington Convention (1992).

MALAYSIA-SINGAPORE POINTS OF AGREEMENT (POA) 1990

Singapore was briefly part of the newly independent Federation of Malaysia (1963–65) before being expelled to preserve the Federation's system of *bumiputera*: ethnic Malay affirmative action. Relations have been intermittently fraught ever since. The POA purported to resolve a dispute over Malaysian Railways land owned by the Malaysian government but running into the territory of Singapore. The crux of the issue related to Malay operation of an immigration checkpoint on the railway at a station within Singapore's borders. The POA's resolution was for the land round the railway to be redeveloped (with 60:40 Malay majority control), allowing the checkpoint to move to the border. All seemed settled, then in 1993, the Malaysian premier baulked.

CHEMICAL WEAPONS ACCORD 1990

In 1969, US President Richard Nixon unilaterally renounced first use of chemical weapons, while a review of their use was initiated by the Disarmament Committee of the United Nations. Iran repeatedly accused Iraq of using gas during their war (1980–88), culminating in the Halabja atrocity (1988), when Iraq used poison gas to kill several thousand Kurdish civilians. By this stage, the United States and the Soviet Union were already engaged in bilateral discussions, resulting in the 1990 Accord. Under the Accord, both countries agreed to reduce their chemical weapons stockpiles to levels equivalent to 20 percent of the amount of the US stockpile at the time of the Accord. Onsite inspections were agreed to confirm destruction. This was conceived as an interim measure, pending achievement of a universal chemical weapons ban through the United Nations.

TREATY ON THE FINAL SETTLEMENT WITH RESPECT TO GERMANY 1990

Die Wende ("the Turnaround") in East Germany happened with dizzying speed. The Peaceful Revolution triggered the fall of the Berlin Wall, then a first truly democratic election led to the landslide election of a pro-unification government (March 1990). The "Two plus Four" Conference was hastily convened in Bonn to resolve the remaining obstacles to reunification, with representatives from East/West Germany, and the four post-war guarantors of the German states: the United States, Soviet Union, United Kingdom, and France. The Soviet Union required security guarantees, and compensation for troop withdrawal from East Germany; Poland required a guarantee for its German borders; the new Germany needed to accept limits on the size of its military and to forswear nuclear weapons. The treaty was signed on 12 September: German unification took effect on 3 October. The treaty came into force on 15 March 1991, returning full sovereignty to the united Germany.

BRIONI AGREEMENT 1991

President Tito had managed to control the powerful separatist forces in post-war Yugoslavia through strength of will, cunning, and dexterity until his death in 1980. Albanians in Kosovo were already demanding autonomy when the collapse of the Soviet bloc (1989–91) witnessed a wave of popular revolution throughout eastern Europe. Croatia and Slovenia moved first, declaring independence on 25 June 1991. The Ten-Day War followed between Slovenia and Yugoslavia: an attempted

Yugoslav invasion was repulsed, before the European Community (EC) brokered a ceasefire. The Agreement reached on the Adriatic island of Brioni dealt a fatal blow to the prospects of the Federal Republic of Yugoslavia: Slovenian and Croatian independence was recognized (if postponed for three months). The rump Yugoslavia was now increasingly dominated by Serbia, and its President Slobodan Milošević, would train its guns on Croatia.

ABUJA TREATY 1991
The Organization of African Unity was founded in 1963, and while perennially criticized as a Dictators' Club, it played an active role in the eradication of colonialism on the continent, and the relief of refugees. Its record on economic development was checkered. The Lagos Plan of Action (1980) countered the Berg Report produced by the World Bank, which laid the blame for Africa's laggard development squarely with the inadequacy of its rulers, instead concentrating on demands for trade equality and additional aid, ignoring governance issues. The Abuja Treaty set up the African Economic Community with the same blinkered mindset. Grandiose in conception, with six regional economic communities (RECs), and a six stage, 34-year implementation, it quickly foundered on

primary objectives, like the establishment of a free-trade area, and few RECs are properly functional.

TREATY OF ASUNCIÓN 1991
At Asunción, Argentina, Brazil, Uruguay, and Paraguay, while remaining members of Latin American Integration Association (LAIA), decided to pursue stronger integration. The treaty created MERCOSUR, the economic organization mandated to implement free trade, and the subsequent Protocol of Ouro Prêto bestowed a legal framework, enabling the negotiation of treaties with other international organizations. Institutions created included a governing Council with rotating presidency, a Common Market Group responsible for policy implementation, and a Trade Commission with oversight of commercial policy and trade dispute resolution. The integration process has been hampered by unilateral actions (like Brazil's "dumping" of Chinese steel) and the collapse of the Argentine economy in 2001.

BELAVEZHA ACCORDS 1991
By the summer of 1991, Soviet leader Mikhail Gorbachev's ambitious program of reform had gone calamitously awry. The Soviet bloc in eastern Europe had disintegrated in a wave of popular

1991–1994

revolutions culminating in the reunification of Germany. The contagion had spread to the Soviet Union itself with declarations of independence by the three Baltic states, with Armenia and Georgia doing likewise in the Caucasus. In August, Gorbachev desperately sought to salvage the Union, revamped as a confederation, but an abortive coup – and Boris Yeltsin's televised heroics resisting it – effectively eliminated Gorbachev's authority, and he resigned. In December, the Belavezha Accords between Yeltsin for Russia, Leonid Kravchuk for Ukraine, and Stanislas Shushkevich for Belarus, abruptly dissolved the Soviet Union, replacing it with the Commonwealth of Independent States (CIS). On 21 December, eleven further ex-Soviet republics signed the Alma-Ata Protocol agreeing to join the new CIS. The Baltic states eschewed the new Commonwealth.

UNITED NATIONS FRAMEWORK CONVENTION ON CLIMATE CHANGE 1992

By 1957, a US oceanographer had concluded the oceans would not be able to absorb the excess CO_2 being generated and observed, and the following year, systematic recording of atmospheric CO_2 commenced in Hawaii and Antarctica. The term global warming entered the public domain in 1975, and in 1988, the Intergovernmental Panel on Climate Change (IPCC) was convened to gather and analyze evidence of the phenomenon. The Framework Convention was signed by 154 nations at the 1992 Rio de Janeiro Environmental Conference, and called for the prevention of "dangerous anthropogenic interference with the climate system" by the stabilization of greenhouse gas emissions. It established national greenhouse gas inventories, which led to emission targets being formulated under the Kyoto Protocol (1997).

TREATY ON OPEN SKIES 1992

US President Eisenhower first proposed the Open Skies concept of "mutual aerial observation" to his Soviet counterpart in 1955. The suggestion was swiftly rejected and lay fallow for decades, until the first President Bush resurrected the concept during the thaw in US-Soviet relations under Gorbachev's leadership. After the fall of the Soviet Union, agreement on Open Skies was reached in Helsinki, signed by 34 countries, covering North America, most of Europe, and the successor states of the former Soviet Union. It allowed for the flight of observation aircraft to monitor potential military activity over the signatory states' territory and territorial waters. Flights may only be restricted by the nation concerned for reasons of flight safety, not for national security.

CIS COLLECTIVE SECURITY TREATY (CSTO) 1992

The collapse of the Soviet bloc and then the Soviet Union itself, with the successor European states gravitating towards the west, left the residual members of the Confederation of Independent States exposed. CSTO was the response. Comprising initially Russia, Armenia, Kazakhstan, Tajikistan, Kyrgyzstan, and Uzbekistan (Azerbaijan, Georgia and Belarus signed up a year later), it was intended as a counterbalance to the North Atlantic Treaty Organization (NATO). However, its equivalent of NATO's Article 5, which proclaims "armed attack against one or more of them in Europe or North America shall be considered an attack against them all," merely asserted that treaty members will prefer political means in the protection of independence. In 1999, three members, Georgia, Azerbaijan and Uzbekistan withdrew.

SOCHI AGREEMENT 1992

The Caucasus region houses a complex ethnic mix, reflecting its turbulent history and a mountainous terrain liable to create "pocket" populations. In Abkhazia, the ethnic Abkhaz formed part of a largely Muslim aristocracy under Ottoman rule, while the peasantry was largely Georgian. In South Ossetia, the roles were reversed with a Georgian feudal nobility presiding over ethnic Ossetians who migrated southward from the 17th century. Reflecting these class differences, in the 1989 census, Ossetians formed the majority population (67 percent) in South Ossetia, while the largest single ethnicity in Abkhazia was Georgian (46 percent). Under the Soviet Union, both regions had autonomous status while forming part of the Soviet Georgian Republic. With the Soviet Union's collapse, both regions formed separatist movements opposed to absorption by the new Republic of Georgia. The Sochi ceasefire brokered by Russia attempted to halt the growing conflict, with peacekeeping forces installed: regardless, conflict soon resumed with renewed intensity.

CHEMICAL WEAPONS CONVENTION (CWC) 1993

The 1925 Geneva Protocol reflected the horror evoked by the use of poison gas in World War I, prohibiting the use of chemical weapons in warfare. However, it did not ban the development, production or stockpiling of such weapons, and a number of signatories reserved the right to their retaliatory use, or first use against nations not party to the Protocol. Following Iraqi chemical warfare against Iran in the 1980s there was a twelve-year consultation by the Disarmament Committee of the

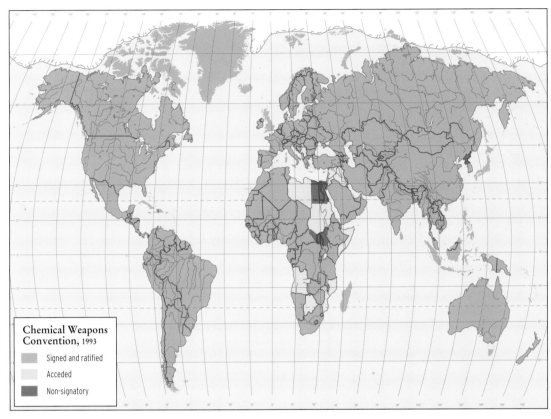

Chemical Weapons
Convention, 1993

Signed and ratified

Acceded

Non-signatory

United Nations, culminating in the CWC. This was the first disarmament agreement negotiated within a multilateral framework to provide for the elimination of an entire category of weapons of mass destruction under universally applied control. It also established the Organization for the Prohibition of Chemical Weapons (OPCW) to implement the wholesale ban on the development, production, stockpiling, and use of chemical weapons.

OSLO ACCORDS 1993
Following Norway's suggestion that it acted as an intermediary in talks between Israel and the PLO, a series of secret meetings were held in London and Norway between Professor Yair Hirschfeld (succeeded by General Uri Savar), representing Israel, and Ahmed Qorei of the PLO, between December 1992 and August 1993. On 19 August 1993 Israeli Foreign Minister Shimon Peres witnessed the signature of an agreement between Savar and Qorei and in September the PLO reaffirmed its recognition of Israel's right to exist; the Israelis recognized the PLO as the sole representative of the Palestinians. On 13 September the Oslo Accords (Oslo I) were signed by Shimon Peres and Mahmoud Abbas in Washington DC. A second agreement, Oslo II, was signed two years later, including provision for the withdrawal of Israeli troops from six West Bank

cities and some 450 towns, and setting a timetable for elections for the Palestinian Legislative Council.

ISRAEL-JORDAN TREATY OF PEACE 1994
King Hussain's Jordan was a minimalist adversary to Israel in the Yom Kippur War (1973–74), and in Black September (1970) was forced to fight a war against the Palestine Liberation Organization bases in its own territory. The king's aspirations to regain the West Bank were clearly untenable, and the nightmare alternatives – Israeli hardliners' claims on further Jordanian territory, or Palestinian expulsion from the West Bank – needed to be averted. The 1994 treaty's passage was smoothed by American forgiveness of Jordanian debt, but it was, nevertheless, very different in tone to the preceding Israel-Egypt Treaty (1979). A border was agreed, with the cession of some occupied land to Jordan. Full diplomatic relations were restored, with mutual respect of sovereignty. Cooperative arrangements were: access to joint water resources; Jordan's input regarding Jerusalem's Muslim Holy shrines; the quest for a solution with regard to Palestinian refugees; and support of the Israeli-Palestinian peace process.

NORTH AMERICAN FREE TRADE
AGREEMENT (NAFTA) 1994
NAFTA was predated by CUSFTA, a free-trade

1994–1998

agreement between Canada and the United States. The earlier agreement had been highly contentious in Canada, with opponents fearing commercial annexation by the much larger neighboring economy. These fears proved largely unfounded, and the first President Bush moved to extend the agreement to its southern neighbor. This aroused public and political concern in both Canada and the United States, particularly centered on job flight to Mexico's low wage economy. When President Clinton inherited the negotiations he secured Canadian support, and passage through Congress and the Senate by supplementary agreements on labor and environmental cooperation to defuse opposition lobbies. In practice, NAFTA was neither the magic bullet claimed by its proponents nor the wrecking ball feared by its critics. Mexico enjoyed an export boom fueled by its *maquiladora* factories, importing parts and exporting finished goods. US and Canadian growth was more modest.

KREMLIN ACCORDS 1994

A Moscow summit between Presidents Clinton and Yeltsin produced the Kremlin Accords, perhaps the watershed of what would prove to be a brief rapprochement between the United States and post-Soviet Russia. There was an agreement on the removal of nuclear armaments from Ukraine (whose president also attended), and that US/Russian long-range missiles would not be preprogrammed to target any state. There were joint pronouncements on human rights, denouncing "aggressive nationalism," xenophobia, and anti-semitism. Various US investment projects in Russia were endorsed. However, in a harbinger of the subsequent Putinist refreezing of relations, Yeltsin sharply opposed former Soviet bloc countries entering NATO – unless they joined en masse – and Russia joined at the same time.

BISHKEK PROTOCOL 1994

Under Soviet rule, Nagorno-Karabakh formed a largely Armenian Christian enclave in predominantly Muslim Azerbaijan. In 1988, with the Soviet Union beginning to disintegrate, the local political assembly voted to join Armenia, but was quickly suppressed by Azeri security forces. On the Union's final collapse, ethnic Armenians in the enclave rebelled against the newly independent Azerbaijan, with the support of newly independent Armenia. Russia supplied the Armenian side with armaments, while Azerbaijan gained support from Chechen and Afghan *mujahideen*. The conflict resulted in thousands of casualties and hundreds of thousands of refugees. In May 1994, with Armenia gaining the upper hand, Azerbaijan reluctantly

recognized Nagorno-Karabakh as a third party to peace talks brokered by Russia. At Bishkek in Kyrgyzstan, a ceasefire was agreed, with return of occupied territory and future mediation through parties from the Commonwealth of Independent States. Fighting has flared up repeatedly in the intervening years.

UN CONVENTION ON THE LAW OF THE SEA (UNCLOS III) 1994

Two previous UNCLOS Conferences (1956, 1960) had established a basic framework for maritime jurisdiction, but skirted the cardinal – and vexed – question of the delimitation of territorial waters. The traditional limit had been 3 miles (4.8 km) from the coast, but without effective governing rules, certain countries had arrogated limits up to 230 miles (370 km). UNCLOS III defined the determination of a baseline (usually the low-water line) and territorial water was deemed to extended outward 13.7 miles (22 km) from the baseline. Beyond territorial waters would be a contiguous zone, where the coastal state retained authority over immigration, customs, taxation, and pollution. Finally, the exclusive economic zone, where the coastal state retained rights over natural resources, extended for 230 miles (370 km). The US hotly disputed the establishment of an International Seabed Authority to oversee exploitation of mineral resources in international water, and remains a non-party to the Convention.

COMPREHENSIVE NUCLEAR-TEST-BAN TREATY (CTBT) 1996

In the 1990s, the strength of popular movements calling for nuclear disarmament, and the post-Soviet rapprochement between Russia and the United States finally created an environment where a comprehensive test-ban was tenable. The CTBT bans all nuclear explosions for any purpose in all environments, and provides for a comprehensive range of monitoring equipment to verify compliance. The treaty has yet to come into force.

KHASAVYURT ACCORD 1996

Chechnya became a battleground of the empires of Russia, Safavid Persia, and the Ottomans in the 18th century. It was finally annexed by Russia in the 1870s, after a brutal 50-year war culminating in mass deportation of native Chechens. Brief independence during the turmoil of the Russian Revolution was cut short when the Bolsheviks invaded. When the Soviet Union dissolved in 1991, the Chechen National Congress was formed, and once more declared independence. The First Chechen War (1994–96) was marked by heavy Russian losses (including almost 2,000 tanks), the assassination of the Chechen president, and Chechen separatist attacks on targets in Russia. After the Chechens retook their capital, Grozny, Russian President Yeltsin agreed a ceasefire. The Accord specified the withdrawal of Russian forces from Chechnya, and the jointly supervised demilitarization of Grozny.

AMSTERDAM TREATY 1997
The Treaty of Maastricht (1992) delineated a blueprint for future European integration. Opening the way to the creation of a (partial) common currency, the three pillars of the integration process were defined: socio-economic/environmental; judicial; foreign policy/security. But it left loose ends, and the collapse of the Soviet bloc (1989–91) in eastern Europe posed the challenge of multiple new potential members, who were culturally distinct, and economically adrift, from the existing Union's western core. Amsterdam enunciated an accession framework for the new states. It improved the efficiency of EU decision-making by increasing the areas where Qualified Majority Voting applied, as opposed to unanimous endorsement. Open borders between twelve member-states were confirmed by the incorporation of the Schengen Convention into EU Law. In recognition of the tensions created by increasing member diversity, "constructive abstention" was introduced in some policy areas, whereby members could opt out of initiatives without preventing co-members from proceeding.

OTTAWA TREATY 1997
The Mine Ban Treaty concluded in Ottawa was unusual in that it was driven by passionate lobbying by non-governmental organizations (NGO) attracting high-profile advocates such as Diana, Princess of Wales. Its objective was the global elimination of anti-personnel landmines. Landmines were often planted indiscriminately, presented a continuing hazard to civilian populations in countries such as Angola, Cambodia, and El Salvador, long after the cessation of hostilities. Ottawa is limited in its scope: it does not address anti-vehicle mines, remote-controlled mines or booby traps. However, it does require signatories to remove landmines on their territory, and destroy stockpiles (other than a small quantity for training purposes). The treaty's design and application has been heavily criticized, betraying its informal origins, and non-signatories include most of the permanent members of the UN Security Council.

POP AIR POLLUTION PROTOCOL 1998
The 1983 Convention on Long-range Trans-Boundary Air Pollution (CLRTAP) spawned a string of supplementary Protocols. Adopted in Aarhus in 1998, this Protocol targeted Persistent Organic Pollutants (POPs), chiefly pesticides, of which DDT, Dioxins and PCBs are prime examples. After entering an ecosystem, POPs work their way through the food-chain by a process known as bio-magnification, with their most intense effects registered in apex predators, often birds of prey and mammalian carnivores – including, potentially, humans – causing wide-ranging damage including birth defects. The Protocol sought to eliminate the production, stockpiling, and trade of POPs, with certain specified exemptions. It also targeted their unintentional creation, and mandated research on contamination and its effects.

ROME STATUTE OF THE INTERNATIONAL CRIMINAL COURT 1998
The phrase 'Crimes against Humanity' (CAH) was first applied in diplomacy by European powers denouncing the Turkish massacres of Armenians (1915). It was then employed as a legal mechanism after World War II, in the Nuremberg and Tokyo trials (1945–46) of war criminals. Subsequently, the United Nations Security Council established International Criminal Tribunals to try the perpetrators of atrocities in the former Yugoslavia (1993) and Rwanda (1994). Each round of prosecutions produced refinements of the definition of CAH, which the Rome Statute sought to clarify. A CAH, it asserts must be "part of a widespread or systematic attack directed against any civilian population," and provides a comprehensive list of qualifying crimes including murder, torture, enslavement, enforced disappearance and deportation, rape, apartheid, enforced sterilization, and forced pregnancy. The Statute came into effect in 2002.

GOOD FRIDAY AGREEMENT 1998
The Protestant Unionist party effectively controlled the political system in Ulster after Irish Independence (1922). The large Catholic minority were excluded by "gerrymandering" of electoral constituencies and suffered discrimination in employment and housing. The police force, the Royal Ulster Constabulary, was heavily Protestant. The Bogside Riots (1969) by Catholics against "Orange" marchers marked a descent into violence, which dramatically escalated after 14 died in the British army's suppression of rioters on Bloody Sunday (1972). The official wing of Sinn Fein, the left-wing republican party with the goal of integration with Ireland, pursued political means; the Provisional Irish Republican Army (IRA) its paramilitary wing, unleashed insurgency and terrorism, particularly bombings, which began to

1998–2001

Ulster's Troubles & The Good Friday Agreement
1970s–90s

Major terrorist activities

1970s

1970s-90s

Real IRA base (late 1990s)

Major incident with date

Results of General Election 1997

United Kingdom Unionist

Ulster Unionist Party

Social Democratic and Labour Party

Democratic Unionist Party

Sinn Féin

blight the British mainland. The Protestants formed their own terrorist paramilitaries, the Ulster Defense Association. The Good Friday Agreement of 1998 brought an end to 30 years of sectarian conflict. It contained proposals for a Northern Ireland Assembly at Stormont with a power-sharing executive, and new cross-border institutions with the Republic of Ireland. There were also proposals for decommissioning of paramilitary weapons and the early release of paramilitary prisoners. A referendum vote in Northern Ireland returned a vote of 71.12 percent in favor of the deal.

ADAPTED CONVENTIONAL ARMS FORCES IN EUROPE TREATY 1999

The Treaty on Conventional Armed Forces in Europe (1989) aimed to achieve balance between the offensive capability of NATO and the then Warsaw Pact alliance. The collapse of the Soviet Union, and the resulting dissolution of the Warsaw Pact, left this treaty in need of overhaul: the "Adapted

Treaty" was the response. Its main thrust was to replace bloc to bloc parity with a series of national and territorial ceilings. In addition, it provides for enhanced systems of inspection and verification, and mechanisms for signatories to either grant or withhold consent for foreign armed forces to be stationed on their territories. The last issue provided a stumbling block, as NATO counterparties to the treaty linked their ratification to Russia's commitment to the withdrawal of its armed forces from Georgia and Moldova. Russia protested and ultimately withdrew from the treaty in 2007, rendering it in Vladimir Putin's description "dead."

EAST AFRICAN COMMUNITY TREATY 1999

In 1967, independent Kenya, Uganda, and Tanzania resurrected the idea of the East African Community (EAC), but it collapsed in 1977 through the stresses created by Kenya's more dynamic economy, and the antics of Ugandan dictator, Idi Amin. The EAC was revived by the 1999 treaty and expanded to include Burundi and Rwanda. The objectives remained broadly similar to those espoused in the Community's previous manifestation, but are yet to be fully realized. Kenya's economic dominance is a destabilizing factor, and the combined weight of the constituent economies is insufficient to provide international bargaining power to the Community.

KUMANOVO AGREEMENT 1999

After the death of Tito (1980), there was widespread civil unrest amongst Albanians (who constituted about 90 percent of the overall population) in Kosovo, which was ruthlessly suppressed by the authorities. As Yugoslavia began to disintegrate in the 1990s, the Kosovo Liberation Army (KLA) was formed, and in 1991 an unofficial referendum by Kosovar Albanians overwhelmingly backed independence from its successor government in Belgrade. Failure to secure independence by peaceful means led the KLA to wage a guerrilla war from 1998, which soon became all-out civil war along ethnic lines, exacerbated by Serbian army intervention. NATO's Operation Allied Force in 1999 forced the warring parties to the negotiating table. At Kumanovo, the Serbian armed forces were forced to withdraw, and the KLA to cease hostilities. A UN peacekeeping force was installed.

NARRATIVE PROTOCOL ON EASTERN AND WESTERN SECTIONS OF THE CHINA-RUSSIA BOUNDARY 1999

During the protracted disintegration of China's Qing Dynasty, Russia acquired vast stretches of Chinese territory from Manchuria to the Pamir Mountains in a string of unequal treaties. Early negotiations in the 1960s to resolve the border question broke down and led to armed clashes in contested areas in 1969. In 1987, as part of his *glasnost* initiatives, Soviet leader Mikhail Gorbachev resumed negotiations and reached substantial agreement in principle with the pragmatic Chinese premier Deng Xiaoping in the dying days of the Soviet Union (1991). However, control of three islands in the Amur and Argun Rivers, and a small strip of border were still to be decided. Finally, in 1999, the Russian leader Boris Yeltsin, under western censure over his tactics against the Chechens, sought better eastern relations through the Narrative Protocol with China's Jiang Zemin. Zhenbao and Yinlong Islands went to China, while Heixiazi island was split 50/50.

COTONOU AGREEMENT 2000

The Lomé Convention (1975) was concluded between the then European Economic Community (EEC) and a total of 71 countries in Africa, the Caribbean and the Pacific (ACP). By its terms, the ACP countries were able to export raw materials duty-free to the EEC, and received development aid, and investment assistance. Lomé was renewed three times, but by the end of the century needed updating, particularly after the United States claimed aspects of its operation violated WTO rules. The Cotonou Agreement was the result, concluded between the European Union and 79 ACP states. Cotonou introduced several innovations: performance-based partnerships for channeling aid; good governance; anti-impunity measures to fight corruption and misconduct; reciprocal rather than one-way trade arrangements.

PATENT LAW TREATY 2000

PLT was concluded in 2000, and came into force in 2005, and is open to the European Patent Organization (established by it contracting parties to grant patents in Europe) as well as parties to the Paris Convention (1883). Its key features are: standardized procedures for filing patent applications; standardization of national and regional applications; Model International Forms applicable to all contracting parties; protections against the inadvertent loss of patenting rights, for instance, by missing filing deadlines; and the implementation of electronic filing.

TREATY OF NICE 2001

The inter-governmental conference in Nice was designed to ready the European Union (EU) for its greatest single enlargement: the accession of the countries of eastern Europe. The creation of a European rapid reaction force was agreed, but the incorporation of the recently drafted Charter of Fundamental Rights into EU law was parked after British objections. A framework and timeline for expansion was agreed, but the associated reforms of the EU voting structure were contentious. Germany's advocacy of a greater reflection of population in member voting allocation was resisted by France, leaving notable anomalies: Luxembourg's relative voting "weight" (votes on the Council per head of population) was left 28 times that of Germany's. Overall, countries such as Britain believed Nice increased the EU democratic deficit, centralizing power in an unaccountable bureaucracy.

OHRID AGREEMENT 2001

The Ohrid Agreement was designed to secure peace by enshrining certain protections for the Albanian minority in Macedonia's constitution and administration. A NATO-supervised disarmament of the insurgent Albanian National Liberation Army was agreed. Key provisions determined that any minority comprising over 20 percent of

The World in 2000

At the beginning of the new millennium political borders were being redrawn all over the world, as old empires collapsed and new states came into being. By 2000, the former European colonies were independent, with Africa comprised of 54 sovereign states. With boundaries created predominantly by the Europeans, there were border tensions between many African countries. In 2000, there was war in the Congo and Eritrea-Ethiopia. Much of Africa was also blighted by poverty and famine. In the same year, market based economic reforms made India, once a British possession, one of the world's fastest growing economies. Brazil, once a Portuguese possession, was also becoming a world player. The USSR had broken up, its republics and satellite states now independent. Much of Europe was part of a political and economic union, the EU. The US, China and the Russian Federation were all "super powers," possessing formidable military strength. But this period of fragmentation was also a time when diplomats worked to establish a global consensus, drafting treaties that addressed environmental and disarmament issues worldwide.

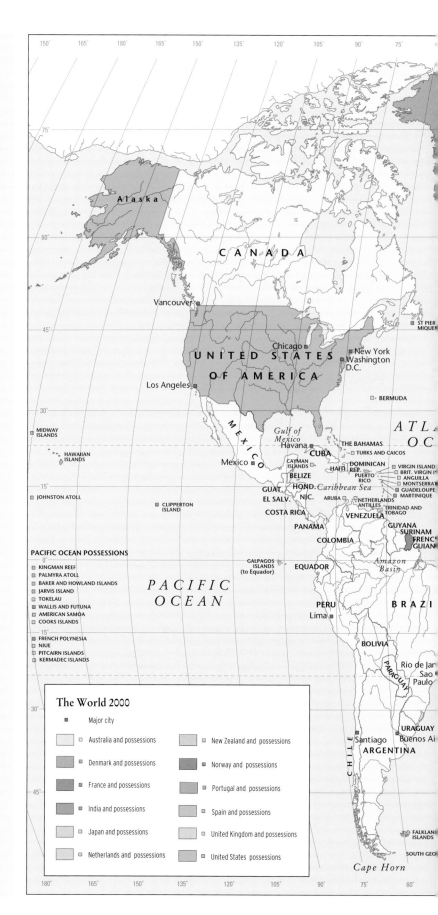

The World 2000

- ■ Major city

- □ Australia and possessions
- □ Denmark and possessions
- □ France and possessions
- □ India and possessions
- □ Japan and possessions
- □ Netherlands and possessions

- □ New Zealand and possessions
- ■ Norway and possessions
- □ Portugal and possessions
- □ Spain and possessions
- □ United Kingdom and possessions
- □ United States possessions

PACIFIC OCEAN POSSESSIONS
- □ KINGMAN REEF
- □ PALMYRA ATOLL
- □ BAKER AND HOWLAND ISLANDS
- □ JARVIS ISLAND
- □ TOKELAU
- □ WALLIS AND FUTUNA
- □ AMERICAN SAMOA
- □ COOKS ISLANDS
- □ FRENCH POLYNESIA
- □ NIUE
- □ PITCAIRN ISLANDS
- □ KERMADEC ISLANDS

2001–2005

Macedonia's population (at the time the country was 25 percent Albanian) would be declared a second people, with an official second language. An important concomitant was the availability of university education in Albanian. Measures were also to be adopted to ensure equitable representation of Albanians in public sector employment. Tensions remain, with the populations tending not to intermix (ethnic Macedonians are predominantly urban, Albanians rural), but a five-year review confirmed the affirmative measures had produced a positive impact in education and employment.

SINO-RUSSIAN TREATY OF FRIENDSHIP 2001

The Treaty of Friendship cemented the rapprochement between Russia and China that had been developing throughout the 1990s. In part, it represented a mutual defense pact, in the (then) unipolar world dominated militarily and economically by America. There was also strong economic complementarity, with China's booming industries needing Russian petrochemicals, and its armies, Russia's top-class military hardware. Equally, Russia needed Chinese capital and industrial know-how, and employment opportunities for its skilled workforce. The treaty also included commitments to a mutual approach on energy conservation, and cooperation in international trade. Finally, Russia recognized Taiwan as an "inalienable part of China."

BUDAPEST CONVENTION ON CYBERCRIME 2001

In 1997, the Council of Europe appointed a committee of experts to deliberate upon the issue of cybercrime, a phenomenon which was both growing and evolving exponentially. The resulting Budapest Convention is a criminal justice treaty that attempts to define cybercrime and to formulate a suite of policies to combat such crimes. The scope of computer-related crime covered includes terrorism, organized crime, hacking, internet fraud, and child sexual exploitation. The Convention both criminalizes such activities, and provides procedural law tools to enable their investigation. It also provides for international police and judicial cooperation on cybercrime. Contracting parties must agree to pass legislation to address specific computer-related crimes, and collaborate with other parties in investigating international cybercrimes.

ASEAN AGREEMENT ON TRANS-BOUNDARY HAZE POLLUTION 2002

In the 1990s, slash-and-burn deforestation in the Indonesian islands of Kalimantan and Sumatra reached the point that, in 1997, the haze created by the fires reached as far as Malaysia and Thailand. This caused a spike in respiratory conditions, and widespread transport disruption. The ASEAN group of countries agreed a Haze Regional Action Plan (1997). In 2002, the Agreement was concluded; it calls for the occurrence of the haze to be mitigated by a range of monitoring and prevention activities, and intensified inter-regional co-operation in promoting sustainable development. Regrettably, Indonesia, the main polluter, did not sign the Agreement until 2014, by which time the haze had reoccurred on four occasions.

GBADOLITE AGREEMENT 2002

Gbadolite was the "Versailles in the jungle" built by the notoriously corrupt dictator President Mobutu of the Democratic Republic of the Congo. He was finally driven from power (1997) by Laurent Kabila, backed by a Rwandan/Ugandan invasion. Kabila then expelled his erstwhile allies, and war recommenced with a number of African countries piling in on both sides. Over the next four years, a (mainly civilian) death toll of millions was incurred through disease, famine, indiscriminate massacres, and occasionally fighting. Several attempts to halt the carnage were attempted: a ceasefire at Lusaka (1999) followed by agreements at at Sun City, Pretoria, Luanda and finally Gbadolite (concluded with Ugandan-backed rebel movements) in 2002. Meanwhile Kabila was assassinated and succeeded by his son in a frequently interrupted peace process.

PRETORIA ACCORD 2002

The Interahamwe was an ethnic Hutu paramilitary group, heavily involved in the Rwandan genocide of ethnic Tutsis in 1994. Following the victory of the Tutsi-led Rwandese Patriotic Front, many Interahamwe fled to the Eastern Congo together with floods of Hutu refugees, disappearing into the chaos generated by the Second Congo War. In April 2002 several of the parties in the war, Botswana, Namibia, Zambia, Zimbabwe and Ugandan-backed rebel groups, signed a peace accord at Sun City, which prescribed the formation of a representative multi-party government for the Congo and a timetable for elections. However, Rwanda and its rebel proxies in the war boycotted the Accord. The subsequent Pretoria Accord was concluded between Rwanda and the Democratic Republic of Congo, in return for an international commitment of support in dismantling the Interahamwe, and of rebel groups formed by deserters from the Rwandan army.

STRATEGIC OFFENSIVE REDUCTIONS TREATY (SORT) 2002

This agreement limited the United States and Russia

to 1,700–2,200 "operationally deployed" warheads apiece. Unlike the previous START treaties, no system of classification of warheads by means of delivery was attempted, nor were any means of verification specified. As the then US Secretary of State Colin Powell observed to the Senate Foreign Relations Committee "the treaty will allow you to have as many warheads as you want."

ASEAN FREE TRADE AREA 2003
The Association of South East Asian Nations (ASEAN) was established with five members (1967); by 1999, membership had expanded to ten countries. In 2003, as part of its 2020 VISION, ASEAN announced its aim to achieve an integrated Economic Community in the intervening period.

TREATY OF ACCESSION EUROPEAN UNION (EU) 2003
The Treaty of Accession was effected between the pre-existing EU member states and ten countries – Cyprus, the Czech Republic, Estonia, Hungary, Latvia, Lithuania, Malta, Poland, Slovakia, Slovenia – concerning their accession to the Union, to come into force on 1 May 2004. Revision of the voting weights by country was made at the same time. The new member states were conferred seats in the European Parliament, and member representatives on the Economic and Social/Scientific and Technical Committees and on the Committee of the Regions. In response to the enlargement, adjustments were made to the system for Qualified Majority Voting.

ACCRA COMPREHENSIVE PEACE AGREEMENT 2003
Liberia developed an unusual variant of colonialism. A colony of freed slaves was established there with the assistance of the American Colonization Society in the early 1800s. From independence in 1847, the country was governed, unbroken, by an elite composed of the descendants of the freed slave emigrés until 1980, when a coup with widespread popular support installed Samuel Doe as the country's first indigenous head of state. Doe's popularity rapidly waned through his blatant favoritism towards his own tribe, a dubious election win, coups, and crackdowns. A rebellion led by Charles Taylor led to Doe's capture and execution and two civil wars, during which Taylor also intervened in civil war in neighboring Sierra Leone. All of these conflicts were littered with atrocities against civilian populations. During the Accra negotiation, Taylor was forced into exile, and a transitional government agreed dividing portfolios between the warring parties. Taylor was convicted of war crimes in 2012.

THE SEED TREATY 2004
The International Treaty on Plant Genetic Resources for Food and Agriculture (Seed) arose from the Biodiversity Convention concluded by the United Nations in 1992. It aims to ensure the conservation of plant genetic resources that underpin world agriculture and provide the bulk of foodstuffs. It recognizes the exceptional contribution of farmers to the conservation and development of such resources and to respect their rights in that process. It seeks to provide access to plant genetic resources to farmers, agronomists and scientists and share their benefits equitably with their countries of origin, in particular, the farmers in those countries. At its core is a multilateral system of access to cultivated plants, jointly operated by all contracting parties to the treaty. In total, 64 key cultivated plants (accounting for c. 80 percent of plant-derived food) are covered, and made readily available to potential users. Wheat, maize, rice, and potatoes are core inclusions, soya, sugarcane, and groundnut surprising omissions.

ENERGY COMMUNITY TREATY 2005
The European Union (EU) imports more than half of its energy needs, including over 80 percent of its oil, and 97 percent of the uranium used in its nuclear reactors. There are particular concerns about the potentially destabilizing effect of "energy politics" on southeastern Europe, where a Stability Pact (1999) and regional Energy Market (2002) were constituted as preliminaries to EU Accession. The Energy Community Treaty was concluded between the EU and eight contracting parties, ranging from Albania to Moldova and Ukraine. Early observers to the treaty were Norway and Turkey. Its objective is to create a seamless Pan-European Energy market by collective acceptance of the EU's accumulated legislation governing security of supply, energy efficiency, renewable energy targets, emissions of pollutants, and transparency in, and liberalization of, energy markets.

KYOTO PROTOCOL 2005
This international agreement is linked to the UN Framework Convention on Climate Change of 1992, and commits its signatories to settling internationally binding emission reduction targets. It was adopted in 1997, and finally came into force in February 2005, following the Marrakesh Accords of 2001, which laid out a framework for the protocol's implementation. In recognition of the greater responsibility of the developed world for the currently high levels of CO_2 emissions, which are bringing about an increase in the global mean temperature, the protocol placed a greater burden on the developed nations under the principle of

2005–2008

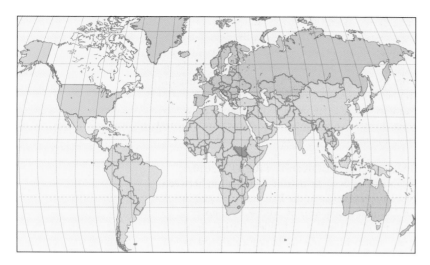

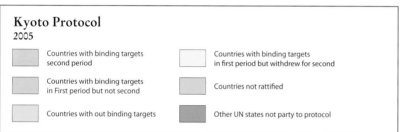

Kyoto Protocol
2005

Countries with binding targets second period

Countries with binding targets in First period but not second

Countries with out binding targets

Countries with binding targets in first period but withdrew for second

Countries not rattified

Other UN states not party to protocol

Muslim north against the Christian south, further complicated by tribal divisions. Neighboring states Libya and Sudan both exploited these conflicts to further their own ambition for dominance in the region. However, after having his own attempts to occupy Chad repulsed in the 1980s, Libya's Colonel Gaddafi turned peace broker to prevent Sudan usurping his position of influence. By 2003, Sudan was dealing, brutally, with its own insurgency in Darfur on Chad's borders, while Chad had once more degenerated into civil war, with Sudan arming its rebels. In February 2006, Gaddafi brokered the Tripoli Agreement between Sudan and Chad, to widespread plaudits in the Arab world. Two months later, the Chadian rebels attacked the capital N' Djamena with Sudanese backing, and the Agreement was, most definitely, off.

WAZIRISTAN ACCORD 2006

Waziristan is a mountainous territory on Pakistan's northwestern border with Afghanistan. Ethnically Pashtun and religiously conservative, it twice rebelled against British rule. When the Americans invaded Afghanistan in 2001, the Taliban began to cross into Waziristan to find refuge. It soon became a base for Al-Qaeda operations across the border, and host to *mujahideen* (religious fighters) from Central Asia. The Pakistani army deployed there in 2002, which soon expanded into a concerted attempt to expel militants, backed by American air strikes. A ceasefire was agreed in 2005 with insurgent leaders in South Waziristan: the Accord was an equivalent deal for North Waziristan, concluded in September 2006. By its terms, the militants agreed to cease cross-border operations in Afghanistan. Foreign jihadists had to leave but those who unable to leave were to "live peacefully." In return, Pakistan's government released captured fighters and promised minimal control in the territory. The Accord was widely denounced as a government cave-in.

ST ANDREW'S AGREEMENT 2006

The Northern Ireland Assembly, the devolved legislature of the province, was repeatedly suspended from the onset of the Troubles in 1972, owing to sectarian political discord, with its administration handled by the British Northern Ireland Office. At St Andrew's the British and Irish governments met with the Northern Irish political parties to hammer out a deal to restore the Assembly. The key stumbling blocks were obtaining a (Protestant) Democratic Unionist Party (DUP) commitment to power-sharing and a (Catholic) Sinn Féin recognition of the Royal Ulster Constabulary. A deadline was set for the appointment of a First Minister and Deputy First Minister and the

"common but differentiated responsibilities." Under the protocol 38 industrialized countries, as well as the EU (15 states at the time) committed themselves to binding targets on greenhouse gases for the period 2008–12; a second commitment period expires in 2020. Canada withdrew from the protocol in 2012 and the US has not ratified the protocol.

TREATY OF ACCESSION 2005

After the ten-country enlargement of the EU in 2003, a significant issue in the further accessions of Bulgaria and Romania was freedom of movement. National measures that pre-existing member states could apply to regulate access to their labor markets were permitted in accordance with a '2+3+2' formula, indicating the length in years of the initial transition period, and the potential periods of extension. The final two-year extension could only be applied in the event of serious disturbances to a national labor market. Further issues were raised concerning corruption and organized crime in the new member states, a situation that was monitored through a Mechanism for Cooperation and Verification set up for an initial period of three years.

TRIPOLI AGREEMENT 2006

Since achieving independence from France in 1960, Chad had experienced one civil war after another. Conflicts were often sectarian, pitting the allocation of the government ministries between the four main parties. In the event, the deadline was met, and Ian Paisley of the DUP accepted the nomination as First Minister, while Sinn Féin's Martin McGuinness became his Deputy. Devolution was formally restored on 26 March 2007.

TREATY OF LISBON 2007
The achievement of a European Union (EU) Constitution to replace the accumulation of treaties was first designated in an annex to the Treaty of Nice (2001). However, progress was halted by successive rejections of the idea in referendums in France and the Netherlands in 2005. When Germany assumed the EU's rotating presidency in 2007, they decided to drive the project forward, resulting in the Treaty of Lisbon. Prominent changes included the wide-ranging extension of the principle of Qualified Majority Voting (QMV) – as opposed to unanimous agreement – to approve policy changes. The treaty instituted a long-term presidency and increased the relative powers of the European parliament. A High Representative of Foreign Affairs and Security Policy was created (similar to the American Secretary of State). Lisbon was rejected by an Irish referendum, but the Irish were invited to reconsider.

ASEAN (ASSOCIATION OF SOUTH EAST ASIAN NATIONS) CHARTER 2007
By its Charter, ASEAN effectively established a constitution, designating ASEAN itself as a legal entity for the first time, with a secretary-general and permanent representatives from the member states. It also enunciates guiding principles for the conduct of its affairs including respect for: territorial integrity and sovereignty; human rights and social justice; multi-lateral trade; and mechanisms for dispute resolution. Political-Security, Economic, and Socio-Cultural Community Councils were set up to implement policy in these areas. The rights and obligations of member states and the admission process for new member states were to be agreed, as well as the remit of its officials and the codes of conduct for its external relations with other states and supra-national organizations.

UNASUR CONSTITUTIVE TREATY 2008
The 2004 Cuzco Declaration announced the formation of the South American Community of Nations (CSN) by the union of the memberships of two pre-existing trade groups: MERCOSUR and the Andean Community, plus three additional members - Chile, Guyana and Suriname. CSN developed a strategic plan for a more formal union, which translated into the formation of UNASUR,

the Union of South American Nations by the Constitutive Treaty concluded in Brasilia. The trappings of union were agreed: a secretariat to be based in Quito, Ecuador, a parliament to be held in Cochabamba, Bolivia, annual heads of state meetings and bi-annual meetings of foreign ministers. Amongst the long-term objectives were a fully-fledged Free Trade Zone, a single currency, a central bank and the building of an inter-oceanic highway.

BARENTS SEA BORDER TREATY 2010
Negotiations over the marine delimitation between Norway and Russia in the Barents Sea began in 1967. The disputed area of c. 68,400 sq. miles (c. 175,000 sq. km) was valuable maritime "real estate" containing substantial proven oil and gas reserves and the richest fisheries in northern Europe.

2010–2017

In addition, its strategic significance was great, particularly to Russia, granting North Sea access to its one all-year ice-free port, Murmansk, and to shipments of its oil and gas from the East Barents and Kara Seas. Norway's claims were based on the median line principle of the UN Convention of the Law of the Sea (UNCLOS). Russia, for four decades, counterclaimed with "special circumstances," which Norway refuted. In 2010, Russia, quite abruptly, showed flexibility: the treaty was the result. Under its terms, the disputed area was broadly bisected with further agreements for joint exploitation of oil and gas reserves and fisheries straddling the divide.

GLOBAL PLAN OF ACTION TO COMBAT TRAFFICKING IN PERSONS 2010

Resolution 2006/27 of the United Nations (UN) Economic and Social Council made an emotional call for action on human trafficking. An effective response entailed cross-cutting of a number of UN bodies, *inter alia* those concerned with Human Rights, Drugs and Organized Crime, Migration and International Labor. UN Secretary-General Ban Ki-Moon announced the Global Plan as a "clarion call… against this terrible crime... which shames us all." It proposes the establishment of a voluntary fund to provide legal, financial, and humanitarian aid to victims, and greater international cooperation in the prevention and prosecution of trafficking.

ARCTIC SEA SEARCH AND RESCUE AGREEMENT 2011

The Arctic Council is an intergovernmental forum established in 1996, with a membership comprising all the Arctic states: Russia, the United States, Canada, Sweden, Norway, Finland, Iceland, and Denmark. The region has been the subject of conflicting territorial claims, which have, perhaps been intensified by increased potential navigability and resource exploitation as a consequence of global warming. Nevertheless, with the Council's mediation, the Arctic states have shown a strong degree of consensus on issues such as environmental protection, tourism, and shipping.

FRAMEWORK AGREEMENT ON THE BANGSAMORO 2012

The Muslim Moros of western Mindanao fought off all the colonial powers until Spanish takeover in 1844, after which they fought a ferocious insurgency marked by frequent attacks by *juramentados* (suicide swordsmen). When the Americans invaded (1898), they bought Moro neutrality with promises of autonomy – then reneged, triggering further rebellion and an infamous massacre of Moro villagers besieged in a volcanic crater. But the

Moros continued to rebel, and fought against the Japanese invaders (1941–45). Under President Marcos (1965–86), fresh rebellions eventually spawned three factions, the Moro National and Islamic Liberation Fronts and Abu Sayyaf. The Autonomous Region of Muslim Mindanao (ARMM) was created in 1989, but collapsed in a welter of electoral fraud and violence. The Framework Agreement concluded with the leaders of the Islamic Liberation Front replaced the failed experiment of ARMM with a more detailed plan for an autonomous Bangsamoro, replete with budgets and a "Basic Law."

MINSK PROTOCOL 2014

In late 2013, Ukrainian President Victor Yanukovych rejected a pending association agreement with the European Union in favor of closer ties with Russia. Massive street protests followed, leading to Yanukovych's flight to Russian exile in early 2014. The turn of events incensed Russia, which considered Yanukovych's deposition a coup, and they quickly engineered the annexation of Crimea, retroactively justifying the action with an unconstitutional referendum. Within weeks, the more pro-Russian eastern Ukraine had sprouted the Donetsk and Luhansk People's Republics, which proved both well-armed and tactically astute. Reverses on the battlefield brought the Ukrainian government to the negotiating table at Minsk in September with the "People's Republics." The Organization of Security and Cooperation in Europe (OSCE) mediated with the support of "non-partisan" Russia. The Protocol set out the terms of ceasefire; but by January it had collapsed.

COMPREHENSIVE ECONOMIC AND TRADE AGREEMENT (CETA) 2014

Canada agreed the abolition of all tariffs with the European Free Trade Association (EFTA) – Iceland, Norway, Switzerland and Liechtenstein – in 2009, after a decade of negotiation, which served as valuable groundwork for its subsequent agreement with the European Union, CETA. The Agreement extends beyond pure free trade, incorporating mutual recognition of regulated professions (such as engineers and accountants), and the facilitation of employee transfers. Certain issues have proved contentious: eastern European countries threatened to veto the deal unless visa restrictions were lifted; while the attendant freedom of EU fleets to fish in Canadian territorial waters was vigorously opposed by the industry in Newfoundland. Allied permissions for investor-state dispute settlements, whereby corporations can sue government over perceived discriminatory treatment have raised concerns in Europe.

MINSK II 2015

Following the collapse of the first Minsk Protocol, a renewed separatist offensive in eastern Ukraine in January 2015 had made substantial gains, forcing the government in Kiev back to the negotiating table. The renewed Protocol, mediated by the Organization of Security and Cooperation in Europe (OSCE) with Russian involvement, was agreed in February 2015. Much of the Protocol was simply a reiteration of the original, modified to reflect the new facts on the ground: an immediate ceasefire and withdrawal of heavy weaponry was mandated; together with the pull-out of "foreign armed formations, military equipment… and mercenaries." There was significant refinement of the terms for implementing local self-governance in the separatist strongholds of Donetsk and Luhansk, and the organization of elections to that end. Minsk II was flouted, repeatedly, but less blatantly than before.

PARIS AGREEMENT ON CLIMATE CHANGE 2015

A framework convention on the stabilization of greenhouse gas concentrations in the atmosphere was signed by over 130 countries post the 1992 Earth Summit in Rio de Janeiro. However, converting this into a binding agreement took over two decades of tortuous, frequently stalling negotiations. The Paris Accord sacrificed potency to achieve overwhelming acceptance and rapid implement (coming into force in November 2016). Its core aim was to limit global temperature increase to "well below" 2° centigrade above pre-industrial levels. This was to be achieved by Nationally Determined Contributions of reductions in carbon emissions by signatories. A ratchet was built in, whereby countries were required periodically to revisit – and improve upon – the reductions initially pledged. The wealthier signatories pledged over $100 billion of aid towards assistance to developing countries in meeting their commitments. From 2023, five-yearly stocktakes are to be conducted to monitor compliance.

TRANS-PACIFIC PARTNERSHIP AGREEMENT (TPPA) 2016

The TPPA was concluded between an array of Pacific seaboard states including the United States, Japan, Canada, Malaysia, Mexico, and New Zealand after seven years' negotiation. Many stumbling blocks to implementation were imposed by the United States, particularly in respect of intellectual property rights, agricultural subsidies, and financial subsidies. Ironically, after America's disproportionately significant role in shaping the eventual agreement, incoming President Trump promptly signed a memorandum of withdrawal in January 2017. There have been indications that China might replace the United States as the prime economy in the Partnership. Other than tariff elimination, the commercial aspects of the Partnership provide for streamlined customs procedures and reduced red tape for small businesses. Also included are attend environmental protection measures, and provisions safeguarding human and labor rights. Japan, who came late to the negotiations, agreed bilateral continuation of tariffs on its automobile exports to America in exchange for reciprocal protections of its agricultural produce.

NUCLEAR WEAPON BAN TREATY 2017

An "unambiguous political commitment" to achieve the prohibition of the testing, development, stockpiling, stationing, transfer, use and threat of use of nuclear weapons, the treaty aims to stigmatize possession of such weapons, rather than establish concrete commitments for their elimination. Nevertheless, the measure provoked intense debate in the United Nations General Assembly, with opposition not just from the nuclear powers, but also from non-nuclear states that perceive their national security to derive from alliances (like NATO), armed by such a deterrent capability. Unsurprisingly, no member of the United Nations Security Council participated in the vote: the United Stated cited the development of nuclear capability by rogue states like North Korea amongst its grounds for opposition. Nevertheless, 121 nations voted in favor of the resolution for adoption, including Iran and Saudi Arabia, widely seen as candidate nuclear powers, and South Africa and Kazakhstan, who have previously possessed nuclear weapons (*see map overleaf*).

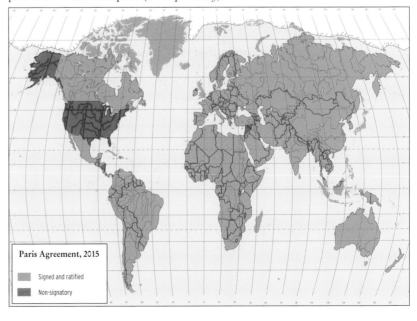

Paris Agreement, 2015

　　Signed and ratified

　　Non-signatory

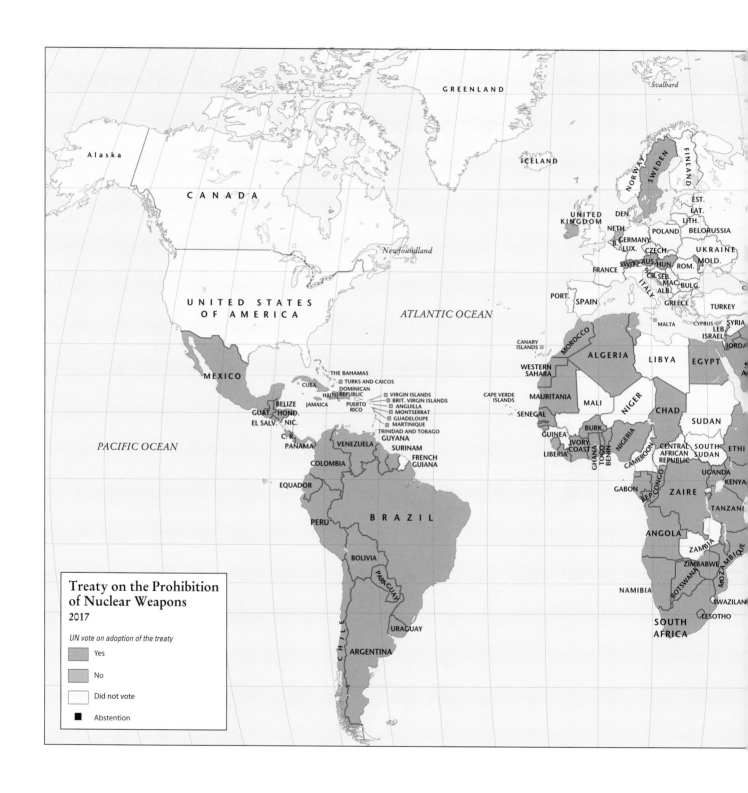

GREENLAND

Svalbard

ICELAND

Alaska

CANADA

Newfoundland

UNITED STATES
OF AMERICA

ATLANTIC OCEAN

MEXICO

THE BAHAMAS
TURKS AND CAICOS
DOMINICAN
REPUBLIC
CUBA
HAITI
JAMAICA
BELIZE
GUAT. HOND.
EL SALV. NIC.
C. R.
PANAMA

VIRGIN ISLANDS
BRIT. VIRGIN ISLANDS
ANGUILLA
MONTSERRAT
GUADELOUPE
MARTINIQUE
TRINIDAD AND TOBAGO
GUYANA
SURINAM
FRENCH
GUIANA

PUERTO
RICO

VENEZUELA

COLOMBIA

PACIFIC OCEAN

EQUADOR

PERU

BRAZIL

BOLIVIA

PARAGUAY

C H I L E

URAGUAY

ARGENTINA

CAPE VERDE
ISLANDS

CANARY
ISLANDS

MOROCCO

WESTERN
SAHARA

MAURITANIA

SENEGAL

GUINEA

LIBERIA

IVORY
COAST

GHANA
TOGO
BENIN

MALI

ALGERIA

NIGER

NIGERIA

CAMEROON

GABON

REP. CONGO

NAMIBIA

BOTSWANA

SOUTH
AFRICA

LESOTHO

ZAIRE

ANGOLA

ZAMBIA

ZIMBABWE

SWAZILAN

MOZAMBIQUE

CHAD

CENTRAL
AFRICAN
REPUBLIC

SOUTH
SUDAN

SUDAN

LIBYA

EGYPT

UGANDA

KENYA

TANZANI

ETHI

NORWAY
SWEDEN
FINLAND

UNITED
KINGDOM
DEN.

NETH.
B. GERMANY
LUX.
FRANCE CZECH.
SWITZ. AUS.
SL.
CR. SEB.
ITALY MAC.
ALB.
PORT. GREECE
SPAIN

POLAND

BELORUSSIA

UKRAINE

MOLD.

HUN. ROM.

BULG.

EST.
LAT.
LITH.

TURKEY

MALTA CYPRUS LEB.
ISRAEL
JORDA

SYRIA

A

Treaty on the Prohibition of Nuclear Weapons
2017

UN vote on adoption of the treaty

■	Yes
■	No
□	Did not vote
■	Abstention

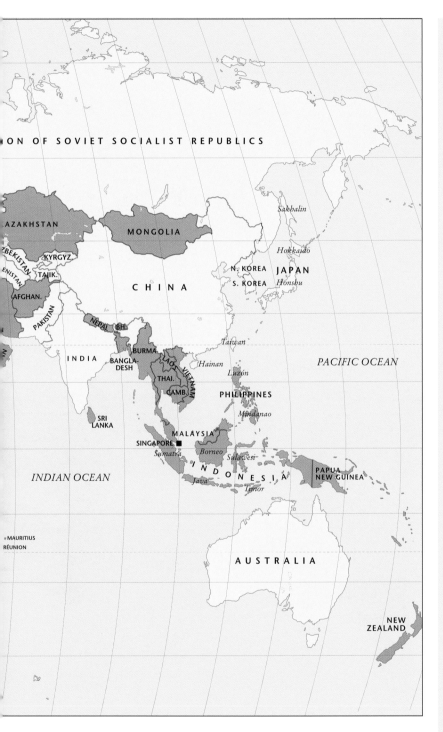

Reference

Glossary of Diplomatic Terms

ACCESSION
The procedure by which a nation becomes a party to an agreement already in force between other nations.

ACCORDS
International agreements originally thought to be for lesser subjects than covered by treaties, but now considered to be treaties by a different name.

ACCREDITATION
The procedure by which an ambassador is certified as his/her country's official representative in another state by presenting "letters of credence," or diplomatic credentials, to the head of state of the host country

AD REFERENDUM
An agreement reached at the negotiating table, which is subject to the subsequent concurrence of the governments involved.

AGRÉMENT
Before a state appoints a new chief of diplomatic mission to represent it in another state, it must be first ascertained whether the proposed representative is acceptable to the receiving state. If the host state finds the appointment acceptable it will convey this by means of an agrément.

AIDE MÉMOIRE
A written summary of the key points made by a diplomat in an official conversation.

AMBASSADOR EXTRAORDINARY AND PLENIPOTENTIARY
This is the chief of a diplomatic mission; he/she is the personal representative of his/her own head of state to the head of state of the host country. The term "extraordinary" was once given only to non-resident ambassadors on temporary missions and was used to distinguish them from regular resident ambassadors. Since the use of the term seemed to imply a higher rank, it was eventually given to all ambassadors, resident and non-resident alike. The term "plenipotentiary" is used to indicate that the appointee is possessed of full power to do the ambassador's normal job.

AMBASSADOR-DESIGNATE
An official named as ambassador, who has not yet taken the oath of office.

AMBASSADRESS
The wife of an ambassador; this term is not used to denote a female chief of mission, who is known as an ambassador.

ASYLUM
In diplomacy this refers to the notion of giving refuge: first, within an embassy and/or its grounds; and second, when one states allows someone to live within its borders, out of reach of the authority of a second state from which the person seeks protection.

ATTACHÉ
Attachés may be junior officers in an embassy or more senior officers, who specialize in certain areas (e.g. trade, culture). An embassy will generally have an army attaché, naval attaché, or air attaché – and often all three, or a single defense attaché. Military attachés liaise with local military authorities.

CHANCERY
The office where the chief of mission and his staff work. Technically the embassy is the place where the ambassador lives, not works, though this may be the same building. Sometimes diplomats use the terms "embassy residence" and "embassy office" to make the distinction clear.

CONCORDAT
An agreement to which the pope is a party.

CHARGÉ D'AFFAIRES AD INTERIM (A.I.)
Formerly, a chargé d'affaires was the title of a chief of mission, inferior in rank to an ambassador or a minister. Today with the a.i. (ad interim) added, it designates the person who acts as head of mission (ambassador) when the post is vacant, or when the ambassador is temporarily absent from his/her post.

CHIEF OF MISSION
The ranking officer in an embassy, permanent mission, legation, consulate general, or consulate – this is always an ambassador when present, or a minister, consul general, or consul when no more senior officer is assigned to the post. A "chief of mission" can also be the head of a special and temporary diplomatic mission.

CONSULAR PROTECTION
The means by which a state can defend the rights of its citizens abroad, in accordance with the laws that apply in the country in question.

CONSULATE
Consular posts are established by a sending state in another state (receiving state). They are established to protect and support citizens who are travelling or residing in the receiving state, and to perform important administrative duties, such as issuing visas. There are four categories of consular posts: consulate-general, consulate, vice-consulate and consular agency. The title of the head of post reflects in principle the category of the consular post in question, for example, a consulate-general is headed by a consul-general. Career consuls are members of the foreign service; honorary consuls, who are familiar with the language and customs of the receiving state, may also be appointed and, while they do not receive a salary, may charge frees for official services.

CONSUL, HONORARY
An individual who performs limited consular functions in a locality where the appointing state has no other consular representation.

CONVENTION
The standard term for multilateral agreements generally concluded within the framework of an international organization, which regulate issues concerning international relations and international law, for example postal, copyright, or maritime laws.

CREDENTIALS
Document from the head of the sending state to the head of state of the host country, which attest that the person designated as extraordinary and plenipotentiary ambassador is entitled by his government to perform the functions of head of mission. They are called "letters of credence" because they request the host head of state to give full credence to what the ambassador will say on his government's behalf. Credentials are handed personally by the ambassador of the sending state to the head of the receiving state at a formal credentials ceremony.

DIPLOMATIC CORPS (CD)
This is the entire body of foreign diplomats, who are gathered in a nation's capital. Together, the accredited heads of mission are presided over by the Dean (Doyen), who is normally the highest ranking head of mission, i.e. the head of mission who has been accredited to that country for the longest period. On certain occasions the Dean will act as the official spokesman for the entire corps, especially on ceremonial or administrative matters. In some Catholic countries, the Dean is automatically the papal nuncio.

DIPLOMATIC COURIER
The person who carries official correspondence between a diplomatic mission and a ministry of foreign affairs as well as between other missions and consulates of the sending state. Diplomatic couriers cannot be arrested; diplomatic bags must not be opened or withheld.

DIPLOMATIC NOTE
This is a formal means of communication between embassies. It is always written in the third person. These notes open with the standard greeting: "The ... Embassy presents its compliments to the Ministry of Foreign Affairs and has the honor to..." and conclude as follows: "The Embassy avails itself of this occasion to renew to the Ministry the assurances of its highest consideration".

DIPLOMATIC PRIVILEGES AND IMMUNITIES
These historic rights ensured that diplomats could legitimately carry out their official duties without impediment from the host country. These rights, which encompass the notion of the "inviolability" of the diplomatic staff and premises, are wide-ranging, included exemption from taxation and the civil and criminal jurisdiction of the local courts.

DIPLOMATIC PROTECTION
Diplomatic protection allows a state to intervene on behalf of its nationals (individuals or legal entities) who have suffered prejudice of some kind at the hands of another state in violation of international law. The nationals in question must have exhausted all local remedies available to them and must not have caused or aggravated the prejudice in question.

DIPLOMATIC RANKS
These are listed in order of precedence:
Ambassador Extraordinary and Plenipotentiary
Ministers Plenipotentiary
Ministers
Chargé d'Affaires ad hoc or pro tempore
Chargé d'Affaires ad interim
Minister-Counselors
Counselors (or Senior Secretaries in the absence of Counselors)
Army, Naval and Air Attachés
Civilian Attachés
First Secretaries
Second Secretaries
Assistant Army, Naval and Air Attachés
Civilian Assistant Attachés
Third Secretaries and Assistant Attachés

DIPLOMATIC STAFF
The members of the staff of a diplomatic mission who enjoy diplomatic status and, with it, certain privileges and immunities.

EMBASSY
This term can be used to refer to the physical building in which the ambassador and his/her staff work (more properly this is called the Chancery), as well as to the staff appointed by a state to carry out diplomatic functions in another state. An embassy may be headed by an ambassador or by a Chargé d'affaires ad interim. Diplomatic activities include political, legal, economic and financial affairs, development cooperation, social issues as well as scientific and cultural activities.

HIGH COMMISSION
A diplomatic mission of one Commonwealth country in another. For example, Canada has a High Commission in Canberra, Australia.

HIGH COMMISSIONER
The chief of a high commission, whose role is similar to that of an ambassador.

INVIOLABILITY
This term can refer to the personal inviolability of a diplomat, or to the inviolability of the premises of a diplomatic mission. The inviolability of diplomats as individuals means that a diplomat cannot be arrested or detained in any way in a host state. The inviolability of the premises prevents any police operation within the mission without the prior consent of the head of mission.

MISSION
This is a generic term for embassy, which also describes the complete range of official representation in a foreign country which falls under the supervision of the ambassador, including civilian and military personnel.

NUNCIO
This term, from the Latin for envoy, refers to the diplomatic representative of the Holy See, a titular bishop accredited as permanent ambassador to a foreign government. Papal Nuncios have the same status as ambassadors or heads of mission.

PACTA SUNT SERVANDA
Latin expression meaning "Treaties are to be honored." The principle that states and international organizations must comply with the provisions agreed in the treaties to which they are party is one of the main pillars of the international legal system.

PERSONA NON GRATA
A Latin expression denoting a representative of a state who is no longer acceptable to the receiving state. Once the head of a diplomatic mission has been informed that a member of the diplomatic staff is "persona non grata," the sending country must then recall this person or terminate his or her activities. If this does not happen, the host country has the right to expel the individual in question

PRECEDENCE
Representatives of states are ranked according to an order of priority, which is determined by both rank and by the order in which ambassadors presented their credentials to the host government. At a ceremony, procession or reception, precedence decrees that each participant will occupy the particular position considered to reflect his or her ranking.

PROTECTING POWER
When two states involved in a conflict break off diplomatic and/or consular relations they will have recourse to a protecting power, representing a third state. The protecting power takes on some of the functions of the diplomatic mission of one of the conflicting parties in the territory of the other, ensuring that diplomatic relations can be maintained at the minimum level.

PROTOCOL
This term most commonly applies to all the forms, uses, and practices of a ceremonial nature observed in diplomatic relations. It is also used to refer to an international treaty that is complementary to a main treaty. Over time, it has come to be used as an alternative term for an agreement.

RECOGNITION
Recognition by an existing state of, for example, a newly created state or of a government which is in effective control of a state. In extending this recognition, an existing state expresses its readiness to establish and maintain diplomatic relations.

TREATY
A formal mutually binding agreement between countries. The term comes from *traiter*, to negotiate.

VICE CONSUL
A junior ranking consular officer.

Further Reading

Adcock, F. and Mosley, D.J., *Diplomacy in Ancient Greece*, London, Thames and Hudson, 1975

Anderson, Matthew Smith, *The Rise of Modern Diplomacy*, 1450–1919, London, Longman, 1993

Bacevich, Andrew J., *American Empire: The Realities and Consequences of U.S. Diplomacy*, Cambridge MA, Harvard University Press, 2004

Barder, Sir Brian, *What Diplomats Do*, Lanham MD, Rowman & Littlefield 2014

Barston, R.P., *Modern Diplomacy*, London, Longman 1997

Benedick, Richard Elliot, *Ozone Diplomacy: New Directions in Safeguarding the Planet*, enlarged ed., Cambridge, MA, Harvard University Press, 1998

Berridge, G.R., and James, Alan, *A Dictionary of Diplomacy*, Basingstoke, UK, Palgrave, 2001

Berridge, G., Keens-Soper, H. M. A. and Otte, T. G., *Diplomatic Theory from Machiavelli to Kissinger*, Basingstoke, UK, Palgrave, 2001

Black, Jeremy, *European International Relations, 1648–1815*, New York, Palgrave, 2002

Black, Jeremy, *A History of Diplomacy*, London, Reaktion Books, 2010

Cable, James, *Gunboat Diplomacy, 1919–1979: Political Applications of Limited Naval Force*, 2nd ed., London, Macmillan, 1981

Cahill, Kevin M., *Preventive Diplomacy: Stopping Wars Before They Start*, New York, Basic Books, 1996

Cooper, Chester L. *In the Shadows of History: Fifty Years Behind the Scenes of Cold War Diplomacy*, Amherst, NY, Prometheus Books, 2005

Copeland, Daryl, *Guerrilla Diplomacy: Rethinking International Relations*, Boulder, CO, Lynne Rienner, 2009.

Craig, Gordon A., and Alexander L. George, *Force and Statecraft: Diplomatic Problems of Our Time*, New York, Oxford University Press, 1983

De Souza, Philip and France, John, eds., *War and Peace in Ancient and Medieval History*, New York, Cambridge University Press, 2008

Freeman, Charles W., *The Diplomat's Dictionary*, 2nd ed., Washington, D.C, United States Institute of Peace Press, 2010

Frey, Linda S. and Marsha L., *The History of Diplomatic Immunity*, Columbus, Ohio State University Press, 1999

Hamilton, K. and Langhorne, R., *The Practice of Diplomacy: its Evolution, Theory, and Administration*, 2nd ed., London, Routledge, 2011

Hill, Christopher and Smith, Michael, eds., *International Relations and the European Union*, Oxford, Oxford University Press, 2005

Kerr, P. and Wiseman, G., *Diplomacy in a Globalizing World*, New York, Oxford University Press, 2013

Keylor, William R., *The Twentieth Century World and Beyond: An International History Since 1900*, 5th ed., New York, Oxford University Press, 2005

Kissinger, Henry, *Diplomacy*, New York, Simon & Schuster, 1994

Lebow, Richard Ned, *A Cultural Theory of International Relations*, Cambridge, UK, Cambridge University Press, 2009

Liverani, Mario, *International Relations in the Ancient Near East, 1600–1100 BC*, Basingstoke, UK, Palgrave, 2001

Mattingly, Garrett, *Renaissance Diplomacy*, Boston, MA, Houghton Mifflin, 1955

Nicol, Donald M., *Byzantium and Venice: A Study in Diplomatic and Cultural Relations*, Cambridge, UK, Cambridge University Press, 1988

Nicolson, Harold, *The Evolution of Diplomatic Method*, London, Constable, 1954

Nickles, David Paull, *Under the Wire: How the Telegraph Changed Diplomacy*, Cambridge MA, Harvard University Press, 2003

Riordan, Shaun, *The New Diplomacy*. Cambridge, UK, Polity, 2003

Sartori, A. E., *Deterrence by Diplomacy*, Princeton, NJ, Princeton University Press, 2005

Siracusa, Joseph M., *Diplomacy: A Very Short Introduction*, Oxford, Oxford University Press, 2010

Symcox, Geoffrey, ed., *War, Diplomacy and Imperialism, 1618–1763*, London, Macmillan, 1973

Te Brake, Wayne, *Religious War and Religious Peace in Early Modern Europe*, Cambridge, Cambridge University Press, 2017

Yurdusev, A. Nuri, *Ottoman Diplomacy: Conventional or Unconventional?*, Basingstoke, UK, Palgrave Macmillan, 2004

Map List

Index

Acknowledgments

Red Lion Media would like to thank the following:

Cartography: Jeanne Radford, Alexander Swanston, Malcolm Swanston
Design: Karen Wilks
Editorial: Elizabeth Wyse
Research: Andrew Avenell, Henry Bewicke, Caroline Chapman
Additional research and advice: Malise Ruthven
Pages 20, 30, 48, 118, 170, 234: with kind permission of www.themaparchive.com
Image page 6: Wikimedia Commons